Figures of Criminality
in Indonesia, the Philippines,
and Colonial Vietnam

Vicente L. Rafael, editor

Figures of Criminality in Indonesia, the Philippines, and Colonial Vietnam

Sponsored by the Joint Committee on Southeast Asia
of the Social Science Research Council
and the American Council of Learned Societies

SOUTHEAST ASIA PROGRAM PUBLICATIONS
Southeast Asia Program
Cornell University
Ithaca, New York
1999

Cornell Southeast Asia Program Publications
640 Stewart Avenue, Ithaca, NY 14850-3857

Studies on Southeast Asia No. 25

Publication sponsored in part by the Joint Committee on Southeast Asia of the
Social Science Research Council and the American Council of Learned Societies

Printed in the United States of America

ISBN 0-87727-724-9

Cover art: Photographs from the journal, *Indie?* 2,45 (February 5, 1919), and from Viện Mac-
Lenin/Viện Lịch Sử Đảng [The Institute of Marxism-Leninism and the Institute of Party
History], *Ngục Sơn La Trường Học Đấu Tranh Cách Mạng* [Sơn La Prison: School of
Revolutionary Struggle] (Hanoi: Nhà Xuất Bản Thông Tin Lý Luận, 19--).

CONTENTS

ACKNOWLEDGMENTS

Special thanks to Benedict Anderson who read and commented on all the papers in the conference and made valuable contributions towards thinking through their connections. From conversations with James T. Siegel arose the initial idea for the conference. Along the way, he also contributed many insightful suggestions for the editing of this collection. Laurie Sears and Patsy Spyer provided important commentaries on the essays, while at the Social Science Research Council, Itty Abraham and David Lelyveld, along with the members of the Joint Council for Southeast Asia, provided indispensable material and intellectual support for both the conference and this publication. The staff and faculty at the International Institute of Asian Studies in Leiden and the Center for Asian Studies in Amsterdam were gracious hosts, providing much in the way of additional funding and accommodations for the conference participants. Deborah Homsher and Erick White at the Southeast Asia Program Publications at Cornell provided timely and precise editorial advice.

INTRODUCTION:
CRIMINALITY AND ITS OTHERS

Vicente L. Rafael

The essays in this volume grew out of a conference on criminality in Southeast Asia held from March 20-22, 1997 at the Center for Asian Studies in Amsterdam under the joint sponsorship of the Social Science Research Council and the International Institute for Asian Studies. However, the region known as "Southeast Asia" is here nowhere close to being fully covered. The papers deal for the most part with Indonesia, two focus on the Philippines, and one on colonial Vietnam. Similarly missing is a consensus on the meaning of "criminality" as well as a common set of methodological approaches for the study of "crime" and "criminals." But it is the sustained attention paid to specific contexts and the differences of approaches and sensibilities that oddly enough make these papers work as a collection. Brushing up against one another, they offer ways to think about criminality comparatively less as a settled object of investigation than as an unsettling figure that attaches itself to the emergence of social types, state formations, and nationalist thought.

In Anglo-American terms, a "crime" is "any act which is punishable by law as being forbidden by the state or injurious to the public welfare," with the severity of the punishment varying with the circumstances of its commission, in particular whether or not it was intentionally carried out.[1] But as jurists and legal scholars have long recognized, this definition and its variations present endless difficulties.[2] Laws, like the state that crafts and enforces them, vary from place to place and change over time. What counts as criminal, to the extent that it is dependent on the workings of the legal and the political, will likewise vary. Similarly, the nature and space of punishment will differ depending on the manner by which not only "criminal acts" are adjudicated but also how "intentionality"—the authorship, as it

---

[1] This definition is so common as to be normative in the Anglo-American tradition, as one can see in the entries under "crime" in the Oxford English Dictionary, *Black's Law Dictionary*, ed. Henry Campbell Black, revised fourth edition (St. Paul, Minn.: West Publishing Co., 1968), William C. Burton, *Legal Thesaurus* (New York: McMillan Publishing Co., 1980), *American Jurisprudence: A Comprehensive Text Statement of American Case Law* (Rochester, New York: Bancroft-Whitney Company, 1938), and the entry on "Crime" in *Britanica Online* of the *Encyclopedia Britanica*, 1994-1998.

[2] See for example, the remarks of Daniel Lev in this volume and sources cited above.

were, of an act—is reckoned. Furthermore, the legal recognition of criminality requires the latter's encoding by the state often with reference to changing public opinions as well as custom and precedent. For this reason, criminal codes call for interpretive protocols and an hermeneutics of enforcement that is beyond the understanding or abilities of any single person. Even professionals from police to lawyers, criminologists to judges, can understand and enforce such codes only in the most partial and uneven manner (hence the common practice of appealing court decisions) and in doing so further add to their complications. Thus the questions— "What is crime?" and "Who are criminals?"— must always be supplemented with: in whose eyes and under what conditions of looking do "crimes" and "criminals" appear?

The constitutive relationship between criminality and the law comes across in the formation of colonial states, the forerunners of nation-states in Southeast Asia. Writing in the 1930s on the British colonization of Burma, John Furnivall reflected on the ironic effects of the colonial state, or what he referred to as Leviathan, in the emergence of crime in those areas it administered:

> When, under Leviathan, the ties of social life are loosed and men become, as it were, free among the dead, one thing is as reasonable as another; theft becomes as reasonable as honesty, provided that it is not discovered. Leviathan may be omnipresent and all powerful, but he does not, like your neighbor, live next door, or like your conscience, nearer still. That is the explanation of the paradox that Leviathan is least efficient where he is most effective; he cannot maintain law and order so well as a society that maintains order without law, and as we have seen, offences multiplied in Moulmien where Leviathan was very active in attempting to maintain order among a motley population, while the quiet stationary provinces with less regulation but a stronger social life continued free from crime.[3]

Furnivall was writing about Tenasserim in the early half of the nineteenth century but could just as well be referring to other places. Most pre-colonial societies in Southeast Asia had codified practices for dealing with social offences. However, Furnivall seems to suggest that such codes did not amount to "laws" inasmuch as these did not emanate from a recognizably modern state. He reads into pre-colonial Burma an idyllic state where disorder was dealt with through the forces of moral suasion and "popular opinion." All this changed with the arrival of the British. Native society was reorganized not for "life" but in the interest of "production."[4] Leviathan turned headmen into bureaucrats and police, thereby undercutting the local basis of their authority. It introduced large numbers of foreign laborers to exploit the forests, fields, and mines, thereby creating a plural society. It thus set the conditions for the emergence of a new sense of equivalence among things so that, for example, "theft becomes as reasonable as honesty, provided it was not discovered." That discovery became, in turn, the business of colonial law as it sought to institute

---

[3] John Furnivall, *The Fashioning of Leviathan: The Beginnings of British Rule in Burma*, ed. Gehan Wijeyewardene (Canberra: The Department of Anthropology, Australian National University, 1991), p. 58. The original essay appeared in *The Journal of the Burma Research Society* 29,1, April 1939, pp. 3-137.

[4] Furnivall, *The Fashioning of Leviathan*, p. 157.

distinctions and boundaries in a place and at a time where everything seemed to be in flux. But instituting the law among a "motley population" could only be done at a remove from these groups. The state enforced the law only by maintaining a gap between itself and the peoples it administered. In doing so, it opened up opportunities for evasion among criminals and all sorts of corruption among police. The "measures for improving the apprehension of offenders was at the same time the cause of the multiplication of offences."[5] There was a sense then that Leviathan, as the keeper of the law, was fundamentally complicitous with the criminal acts which it sought to control.[6]

In the wake of Furnivall, much of the significant scholarship on criminality in Southeast Asia has tended to stress the conditions under which a distinctly modern notion of crime becomes thinkable.[7] These include the penetration of the capitalist economy, the formation of the colonial and, later on, national states, and the socio-economic transformations that gave rise to new sources of disruption and inequality especially in the later nineteenth and the twentieth centuries. Criminality in the form of smuggling, social banditry, prostitution, sedition and revolt, and so forth emerged as important responses to new historical forces in Southeast Asia. These acts were, of course, distinct and by no means commensurate with one another, although their categorization as "crimes" placed them within the common reach of a centralized legal apparatus and unevenly formalized modes of enforcement and punishment.

---

[5] Ibid., p. 52.

[6] For a related perspective that draws on the history of early modern Europe see Charles Tilly's classic essay, "War Making and State Making as Organized Crime," in *Bringing the State Back In*, ed. Peter B. Evans, Dietrich Rueschemeyer, and Theda Skocpol (Cambridge: Cambridge University Press, 1985), pp. 169-191.

[7] Such scholarship might include those studies that treat criminality either directly (for example, smuggling, prostitution, gambling, banditry) or indirectly (for example, social banditry, peasant movements, rebellions and nationalist agitation construed as sedition) whereby the criminality of actions hinge on who is doing the looking and judging. A very partial and uneven list might include Harry Benda, "Peasant Movements in Colonial Southeast Asia," *Asian Studies*, 3 (1965): 420-434; Onghokham, "The Inscrutable and the Paranoid: An Investigation into the Sources of the Brotodiningrat Affair," in *Southeast Asian Transitions*, ed. Ruth McVey (New Haven: Yale University Press, 1978), pp. 112-157; Reynaldo Ileto, *Pasyon and Revolution: Popular Movements in the Philippines, 1840-1910* (Quezon City: Ateneo de Manila University Press, 1979); David Sturtevant, *Popular Uprisings in the Philippines, 1840-1940* (Ithaca: Cornell University Press, 1976); Greg Bankoff, *Crime, Society and the State in the Nineteenth Century Philippines* (Quezon City: Ateneo de Manila University Press, 1996); James C. Scott, *Weapons of the Weak: Everyday Forms of Peasant Resistance* (New Haven: Yale University Press, 1985); James Rush, *Opium to Java: Revenue Farming and Chinese Enterprise in Colonial Indonesia, 1820-1910* (Ithaca: Cornell University Press, 1990); the essays in Alfred McCoy, ed., *An Anarchy of Families: State and Family in the Philippines* (Madison: University of Wisconsin, Center for Southeast Asian Studies, 1994); R.B. Cribb, *Gangsters and Revolutionaries: The Jakarta People's Militia and the Indonesian Revolution, 1945-1949* (Honolulu: University of Hawai'i Press, 1991); Benedict Kerkvliet, *The Huk Rebellion* (Berkeley: University of California Press, 1977).

This list is by no means exhaustive. Most of those I cited above deal with criminality during specific historical eras and do not address more contemporary manifestations of crime (except some of the essays in the volume edited by Alfred McCoy), although they of course establish important analytical terms for doing so. Indeed, there seems as yet very little by way of a sociology of crime or an anthropology of criminality in Southeast Asia for reasons that I cannot account for here. But one recent exception is James T. Siegel, *A New Criminal Type in Jakarta: Counter-Revolution Today* (Durham: Duke University Press, 1998).

Different states employed different measures to cope with the outbreak of crimes, but most included technologies of surveillance, incarceration, deportation, discipline, and reform, as well as the execution and/or coaptation of those judged to be criminal. One might supplement Furnivall's observations then by saying that just as the law is productive of crime, so is criminality an enabling condition for the materialization of the law and its powers of recognition, the very powers which make up the substance of "the rule of Leviathan."[8]

But we might ask: are there ways by which criminality is also linked to something other than the laws of colonial and national states? While the reciprocal relationship between criminality and state formation as mediated by the law seems to have been a constitutive element in the making of all the nation-states in the region, are there instances when criminality falls short of or exceeds this economy? Is crime always reducible to its social effects and harnessed to the production of social types? Does the disruptiveness inherent in criminality inevitably lead towards a conservative resolution? Must it always reiterate the power of the government and its legal institutions to determine the limits of sociality?

And what of the category "political crimes?" Furnivall nowhere addresses this notion. Indeed, his focus on the colonial state (and the incipient nostalgia for a pre-colonial order of things) obscures the ways by which something analogous to "crime" may also arise in societies that have not been, or at least not yet, fully colonized by the state. How and why does criminality become politicized both within and outside of the state? How do modes of incarceration, for example, or prison architecture contribute to politicizing criminals and criminalizing politics? What role do popular culture and mythology play in converting criminal acts into seditious ones? Why is it, for example, that bandits may be regarded as proto-nationalists in one place and time, but regarded as threats to the community's very identity at others? Conversely, at what point do criminals become political operatives, using the law and state agencies to further their interests? In other words, what are the different but related ways by which states and societies make use of criminality and the bodies of those deemed criminal? Although Furnivall argues that criminality is an inevitable, even indispensible, part of colonial (and as the papers in this volume argue, national) state formation, there is also a sense that it is an enabling element in the reproduction of community identity and its mythologies.

The papers in this collection broach many of these questions and so share overlapping concerns with the productive and contradictory features of criminality. For this reason, we can also read in many of them an explicit or implicit awareness of the practical impossibility of exhausting criminality's meanings. In some of the essays, for example, there emerges a notion of criminality as that which brings with it the sense of the unknown or the unexpected intruding into the realm of everyday life. It thus becomes the locus of collective anxiety, stirring mass attention not only because of its capacity to invoke the law but also to override its powers of recognition. In other papers, the "criminal" in its colonial prototype or nationalist articulation comes across as a figure of fear and potency. At times, it is a recurring foreign presence who, in crossing borders, has the effect of drawing different individuals and groups together to issue a common response. It is this figurative and, one could say, fantastic aspect of criminality that suggests its capacity to excite,

---

[8] Furnivall, *The Fashioning of Leviathan*, p. 40.

politicize and even in some instances entertain. It thus alludes to criminality's elusiveness and indeterminacy.

In the first essay, Rudolf Mrázek posits the phantasmatic moment that comes before (and so continually informs) the formation of a notion of criminality. He begins not with a definition of criminality in colonial Java but with an ironic explication of colonial optics. Ranging from such technologies as dactyloscopy, telescopes, photography, trains, and airplanes, he delineates a Dutch obsession with mapping native bodies and spaces. That obsession in part arose from a belief that new technologies allowed for a greater precision of knowledge about, while also affording a safer distance from, its objects. Dutch dreams of technological mastery over the Indies hinged on modes of apprehension that were meant to keep natives simultaneously near and distant, safe and "clean" for colonial consumption. It was as if the extension of vision and the accuracy of mapping (for instance through landscape photography, fingerprinting, and street lighting) had less to do with actually seeing the natives as with elaborating Dutch notions of power having to do with increasing access to a world now made visible.

In Mrázek's examples, we see a kind of surveillance that is not yet, or not quite, attached to disciplinary projects. As such, optical technologies generated a sense of transparency which proved to be problematic. On the one hand, they gave rise to the fear of coming into contact with something that might evade Dutch recognition; or the possibility of being seen by the natives while looking at them. On the other hand, such fears further incited fantasies of power in the tropics which often required violent resolutions. In Mrázek's essay, we see how the anxieties produced by technologies of visibility may lead those in power to anticipate the emergence of "criminals" as a way of giving shape to what they apprehend but cannot, as yet, comprehend. The emergence of such figures, then, had as much to do with the establishment of law as with the investment in machines of seeing that fed upon European ideas about power and its possible failures.

We might think of the *jago* in nineteenth-century Java as prototypical of the "criminal" figure conjured up by the Dutch. Indeed, as Henk Schulte Nordholt and Margreet van Till show in their essay, the precise place of the *jago* in colonial society is difficult to determine. Described in colonial sources as notorious bandits, they were also influential within Javanese communities. Commanding prestige and deference, they were thought to be endowed with personal prowess and magical abilities that put them in touch with sources of power beyond the purview of Dutch authorities. Yet, the *jagos* were also known to serve as "spies" and local police agents of the Regent.

Ambiguously situated, the *jago* could not readily be assimilated into the terms of colonial law. One is struck, for example, at the excitement and anticipation stirred by the appearance of two infamous *jagos*, Sakam and Si Gantang, or at least those who were thought to be them, during their trials. As reported in newspapers, they evoked curiosity as much as dread, pleasure as much as fear. It was as if they had become figures of entertainment. Rendered into subjects of rumor and sensation, their publicized appearances had the effect of connecting different strands of the plural society. Thus it seemed less important that the agents of the law could not even identify these *jagos* (as they often captured the wrong man), for such mis-apprehensions seemed to enlarge the legends and the interest that surrounded them.

It is tempting to see analogies between the Javanese *jago* of the nineteenth century and the Philippine criminal of the later twentieth. Both tend to be mythologized as "social bandits" and, in the Philippine case, as proto-nationalists. And Filipino criminals, like Javanese *jagos,* have their share of amulets, magical powers, and reputations for violence. However, just as Schulte Nordholt and van Till have drawn attention to the uncertain location of the *jago,* so John Sidel in his essay points out the problems of equating Philippine criminals in the Tagalog regions of Cavite and Manila with social bandits. Contrary to their image as Robin Hood-like characters in popular films, such criminal types as Nardong Putik and Don Pepe Oyson relied on the patronage of influential families, police, and national politicians to establish and expand their respective rackets. Local elites in turn relied on such criminals to aid them in intimidating rival families and harassing other opponents especially during electoral contests. And where the police and the military were concerned, they routinely expected a share in the rents extorted by these criminals in exchange for protection.

We can see then some important similarities between the figures of the Javanese *jago* and the Tagalog criminal despite their distinct historical formations. Sidel points out that the Tagalog criminals he examines always worked under the protection of patrons even if they themselves acted as patrons to those under their command. Securing the protection of those with considerable resources and influence was one of the most pressing tasks of the Filipino criminals. *Jagos* have also availed themselves of the patronage of those above for whom they provided services in exchange for protection, but not, it would seem, to the same degree as that of the lowland, Tagalog criminal that Sidel describes. Though their loyalties might change, the fact remained that the Tagalog criminal was always dependent on the sponsorship, tacit or otherwise, of those above him. In this way, the twentieth-century Tagalog criminal as described by Sidel is distinct from the *jago* while sharing some similarities with him. The same could be said about another more contemporary Indonesian type, the *preman.*

In his essay, Joshua Barker describes the *preman's* primary concern with cultivating the space of his extorsive activities. While he may seek the patronage of the socially powerful, Barker suggests that he is equally concerned with securing the borders of his influence. Planting his "flag," the *preman* in Bandung (as distinct from Jakarta) operates in relative autonomy, exacting tribute from those who cross into his domain, especially foreigners. Where the Tagalog criminal seeks access to patronage and relies on relations of mutual dependency, the *preman* is concerned with controlling his territory and projecting an aura of independence from others. In fact, even when the *preman* might at times rely on the help of the military, as Barker points out, this reliance is at best guarded and provisional. Among Philippine criminals, no such equivocation exists: criminality is inconceivable outside of relations of patronage and reciprocity, or so it would seem.

Yet criminals in the Philippines, like *jagos* in Java, have also been the locus of a certain popular fantasy. Sidel details the myths that surround the portrayal of criminals in films. Unlike *premans* whose origins seem to be of little account, Filipino criminals are portrayed as victims of a prior injustice. Their turn to criminality is thus motivated by insupportable circumstances suffered at the hands of cruel authorities. Jose Rizal's late-nineteenth-century novels, *Noli me tangere* and *El Filibusterismo,* anticipated and arguably established the terms for such a mythology. Such characters as Elias, Cabesang Tales, and various other "social bandits" forced into a life of crime by the injustices they suffered are echoed in the film portrayals of Nardong Putik and other criminals. Criminality here is understood as a kind of response: a form of revenge against those deemed responsible for the criminals' situation.

As the agent of vengeance, the Filipino criminal is thus the carrier of a message and the embodiment of popular fantasies about justice. He is thereby endowed with the nationalist desire to reverse a history of oppression and victimization. His violence, cast as a response to this history, becomes more than just an instrument of intimidation and extortion. In this way, the criminal's dependency on patronage is mystified and turned into a basis for mass identification. In the realm of popular culture, the criminal comes across as a proto-nationalist. The recent election of Joseph "Erap" Estrada as the thirteenth president of the Philippines further bears out this link between nationalism and criminality. Building a political career on the basis of his reputation as a movie star typecast into playing the role of a lumpen turned vigilante crime fighter, Estrada as vice-president headed an anti-crime commission that was itself charged with committing various crimes. Police operatives were accused of the massacre of gang members while at the same time engaging in kidnapping and extortions. More recently, Estrada in his speeches has pledged to fight crime while appointing criminal cops to head his anti-crime efforts and Marcos cronies to positions of influence.[9] Yet, his previous opposition to the renewal of the United States Bases Treaty (which has since changed), his image as an advocate of the masses, and his use of street Tagalog at the expense of proper English has made him remarkably popular among nationalists on the left and the right.

The figural quality of the criminal—his genesis, in part, in a collective fantasy that exceeds legal definitions and state sanctions—can also be seen, albeit with vastly different consequences, in the *maling* or thief in West Java. Barker's ethnography of the *ronda* or nightwatch describes how a "culture of security" emerges in response to the anticipated appearance of thieves. Tracking what he calls the "territorializing practices" of the *ronda* in a Bandung neighborhood, Barker shows how the fear of thieves make possible the mobilization of the community and the reproduction of its borders. For, once caught, thieves are beaten by most of the men in the neighborhood. It is not clear that analogous practices have existed in other parts of Southeast Asia.[10] Here, according to Barker, the *maling* is less a criminal who is dealt with by the law than he is "something less than human" and therefore radically foreign to the community. Unlike the *jago* or *preman* who lives on the edge of society, the thief comes to represent all that "stands outside the neighborhood." Conceived from the perspective of the neighborhood as a foreign figure, the thief becomes the recipient of collective violence. Beatings in this case become the language deemed most appropriate for addressing the thief. Blows "territorialize" his body, converting

---

[9] See for example, President Estrada's inaugural speech in "Unang Talumpati sa Bansa ni Pangulong Joseph Ejercito Estrada," *Philippine Daily Inquirer,* June 30, 1998, p. 1.

[10] Greg Bankoff in *Crime, Society and the State in the Nineteenth Century Philippines,* pp. 129-30, mentions the existence of a "regular nightwatch of garrison troops" who patrolled the streets of Manila (most likely Intramuros) as early as the 1590s. The system was extended to outlying towns and came to be known as *bantayan,* a Tagalog word from *bantay,* to watch. As an early mode of colonial policing, the *bantayan* never seemed to be any more than a poorly funded, ragtag band who could not keep up with bandits and often joined the latter's ranks. There is, as yet, no study of how thievery has been handled on the local level in the Philippines, much less a history of the ways its been perceived by rural neighborhoods.

it into a series of signs that can be traced back to the community. In this way, his foreignness comes to be recognized and domesticated.[11]

The foreignness of the thief elicits a language of violence in Java. In the Philippines, the nightwatch as institution for defining neighborhood identity never took on the importance that it has for Java. Thieves do not arouse the kind of collective anxiety among Filipinos and their apprehension does not usually trigger collective violence. Indeed, thievery tends to be mythologized along different routes, as we saw earlier, or in the late nineteenth century in association with a kind of seditious activity or writing—what the Spanish colonial authorities referred to as "filibusterismo," (which originally meant "piracy") or what the Americans called, probably on the suggestion of conservative Filipinos collaborators, "bandolerismo." In the Philippines then, there are other contexts for understanding "thievery." While it often refers to the taking of what does not belong to one (the way, for example, the Marcoses and their cronies were widely perceived as thieves and plunderers of the nation's wealth), there is also a nationalist context for understanding "thievery" as the appropriation of that which belongs to the dominant other. If the thief appears to be foreign at all, it is therefore in the eyes of those who are retrospectively regarded as foreign rulers themselves rather than among Filipinos.

The link between "foreignness" and criminality also arises in relation to the "Chinese." Such a relation, however, differs between the Philippines and Indonesia. Where anti-Chinese riots are frequent in Indonesia, most recently during the weeks leading up to the ouster of Suharto, the last anti-Chinese riot in the Philippines occurred in the late seventeenth century and was promoted by Spaniards, not natives. Only at one other time were the Chinese expelled from the Philippines: in the aftermath of the British Occupation of Manila from 1762-64, and then only temporarily. Conceding their economic importance, the Spanish eventually allowed them to return in the early nineteenth century. Indeed, from the inception of Spanish rule, the Chinese have been targeted for Christian conversion and assimilation by way of inter-marriage with native women. One result was the emergence beginning in the 1750s of a small but economically affluent and, in time, politically influential group of Chinese mestizos from whose ranks many of the early nationalists came. Yet, many of the latter also came to disavow their Chineseness, revising their mestizo-ness upwards, as it were, in Hispanic terms while seeking to speak on behalf of the natives. Hence, in the face of persistent anti-Chinese racism, much of the Filipino elite today bear some Chinese ancestry.[12] In both Indonesia and the Philippines, the "Chinese" intimate a familiar foreign presence. But in the latter, the "foreign" is also that which has been converted and given a recognizable place in society rather than targeted, as in the former, for violent domestication.

In recent years, however, a new means for converting the foreignness of the "Chinese" in the Philippines has arisen by way of a criminal act: kidnapping. In her essay, Caroline Hau suggests how the kidnapping of the Chinese, for the most part restricted to the Metropolitan Manila area, resonates in nationalist thinking about the proper place of the foreign. There is a strain in nationalism that regards the Chinese

[11] See also James T. Siegel, *Solo in the New Order: Language and Hierarchy in an Indonesian City*, (Princeton: Princeton University Press, 1986), pp. 34-58 for a related discussion of the *ronda* in another part of Java.

[12] The best account of the Chinese in the Philippines is Edgar Wickberg, *The Chinese in Philippine Life, 1850-1898* (New Haven: Yale University Press, 1965).

as "the foreign trace of colonial history" despite the fact that many of the most prominent nationalists are themselves part Chinese. Thus the essential indeterminacy of "Chineseness" in a Filipino context. "Chinese" comes to be imagined as the repository of that which is alien residing within the Filipino body politic. Such thinking has as its corollary the popular belief that the Chinese are the very embodiments of capital. Associated with money, they are seen as an alien force which exploits Filipino labor.

The link between the foreignness of the Chinese and money as capital raises the question: what kind of crime is kidnapping? Is it a way of responding to an alienating presence, and therefore not a crime at all but a form of revenge? Or is it a "growth industry"—part of a culture of entrepreneurship geared towards making profits? Kidnapping for ransom, as Hau argues, commodifies the Chinese body, converting its strangeness into an object for exchange. Here, the foreign is that which circulates by virtue of being substitutable for money. On the one hand, kidnapping when viewed within a nationalist context converts the Chinese capitalist into an object with which to pay off his debts to Filipino labor. In this way, the crime conveys a phantasm of revenge. On the other hand, within an entrepreneurial context, kidnapping turns the Chinese body into a sign that can be given an equivalent value and thus made productive of a surplus that continually returns, introjecting itself into the very realm in which it is deemed alien. Either way—as a payment for that which had been "stolen," or as a bearer of surplus value—the "Chinese" is invested with the sense of being more than what he or she originally is. S/he is an other who becomes more than an other without becoming part of oneself. His/her perceived excess is thus domesticated into that which can circulate among and be recognized by those who think of themselves as "Filipino." The "foreign" is transformed into an element of oneself without, however, ceasing to be foreign. It is as if to say "we are Filipinos" to the extent that we are able to respond to the "Chinese" by setting their equivalent value and thereby putting them in circulation and insuring their return. Thus is the foreigner neither exterminated nor expelled but given a place in the imaginative and political economies of the nation-state.

In colonial Indochina, we can discern as well a link between criminality and nationalism in the early twentieth century. One of the sites for forging this link was the colonial prison. After a spirited engagement with the recent scholarship on prisons, Peter Zinoman in his essay demonstrates the discontinuity between the French metropole and the Indochinese colony where the disciplinary projects of modernity were concerned. This gap was particularly acute in the colonial prison.

Zinoman alerts us to the central contradiction often remarked on by Vietnamese nationalists themselves: that under French rule, prisons became "schools" for producing anti-colonial revolutionary leaders. In part such developments arose from French racist regard of the native as incorrigible and impervious to change. Such attitudes led to the construction of prisons that were decidedly un-panoptic. The segregation of European from native prisoners, and the use of native guards for the latter, along with the continued use of pre-colonial architectural designs and punitive practices allowed for unregulated mixing among prisoners and collaboration between prisoners and guards. In the 1930s, then, a "custodial mode of incarceration" led to forms of punishment detached from reform and surveillance. Colonial prisons, as Zinoman argues, were less sites for the formation of disciplined subjects as they were places for inciting nationalist desires for the modernizing technologies withheld by the colonial state. Here, incarceration is related to criminality in a highly politicized manner. Retrospectively regarding prisons as pedagogical sites for cultivating revolutionary consciousness, Vietnamese nationalists saw their "criminalization" by the French as the condition with which to overturn colonial rule.

Zinoman's essay is a significant departure from the rest of the papers in this volume. Aside from being the only paper that deals with Vietnam under the French, it is also the only one which does not directly take up the question of criminality or criminals but rather the space of their punishment. His contribution comes closest methodologically to a social history of prisons, the study of which, as he points out, is sorely wanting in the scholarly literature on Southeast Asia.[13]

With the essays of Daniel Lev, John Pemberton, and James T. Siegel, we return to the motifs raised in Furnivall's discussion of Leviathan, though with a difference. Furnivall argued that the processes of state formation were also those which set the conditions that contributed invariably to the spread of criminality. Only with the emergence of a modern legal apparatus do we also witness the appearance of crimes, that is, offences whose definitions are decided by the law rather than by "custom" or "public opinion." Lev, Pemberton, and Siegel make stronger claims. Lev argues that post-colonial Indonesian history has long been characterized by a constitutive relationship between the administration of the law and the normalization of corruption, and therefore between the consolidation of state power and the preservation of class hierarchy. In his conversation with a Javanese lawyer just a year before Suharto's resignation, Pemberton lends a striking intimacy and uncanny immediacy to the "open secret" of everyday corruption whose historical outlines had been laid out by Lev. Siegel, discussing the "Petrus" killings of 1983-84, claims that not only is the New Order State complicitous with criminals; its leaders, beginning with the former head Suharto, were part of a new criminal type themselves.

Lev chronicles the progressive corruption of a colonial legal system deeded to the postcolonial state, first under Guided Democracy and most stunningly under the New Order. Under Sukarno, the Indonesian state chose to stress the "most repressive side of the colonial legal structure" as criminal procedure became increasingly politicized. The entire legal apparatus was given over to the silencing of critics and to serving the interests of the state. In exchange for their complicity, judges and prosecutors were given license to use their positions for personal gain.

Under Suharto's New Order, the "impressively predatory" workings of Guided Democracy's legal system became even more pronounced. Prosecutors have acted like extortionists, and public lawyers, judges and police, along with other bureaucrats, have routinely engaged in elaborate protection rackets. And despite their reluctance, defense lawyers often have been compelled to submit to such practices. Not surprisingly, the Chinese have been particularly victimized by being arbitrarily charged with offences, then forced to pay substantial bribes to avoid prosecution. Civil cases have been auctioned to judges, decisions sold to the highest bidder, and those who are well connected have been routinely let off from prosecution. Hence, the institutionalization of corruption was an integral aspect of

---

[13] For rare exceptions, see Bankoff, *Crime, Society and the State in the Nineteenth Century Philippines*, pp. 155-187; and Michael Salman, "'Nothing Without Labor': Penology, Discipline, and Independence in the Philippines Under United States Rule," in *Discrepant Histories: Translocal Essays on Filipino Cultures*, ed. Vicente L. Rafael (Philadelphia: Temple University Press, 1995), pp. 113-129.

the subordination of the legal process to the dictates of the state. At the same time, the commodification of criminal procedure protected the wealthy from prosecution and thereby consolidated ever growing class divisions. Thus did Suharto perpetuate his rule while fending off demands for reforms. And even with Suharto's departure, the normalization of corruption has become so pervasive and deeply entrenched as to be taken for granted by most of Indonesia's population.

The corruption of the legal system is not, of course, particular to Indonesia. Such practices undoubtedly occur in other places in Southeast Asia to a greater or lesser extent. We can think, for example, of the Philippine judiciary under Marcos's New Society which was used to silence critics and safeguard the privileges of cronies. More recently, President Estrada's vow to rid the country of "hoodlums in uniforms and robes" acknowledges the pervasiveness of bribery and corruption in the legal system. Recent developments might lead one to think that Philippine courts have sometimes shown a semblance of integrity. For example, it has been possible to convict members of the military who were involved in the assassination of Benigno Aquino in 1983 (though not the actual figure who gave the order), as well as those who were involved in the coup attempts during the Aquino years (though a number of them have since been released and are now in Congress). Similarly, Imelda Marcos and two of her children have been convicted of tax fraud, though it is highly unlikely that they will do any jail time. The wealthy and well connected may be tried and even on occasion found guilty, but they are almost never punished. For the overwhelming majority of the people, the courts remain forbidding and the bribery of officials remain the most expeditious way of avoiding the considerable expense and untold complications of litigation. Hence, attempts at reforming the Philippine judiciary in the wake of Marcos and the depoliticization of the military have proved largely ineffective. Similarly in New Order Indonesia corruption seems to have been so thorough a part of the legal culture as to foreclose the possibility of change in the near future as John Pemberton's essay makes clear.

"Boundaries blur," Pemberton's Javanese interlocutor shrewdly observes, between criminals and judicial officials, ranging from judges to petty bureaucrats, police to military in contemporary Indonesia. Practices of corruption have become so routine that the only difference between the past and present is that "they're even bolder now," no longer embarrassed to trade everything from detention to decisions for cash. "They" here includes "we," that is, the Javanese lawyer himself who despite his initial outrage has grown wearily accustomed to submitting to the demands of what amounts to a judicial marketplace. Legal matters become subject to a kind of "fantastic" calculation all the more shocking, as Pemberton observes, for being so commonplace to the point that plaintiffs and their lawyers anxious to avoid losing a case now regard it as their "right" to pay off judges. Thus when asked to whom the term "criminal" properly refers to, the lawyer responds without irony: "They [and therefore 'we'] are all criminals."

The "open secret" of corruption, as Pemberton points out in his commentary, informs the identity of the new criminal type in Indonesia. Unlike the old or "classical" criminals like the *maling* or the *jago* who relied on physical strength and magical skills to impose their will on others, the new criminals announce their criminality in the uniforms they wear and the public offices they occupy. Putting aside any sense of embarrassment, they openly demand money, which is to say, they readily reveal the motive force that drives the entire *aparat* for which they serve as agents. As such, the very nature of scandal changes. What is scandalous is no longer that which was hidden and which then suddenly becomes visible and public. Rather, it is the fact that "everyone knows" and, therefore, that everyone is implicated, the accuser the same as the accused. The devastating events of 1998 has only confirmed this "open secret"; but the "revolution" that, as the Javanese lawyer remarks, would be required to undo its effects seems very far indeed from taking place.

Siegel's contribution further interrogates the criminal foundations of the New Order, though from another angle. He focuses on the events of 1983-84 known as "Petrus" in which soldiers in mufti killed reputed criminals, stabbing them repeatedly then leaving their corpses on display for people to discover. Siegel situates this event in relation to a history of massacres carried out by Indonesians against fellow Indonesians on the one hand, and to the prominence of the notion of *kriminalitas* under the New Order on the other. Both have to do with ideas about death that the state has sought to control.

New Order-sanctioned publications such as *Pos Kota* and *Tempo* crystallized the category *kriminalitas,* endowing it with a reference specific to the regime. Under Suharto, it became a way of figuring a pervasive fear: that a force related to the Indonesian Revolution—at times thought of as the *rakyat* or "people," as it is closely associated with another term, "communists"—might return to seek vengeance against a regime that has killed so many of its own citizens. The criminals of *kriminalitas* were imagined to be among the envoys of a repressed past, signs of a return which conjured up a realm of power that had to be overcome. Such became the case when criminals were portrayed as killers or started turning up dead. In fact, most of them were not murderers but rather petty criminals who had worked for the ruling party to intimidate and threaten opponents whenever called upon to do so. But on those occasions when they were depicted as murderers, they attracted national attention. What drew people to them, and what shaped their tabloid depiction, was the sense that they provided a link between their dead victims and the living who heard about or saw the corpses. Being the last ones to see their victims alive and the first ones presumably to see them dead, the criminal is thought to retain a memory of the dead as if he were a photograph that kept an absence continually present. The attraction then to the criminal lies in his capacity to occupy a position midway between life and death, and thereby draw on death as the basis of his power. It is precisely this middle position that the government sought to claim for itself.

In killing these criminals, the agents of the state made it a point to stab them repeatedly and then display their corpses. In so doing, Siegel argues, the state simultaneously identified with the criminals and set themselves apart from them. The corpses were made to convey a message about the authority of the government. The murder of so-called murderers allowed the state to absorb the power that they thought inhered in *kriminalitas,* the very power of death that issued from the corpses. Admitting to this crime, Suharto and others came to appropriate this power. Thus does *kriminalitas* bring with it the what Siegel calls the "nationalization of death."

However, such a process was potentially endless. Inasmuch as death, the source of *kriminalitas'* power, is inexhaustible, it is beyond the reach of the living, including the government. For how else could death, even in its nationalized form, be powerful except as that which surpasses historical life? Thus arose the necessity of killing not once, but over and over again.

The state in Indonesia has been haunted by the fear of revenge, a fear that is all the more remarkable, as Siegel points out, given the absence of any "culture of vengeance," at least as of 1997, among the children of those victimized during the 1965 massacres. *Kriminalitas,* as we saw, is a way of figuring this fear. Another way of dealing with this fear is by means of censorship. Henk Maier in his essay recounts the history of state censorship involving the banning of the books of Pramoedya Ananta Toer. Deftly demystifying the rhetoric and practice of censorship in Indonesia, Maier asks: what is it exactly that the state fears in Pramoedya?

The criminalization of Pramoedya has a long history. Already under Sukarno he had been imprisoned for his writings sympathetic to the Chinese. Under Suharto, he spent long years in Buru, as is well known, where he began working on his historical novels. While not directly about the Revolution, the Buru tetralogy focused on the progressive origins of Indonesian nationalism and has thus kept alive a history of the movement long suppressed by the military regime (many of whom had served in the Dutch colonial army ordered to smash the anti-colonial activity). His recent memoirs of imprisonment continue his critique of official versions of the past and have been banned by state censors concerned with the circulation of what they regard as "code books" that encrypt "communist doctrines." Like the Dutch described in Mrázek's essay, Indonesian censors imagine in such writings the emergence of figures that return from a realm over which they have no control.

By writing, Pramoedya poses a security risk. The New Order has feared in Pramoedya the possibility of something coming back: the specter of revenge arising out of a history of massacres. The author is punished not for what he has actually done, but for what his writings might give rise to. As Maier puts it, paraphrasing Pramoedya himself, imprisonment and censorship involved a logic of "first the punishment, then the crime." Never having been given a trial, Pramoedya's crime has never been specified, only assumed.

We might think of the banning of Pramoedya's books within the context of *kriminalitas.* In censoring him, the state acknowledges implicitly the existence of another source of power. It is one that arises, we might assume, from "literature," one that surpasses the official rhetoric of the government and the commercialized discourse of popular culture, reaching back to the revolutionary origins of the nation (and the Indonesian language). In this sense, it is a literature that connects with a long history of deaths and thus seem analogous to the power of criminals. Censors see Pramoedya's writings as inciting authority to act and respond to what it deems a threat. This happens because literature comes to be invested with the capacity to evoke specters of revenge. Censorship then seeks the containment of literature as a way of putting such ghosts to rest. But precisely because literature, as in Pramoedya's writings, is thought to surmount control (for what need would there be to interdict something that is not, by its very nature, always transgressive?), its power could not be exhausted by the New Order regime. Thus the need on the part of the state to ban the books in the same way that it has had to kill "criminals": over and over again. It is this ghastly equation of "literature" with criminality and death that helps to explain why the state and its allies, despite the fall of Suharto, continues to fear a man in his seventies who, as of this writing, remains under suspicion and city arrest, forbidden to travel without the permission of authorities.

"Literature" seems like an odd place to end a collection of essays on criminality, especially since it seems so far removed from where we began, with "Leviathan." But the fact that criminality traverses both the social and the phantasmatic, the legal and the fictional, informing both the materiality of state institutions and the spectral returns of the past is an indication of its persistent figurality. The *jago,* the thief, the Philippine criminal, the *preman,* the "Chinese," the "foreigner," the "criminals" of *kriminalitas,* the prisoners of Indochinese jails, the "criminal" Pramoedya: all these are incommensurable figures whose socio-historical depth sets them apart from one another. Yet, their appearance in part owes something to the recuperative powers of the state—colonial, and then national—that renders them recognizable, however tenuously, within some notion of criminality. Related to one another by virtue of their reference to a modern conception of the law, they have also stirred nationalist imaginings and so play important roles in the formation of modernity in these countries of Southeast Asia. At the same time, figures of criminality, as we saw, are subject to historical revisions and interpretive ambiguities, feeding on and off rumor and publicity, sensational pleasures, open secrets, phantasms of revenge, and anxieties about the foreign. Criminality thus renders fugitive the very criminals that states seek to subsume. They always escape, it would seem; but for this very reason, they are always poised to return in one form or another.

FROM DARKNESS TO LIGHT: OPTICS OF POLICING IN LATE-COLONIAL NETHERLANDS EAST INDIES

Rudolf Mrázek

And all the instruments, each for a particular need, were invented by scientifically minded travelers to allow them to stand on their own; for instance, a funnel made of glazed tin, with a wide opening, and with its ending narrowing into a stopper bottle—a device to be placed on open galleries and other exposed parts of a house, under lamps and all kind of lights, to catch a large number of insects in short time.

(Official Guide to Colonial Exhibition in Amsterdam 1883)[1]

1. DACTYLOSCOPY

A textbook, written by Anthonie Cornelis Oudemans, published first in 1873 and frequently reprinted, opened with:

Once upon a time, there lived in Java, close to the sea, a man who had a great knowledge about all the matters of the earth, stars, sun, moon, etc. In the same place, there was also a regent, and he had a son, whose name was Abdullah . . . [2]

---

[1] *Officiële Wegwijzer voor de Internationale Koloniale en Uitvoerhandel tentoonstelling, te Amsterdam in 1883* (Amsterdam, no publisher, 1883).

[2] J. A. C. Oudemans *Ilmoe alam of wereldbeschrijving voor de Inlandsche scholen* (Batavia: Landsdrukkerij, 1873).

It was a science primer. The usual topics were dealt with in the textbook. Yet, one item was granted extra space. Two big chapters dealt with *kijker*, a "looking glass" or, as the textbook put it, "a Dutch looking glass."[3]

The wise white man at the beach instructed the regent's son how the Dutch looking glass worked. He aimed it at a distant coconut tree and after some tinkering, the tree was pulled into focus, made distinctly visible. The reality was captured. One might aim this looking glass at everything.

But now, the regent's son looked into the glass, then at the white man, and said:

> But, sir, can I ask you something; the image of the coconut palm appears turned around, with its leaves downwards, but my father has a binocular, and also a taller glass, and through them one can see trees as not reversed.[4]

At this moment, we realize how early in the modern era this book was written; how very "close to the sea" still the white man lived. "Your father," the white man answered Abdullah, "has more advanced instruments. That's why."

"Picture no. 2" in the textbook showed the Dutch looking glass with the coconut tree, upside down yet safely focused and contained. Oudemans's was a rosy textbook. "Picture no. 1" in the book showed a "Map of Java," even cleaner and more cheerful in its style and message than "Picture no. 2." Straight, abstract lines intersected at points marked by single digits or letters of the alphabet. In the same style, only purer, there were several maps of the Javanese heaven in the latter part of the textbook. In these maps the tropical stars were labeled not with letters and digits but with Latin names.[5]

A. C. Oudemans was a lucky man. He spent the years between 1834 and 1840 as the principal of the Dutch elementary school in Batavia, and he died during a quiet retirement in Holland. He was a father blessed with perfect sons: Jean Abram, a doctor of medicine, botany, and mycology, was a professor at the University of Amsterdam; Antoine Corneille, a chemist, served one time as a director of the Delft Institute of Technology; Jean Abraham Chrétien became one of the most prominent Dutch astronomers of his time.[6]

Particularly the last of Oudemans's three children was almost like his father's textbook. Born in Amsterdam, Jean Abraham Chrétien received his early education in Batavia. In 1852 in Holland he defended a doctoral dissertation on the determination of the latitude of Leiden,[7] and in 1857 he was appointed "head engineer of the geographical service" in the Indies with the task of mapping the colony by astronomical means.

In the following decades, J. A. C. Oudemans became one of the most respected, and best paid, men in the colony:

---

[3] Ibid., pp. 100ff.

[4] Ibid., p. 101.

[5] Ibid., p. 181.

[6] Lewis Pyenson, *Empire of Reason: Exact Sciences in Indonesia, 1840-1940* (Leiden: Brill, 1989), p. 21.

[7] Ibid., p. 21.

one needs at least five hundred guilders per month here to live decently . . . and this sum did not take account of capital expenses necessary for setting up a household.[8]

He was a white wise man who lived still very close to the sea, in large part because access to the interior was so difficult to achieve:

> Except for Java, no big roads or horses are to be found, the coasts in various places are unapproachable and the inlands do not offer anything but marshes . . . [We] have to drag [ourselves] with chronometers and [other] instruments from one place to the other. For each expedition we depend on the solution to the big question: How shall I get to the places to be defined (geographically)?[9]

Oudemans depended upon steamers, the technologically most *à jour* things, and he could become very angry when a ship was not available to him at an appointed place. At the same time, he was fond of using what he strongly believed were "native" symbols of authority—palanquin and cane.[10]

His, clearly, was a most intense scientific pleasure: to penetrate the dark interior, to measure the islands by means of pure rationality. A high-soaring pleasure. In his mapping and triangulating Indies, Oudemans used the newly laid submarine transcontinental telegraphic cable and sent signals over various segments of the line between Perth and Berlin.[11]

Oudemans left the Indies to return home to Holland in the early 1890s, with his huge job, of course, just begun. The last thing we hear about J. A. C. Oudemans in connection with the Indies is as cheerful and uplifting as his life and as his father's textbooks:

> As early as 1881, he observed that the meter used in Java (which he himself had delivered in the 1850s) was not calibrated directly against the one in Paris; neither had it been corrected for temperature variations.

In 1894, Oudemans acquired a new, true, and perfect platinum-iridium meter. This he kept in his new laboratory in Utrecht, Holland, of course. The colony was provided with a glass copy.[12]

Mapping was an art in the late-colonial Indies—increasingly so as the colonial crisis deepened. Each new edition of a map called for a literary review. Cultural personages were involved, and the language of the reviews was of the kind one might expect from writers of *belles-lettres* :

> The map is networked according to Flamsteed's projection. Thus our Indies possessions festoon the Equator as the poetical expression of Multatuli had

---

[8] Oudemans in a letter quoted in Pyenson, *Empire of Reason*, pp. 24-25

[9] Ibid., p. 26.

[10] Ibid., p. 179, and see photos pp. 28, 35.

[11] Ibid., pp. 32-33, 37.

[12] Ibid., p. 44.

it; their extreme points reach to the 6° in the north and to 10° in the south . . .
There is no overloading, there is great clarity and readability, true harmony
of all the tones and colors![13]

Poor maps could be criticized as *ontaarden*, "degenerated":

> Not merely did the solemnity of the drawing disappear, but with each
> single map [of the collection] an unnatural mixture of colors becomes more
> gross . . . [14]
> I found it in a bad taste to crowd a map with all the colors of the
> rainbow. I found it childish to paste a coffee plantation with the color of
> coffee, a tea plantation with a light-tea color. The color of this land is green.
> Light-green are the rice fields, dark-green is the rest.[15]

Geometrical beauty was appreciated, and this appreciation increased as the
Indies reality grew messier. In another late nineteenth-century textbook, this time
written exclusively for "native" children, the narrator explained to the little Javanese
students that their island was

> a very elongated rectangle, thus in your textbook it had to be a little
> shortened . . . [16]

Sumatra, in the same textbook, had "a shape almost the same as the island of
Java, except that its position lengthwise is from the west to south-east."[17]
In the West, it took the barbarous war of 1914-1918 and a great and failed
revolution before the European avant-garde came up with ideas like "linear city"[18]
or began to think, as the Dutch painter Piet Mondriaan did think, in terms of "holy
mathematics"[19] and all-powerful "circles in connection with triangles and squares."
A great part of this intellectual and imaginative development had to do with "an
attempt . . . to obtain [a] knowledge . . . about the 'ascending path, away from
matter . . .'"[20] The colonial Indies, in that sense, marched a few decades ahead of the
ailing and anxious West.

---

[13] Review by M. T. H. Perelaer of the book *Kaart van Java met aanduiding der spoor- tram- en
andere wegen* by H. H. Stemfoort and Hora Adema, and of the book *De nieuwe Atlas van de
Nederlandsche Bezettingen in Oost-Indië naar de nieuwe bronnen samengesteld en aan de Regeering
opgedragen* daor J. W. Stempoort en J. J. ten Siethoff, kapiteins van den Generalen Staf van het
Nederlandsch Indische leger. *De Indische Gids* 7,2 (1885): 1614-1615.

[14] H. Ph. Th. Witkamp, "Een voorbeeld zonder voorbeeld," *De Indische Gids* 8,2 (1886): 1627.

[15] Ibid., p. 1628.

[16] W. van Gelder, *Dari Tanah Hindia Berkeliling Boemi: Kitab Pengadjaran Ilmoe Boemi bagi sekolah
anak negeri di Hindia-Nederland,* 3rd. ed. (Wolters Groningen, 1892), p. 1.

[17] Ibid., p. 46.

[18] The phrase describes a 1930s design by architect J. Leonidov for the new Siberian city of
Magnitogorsk. See *Sovjet Architectuur, 1917-1987* (Amsterdam: Art Unlimited Books, 1989), p.
27.

[19] Els Hoe, "Piet Mondrian," in Carel Blotkamp, ed., *De Stijl: The Formative Years* (Cambridge,
Massachusetts: The MIT Press, 1986), p. 59.

[20] Marty Bax, "Mondriaan and his Friends," in *Piet Mondriaan: The Amsterdam Years*
(Amesterdam: Gemeentearchief Amsterdam, 1994), p. 40.

Thinking about what a perfect late-colonial Indies map might be—logical, beautiful, and powerful—dactyloscopy comes to mind.

The origins of dactyloscopy are traced to Josef Purkine, Czech scholar and nationalist, who in 1822 discovered under his microscope a breathtaking, orderly pattern of lines on the skin of human fingertips.

> He distinguished nine principal categories. Thus, he laid the foundation for the present dactyloscopic methods of registration . . . [21]

Three-quarters of a century later, this system of dactyloscopic registration as used in the Indies would be called "system Henry," named after the "chief inspector of the London police, Sir Henry."[22] The dactyloscopic "operators" taking the fingerprints ("each operator must work in a neat and orderly manner"[23]) became the late-colonial renaissance men *par excellence*: cartographers, engineers, dreamers, and policemen all at the same time.

The word for fingerprints in Dutch was *vingersporen*, "finger-traces" or "finger-tracks":

> By the government decision dated 23 July, 1898, no. 27, and another one dated 17 July 1905, no. 20, offices of judicial anthropometrical identification . . . were established in the principal cities: *Batavia, Semarang* and *Surabaya* . . .
>
> In 1901, the anthropometry was supplemented with *photography* . . .
>
> By the decision of the governor-general of 15 March, 1917, the Central Office of Dactyloscopy began to work with the police in Batavia. [24]

The Indies dactyloscopy manual from 1917 called the piece of paper where fingerprints were stored *slip van Simin*, "Simin's tag." "Simin" was chosen as a typical native name. One copy of each set of prints was kept in the central office in Batavia, the other in local police dactyloscopic files.[25]

An Austrian philosopher, Ernst Mach, wrote that "the mind feels relieved, whenever the new and unknown is recognized as a combination of what is known."[26] Robinson Crusoe also felt good enough on his island so long as he could continue "stating and squaring everything by reason."

The Dutch experts spoke about a "dactyloscopic sieve."[27] It was hoped that the unruly flow of native people between Java and the rest of the Indies might be

---

[21] D. H. Meijer, "Dactyloscopie voor Nederlandsch-Indië," *Koloniale Studiën* 10,2 (1926): 912.

[22] I. H. Misset, *Departement van Binnenlandsch Bestuur Politieschool. Het Centraal kantoor voor de dactyloscopie bij de Politie* (Weltevreden: Visser, 1917), p. 20; see also Sir E. R. Henry, *Classification and Uses of Fingerprints* (London: Darling and Son, 1913).

[23] Misset, *Het Centraal kantoor voor de dactyloscopie bij de Politie* , p. 20.

[24] Ibid., p. 7.

[25] Ibid., p. 23.

[26] Robert Musil, *On Mach's theories* (Washington: Catholic University of America Press, 1982), p. 29.

[27] H. J. Spit, Directeur van Justitie in *Volksraad*, July 10, 1929 (Handelingen van den Volksraad, 1929-30), p. 775.

"strained" through dactyloscopic methods. Medan in East Sumatra, the biggest plantation center, and Semerang, Surakarta, and Yogyakarta, the Javanese towns where most of the plantation labor force originated, were the prime candidates for being "dactyloscoped."[28] Some argued that with dactyloscopy, at last, a modern labor system had arrived in the Indies, replacing the *poenale sanctie*, a crude forced labor system:

> came the Dactyloscopic Institute . . . All the contract workers began to be registered by the means of fingerprints.[29]

The fingerprints could truly be appreciated only under a microscope. Dactyloscopy, therefore, was a historical moment not merely for the Dutch colonial mapping, but for the Dutch Indies looking glass as well. And there would be no limit to the new vision:

> Of whom shall the tags be required?
> In the government instruction it was stated: "of persons suspected of criminal offense and of breaching the rules . . . of all suspected individuals in the Netherlands Indies . . . [30]

The poetics of the triangulated maps in the early textbooks thus reappeared in a timely form and reached their high point. This huge archipelago, through which Oudemans Jr. had dragged his theodolites, this unwieldy colony entering an uncertain new century, was about to be pinned down cleanly and by whole numbers. This was a digital dream:

> With a pair of fingers we get 2x2=4 variation . . . With three fingers the number arises to 2x2x2=8 variations.
> So it follows, with ten fingers there is 2x2x2x2x2x2x2x2x2x2=1024 variations.
> Given to the 1024 possibilities, the tags can be divided in 1024 classes: System *Henry*, of these 1024 classes, made thirty-two series with thirty-two numbers for each possibility . . . Because in each fingerprint, twenty details can be distinguished, then we arrive, with ten fingers, at the number of combinations 20^{10}=10,240,000,000,000 . . . [31]

Here we find the amazing potential for producing a long-distance map, the best thing any ruler might ever have hoped for, a touching map—a one-way touching. The Indies dactyloscopy manual of 1917 explained what might be achieved after dactyloscopy was solidly installed in the Indies:

---

[28] Ibid.

[29] H. Meijer, *De Deli Maatschappij: driekwart eeuw koloniaal spoor* (Rutphen: De Walburg, 1987), p. 74.

[30] Misset, *Het Centraal kantoor voor de dactyloscopie bij de Politie*, p. 18.

[31] Ibid., pp. 20-23.

In London, a thief climbed over the door that was outfitted at the top with nails. Thus, he entered a warehouse, where he committed a serious crime.

On his way back, as he climbed over the door again, he got himself caught by one of the nails between his ring and his ring finger. By the weight of his body, he fell to the ground and left the ring and a portion of his finger's skin on the nail behind.

At the dactyloscopic central station of Scotland Yard, people made a print from the finger skin and checked it against the collection of the central station. The man was arrested and his wounded finger provided a proof of his guilt beyond any doubt.[32]

From these millions of Simin's tags, an Indies *waarschuwing register,* a "caution register," could be compiled:[33]

The collection and storing of the tags at the central bureau can be compared with compiling a dictionary. If one wishes to find a word, one simply turns a page, and the word must be there . . . [34]

Fingerprints might be photographed, and enlarged.[35] The "natives" could be made to stand still; and it is better than photography:

To be able to photograph somebody well and quickly, registering each possible step, one must have at one's disposal special equipment, and that is not always available . . . It is very difficult to identify even a white man on a photo; to identify a native is for a European often impossible . . . Therefore, the identification tags with their combinations should be put to use . . . Also, if the measure is to have a general success, dactyloscopying has to be declared compulsory by the government . . . [36]

It was suggested that dactyloscopy would render the "natives" as individual as their fingerprints: ". . . not two fingerprints look one like the other."[37] From now on in the Netherlands East Indies "natives" would be as eternal, or as temporal, as they were mapped: "They [the fingerprints] do not change; they remain unchanged since before the birth, till shortly after the death . . . "[38]

---

[32] Ibid., p. 26.

[33] D. H. Meijer, Bandoeng, November-December 1926, "Dactyloscopie voor Nederlandsch-Indië," *Koloniale Studiën* 3,2 (1919): 167-168.

[34] G. H. A. Hoedt, "Naschrift," *Koloniale Studiën* 3,2 (1919): 167-168.

[35] Misset, *Het Centraal kantoor voor de dactyloscopie bij de Politie,* p. 29.

[36] A. van den Bovenkamp, "Het dactyloscopeeren als algemeene Regeeringsmaatregel ter tijdelijke vervanging van een Burgerlijken stand voor de Inlandsche bevolking," *Koloniale Studiën* 3,2 (1919): 156-164.

[37] Misset, *Het Centraal kantoor voor de dactyloscopie bij de Politie,* p. 23.

[38] Ibid., p.23.

2. THE FLOODLIGHT

"Two eyes, often, are not enough to watch them," the Dutch Indies post and telegraph union journal wrote in 1906 about "native" co-workers.[39] Whenever two eyes were not enough, or when they appeared vulnerable, glass and glass cases were used.

Already at the first Amsterdam big colonial exhibition in 1883, a special lighting artfully filtered through glass was highly praised:

> We step inside, into the Indies division. What a soft and jolly light! We cry out and, looking up, we notice a white cloth arranged in pleats and spread all over the hall under the ceiling. As if the light were falling down through a web of white palm leaves: it is an ivory light. The firm of De Heyder en Co. made this cloth without using any impregnation.
>
> Even if a tropical rain might ever fall here, and should it leak through the glass panes of the roof and through the cloth, the rainwater would leave no smudges on the floor.
>
> The soft light by itself would be enough to justify the whole enterprise . . . [40]

Maps, logically, proved to be the objects most amenable to being placed under the glass:

> Maps, models, drawings, photographs, samples . . . graphs . . . collections of insects (no less than a hundred glass bottles with these enemies of a sugar planter) . . . [41]

As the colonial times evolved, the trend accelerated. At the "last and greatest"[42] colonial exhibition, in Paris in 1931, the glassed, glass-cased, and artfully lighted maps virtually monopolized the show. Shortly before the opening, a fire destroyed the Dutch Indies pavilion.[43] In forty-one days, the pavilion was rebuilt and became famous as a "Phoenix pavilion."[44] As most of the massy three-dimensional artifacts to be exhibited had vanished in flames, the "Phoenix pavilion" was filled with:

---

[39] "De inlandsche klerken en javaansche bestellers in onzen dienst," *Orgaan van den Bond van Ambtenaren en Beamten bij den Post-, Telegraaf- en Telefoondienst in Nederslandsch-Indië* 2,9 (December 1906): 340-343.

[40] *Officiëele Wegwijzer*, p. 14

[41] J. F. Scheltema, "Nederlandsch-Indië en de Wereldtentoonstelling te Parijs," *De Indische Gids* 22,2 (1900).

[42] Marieke Bloembergen, "Exhibiting colonial modernity: De exposities van de Nederlandse koloniën op de wereldtentoonstellingen (1880-1931)," unpublished PhD prospect, University of Amsterdam, 1995, pp. 3-4.

[43] *Nederland te Parijs 1931: Gedenkboek van de Nederlandsche deelneming aan de Internationale Koloniale Tentoonstelling* ('s Gravenhage: Van Stockum en Zoon, 1931), p. 46.

[44] Bloembergen, "Exhibiting colonial modernity," p. 14 and 14n.

. . . chiefly photographic material . . . sent quickly to Europe through our unsurpassed air mail connection. New entries of a larger size and greater weight could not be sent . . . [45]

The memorial book still exudes the pavilion's spirit. It opens with a photographic portrait of the Dutch Queen; next, there are plans of the exhibition, air photographs of the Paris fair grounds, other photographs, maps, and photographs of maps:

> Netherlands Indies as compared with Europe; Steamship connections in the Indies; Development of the air traffic in the Indies.[46]
> Special interest was attracted by the "staircase of abundance" with a map of the Netherlands Indies archipelago as its backdrop, fifty steps, each with a couple of human figures carrying typical products, also to be located by a special sign on the map . . .
> On the left side of the hall, there was a map of radio-connections of the Netherlands Indies with the world; the map was supplemented with a system of dioramas.[47]

There were more photographs of maps, in Paris, than maps themselves. Irreplaceable originals had vanished in the flames. But, again, the importance of photographs and maps in the Phoenix exhibit merely demonstrated a quickening of a long evolving trend. Already in 1883, back in Amsterdam, two groups of "natives," one from the West Indies and the other from the East Indies, had been brought to the fair grounds and placed so that they could easily be watched by visitors. A celebrated scholar of the time, Roland Bonaparte, arranged for portraits of several individuals in the groups be taken by an Amsterdam photographer: three photographs of each man, woman, or child were taken: *en face*, left profile, and right profile.[48]

This was, of course, just a rudimentary gallery of "wanted natives" and "wanted colony." At the last and biggest Paris exhibition, held in 1931, the gallery was more extensive:

> There were seventy-eight heads of folk types from all the parts of the archipelago. The heads are made by the hand of a well-known Javanese painter Mas Pirngadie, presently on an assignment at the Batavia Museum. He painted from photographs, and thus these are no character studies, as that would not fit these maps, but pure ethnological plates.[49]

Landscapes were flattened in photographs and maps, and the photographs and maps were placed behind a glass. Faces and peoples were flattened. Buildings were smoothed into facades:

---

[45] *Nederland te Parijs 1931: Gedenkboek*, p. 31.

[46] Ibid., pp. 11-18.

[47] Ibid., p. 57.

[48] Some of the photos are located and were exhibited in the Rijksmuseum, Amsterdam, March, 1996.

[49] *Nederland te Parijs 1931: Gedenkboek*, p. 49.

sugar cake creations with silly little pavilions . . . triumphs of stucco. While in 1889, it looked like iron was winning against stone of the earlier time, now plaster has the last word . . . [50]

There was no Nero in the Indies, no burning of Rome. Just a light diversion. An extraordinary Indonesian writer of the period, Mas Marco Kartodikromo, described in 1914 a big colonial exhibition in Semarang as "showing off a perfect fake."[51]

H. F. Tillema is sometimes considered the founding father of modern Indies photography. His works were also part of many of the great colonial exhibitions of the time. He owned a pharmacy in Semarang, early in the century, and was a public figure in the city. He left the Indies just before World War I started, and he spent the rest of his life very close to the beach, at Bloemendaal, north Netherlands, in the house he called "Villa Semarang."[52]

Tillema is best known for his *Kromoblanda,* a five-volume opus filled with photographs, statistics, and charts, so many that the work is often considered "unreadable."[53] Tillema also collected photographs by others and classified and stored them in a "photo central,"[54] a kind of a photo register open to newspapers, museums, and anybody willing to pay. Tillema's services were acknowledged when he was made a Knight of the Order of the Netherlands Lion in 1939 and a *doctor honoris causa* at the University of Groningen in 1940.[55]

Kromoblanda is a journey: as Tillema travels, the Indies, through the lenses of his cameras, becomes nakedly exposed. The volumes open with a number of photographs of jungle, temples, native women with bared breasts, and volcanoes. One caption repeats under these photographs: "—blinded by the glare of majestic tropical nature."[56] Then, as one turns the pages, and Tillema goes on with his journey, the scenes photographed become progressively ordered, lines stand out sharper, shapes become more angular. The man behind the camera is no longer so blinded, and eventually—it becomes clear that this was the motivation and the aim of the journey—the camera gets it all as it should be.

Like on a perfect map, there is a measured proportion of shade and light, and geometrical beauty, at the end, is dominant. Landscapes and peoples are caught by snapshots, which means they are given no time to move unmanageably or independently.

---

[50] Scheltema, "Nederlandsch-Indië en de Wereldtentoonstelling te Parijs," pp. 954-955.

[51] Mas Marco Kartodikromo, "Koloniale tentoonstelling boekan boetoehnja orang Djawa," *Doenia Bergerak* 1,20 (August 1914): 3.

[52] E. Vanvugt, *H. F. Tillema (1870-1952) en de fotografie van tempo doeloe* (Amsterdam: Mets, 1993), pp. 28, 37.

[53] Ibid., p. 37

[54] Ibid., p. 160

[55] Ibid., pp. 29, 158-159.

[56] H. F. Tillema, *"Kromoblanda": over 't vraagstuk van "het wonen" in Kromo's groote land,* vol. I ('s Gravenhage: Uden Masman etc. 1915-1923), pp. 7-12.

One whole volume of *Kromoblanda* is filled by photographs of bathrooms: modern, shiny, tiled, a harmony of straight lines and bright light.[57] In a dramatic contrast, on the same page, there are photographs of the most messy latrines of the "natives" and also photographs of the "natives" themselves. All this is well lighted.[58] Many of the natives, indeed, are photographed in the most private act. As one Tillema's biographer put it, "The Tillema-archive is a monument of Indies scatography."[59]

Later in his life, in 1930, Tillema wrote advice on how to "film and photograph in tropical forest."[60] First of all, one should think of taking a big white sheet of cloth to be used as a backdrop. The mats of "natives" could be used, but they might not always be available. There were other challenges, Tillema warned, that still faced a photographer in the wild. Heat and humidity threatened the camera, lenses, and film; there were "myriads of annoying insects" and "sunlight."

With Tillema, once again, a pioneer, a daring colonial, was on the move:

> an amateur on a journey in uncivilized regions . . . has no place to rest, nowhere to buy anything, a little screw, a nail, a piece of copper or an iron wire, a tool, in a word, he lives and works in a photographic vacuum![61] . . . in a rimboe [forest], one has to walk. For this, one needs shoes that one cannot buy in the fatherland. So called "Acheh" shoes [used by the Dutch in the Acheh war 1873-1903]—available in the Indies in many shops—are excellent . . . Every Indies military man can give a good information about this matter.[62]

Infections and bacteria posed a grave danger to the man and, at the same time, to the man's technology:

> Also . . . infections . . . dysentery . . . "vaccination" . . . must be repeated each six months . . . [63]
> All the precautions notwithstanding, a number of fungus or bacteria colonies may develop which can spoil the final picture . . . [64]

While on the mission, one had to take a good care of oneself as well as one's technology:

---

[57] See especially ibid., vol. 4, part 2, p. 523; vol. V, part 2, pictures nos. 21-22, pp. 454-457, 782-783, 884.

[58] See also J. A. A. van Doorn, *De laatste eeuw van Indië: Ontwikkeling en ondergang van een koloniaal project* (Amsterdam: Bert Bakker, 1994), p. 156, quoting F. W. M. Kerchman (red.) *25 Jaren decentralisatie in Nederlandsch-Indië 1905-1930* (Semarang, 1930); G. Flieringa, *De zorg voor de volkshuisvesting in de stadsgemeenten in Nederlandsch Oost Indie: in het bijzonder in Semarang* (Den Haag: Nijhoff, 1930).

[59] E. Vanvugt, *H. F. Tillema*, p. 35.

[60] H. F. Tillema, "Filmen en fotografeeren in de tropische rimboe. Met foto's van den schrijver," offprint from *Lux-de camera* 1930.

[61] Ibid., p. 97.

[62] Ibid., p. 103.

[63] Ibid., pp. 100-101.

[64] Ibid., p. 108.

Lenses. One takes lenses of a greatest possible "light strength." I used a f2.9 focus 12.5cM. Dallmeijer, which worked well . . . [65]

This all being carefully done, the journey makes sense. Subjects are taken in:

Soedah! [Finally done!] I also noticed that a primitive peoples, like we in our youth, have never learned in school to sit still, even for one second! Thus, one is forced to work at a very slow pace, with 1/8 second opening. Whenever light permits, one takes a short-time exposure . . . Hands are sticky with sweat. This is not just very annoying, but also very dangerous for the film. After some training, however, we will make it.[66]

In 1935, Tillema made one more Indies trip, once again as a camera expert. This time he traveled to the deepest interior, to film the tribes of Apo Kaya in Central Borneo.[67] In his report on this adventure, he appeared particularly excited about one item. "It had been of scientific interest," Tillema wrote,

to discover whether there still remained some women who knew how to weave as it used to be done when they were young. In fact, I was anxious to obtain a filmed record of the whole process . . . De Rooy [a local Dutch official and Tillema's partner in the project] gets on marvelously with those people and by tact and sympathy . . . [he found] one very old woman who still knew how to weave, but [was] unwilling to give us a demonstration, because the spirits would not approve.

Tillema and De Rooy quickly decided upon

providing an active force which would neutralize the power proclaimed by tradition . . . tin of salt . . . some sewing needles, thread, a couple of pieces of velvet, a few hands full of tobacco and some other little items . . . Instead of one old woman, three of them turned up . . .

The weaving and filming were completed; the camera captured it. Then it was an easy thing, as just by the way of an afterthought, that

De Rooy purchased the last Dayak loom and the last woven piece of material and presented both to the "Colonial Institute" at Amsterdam . . .

Who can imagine, wrote Tillema,

---

[65] Ibid., p. 105.

[66] Ibid., pp. 106-107.

[67] H. F. Tillema, *Apo Kajaan: een filmreis naar en door Centraal Borneo* (Amsterdam: Van Munster, 1938) ; also H. F. Tillema, "The etiquette of dress among the Apo-Kajaan Dayaks," offprint from *The Netherlands Mail*, vol. 2, no. 3-4 (1935). For photo of Tillema with camera, see E. Vanvugt, *H. F. Tillema*, p. 150.

my delight . . . after . . . suspense for about a year . . . to see the negative film developed and soon thereafter to watch on the screen the little women . . . intent on their work.[68]

Sometimes, this appeared like the Marinetti's avant-garde futurist dream:

We disengage ourselves today . . . [instead of] chaos [we] substitute . . . mechanical splendor; [we make] the sun relit . . . [we achieve] healthful forgetfulness [through] controlled force . . . speed . . . light.[69]

Marinetti and Frankenstein. The Indies maps and photographs, images through the camera, under the glass, and illuminated by a man-made light, were acquiring a cheerful, liberating, and ghostly life of their own.

Mr. Scheltema, a Dutchman and an Indies hand, visited the Paris exhibition of 1900, and, in the Dutch pavilion, as he later wrote, was particularly excited about

a railway map with illuminated images of most picturesque and, from the point of view of construction, most significant sections of the train connection between East and West Java . . . [70]

If Mr. Scheltema had lived long enough to see the "last and biggest" Paris exhibition of 1931, he might have enjoyed, in the midst of a severe world and colonial economic depression, something even more impressive. "An endless wonderment," in Paris in 1931, was awakened

by a show designed by ir. Utermark and constructed by the Technical Service of the Colonial Institute that offered a map of the piece of world between Amsterdam and the archipelago displaying to large numbers of visitors the weekly air-way KLM connection between the Netherlands and the Netherlands Indies . . .

Segment by segment, the route lighted up with twelve place names, a yellow lamp for an outbound plane, a blue lamp for a homebound plane, and a green lamp for the meeting point in Djask.

. . . moving incessantly, the miniature airplanes have a great power of attraction . . . Another electric map demonstrates truthfully, by lamps automatically lighting up, a difference between a journey by ship and by plane to the Netherlands Indies . . . all is made even more interesting by the airfield at Tjililitan, Batavia, in miniature, which is a part of the complex. [71]

---

[68] Ibid., p. 2-5. See also the photo by Tillema of an Apo-Kajan woman at a sewing machine in Vanvugt, *H. F. Tillema*, p. 163. See also a comment in *Volksraad* about Tillema being helped in the adventure by the colonial government *"militair transport."* Speech of Van Helsdingen in *Volksraad* on July 22, 1938, *Handelingen van den Volksraad*, 1938-39, pp. 371-372.

[69] Marinetti's Futurist Manifesto as published in *Figaro*, quoted in M. McLuhan, *The Mechanical Bride: Folklore of Industrial Man* (London: Routledge and Kegan, 1967), pp. 88, 90.

[70] Scheltema "Nederlandsch-Indië en de Wereldtentoonstelling te Parijs," p. 969.

[71] *Nederland te Parijs 1931: Gedenkboek*, p. 54.

Competing for visitors' attention, just across the hall from the air-route map, there was:

> a 14 meter long, 4 meter broad, and 1.5 meter deep pit with a grotesque relief map of the main island of the Netherlands Indies archipelago on the bottom, on a scale of 1:80,000 in the horizontal direction and 1:8,000 in the vertical direction.
>
> The aim of the map is, among other things, to point out the tourist qualities of Java; little electric trains move through the map, and, as they pass the crucial points, fourteen dioramas suddenly light up.[72]

The illuminated maps, like Tillema's snapshots, were an entertainment, but they were not marginal. In them, more than in anything else, the late-colonial paradigm came to be intensely expressed—as if the whole dynamics of the colony centered in them. Attractive, self-contained, and frivolous, the patches of light manifested what the whole colony increasingly wanted to be.

There had been "multicolor fountains" and "Edison feasts" in vogue in the Indies since before World War I.[73] Journals gave witness to the extraordinary popularity of "electric pictures." Modern buildings in an Indies town, selected with care, were illuminated on a special night—*floodlighted* as the popular English word described it. Modern facades glowed as if they were only facades. Sometimes, and this seemed to be preferred, only a building's contours were illuminated. Nothing but clean, sharp lines stood out of the darkness.[74]

The Technical Institute in Bandung was a special subject for floodlighting, as well as city halls, banks, and railway company headquarters.[75] The journal for "local technique," its volumes throughout the 1930s filled with these electric pictures, celebrated Surabaya at night, "the most amazing city illumination . . . white and orange glare."[76]

Movies appeared in the Indies, reportedly, on St. Nicholas Day, December 5, 1900. The first movie was reportedly shown in the Tanah Abang quarter of Batavia as a light diversion for better society. The attractions of the first show were

> shots of the Queen Wilhelmina and Duke Hendrik in The Hague, scenes (probably fake) from the Boer War in Transvaal, and pictures of new consumer products from the fair in Paris.[77]

---

[72] Ibid., p. 61.

[73] *Alles Electrisch* 1,1 (June 1931), title page; see also *Alles Electrisch* 1,2 (August 1931), title page; *Alles Electrisch* 1,3 (September 1931), title page.

[74] *Alles Electrisch* 1,3 (September 1931), title page.

[75] For "electric pictures" of Technische Hoogeschool on the Queen's birthday in 1923 and 1924 see Jaarboek THS, *Lustrum Uitgave* (Bandoeng, 1935), title page.

[76] *Locale Techniek* 5,6 (June 1935): 20.

[77] Michael Kaden, "An Evening Breeze from Southeast," unpublished paper from the proceedings of the European Conference of Southeast Asian Studies, Leiden 1995, p. 1.

Soon, enormous movie houses, often "enormous movie bamboo tents,"[78] were built throughout the Indies. During the next decades, some of the most modern structures in the colony, including the first air conditioned homes, were movie houses.[79]

Dutch, Chinese, French, and soon American movies, all with Malay subtitles, became wildly popular.[80]

> Jasmine of Java, Mystery of Borobudur, Clear Moon, Fatimah, Halfhearted [the first Indies jungle film], Dagger of Mataram, Zoebaida, Laughing Mask, Tom Mix . . . [81]

This was a serious colonial project. Prof. Treub, one of the foremost apologists of the empire, visited a new labor camp for the native workers in the Batavia harbor, in 1923, and he was excited:

> The terrain is spacious . . . there is an opportunity for enlarging . . . naturally . . . cinematograph is not missing . . . [82]

The public at the movies, naturally, sat in the shadows. Many officials complained about "natives" acting "nonchalant" in their *kambing* (goat) sections even "while the 'Wilhelmus' [Dutch anthem] was played,"[83] or "whistling ditties while the image of the Queen was on the screen."[84] Some worried about the spectators viewing Western movie stars in their underwear.[85] Precautions were taken in 1912 to see that films with "murder, robbery, adultery, and matters of that sort—can in no case be permitted."[86] The Film Law of 1916 banned the movies that might be subversive to "public order and morals."[87] Groups of vigilantes were formed, in 1918, to help the police to watch the movies.[88]

---

[78] Walraven on Java around 1918; *Fakkel* I,9 (Jul-Aug 1941), p. 704.

[79] Dipl. Ings. B. de Vistarini, "Luchtconditioneering en bouwkunde," *De Ingenieur in Nederlandsch-Indië,* Jg.V, No. 11 (November 1938), p. VI, 45. See also ir. P. Timmerman, "De bevordering van lucht-conditioneering door de electriciteitmaatschappijen en het verbruik van electrische stroom in Nederlandsch-Indië," *De Ingenieur in Nederlandsch-Indië,* Jg. V, No. 11 (November 1938), p. VI, 47.

[80] Soeluh van den Berg, "Notabele ingezetenen en goedwillende ambtenaren: De Nederlands-Indische filmkeuring, 1912-1942," in *Jaarboek Media Geschiedenis* 4 (1992), pp. 157, 160. Nio Joe Lan, "De vestiging van een Indische Filmindustrie," *Koloniale Studiën* 25,4 (1941): 388-389.

[81] Nio Joe Lan, "De vestiging van een Indische Filmindustrie," *Koloniale Studiën* 25,4 (1941): 394-400.

[82] M. W. F. Treub, *Nederland in de Oost: reisindrukken* (Haarlem: Willink, 1923), pp. 249-250.

[83] See e.g. "Van eerbied gesproken!" *Nationale Commentaren,* Jrg. 4, No. 39 (September 27, 1941): 3817.

[84] "VERSCHRIKKELIJK," *De Beweging* 6 (February 8, 1919): 101.

[85] Sir Hesketh Bell after visiting the Dutch Indies in 1926 in his *Foreign colonial administration in the Far East,* London 1928, pp. 121-122, quoted in S. van den Berg, "Notabele ingezetenen en goedwillende ambtenaren," p. 157.

[86] Ibid., p. 148.

[87] Ibid., p. 149.

[88] Ibid., p. 150, for more detail see ibid, pp. 150ff.

Yet, even the shadow in the Indies movie houses was man-made. The electric-light switch was in professional hands. These indeed are the most disturbing images of the late-colonial period: the people floodlighted and the rulers watching the light effect.

H. Maclaine Pont, an Indies architect, the builder of the Technical Institute in Bandung, among other things, recalled in 1916 how he had completed a new central office for a tramway company in Tegal, Central Java, and how he celebrated with his Javanese workers:

> Several *wayang* [shadow-puppet theater] troupes entertained the festive crowds; towards the evening, the terrain was electrically illuminated and an open-air cinematograph began. After a while, a heavy rain started and poured down, and a great deal of the terrain was soon deep under the water . . . yet . . . between two thousand and three thousand spectators remained and they stood in the water and watched until the last film was at its end...[89]

In the same journal, the same year, an elaborate account was published by one C. M. Vissering of the Batavia colonial exhibition of 1916:

> Batavia's biggest square is temporarily recreated into a fair, a platform is erected for the Resident of Batavia, other officials and their dames. . . below, a group of native chiefs from the most outlying lands of our Empire of Great Insulinde.[90]

There were chickens, birds of prey, rabbits, and crocodiles on the square, "a pack of old apes with indescribably melancholic deep-set eyes; they look out, as if sick with nostalgia for their forest." There were also clowns, orchestras, and stands selling the produce of village industries.[91] But the high point came at twilight:

> As soon as darkness wins over, both of the main entrance gates and the whole front part of the square glitter reflecting a glow coming from the motley lights of the cinematographs . . .
>
> An immense crowd sits on the ground in their best plumage of white *baadjes* [coats], colorful sarongs, and tidy head clothes . . .
>
> Amidst the crowd, there are little *warong* [stalls] stands, whose little lamps, whenever the beam of light from the movies fall in other direction, create red, yellow, and orange glimmers across the multitude.
>
> There is, in this immense human mass, nothing but light, color, and peace; first of all, peace, picked up by the colors and the light, each time the scene brightens by a sudden radiation from the big movie theater, as the cinematographic mechanism throws a broad stream of light over the whole square; now, everybody is garish, then everybody is carmine red, then deep blue, then fiercely orange . . .

---

[89] H. Maclaine Pont, "Het nieuwe Hoofdbureau der Semarang-Cheribon-Stoomtram Maatschappij te Tegal," *Nederlandsch Indië oud en nieuw (1916-1917)*, vol. I, no. 0 (promotional issue), p. 98.

[90] C. M. Vissering, "Een Pasar Gambir," *Nederlandsch Indië oud en nieuw (1916-1917)*, p. 399.

[91] Ibid., pp. 399ff.

For us, it is a joy of a show! That look of a placid happiness of the hundreds; that picture that repeatedly emerges out of the darkness in the vehement lighting by the cinematograph . . . always the same amazing multicolored still life, and the little *warong*'s little flames flickering orange and red.[92]

When this is over:

The native chiefs and the native workers return to their solitary distant regions; they will live again in their *kampong*, [native quarters] work with their primitive tools, and do their pure handiwork of peace; for us, Westerners, they left behind images of a culture ennobled through work.[93]

3. THE SUBLIME

There is a novel by Louis Couperus drawn from the lives of early twentieth-century Dutch officials and planters who had retired from the Indies and returned to live in The Hague. Entitled *Old People*, the whole story is about aging and how one might possibly evade it. This is how the novel ends: "His fair and delicate face bent low over his papers; and so close to the lamp, it could be seen that he was growing very gray at the temples."[94]

The imperative for the act of looking—this was the hero's chief discovery and lesson—was to remain in the shadows. To avoid being seen, in full light at least, was as important as to see.

The Indies Dutch were determined not to let the "natives" see their masters watching. There were very few Indonesians among the surveyors in the colony.[95] Even the most trifling matters of government were veiled by an extraordinary and oft-noted secretiveness.[96] Optical tools came to be important also as shields. Everything, or so it was hoped, might become a theodolite, or a telescope. One might get inside to hide and watch.

Trains became such an optical tool. Late-colonial trains "glided through countless turns between the majestic mass of the landscape."[97] As they sledded on the iron rails, the land along the tracks, and as far as one could see from the train, sledded back with the same smoothness and speed as the train. The landscape

---

[92] Ibid., pp. 406-407. For *lichteffecten* see also report on a student festivity evening in Bandung in 1939. *Ganeça* 10,1 (February 1939): 3.

[93] C. M. Vissering, "Een Pasar Gambir," p. 407.

[94] Louis Couperus, *Old People and the Things that Pass* (Leyden, London: Sythoff, Heinemann, 1963), p. 265.

[95] It was not before 1909 that non-Europeans were first received into a training for *landsmeters*. See C. Fasseur, *De Indologen. Ambtenaren voor de Oost, 1825-1950* (Amsterdam: Bert Bakker, 1993), p. 258. Another source says it first happened in 1913. See L. C. F. Polderman, "Het kadaster in Nederlandsch-Indië," *Koloniale Studiën* 3,1 (1919): 84-85.

[96] M. T. H. Perelaer, "De geheimzinnigheid uwer staatslieden in bestuurszaken," *De Indische Gids* 7,2 (1885): 1597-1598; see also "De geheimzinnigheid in het Indische bestuur," *De Indische Gids* 16,1 (1894): 911-912.

[97] M. Buys, *Batavia, Buitenzorg en de Preanger-Gids voor bezoekers en toeristen* (Batavia: Go Kolff &Co. 1891) quoted in *De Indische Gids* 14,1 (1892): 896.

alongside the train was often the most modern strip of the colony, created at the same time as the train, with the same design, and largely for the sake of the train. It was a most easily and comfortingly watchable modernity. As the fuel was still coal, travelers were well advised to pull up the window—unless they wanted to "leave the train black with soot"[98]—and watch the land along the tracks from behind the window glass.

H. P. Berlage, the most celebrated Dutch architect of the early twentieth century, visited the Indies in 1924. Berlage enjoyed the trip across the seas. After disembarking, he noted that Batavia was much of what he had expected and believed in: a modern colony on the march. He was just a little nervous before he set out further on a trip into the colony's interior:

> I went to the station very early, anxious about surprises of a train trip in the Indies . . . Javanese crowds waited for the train . . . in swarms, they stormed it . . . [yet, on a second look, they were coolies] you could trust them even with your minutest luggage . . . My high respect and admiration goes to the Javanese servants . . . Oh! that always so delightful calm and silence of theirs . . . [99]

As the train pulled out of the station, Berlage pulled his window up: "the aspects are fleeting . . . cinematographic . . . palm groves, *kampongs*, bridges, green sawah rice fields . . . blue and hazy horizon . . . "[100]

As far as Berlage could see, beyond the window glass and framed by the window framed there lay the *mooi Indië*, "beautiful Indies," a late-colonial image often more significant than the colony itself. Retiring Dutch officials and planters, especially, liked to take "the beautiful Indies" back home. They would carry home pictorial souvenirs, the colony captured in a little hangable painting, and photographs, a panorama of rice-fields, coconut trees, buffalo boys, mountains, with a red shining sun.

There were strict rules for the "beautiful Indies"; to be beautiful, a picture must contain no suggestion of waving time, no trembling of the air, no hidden energies, nothing hinted at in the shadows. The trees, houses, fields, mountains, and the people had to be distinctly outlined. The perspective should swell forward, and everything should offer itself to be seen. As in Roland Bonaparte's or Tillema's snapshots, or in the maps, there was a distinct police quality in the beauty of this craft.[101]

Berlage traveled to Bandung and noted that, "The trip by train through Praenger is one of the most beautiful in the world."[102] "A wonderful road network," he wrote,

---

[98] Treub, *Nederland in de Oost*, p. 268.

[99] H. P. Berlage, *Mijn Indische Reis: Gedachten over cultuur en kunst* (Rotterdam: W. L. en J. Brusse's, 1931), p. 36.

[100] Ibid., pp. 36-37.

[101] Angus McIntyre, "Sukarno as Artist-Politician," in *Indonesian Political Biography: In search of cross-cultural understanding* ed. Angus McIntyre (Clayton: Monash Papers on Southeast Asia, 1993), pp. 166-167.

[102] Berlage, *Mijn Indische Reis*, p. 49.

... the most modern means of transportation, not only in the horizontal, but also in the vertical direction . . . [103]

The Netherlands was so flat a place! Others complained about it as well:

the Indies has three dimensions as against the flat and low Netherlands with only two . . . [104]

In the Indies, a modern Dutch man or woman might feel complete. This state of completeness might be what Berlage, at the rail head in Bandung, appeared close to attaining: "*Ueber allen Gipflen*, in a purple-gray depth, the splendid land of Java . . . "[105] Many made the journey before and after Berlage. For a trip like that, clearly, there was no better venue than the Praenger railway and Bandung at its end. As an anonymous Dutch writer put it more than a decade later in 1939:

Bandung . . . Indeed, no Indies town gives Westerner so sure a feeling that he is among his own . . . its segregation in the design . . . always secluded sphere . . . provincial . . . small and un-monumental . . . cheerful and nice . . . historically uninteresting, closed . . . among its (indeed beautiful) mountains . . . [While] the genuine Indies . . . the heaving tropical land . . . lays far and deep, "in the warmth" . . . reachable and playable with airplane . . . [106]

It is appropriate that an "airplane" would be mentioned in the last quote. Just a few years after Berlage's visit, the airplane arrived as a technological—and optical—tool in the Indies, welcome as the train and capable of transporting passengers along a path even more pleasantly distant from the real ground.[107] Like the train, the airplane glided smoothly through the mass of landscape, climbing higher and higher, in the same anxious search for the third dimension.

The arrival of the airplane marked one more cheerful moment for the colonials. It must have felt as if Holland of the Golden Age was about to rise again, this time reaching out not only to the "beautiful Indies," but ultimately extending around the "beautiful world." One passenger recorded that "The first day [from Amsterdam] we flew to Prague, then, second day, to Belgrade, on the third day, tough luck! . . . thermometer's gone . . . "[108] Planes leaving from Amsterdam soared and glided above, "over the blue Danube . . . "[109]

---

[103] Ibid., p. 110.

[104] *Ganeça* I, 6 (November 1, 1922): 83.

[105] Ibid., p. 110.

[106] "Batavia en Bandoeng," *Kritiek en Opbouw* II,1 (February 16, 1939): 4.

[107] Picture #28 in Rusman. See E. Rusman, *Hollanders vliegen: tien jaar Amsterdam-Batavia door de lucht* (Baarn: Bosch en Konning, no date), p. 33.

[108] Rusman, *Hollanders vliegen*, pp. 15-16.

[109] Charles M. Morrell, "The 100th Flight: The Royal Dutch Airways Great Achievement," *The Java Gazette* (1940) (special issue), p. II.

> Jupiter temple, Athens, pyramid of Cheops . . . the sphinx . . . Dead Sea
> . . . Cashmere Mosque in Baghdad . . . [110]
> finally 24th November over Batavia; the whole distance 127 hours 16
> minutes; over 20 flight days; average speed 120.75 km per hour.[111]

One of the early passengers on the KLM flights wrote "an appreciation"
describing how on that kind of trip one might

> . . . obtain a true bird's eye view. From the vantage point of the aeroplane
> you see in this manner the primeval forests of Sumatra and Burma, the deep
> blue of the Malaccan Archipelago [sic] . . . [112]

It was noticed in the last decades of the colonial period that the "Indies public"
"became 'airminded' faster and more completely than the public in an average
Western country."[113]

From the planes, one might see volcanoes little as toys. The volcanoes seen from
an airplane fitted into the panorama of the "beautiful Indies." And nature itself was
captivated by the new wonderful illusion; as first passenger planes appeared in the
colony, the terrible Krakatoa came to life again, perfectly in time for the first air
tourists to see it:

> . . . special "sight-seeing-flights" . . . Among the latter, the most popular
> are flights from Bandung over the Tangkung Prahu craters, from Batavia
> over the bay of Tandjong Priok and the little islands, from Surabaya over
> Bromo and the Sand Sea. The flights that KNILM [the sister company of
> KLM in the Indies] organized during the explosion of Krakatoa at the
> beginning of 1929 were unforgettable for all participants.[114]
> . . . A toilet is available in each airplane; as the cabin is suspended under
> the wings, the passengers can have an undisturbed view through the large
> windows with unbreakable glass . . . [115]

Through the unbreakable glass of the planes not merely volcanoes and the rest of
the landscape, but also the people of the land were made most distinctly and safely
visible: "The Papuans have a particularly great interest in Dragons traveling by air:
the first airplanes that they ever had an opportunity to see."[116]

Soeroso, one of the Indonesian deputies in the *Volksraad*, an advisory council of
the governor-general, complained in July 1938 that governmental support of the
Indies air traffic was overzealous and made no sense to the "indigenous population":

---

[110] Rusman, *Hollanders vliegen*, pp. 17-19.

[111] Ibid., p. 18.

[112] *Gedenboek, KLM Air Line Amsterdam* (Batavia, KLM), p. 23.

[113] *10 vervlogen jaren* (Batavia: KNILM, 1938), p. 7.

[114] *KNILM* (Koninklijke Nederlands Indische Luchtvaart Maatschappij) *Reisgids 1930* (Batavia: KNILM, 1930), p. 11.

[115] Ibid., p. 13.

[116] *10 vervlogen jaren*, p. 16b.

I was [in 1928] of the opinion that the introduction of the air transport had no significance for the indigenous population . . . We are now ten years further, but yet not a single *tani* [peasant] or coolie has made use of an airplane. . .[117]

Soeroso's Dutch colleagues and other experts responded in the *Volksraad*, arguing that he was wrong to discount the significance of air traffic to the indigenous population for three reasons. First, there was "the imperial interest" excited by the appearance of the airplanes.[118] Second, "the indigenous people" were sending a great number of postcards through airmail.[119] And third, air travel made sense "for all the races" in the colony, and "for all the nationalities without an exception," if one only looked at it as at an amusement:

Number of passengers in air transportation between 1 November 1928, and 1 November, 1929: Batavia-Bandung: 3953; Bandung-Batavia: 4303; Batavia-Semarang: 997; Semarang-Batavia: 1002; Extra- and sight-seeing flights: 3514; Total: 13,769 . . . Passengers of every sex, nationality, race, of all ages and classes, could be found among the KNILM regular clients.[120]

In advertisements for "observation vacation cruises" found in the memorial books of KNILM through the 1930s, the celebrated "Javanese princess," Kartini—a forerunner of "native emancipation," and an author of letters that her Dutch mentor published under the title *Door duisternis tot licht*, "From Darkness to Light"—became a regular feature:

The photo shows an excursion by the Kartini-schools in Semarang . . . sight-seeing flight over Semarang . . . [121]
Interest by the youth . . . Visit of the Kartini-school to the airfield Simongan . . . [122]

In Lembang, a town located yet another half an hour by car further up above Bandung, there was a hilltop with magnificent views topped by an observatory. The telescopes of Lembang were as famous in the Indies of the 1920s and 1930s as the Bandung railway. The Lembang observatory was built by K. A. R. Boscha, one of the wealthiest Dutch tea magnates of the Indies. Boscha lived on his Javanese plantation at Malabar, near both Bandung and Lembang. When Louis Couperus visited him, in 1924, Boscha's Malabar estate boasted, among other things, "a dainty little electric grill . . . electric piano . . . generator by the . . . river . . . seismograph which recorded any tremor of the ground which was still volcanic."[123]

---

[117] Soeroso, February 5, 1938. *Handelingen van den Volksraad, 1938-39*, p. 364.

[118] De Hoog, February 5, 1938, *Handelingen van den Volksraad, 1938-39*, p. 377.

[119] Soeroso, March 5, 1938, reacting in *Handelingen van den Volksraad, 1938-39*, p. 889.

[120] "Een jaar Luchtverkeer, 1929-1930," *KNILM Reisgids 1930* (Batavia: KNILM, 1930), p. 10; see also *10 vervlogen jaren*, p. 45.

[121] *10 vervlogen jaren*, p. 45.

[122] *KNILM Reisgids 1930* (Batavia: KNILM, 1930), p. 57.

[123] L. Couperus, *Eastward*, trans. J. Menzies-Wilson and C. C. Crispin (London: Hurst & Blackett, Ltd., 1924), pp. 166-167.

Boscha, the son of a Dutch physicist and at one time the director of the Technical Institute in Delft, studied civil engineering, but never finished school. Rather, he became an "enthusiastic amateur."[124] He arrived in the Indies in 1887, and by the 1910s he had become the colony's tycoon. At this moment, he decided to build Lembang and to dedicate it "exclusively to science."[125] By the mid-1920s, there already were amazing machines on the Lembang hill:

> The 16-cm Secretan refractor . . . 11-cm Zeiss comet-seeker and . . . the 60-cm double refractor-with one barrel for visual work and one for photography.
> Around the double refractor . . . rose a round, domed structure of reinforced concrete . . . The floor beneath the telescope changed elevation by means of an electric motor, to accommodate observers.[126]

Boscha "decided to set up the finest observatory in the Southern Hemisphere."[127] The Dutch skies were obscured most of the year; thus, this was another effort to compensate for the two-dimensionality of the motherland. Boscha's observatory, even before it began to work, was hailed as "a monument of the Dutch culture in this land."[128]

Recreational star-watching at Lembang soon became as popular as the air-cruises and sight-seeing railway trips, and often the activity was offered as part of the same package. Every day at Lembang one encountered "the same show: youngsters . . . on vacation . . . elders . . . natives, who were attracted by rumors about the great looking glasses . . . "[129]

But then as the colony developed, and as the Great Depression set in, it became necessary for people to economize, even on Lembang. For this reason, some of the most spectacular technologies planned for the hilltop were never put to work.[130] Yet what seemed to matter most was to keep on gazing. For so long as one was star-watching, one might survive and not notice the Depression or even the final destruction. When the Dutch Indies was crushed under the Japanese onslaught of 1942, Joan Voute, the Dutch director of the Boscha observatory at that time

> also went into internment, but he returned to the observatory at the request of the Japanese astronomers who took charge in 1943. There he carried out observations of double stars with the tacit approval of the *chargé d'affaires*, Masai Miyadi. Under the Japanese administration, Voûte measured 11,000 pairs, first with the 37-cm telescope and then with the largest one, which the Japanese remounted . . . [131]

---

[124] Pyenson, *Empire of Reason*, pp. 56-57, 134.

[125] According to Cornelis Braak, acting chief of observatory in Batavia the new observatory should "'limit its work exclusively to science'; the practical side of things would be left to Batavia." Quote from June 1920. Pyenson, *Empire of Reason*, p. 55.

[126] Pyenson, *Empire of Reason*, p. 71, 71n.

[127] Ibid., p. 57.

[128] Prof. Dr. J. Clay on "De zonsverduistering van 21 September j.l. en te beteekenis van de expeditie ter waarneming van het Einstein-effect," *Ganeça* I,5 (October 15, 1922): 68, 96.

[129] G. A. van Bovene, *Nieuws! Een boek over pers, film en radio* (Batavia: G.Kolff), p. 52.

[130] Pyenson, *Empire of Reason*, p. 77.

[131] Ibid., p. 82.

Like trains and planes, telescopes were a shelter. They let a gazer hide and watch the "beautiful Indies," the "beautiful world," and "beautiful stars" from behind the glass, a kaleidoscopic illusion "aimed upon the southern skies . . . beneath. . . the city of Bandung . . . with its thousands of visible stars, the vault of heaven . . . "[132]

Most sublime in that universe were the Indies late-colonial *dealuxe* mountain hotels. In a typical tourist folder, next to one or two photographs of half-naked (preferably Balinese) hotel maids, declarations (often facsimiles) were published, certified by doctors' signatures and governmental stamps:

Certificate I
Result of the bacteriological, chemical, microscopical analysis of DRINKING WATER from the BROMO HOTEL at Tosari, taken by Doctor J. Schut in sterilized bottles at Tosari the 2nd of May 1925. The bacteriological analysis gave on plates of agar-agar by a temperature of 30 degrees Celsius: after 2 days 12 germs per cc.; after 3 days 18 germs per cc. The germs were bacillus vulgatus, which is harmless. The total number of germs per cubic centimeter is low. The water is clear, of good taste and meets the requirements of good and trustworthy drinking water . . . it can be drunk without being boiled. Soerabaia, 20th May 1925. Chem.Bact.& Serol.Laboratorium. v/h Lab.v,Suikerindustrie.

Certificate II
Result of the renewed analysis of Drinking Water on the 30th December 1925. Conclusion: The quality of the water is A 1. The chief of the Governments Laboratorium. [133]

Microphotographs of cerebral malaria were highlights of the First Exhibition for Hygiene that opened late in 1927 in Batavia: "The richness of colors of the sick tissue and the changed organ are a constant attraction, and they never fail to make an impression on the *massa* . . . "[134]
Like the toy trains displayed at the Paris exhibition, and like the colony perceived through the Lembang telescopes, the insides of human bodies moved obviously, brimming with the man-made light:

Fascinating was the way in which Prof. H. M. Neeb in his exhibition "stand" demonstrated the process of infection by hookworms: an almost life-size picture showed schematically the blood-vessel and intestinal system of a human. By pushing a button, one can see a tiny electric light that represents a hookworm larva, moving in through the cuticle on the foot, into the body. It climbs upwards through the blood vessels, enters the heart, the lungs, the pharynx, the oesophagus, the stomach, and, thus, the intestinal canal.[135]

---

[132] G. A. van Bovene, *Nieuws! Een boek over pers, film en radio*, p. 53.

[133] *Bromo-Hotel-Tosari* (Tosari: Bromo Hotel, 1926?) (tourist folder), pp. 20-21.

[134] M. A. J. Kelling, "De Eerste Hygiëne Tentoonstelling in Nederlandsch-Indië," *Koloniale Studiën* 11,2 (1927): 346-348.

[135] Ibid., pp. 355-356

If there was some vigor left to the Dutch in the colony of the 1920s and especially the 1930s, it was in the intensity of moments like these.

Early in 1933, the Dutch community in the Indies passed through a brief, yet violent shock. There was a mutiny among the Dutch and Indonesian crew of *De Zeven Provinciën* (The Seven Provinces), a battleship in the waters just off Java. The commander of the Dutch naval aviation, P. J. Elias, recalled later in his memoirs how the mutiny was dealt with.

At one point, captain Elias wrote, the mutinous ship was almost lost to the pursuers. However, on the ship "a young officer pulled it off . . . got into the radio room at the last moment and sent notice . . . to the naval air forces about the position of the ship.[136]

An ultimatum was sent, but ignored by the ship. Then it was decided that the ship would be bombed, first from an airplane with an 800-kilogram bomb, and then, in the event that the bomb should miss, from a submarine armed with a torpedo:

> between 8.53 and 9.02 the instruments gave their summations . . . on various wavelengths . . . no white flag . . . Coppers, a young bellwether air-fighter, just before the end of his six-year service turned, grabbed the chance. At 1,200-meter altitude his Dornier began its foray. Then the ship came into the viewfinder of the bombsight . . . Zero! direct hit . . . exactly on target . . . flames. In a fraction of a second . . . they learned . . . The mutineers in panic gave themselves up . . . [137]

This was how the mutiny was seen, and how powerfully the seeing worked. This is also, perhaps, as far as this story could go. The mutineers' ship was pulled into the looking glass and held there, either upright or upside-down. From that moment, the mess of the colony "far and deep in the warmth" could safely be—as Oudemans, or Kant, might say—"subsumed under the concept of Quantity."[138] As captain Elias put it more succinctly: "Zero! direct hit." They had no chance.

---

[136] Jhr. P. J. Elias, *Dan liever de lucht in. Herinneringen van een marinevlieger* (Amsterdam: van Kampen en Zoon, 1963), pp. 83-84.

[137] Ibid., pp. 83-86. There is a photo of *Zeven Provinciën* in the book, an air-photo, naturally. Ibid., p. 113.

[138] "The first one of the physiological principles subsumes all phenomena, as intuitions in space and time, under the concept of Quantity . . . " Immanuel Kant, *Prolegomena: To Any Future Metaphysics That Can Qualify as a Science* (La Salle: Open Court, 1902), p. 65.

COLONIAL CRIMINALS IN JAVA, 1870–1910

Henk Schulte Nordholt, Margreet van Till

INTRODUCTION

In this article we present a few cases in order to make a simple argument that runs as follows: although "law and order," or "peace and tranquillity," were from the 1830s onwards the cornerstones of colonial ideology, in practice colonial rule was based on terror and intimidation all over Java; not only rural Java, but especially the very centers of the colonial state—the areas of Batavia and Buitenzorg (Bogor)—were heavily dominated by local violence. As part of its own formation, the colonial state gave birth to criminals. It counted and flogged persons defined as criminals, and it ceded specific spaces to them in which they could operate. Through policing, terror, and convict labor the Dutch were only capable of, and interested in, controlling some of the criminality their colonial state had helped to create. Moreover, an attitude of fear and notions of injustice were fundamental characteristics of the mental framework of colonial society.

VIOLENCE AND POTENCY

Both colonial administrative concepts, which focused on the Javanese village as the static basis of rural society, and colonial Javanology have helped to create an image of Java that emphasizes harmony and self-constraint as basic features of the Javanese character. In old Java emphasis was indeed placed on balance, unity, and the divine origin of royal rule, but political practice was often in sharp contrast with this ideal. Internal divisions, feuds and the fragmentation of power, and insecurity marked daily life. Although royal power was supposed to be derived from supernatural and suprahuman sources, it also consisted of unstable and indirect control over a scarce and shifting reservoir of manpower. It was possible for a strong person, whether invested with princely dignity or not, to gain considerable prestige if he was capable of attracting followers, had the necessary resources at his disposal, and, at the same time, could enact and stabilize (not legitimize) his position through the staging of rituals. These "men of prowess" were the principal actors within the complex map of overlapping "contest states" in Southeast Asia.[1] They struggled with each other over scarce resources like labor, food, access to trade, wealth, and protection. Both temporary protection and relative security were especially scarce commodities that a powerful leader could offer in exchange for a tribute of labor and loyalty. Noble elites with their fluid alliances were constantly engaged in a struggle over these resources with the consequence that bonds between leaders and followers had to be re-established time and again.

It is misleading to use the word "state" in this context, because state making results, at least, in an effort to establish a monopoly over taxation and violence. Instead, "mandala" or "negara" seems more appropriate, even though due to the influence of Clifford Geertz, the meaning of "negara" has almost exclusively been defined in terms of royal ritual.[2] Warfare and ritual had, in fact, a great deal in common. Wars between lords were mostly waged to impress opponents, to damage their prestige, and to increase the number of one's own followers. Skirmishes, raids on traders, cattle rustling, and the sabotage of irrigation works all had a similar purpose. Although the number of direct warfare victims was on average probably not very high, mass killings did sometimes take place. The long-term consequences of warfare, such as bad harvests, migration, and diseases, could, however, produce a considerable numbers of victims as well.

Not only kings and princes were at loggerheads with one another, since there were also violent disputes over land, water, daughters, and cattle among the local population as well. In the "mandala" form of political organization people were used to living in a permanent state of insecurity in which the possession of power was of crucial importance. We suggest, therefore, that power should be understood in terms of potency. Potency implies a divine-cum-ancestral origin, the ability to use physical violence and control natural forces, and is characterized by strong sexual connotations.[3]

A different reading of classical Javanese literature and another way of perceiving *wayang* performances shows a world full of sex and violence, which was, no doubt, more or less familiar to the audience. Colonial Javanology (as reflected in the works of Zoetmulder, De Serrurier, Hazeu, Rassers, and Kats) searched for underlying structural or literary themes and the contours of Ur-Java, and was not, therefore, very interested in the endless repetition of battles—disturbing the real content of the stories—and grossly overlooked the sexual dimensions—the dirty parts—of many of the stories. Discussing the meaning of the *linga* was a bit embarrassing to these scholars, and if it was discussed the *linga* was conservatively interpreted in terms of "fertility," not potency. That power should be interpreted in terms of potency, however, is illustrated by the following story from Bali:

---

[1] O. W. Wolters, *History, Culture, and Region in Southeast Asian Perspectives* (Singapore: ISEAS, 1982); M. Adas, "From Avoidance to Confrontation: Peasant Protest in Pre-Colonial and Colonial Southeast Asia," *Comparative Studies in Society and History* 23 (1981): 217-47.

[2] C. Geertz, *Negara: The Theatre State in Nineteenth Century Bali* (Princeton: Princeton University Press, 1980). For a Balinese response "avant la lettre" to the idea of the "theatre state" see H. Schulte Nordholt, "Leadership and the Limits of Political Control: A Balinese 'Response' to Clifford Geertz," *Social Anthropology* 1 (1993): 291-307.

[3] See H. Schulte Nordholt, *The spell of power: A history of Balinese politics, 1650-1940* (Leiden: KITLV Press, 1996), Chapters 2 and 5.

Prince Panji, the oldest son of king Agung of Mengwi was suddenly faced with a revolt by disloyal lords, when his father was on campaign in East Java (for, strong rulers had to be on the road all the time). According to VOC reports, and Balinese babad and temple shrines Panji died in 1713 in a pitched battle together with two to three hundred of his followers. Local tradition tells that, to finish it off the victorious enemy took Panji's testicles and crushed them between two stones. Only then his power was gone.[4]

There was in this respect no fundamental differences with Java. Both the fact that violence was a normal experience of everyday life and the interpretation of power in terms of potency are useful for achieving a better understanding of the appearance of the notorious rural criminal in colonial Java: the *jago*.

RURAL *JAGO* : THE SETTING[5]

Onghokham has drawn attention to the *jago* as a rural power broker who operated in the shadow of the colonial state, but whose genealogy goes back to earlier periods when the distribution of power/potency was more fluid and local strongmen played vital roles in regional politics.[6] The main character in Pramoedya's novel *Arus Balik* is such a figure.[7] The *jagos* were used by noble houses in order to mobilize and control the local population, but they were also potential sources of discontent and rival power centres. Strongmen were, in other words, a vital part of the precolonial political system.

After the Java War (1825-1830) and during the early years of the so-called Cultivation System, which was designed to extract an agricultural surplus from Javanese peasants, important changes in the organization of regional rule were introduced.[8] The Dutch managed to establish a power monopoly that was not seriously challenged until the Japanese invasion in 1942. They introduced and gradually expanded a centralized bureaucratic apparatus which did not, however, reach beyond the regional level. The Bupati, or "Regent"—a strange title for a hereditary official of noble descent which was derived from the urban anti-royal

---

[4] Nordholt, *The spell of power*, p. 29.

[5] This section is a summary of H. Schulte Nordholt, "The Jago in the Shadow: Crime and 'Order' in the Colonial State in Java," *Review of Indonesian and Malaysian Affairs* 25 (Winter 1991): 74-91. Other terms for *jago* are *jawara*, *bromocorah*, or *jagabaya*, indicating a mixture of local police and rural strongman or criminal. Also see A. Teeuw, *Indonesisch-Nederlands Woordenboek* (Dordrecht: Foris, 1990), p. 265; J. Rush, *Opium to Java: Revenue Farming and Chinese Enterprise in Colonial Indonesia, 1860-1910* (Ithaca/London: Cornell University Press, 1990), p. 258.

[6] Onghokham, *The Residency of Madiun: Priyayi and Peasant in the Nineteenth Century*, PhD Dissertation, Yale University, 1975; Onghokham, "The Inscrutable and the Paranoid: An Investigation into the Sources of the Brotodonigrat Affair," in *Southeast Asian Transitions: Approaches through Social History*, ed. R. McVey (New Haven: Yale University Press, 1978), pp. 112-57.

[7] Pramoedya Ananta Toer, *De stroom uit het noorden* [*Arus Balik*, trans. Henk Maier] (Breda: De Geus, 1995).

[8] See W. F. Wertheim, *Indonesië: van Vorstenrijk tot Neo-Kolonie* (Meppel/Amsterdam: Boom, 1978), pp. 35-52, for an illuminating illustration of the articulation of old patrimonial practices with new Napoleonic-bureaucratic standards in colonial Java.

commercial elite in the Dutch Republic—was in control at the regional level and he was initially invested with a broad range of privileges. As long as he ran the system smoothly his "older brother," the Assistant-Resident, had no inclination to ask awkward questions. There was from the Dutch perspective, moreover, a clear picture of what local Java looked like. It consisted of relatively autonomous and egalitarian village communities in which communal values were more important than individual interests. The village became the lowest unit of colonial administration, and its leader had to fulfill a range of administrative tasks concerning taxation, corvée labor, and the cultivation of export crops.[9] Since both Bupati and village leaders were protected by their Dutch superiors as long as they fulfilled their obligations, and no major disturbances took place, the bargaining power of the local population was reduced significantly.

Officially there was no longer a place for a variety of local strongmen in this simplified picture of colonial administration. There was, however, ample space for brokers in violence, even if their room to maneuver was redefined. One of the results of the colonial reorganization of political administration was that the number of officials that a Bupati had at his disposal was much smaller in comparison with earlier times when a large number of followers filled the dynamic, hierarchical networks around leaders and their entourage. It was in this shady area outside official control and knowledge that new forms of local violence emerged.

RURAL *JAGO*: THE CASE OF KEDIRI (1870S)

> In Java, the business of a thief is an occupation which belongs to the village institutions, which provides many people with a job, some with an investment, and offers many benefits to its protectors.[...] No headman considers his village complete and in good order if it does not have at least one thief, often several, who are under the command of the oldest and cleverest thief, who is called *Jago*.[10]

With these words C. A. A. Amand, a private tobacco planter at Kediri, East Java, informed the colonial authorities in 1872 about a situation in rural Java where cattle rustling, intimidation, arson, fraud, and physical violence occurred daily, a situation that was, moreover, beyond Dutch control.

Being unaware of these practices, the authorities reacted with astonishment. The Governor General in Batavia ordered the Resident of Kediri to investigate the matter, and the latter had to admit that "the story told by Amand, though sounding very odd and unpleasant, contains a lot of truth, previously unknown to our officials."[11] Amand had revealed the existence of a network of *jagos* which was not confined to Kediri but was probably spread all over Java. Similarly P. C. C. Hansen concluded that "gangs of criminals and robbers are spread over the whole of Java, and they

---

[9] On the image of the traditional village in nineteenth-century Java, see Onghokham, *The Residency of Madiun*, and J. Breman, *The Village on Java and the Early Colonial State* (Rotterdam: Erasmus University, 1980).

[10] Algemeen Rijksarchief The Hague (ARA), Archive Ministerie van Koloniën (MvK), Verbaal (V) July 3, 1872/30; letter Amand April 17, 1872.

[11] ARA, MvK, V June 1, 1874/36, Resident Bosscher to Governor General, March 25, 1874.

form as it were a distinct society whose members are known to each other..."[12] How, or for what reason, someone became a *jago*—literally: fighting cock—is not known, nor whether *jago* qualities were considered hereditary within a family. Probably physical strength, guts, and "mystical talents" were the individual characteristics that facilitated becoming a *jago*.

One became, according to Amand, an "acknowledged" *jago* after having completed an apprenticeship period. This consisted of assisting senior *jagos* with their thefts and other enterprises, and, more importantly, learning specific knowledge (*ngelmu*) from respected gurus or teachers. To be apprenticed with various teachers was fairly common among young men in Java. When they visited several Islamic schools (*pesantren*), pupils also learned fighting techniques (*silat*) and special knowledge that a *jago* needed: the *ngelmu* to be able to disappear, to become invulnerable, or to evoke spirits that bring people into deep sleep, for instance. At the same time the pupils formed a "police force" that protected the *pesantren* and its surroundings. The period of apprenticeship of a *jago* was concluded with a period of asceticism and solitude followed by a ritual meal (*selamatan*). Wandering about in areas further away from home formed the next phase in the process of becoming a *jago*. One thus gathered experience and made contact with other *jagos*, who taught their young brethren further tricks of the trade.

This process reveals the networks in which *jagos* operated and the guild mentality that characterized them. For, when the first contacts were carefully established, a mutual bond was sealed with a reciprocal promise or oath. The oath takers drank together from a jug of water—sometimes mixed with a few drops of blood—and promised to help one another. Such an oath could encompass as much as one liked. The sanction consisted of the threat that the water drunk would turn into burning poison if one of the sworn men should violate the oath. Depending on both the extent of his contacts and alliances under oath, and his personal fame as an experienced and respected *jago*, an established *jago* could have contacts over a wide area. From these contacts he could, on a contract basis, recruit helpers or specialists for particular jobs. Large and permanent bands of *jagos* were either very rare or did not exist. Most *jagos* worked individually, even though they had assistants and pupils.

This network functioned so well that the Dutch authorities in Kediri appeared incapable of penetrating it. As soon as they were threatened by outside forces, the *jagos* closed ranks.[13] And threats of violence were very often intimidating enough to convince the local population to remain silent. For those who have hoped to recognize in the *jago* a Javanese Robin Hood, it is without doubt disconcerting to learn that the main target of the *jago* was the small peasant.[14]

Cattle rustling, in particular, formed an important source of income for the *jago*. Despite the fact that people increasingly kept cattle in their compound during the night, *jagos* appeared to be very skillful in taking these animals away by digging a hole under the wall without making any noise. Apparently the sleep *ngelmu* worked

---

[12] Boeka [P. C. C. Hansen], *Uit Java's binnenland: Pah Troena* (Amsterdam: Van Rossen, 1901), pp. 332-3. For a study of Hansen's work, see M. Bloembergen, *Een koffieopziener in de desa: P.C.C. Hansen en zijn beeld van Java's binnenland*, MA thesis, University of Amsterdam, 1993.

[13] See C. Poenssen, "Iets over Javaansche dieven," *Mededeelingen Nederlandsch Zendingsgenootschap* 22 (1878): 99-146.

[14] On the image of Robin Hood see John Sidel's contribution to this volume.

well, and the victims wisely kept quiet for fear of the *jago* and possible reprisals. Sometimes *jagos* operated even in broad daylight. The great advantage of cattle theft was that the loot could walk away by itself. Together with opium smuggling, the trade in stolen cattle proved to be a lucrative business.[15]

It was striking that towards the end of the year (i.e. from October until December) the number of cattle stolen increased dramatically in Kediri. This can only be explained by turning to an examination of the relationship between *jago* and village chiefs.

As mentioned above, the position of the village chief was strengthened as a result of colonial rule. At the same time, the regional administration was so depleted of personnel that it was unable to perform its police duties. Kediri with 560,000 inhabitants in 1870 was divided into five regencies and thirty districts, and was served by a contingent of over 170 Javanese administrative personnel, half of whom consisted of so-called *oppas* (messengers and policemen). Cattle theft and other activities that were categorized as criminal were kept secret from the Dutch officials as much as possible, while at the village level, chief and *jago* came to an agreement. The relationship between chief and *jago* resulted in a modus vivendi that offered both partners enough room to maneuver, while the costs were shifted onto the shoulders of the weaker peasants.

In virtually every village in Kediri, *jagos* lived "as ordinary desa [village] people, unrecognizable among the population, but very much feared and respected."[16] Strangers would not have been able to point out the *jago*, but everyone in the village knew who he was. He was not necessarily born or brought up in the village of his residence; he could settle there. This relocation became permanent once the *jago* concluded an arrangement with the village chief. The *jago* promised not to undertake any actions against villagers and to protect the village against theft and violence to the best of his abilities. He sought to achieve this end through his contacts with his oath brethren.

In exchange for his services the *jago* was exempted from corvée labor and land tax. The *jago* became a well-respected local hero as long as he left his own people in peace and managed to prevent his colleagues from visiting his village. When he himself went out he would go and steal from villages without local strongmen or from villages with whose strongmen he had no agreement.

The village head also profited from the presence of the *jago*. He could insist on receiving a share of the stolen goods which the *jago* wanted to sell in his village, for instance one hindleg from each stolen cow that was slaughtered. This was the price a *jago* had to pay for anonymity, in case colonial authorities might investigate a theft. Officially a theft had to be reported to the district head, who usually sent the village chief out to investigate the case. The latter would receive a letter which had to be signed at the offices of the neighboring districts. In most cases, eventually the village chief returned empty handed, without a thief but with a letter full of signatures. The letter was evidence that he had really done his utmost, but to no avail. In turn, the district head could show his superiors the letter which proved that he had taken all the necessary steps to find the culprits.

Local solutions were, therefore, a bit more promising for the victim of a theft. If someone in the village had been robbed and the *jago* was not able, or not willing, to

---

[15] Also see Rush, *Opium Farms*.

[16] Letter Amand, April 17, 1872.

prevent the theft, then the *jago* was asked to insure that the cattle were returned. The *jago* received from the victim a sum of money to finance his trip and with this he visited the opium dens in the neighborhood, put his ear to the ground, and established new contacts as well. In most cases he returned without success. The cattle had long since disappeared, and the *jago* did not want to have an argument with a colleague. Sometimes the *jago* did manage to find the stolen animals and negotiated a payment of ransom.

In another important respect the *jago* was of service to the village head. The land tax was collected once a year in December, but village chiefs had already collected it much earlier in order to have ready cash on hand to pay off debts, to gamble, or to speculate. Despite the fact that the village chiefs collected on average about 20 to 30 percent more than they were officially allowed to, it often happened that they had run out of money by December. At this point the *jago* could offer some help. By stealing and selling cattle, after which the money was divided on a fifty-fifty basis between the village chief and the *jago*, these allies could insure that the village chief's deficit was settled just in time. This general situation explains the increase in cattle rustling towards the end of the year.

As has been indicated above, the most important quid pro quo a *jago* received from the village head was absolute protection in case the colonial authorities would initiate serious investigations. Nobody was allowed to betray the *jago*.

When colonial officials in Kediri suspected that stolen goods were kept in a certain village, the Assistant Resident and the district head paid a visit to that village. When the village head heard about it, he ordered the *kentong*—wooden alarm block—to be beaten, which was after all the proper way to call the villagers together. The officials "heard nothing special in the sounds of the beats. Every villager, however, would hear immediately from the signals that a police investigation was to take place."[17] There were even special signs to indicate the type of stolen goods that the Dutch were searching for.

What was taking place here was not only a conspiracy against the colonial authorities, but also against the population itself. If a *jago* was by chance arrested, the "traitors" who had mentioned his name to the authorities ran the risk that their house would be burnt down. "One knows that the brothers of a caught villain would take revenge," wrote Amand.[18] In case a village head was unable to protect his *jago* sufficiently, or when he had broken off his relationship with a *jago*, his house went up in flames.

It should be emphasized that the distinction between village head and *jago* was not absolute nor institutionalized. There is evidence that in the course of the nineteenth century a new group of *jago*-like people managed to push old village elites aside in order to become village heads themselves.[19]

The local population appeared unable to defend itself. Running away, migrating to empty land, or seeking protection from a more benevolent lord were all old strategies that were no longer possible. The colonial regime had produced uniform

---

[17] ARA, MvK, V August 8, 1873/22, Letter Amand, December 1, 1872.

[18] Ibid.

[19] "Historische nota over de dessabesturen op Java," *Koloniaal Verslag* (Den Haag: Algemeene Landsdrukkerij, 1877), Bijlage N. During the era of the so-called Cultivation System, villages chiefs-cum-*jagos* played a central role in mobilizing tribute and labor for the emerging colonial state.

administrative rule all over Java. The institution of new formal restrictions limited the possibilities of migration, while complaints about thievery to the colonial authorities usually did not help much either. The Javanese administrators even discouraged the complainants from taking further steps because it was in their bureaucratic interest that activities labeled as "criminal" should get as little publicity as possible. Colonial law, therefore, brought no justice.

Should a *jago* be arrested and brought before a magistrate, it proved extremely difficult to find people who were willing to testify against him. Only after assurances were made that the accused would not be set free for a long time, and only if his friends were not considered too dangerous, was it sometimes possible to elicit testimony. Very often false testimonies, offered at the behest of the village chief, exonerated the *jago*, and the testimony could accuse completely innocent villagers of being the real culprits. The best defense the average villager had against this organized force was either to buy it off or to keep quiet. As Hansen concluded: "To be able to sleep quietly, that was the great advantage of being poor; one need not fear thieves."[20]

Moreover, the regional administrators themselves had to maintain a tentative and fragile balance with the *jagos* and village heads as well. The Regent, or Bupati, could influence the regional administration of justice to a great extent. It was in his interest to acquit for "lack of evidence" some of those who were accused and came before him. *Jagos* were, after all, useful as spies (*weri*) and local agents of the Regent. In this way, as he was stimulated by, but functioning outside the direct control of European administrators, the *jago* was able to create his own power base in the shadow of the colonial state.

The trade in stolen cattle entailed an extended network of contacts and transactions. Here the relationship between *jago* and *tauké* (boss) was important.[21] Instead of slaughtering cattle and selling the meat in the same district where it was stolen, it was more advantageous to take the animals to a neighboring district where a good price could be obtained and there was little risk of recognition. The transportation of stolen cattle proceeded along a series of intermediate stations in remote places—often still uncleared land—in which the thieves slept during the day and traveled by night. The final destination was the *tauké* who lived in the border areas and bought the stolen cattle. He often had already provided cash advantages and maintained permanent relationships with several *jagos*. At this point the trade in stolen cattle and opium smuggling clearly coincided.[22]

Having bought the cattle, the *tauké* crossed the border with forged papers on his way to the cattle market. The forged papers were obtained from *magang* (apprentices without a salary) at the district office who had access to official papers and stamps and who could in this way make some money.

Taukés were a typical group of non-official intermediaries and consisted of Chinese traders and/or agents of opium farmers, Javanese drop-outs who had failed to make a career in the colonial administration, and "fallen" Indo-Europeans, as well as village heads. To what extent Regents were involved in this network remains unclear. Sources and evidence suggest that the Regent of Blitar (in Kediri) knew

---

[20] Boeka, *Uit Java's binnenland*, p. 48; see also pp. 249ff. and 358ff. for an "insider's" view on court procedures.

[21] In his letter from April 17, 1872, Amand uses the word *toko* (shop) to indicate the *tauké*.

[22] See Rush, *Opium Farms*, pp. 65-82.

much more about the wheelings and dealings of *jagos* and *taukés* than what he told his European superiors. The Regent, Raden Adipati Ario Adinegara, served from 1851 until 1869, and while in office he was in complete control over his domain. Gradually he had extended his influence into Blitar villages by manipulating the election of village heads. It was said that nearly all village heads in Blitar owed their position to the Regent and that they had to pay for this privilege. The Regent did not choose well-respected senior villagers as village heads, but rather seems to have preferred appointing relative outsiders like *magangs* and even stable boys of Javanese and European administrators.[23] Thanks to his connections with his village heads, Raden Adipati Ario Adinegara knew everything about the *jagos*. Moreover, considering his private ownership of some two thousand head of livestock, he probably maintained good relationships with several *taukés*.

The Regent allowed the predatory collusion between *jagos*, village heads, and *taukés* to continue, provided that it did not go too far (i.e. that it did not bring him into trouble with his European superiors), that he received a share in the profits, and that the *jagos* were prepared to do some dirty work for him.

The extent to which the Regent was able to keep things quiet is illustrated by the following case. People from a village in Blitar went to the Regent with complaints about their village head, in itself a risky and courageous step, but the Regent sent them away and forbade them to move to another area. When, some time later, the Assistant-Resident, accompanied by the Regent, visited the village during an inspection tour, the villagers made a last and desperate effort to make their complaints known. Unfortunately the Dutch official did not understand Javanese and left the village without the slightest idea of their concerns or complaints.[24]

Now and then, of course, the Regent had to demonstrate his authority. He did this by summoning the most notorious *jagos*, lecturing them seriously about their bad conduct, compelling them to renounce their evil deeds in the mosque, and finally concluding by giving them a team of buffaloes so that they would no longer have a reason to steal. Later during an inspection tour, he would call on these people and investigate whether they still lived a decent life. In this way the Regent protected his position and reinforced the overall system of extortion.

Apart from supporting extensive sugarcane fields, Kediri also experienced a tobacco boom beginning in the 1850s. In Blitar about fifteen European entrepreneurs bought tobacco leaves from the population and processed them in drying sheds, which numbered three hundred. The tobacco boom injected large amounts of cash into the general population and attracted twenty to thirty thousand seasonal workers from Central Java at harvesting time. European reports mentioned in this context an increased prosperity evident from an increase in livestock owned by the general population.[25]

---

[23] "Historisch nota," *Koloniaal Verslag* 1877.

[24] A. Courier dit Dubecart, *Feiten van Brata-Joeda* (Semarang, 1872), p. 174.

[25] See J. Huyser, "De vrije tabaksindustrie in Kedirie," *Tijdschrift van Nijverheid en Landbouw in Nederlandsch-Indië* 13 (1868): 48-57; P. Huyser, "Iets over de assistent-residentie Blitar," *Tijdschrift van Nederlandsch-Indië*, Nieuwe Serie 3 (1874): 319-24; J. de Mol van Otterloo, *De vrije arbeid te Rembang en Kediri* (Utrecht, 1859); H. Staverman, "Beschrijving van de tabakscultuur in Kediri," *Tijdschrift van Nijverheid en Landbouw in Nederlandsch-Indië* 13 (1868): 39-56. In 1874 the total tobacco production amounted to 2,400 tons covering approximately 4,900 hectares (12,000 acres). About 11,000 plants could be grown per hectare for which the entrepreneur paid 120 to 150 florins.

In the early 1870s, however, things got out of hand. Due to excessive rainfall the tobacco crop failed, and thousands of seasonal workers lost their source of income yet did not want to return home empty handed. Village heads were also in trouble since they still had to collect and hand over the land tax to their colonial administrative superiors. As a result, cattle theft took on proportions too great to be concealed anymore. On top of this, the old Regent of Blitar had retired, so the last authority who could have prevented excessive theft was no longer available.[26]

After the appearance of the first newspaper articles describing theft and unrest in Kediri, the Resident claimed that the reports were exaggerations. But after Amand had written his letters to the Governor General and a new Resident had been appointed, the colonial government decided to solve the "Kediri problem," even though Amand had made it clear that the situation he described was widespread across Java. The new Resident of Blitar let it be known that he was going to make a clean sweep and threatened his Javanese officials with dismissal if there were no quick results. Of course the resulting operation had the appearance of success. Cattle rustling declined and forty-two people were arrested. Among these, real *jagos* constituted only a minority of ten, while nineteen were *taukés,* and eleven were village heads and *taukés.*[27] Moreover, the colonial state reacted to the problem with typical bureaucratic measures: by expanding the bureaucracy and debating an increase of rules and procedures. The number of Javanese administrative personnel was increased from 170 to 360.[28] A bureaucratic cover-up was also instituted. When the Resident of Kediri suggested that Amand's letters should be published in order to draw attention to the situation elsewhere in Java, the Governor General decided to shelve the proposal. He considered it "inexpedient" to mention the troubling situation in the yearly *Koloniaal Verslag* (Colonial Report). A state of deliberate ignorance was maintained.

BATAVIA - BUITENZORG (BOGOR): TERROR AND ENTERTAINMENT

> Maling! Maling! Toeloeng! Toeloeng!
> Peghang maling!
> Brenti! Dijem! Djangan lari!
> Kaloe ko-e lari, ko-e saja pasang.
> Nanti ko-e saja pedang.

---

[26] Due to a series of articles in the *Soerabajasche Courant* by Agathon Coerier dit Dubecart which revealed the Regent's less pleasant aspects, the Regent asked for, and was granted, an honorable discharge. Coerier dit Dubecart, whose articles were separately published in 1872, landed in prison for slander. See also D. Hartoko, "Mitos di Lebak, kenyataan di Blitar," in *Studi Belanda di Indonesia—Nederlandse studiën in Indonesië,* ed. K. Groeneboer (Jakarta: Djambatan 1989), pp. 71-7. Around the same time a lot of tobacco sheds went up in flames. This had very little to do with protest or theft, but was the work of the local supervisors of the tobacco companies who had committed such extensive frauds that the discrepancies between their bookkeeping and the actual content of the sheds could no longer be concealed. Therefore they burned down the sheds in order to insure that the evidence of their fraud went up in smoke.

[27] The identity of two of these arrested men is unknown. ARA MvK V August 8, 1873/22.

[28] ARA MvK V June 1, 1874/36. There was, of course, also a quarrel over procedures. The Minister of Colonies denied the Governor General the right to take these decisions without prior consultation because there was no room for it in the budget.

Toeroet sama saja.
Djangan djalan di blakang saja.
Djalan di moeka saja. Lekas sedikit.
Mana roemah gherdoe njang paling deket?
Disana di djalan prapat-an.
Toeloeng saja, bawak ini orang maling ka gherdoe.
E orang gherdoe!
Peghang ini maling.
Bawak dija pada poelisi.
Apa dija tida moesti ko-e iket?
Dija nanti lari.
Di mana ada orang poelisi?
Di mana ada kepala poelisi?
Dia-orang tida ada di sini.
Dia-orang ada di kotta.[29]

If the penetration of the formal institutions of the colonial state into rural Java had been limited in its success, what was the situation in the area around the very center of the colonial state, Batavia and the residence of the Governor General, Buitenzorg ("Care free")? In a way this part of West Java was the most colonized area of the Indies, for it counted among its inhabitants descendants of former slaves who came from many islands of the archipelago, Chinese settlers, Arabs, a small European community, and a larger mestizo population, Sundanese from the Priangan, and seasonal migrants from Banten and Cirebon.

From the time the so-called "empty lands" around Batavia were conquered by the Dutch and (re)populated in the early seventeenth century, large tracts of land were leased, granted, and later sold to private persons. It was under the reign of H. W. Daendels and T. S. Raffles (1808-16) that many more private estates were created by selling so-called domain lands, including Bogor, Krawang, Pamanukan and Ciasem, Kandanghauer, and Indramayu West. These estates were privately run by their owners or their representatives, and as a result the colonial state had no influence in, nor control over, these areas. The owners were entitled to demand labor from the local population (officially one day per week) and to levy a special tax, the so-called *cuké* which amounted to 20 to 40 percent of the rice harvest.[30]

Ironically the centers of the colonial state formed only tiny islands in a sea of private estates, state agencies were largely absent, and colonial control could not be imposed. For as long as the private estates existed they were notorious for their

---

[29] P. Pieters, *Praktische Indische tolk: Spreken in Hollandsch-Maleisch en Javaansch* (Amsterdam: Van Holkema & Warendorf, 1903), p. 219. Opening lines of lesson sixty-eight, on "Theft and Police" (Tjoeri-an Poelisi), in a language course book (Dutch–Malay–Low– and High Javanese): "A thief, a thief, help, help. Stop the thief. Stop, shut up, don't run away. If you run away, I'll shoot you. I will hack you down. Come with me. Don't walk behind me. Walk in front of me. Come on, quick. Where is the nearest guard-post? Over there at the cross roads. Help me to bring this thief to the guard-post. Hey there, guard. Keep this thief. Bring him to the police. Shouldn't you tie him up? He will escape. Where is a police man? Where is the head of police? They are not here. They are in town."

[30] It is beyond the scope of this paper to go into detail about the exploitation of the population on these estates and the changes that occurred within them over time. For one of the best insider accounts see the novel by E. F. E. Douwes Dekker, *Het boek van Siman den Javaan: Een roman van rijst, dividend en menschelijkheid* (Amersfoort: Wink, 1908).

endemic violence. From the time of the reign of Surapati, the wandering ex-slave, mercenary soldier, gang leader, and eventually king, in the late seventeenth century, until the Indonesian revolution of 1945-49 with its gangster revolutionaries, no outside power ever succeeded in establishing a monopoly of power over the area, which in 1900 covered over one million bahu (1 b. = 0.7 ha.) and in which one and a half million people lived on about 345 estates.[31] While the Javanese countryside was dominated by local *jago*, the Batavia-Buitenzorg area was to a large extent controlled by so-called *preman* (from the Dutch *vrij man*, meaning free or independent man).[32]

We are not sure what caused the increase in criminality which was reported by colonial sources during the second half of the nineteenth century.[33] Was there really an increase in theft or was the increase a result of a more sophisticated way of producing statistics? It is in this respect amazing to see how little colonial officials actually knew about what occurred on the private estates, and yet how much statistical information was produced at the same time. Was there a correlation between increased immigration and the expansion and "rationalization" of estate agriculture, which resulted in more pressure on the population? Did the colonial state become more aware of the fact that the situation on the estates did not quite correspond to those appropriate for a civilized colony? As the influx of Europeans increased and white women started to migrate to the colony as well, new notions of public order emerged which were concerned with the protection of the demographically expanding white ruling class. This might well have been a factor in prompting more reports of criminality.

In 1903 especially another increase in criminality was detected, and in these early years of the Ethical Policy, when the uplifting of the native received much support, the problem of criminality was analyzed in crudely racist terms. Chinese and Arab landowners were primarily held responsible for the bad living conditions on the estates due to their usurious practices, while Lombroso[34] would have been ecstatic about the species of "born criminals" discovered by the Dutch in the social jungle outside of Batavia, "born criminals" who were believed to consider criminality simply as sport.[35]

There was indeed among the Batavians a culture that held in high esteem physical strength and bravado, which was celebrated in later years through the acquisition of motorbikes and rifles.[36] Where the state was absent and judicial

---

[31] H. van Kol, *Uit onze koloniën* (Leiden: Sijthoff, 1903), p. 813; ARA MvK, "Nota over de Particuliere Landerijen Bewesten de Tjimanoek," by E. von Zboray, 1947 (KIT 513); A. Kumar, *Surapati: Man and Legend* (Leiden: Brill, 1976); R. Cribb, *Gangsters and Revolutionaries: The Jakarta People's Militia and the Indonesian Revolution, 1945-1949* (Sydney: Allen & Unwin, 1991).

[32] See also Joshua Barker in this volume.

[33] Jakarta, Arsip Nasional Republik Indonesia (ANRI), Arsip Batavia, Algemene Verslagen 1896-1882.

[34] A Lombroso is an Italian psychologist who classifies criminals according to their physical appearances or characteristics.

[35] P. Bodemeijer, *Waaraan de achteruitgang van de bevolking in het district Bekasie en de daarmee gepaard gaande moord- en roofpartijen te wijten is* (Salemba, 1905); W. de Veer, *Particuliere landerijen en de openbare veiligheid in de residentie Batavia* (Batavia: Javasche Boekhandel en Drukkerij, 1904).

[36] See, for instance, the short stories by Vincent Mahieu, *Tjies* (Amsterdam: Querido, 1987 [1958]), and the references to the culture of violence in E. du Perron, *Het land van herkomst* (Amsterdam: Van Oorschot, 1973 [1935]).

procedures proved to be unreliable, one had to rely on one's own ability to cope with threats and violence.

For the lower classes public life in Batavia was characterized by thefts, robberies, and frequent fights among soldiers or gangs of Indo youths. On the other hand, Batavia formed the capital of the Indies and, even more so, Bogor was the center of an extremely dull and over-regulated social world of the colonial elite. Nothing much happened there except for the regular and boring visits which socially knit the colonial hierarchy together through some dancing, a bit of theatre, occasional horse races, and a lot of idle socializing and gossiping. No wonder that criminals and their actions, and especially their trials, created public sensations which were also infused with hidden sexual connotations—after all criminals and their actions stood for excitement and everything that was unruly and forbidden. Consequently, through the self-interested assistance of the colonial press, criminality was turned into entertainment.

SAKAM (1886), OR HOW TO GET RID OF AN ELUSIVE BANDIT[37]

In August and September of 1886 the Batavian authorities were lucky. During the night of August 26th, the famous thief Arkam, also known as the boss of the market (*pasar*) of Serpong, surrendered himself to the local indigenous authority, Demang of Kebayoran. Three weeks later, two men from Banten armed with revolvers were arrested in Gang Petjenongan. One of them was possibly the famous robber Sakam.[38] Arkam disappeared into anonymity, but Sakam became the talk of the town in dull Batavia for at least a year.

Police spies recognized Sakam, but other witnesses were less sure about his identity. After being confronted with the arrested man, who looked fixedly at him, a witness from Tangerang concluded: "This can't be Sakam because he certainly would have disappeared when they wanted to arrest him."[39]

In April of the following year, after half a year of detention, the trial began. Because he was accused of having committed two murders, Sakam's case was handled by the so-called Omgaand Gerecht[40] in the old town hall (*gedung bicara*) of Batavia. As a large crowd of more than a thousand people gathered outside the hall, the suspect was brought by thirty-six soldiers to a courtroom packed with Europeans.[41] One wall of the courtroom was covered with a huge and ugly two hundred year old painting called "Judgment of Salomon,"[42] and this was not without symbolic significance since confusion increased as the trial proceeded.

The Batavian police claimed that they had known that Sakam was coming to Batavia and so had arranged that a police spy would accompany him. Once Sakam fell asleep, his holy dagger (*kris*), which could make him invisible, was taken from

---

[37] Based on *Algemeen Dagblad voor Nederlandsch-Indië* (AD), August 1885 - November 1886, Jakarta, Perpustakaan Nasional.

[38] *AD*, August 28, 1885 and September 15, 1885.

[39] *AD*, September 17, 1885.

[40] The Omgaand Gerecht consisted of two European judges (chairman and secretary) and four indigenous members, plus the *jaksa* (prosecutor) and *penghulu* (Islamic official) of Batavia.

[41] *AD*, April 8, 1886.

[42] *AD*, April 9, 1886.

him by a female spy and he was subsequently arrested. The suspect, however, claimed that he was not Sakam at all, but Soeheirie, a police spy from Banten! Moreover, officials from Banten denied that the man was Sakam, while some of the witnesses, contrary to earlier statements, testified that they did not recognize the suspect as Sakam. The only witness who maintained that the suspect was indeed Sakam was the widow of one of Sakam's victims.[43]

Obviously there was something fundamentally wrong in the ranks of the colonial authorities, because the testimonies of the Batavian police and the officials from Banten contradicted each other. Consequently, part of the court sessions were held behind closed doors.

After one week the man called Sakam, or Soeheirie, was suddenly acquitted. The reporters of *Algemeen Dagblad* expressed surprise at this acquittal due to the fact that several witnesses had never been heard from, while other witnesses had changed their minds during the trial. Moreover, the suspect himself had changed identities for he was no longer "Sakam," but appeared, instead, to be "Soeheirie." On top of that, the individual who faced legal charges was no longer Sakam/Soeheirie, but the widow who was accused of giving false testimony!

It was quite an embarrassing defeat for the Batavian police because their spy was classified as a liar. To make things even more complex, it was confirmed that Soeheirie was indeed a police spy who was sent from Banten to Batavia in order to look for Sakam! When he met the Batavian police spy during his trip, he was caught and delivered to the Batavian police as Sakam. So, one spy had caught another spy, and it turned out that there had been no Sakam at the trial. Or was there?

When the trial was over and Soeheirie left the town hall he was immediately surrounded by a large crowd among whom there were a number of *haji's* who treated him with respect by not only making a *sembah* (respectful greeting), but by offering him presents as well. Furthermore, they accompanied him to a holy grave in Luar Batang where a goat was sacrificed.[44] Was this the usual way to deal with an ordinary police spy? Had the widow been, after all, correct all along?

After a short time newspapers started to report on new activities by Sakam in Banten.[45] In addition, there were apparently several Sakams plying the roads. When a young police spy, who was on his way from Serang to Batavia and who had run out of money, sat down in a food stall (*warung*) people suddenly thought that he was Sakam. They offered him everything he wanted—rice, fish, tea, cake—saying: "Eat, Sakam eat, but do not hurt us." They even put copper coins on his empty dish.[46]

By late October the police had put a price of 2,000 florins on Sakam's head, and this action produced successful results. A certain Biroe, an ex-convict laborer who had spent some time with Sakam in jail and who was currently accompanying him in the area of Tangerang and Cikandi, finally betrayed his mate. Biroe went to the Bupati of Serang to inform him of Sakam's whereabouts, and the latter gave him instructions and sent him back to Sakam's hiding place in a sugar cane field near Serang. Because of the *kecapi* fruit (Sandoricum koetjape) which Biroe gave Sakam that night, he fell ill. Biroe also managed to seize Sakam's rifle along with his other

---

[43] *AD*, April 10 and 13, 1886.

[44] *AD*, April 15, 1886.

[45] *AD*, May 3, 1886.

[46] *AD*, August 17, 1886.

weapons, and when Sakam was finally asleep early in the morning, the officials from Serang arrived to arrest him.

A second trial was never held for Sakam. On the way to Serang he was strangled due to the manner in which he was tied up on a bamboo frame.[47] His timely death saved the colonial authorities from confronting any further embarrassing situations in their own courtroom.

SI GANTANG (1903) AND THE MOCK STATE

The same qualities of elusiveness and public entertainment characterized the trial of Si Gantang, although this time they were combined with an explicit negation of colonial authority.

In a series of editorials entitled "Onze Mafia" (Our Mafia) the newspaper *Bataviaasch Nieuwsblad* focused on a certain Si Gantang who was perceived as the personification of a sudden increase in crime.[48] Si Gantang was an escaped prisoner who had spent six years in jail after being sentenced to death. Like Sakam he created a great sensation in the press, the more so since he successfully mocked the powerless colonial authorities. Each time he showed up in public he wore the cap of an Assistant Resident, while his followers were dressed in uniforms similar to those of the indigenous colonial police. When the Dutch decided to arrest him and sent the military police after him, he showed his bravado once more. Sources quoted him as saying that he was pleased that he finally would meet a worthy adversary in contrast to the useless native police. Nevertheless, he continued in a mocking tone, it was a pity that even the military police ran out of ammunition so quickly. Still, he was willing to lend them some of his own bullets if necessary.

Si Gantang not only imitated the appearance of colonial authorities and organized his own independent political administration, he also collected his own taxes and demanded regular services from the local population. They had to pay their taxes with either money or cattle, and part of their services consisted of forced burglary. While these services were being performed, the members of Si Gantang's gang were located at strategic locations in order to prevent outside intervention. Besides robbing the peasant population—again, no similarity to Robin Hood—Gantang's gang also plundered the mansions of Chinese and European estate owners. The only thing these landowners could do to prevent assaults on their estates was to buy security and protection from strongmen like Si Gantang.

Gantang and his gang had a special relationship with indigenous officials, such as the Demang of Bekasi, whom he bribed in order to release arrested fellow thieves. It is even said that Si Gantang had European accomplices who provided him with information and weapons. Compared with the relationship between the Regent and rual *jago*, it seems that the Demang of Bekasi was in a much weaker position vis-à-vis the local strongmen around Batavia, who had a comparatively stronger base of authority in the area.

Like Sakam, Si Gantang aroused a lot of (sexual) excitement within the colonial society which he was so forcefully ridiculing:

---

[47] *AD*, October 20, 1886 and November 1, 1886.

[48] AD, November 14, 19, 21, 30, and December 1 and 15, 1903.

> We saw quite a few Europeans, even young ladies, on their way to *pasar* Tjelilitan [Cililitan]; they were all eager to see the Chinese shop owner who had found himself in such a delicate position when he was robbed; they all had to see the door of the shop which was badly damaged by blows of the axe and by bullets; maybe they hoped, the young ladies I mean, to see Gantang suddenly appearing from the bushes on the roadside, furiously screaming. It's all emotions that matter these days.[49]

The success of Si Gantang apparently convinced other robbers to use his name and fame. As in the case of Sakam, this both helped to increase the status of Gantang and caused even more confusion about his real identity and residence.

According to the *Bataviaasch Nieuwsblad*, Gantang had his headquarters in *kampong* (neighorhood) Pondok Gede, about ten miles from Batavia, and yet despite its proximity to the center of the colonial state, police authorities seldom went there. According to another newspaper, the *Javabode*, Si Gantang was no longer active and currently lived somewhere in the cool Priangan mountains among retired colonial officials.[50]

Eventually Gantang, or someone identified as Gantang, was caught in a *desa* near Kendal, a town on the north coast of Central Java. The man was accidentally recognized by a Batavian who had moved to Kendal. Because it would be far too conspicuous for the European police to enter a *desa* in great numbers, the police officers were disguised as hunters. While the "hunters" were on their way, the local town head was ordered to assemble the male population of the neighborhood under the pretext that they were to be registered for taxation. During this assembly the "hunters" arrested a certain Si Oenoes whom they identified as Si Gantang. The final identification of the suspect was, however, complicated by the fact that one of the guards had smashed in Si Oenoes's face. But on the whole the suspect looked like a real bandit: he was 1.8 meters tall (which was quite big actually) and had an impressive moustache, while his body bore the signs of an eventful past, with scars on his face and back (due to beatings with rattan in jail). He had also traces of a venereal disease.[51]

Unlike Sakam, Si Oenoes/Si Gantang survived his trip to Batavia. Surprisingly, his trial did not attract much publicity nor was he put to death, although Si Gantang had already been sentenced to death two years earlier. Until the very last moment Si Oenoes/Si Gantang kept stirring up emotions. All the time during his journey by train to the location where he was put to work as a convict laborer, he was grinning in an insolent way at some European ladies. That must have been a horrifying thrill for them.

But was this person really Si Gantang? Or had the police simply arrested another criminal to stand in for Si Gantang in order to reinforce its authority in the eyes of a concerned and skeptical public? The authorities were eager to pretend that the chaotic, unruly conditions that persisted under their jurisdiction could in fact be attributed to one particular bandit. Once he was arrested and tried, they hoped and

---

[49] *BN*, December 1, 1903.

[50] *Javabode*, November 21, 1903. For a cynical comment on these rumors see *BN*, December 15, 1903.

[51] Like tattoos today, scars were part of the attire of many local strongmen; see Sidel and Barker in this volume.

proclaimed, peace would be restored. We do not know how many Si Gantangs there actually were, but the surroundings of Batavia were, or at least seemed, quiet again for a short while once there was an arrested criminal called Si Gantang in chains, or, indeed, living among retired officials in the Priangan.

Sakam and Si Gantang were not, however, exceptional criminals, because almost every year another local strongman forged a brief but tumultuous criminal career and received abundant press coverage in the process. Perhaps one of the most famous among these other cases was the legendary Si Pitung, who was active in the years 1892-93, and who after his death became a kind of cultural hero of the *orang Betawi*, the long established inhabitants of Batavia. As the leader of a small gang, Si Pitung robbed the houses of wealthy landowners. He was renowned for his bravado, especially since he had managed to escape from prison and, like many of his colleagues, was believed to wield magical weapons and powers. Si Pitung must have been an active womanizer as well, and in this respect there is an interesting quote from an interview by Damardini.[52] The informant could not understand why Si Pitung was accused of committing rape during the burglary of a house, because as a *jago* he could get all the women he wanted, couldn't he? As the archetype of the Batavian bandit—alternatively interpreted either as the romantic personification of Robin Hood or as a proto-nationalist resistance leader—Si Pitung became the main character in numerous ballads, theatrical stories, and movies.[53]

There are also indications that myth-making concerning bandits had already started during their respective lifetimes and contributed to their elusiveness. In this respect newspapers referred to a popular novel about Rinaldo Rinaldini, an Italian bandit, which was very popular among the youth of Batavia.[54] Rinaldo Rinaldini's story and the careers of Si Pitung, Sakam, and Si Gantang show numerous similarities: the frequency of their disguises, the inability of people to recognize the bandits, the betrayal by close friends, and the many escapes from both jail and execution. The mixture of Italian mafia stories and rumors about local bandits suggests that the people in Batavia were eager to romanticize the local *preman*. And these local strongmen were perhaps equally willing to live up to the images of them produced by the press.

PUNISHMENT

> Oekoem mati, boenoeh, ghantoeng, potong leher, pasang
> dalam rante, oekoem sapoe, boei, oekoem boei, kerdja
> paksa, lepas, potong ghadji, denda.[55]

---

[52] P. Damardini, *Ceritra Si Pitung sebagai sastra lisan* (MA thesis, Universitas Indonesia, Jakarta, 1993), p. 134.

[53] M. van Till, "In Search of Si Pitung: The History of an Indonesian Legend," *Bijdragen tot de Taal-, Land- en Volkenkunde* 152 (1996): 461-82. Si Pitung's grave is still regarded as a powerful place, and he is the only old-time bandit for whom a museum was established.

[54] *Bataviaasch Nieuwsblad,* November 11, 1903. *Rinaldo Rinaldini, Goeverneurs Volksboeken* vol. 31-66 (Leiden: 1885). In contrast to the Batavian bandits, Rinaldo Rinaldini had the ambition to liberate the population from oppression.

[55] Pieters, *Praktische Indische tolk*, p. 225. Opening lines of chapter 69, "Punishment" (*Oekoeman*): "Death penalty, to kill, to hang, to cut one's throat, to put in chains, to flog, prison, imprisonment, forced labour, release, deduction of salary, fine."

Si Pitung came to his end at the graveyard at Tanah Abang where he was finally trapped and killed by the Batavian police who had been after him for more than six months. In comparison with rural Java, the local strongmen or *jago* in and around Batavia formed a direct threat to the European community, and this was the reason why their existence could not be so easily ignored. Their activities were also perceived as an embarrassment by the authorities of a colonial state that was gradually expanding its ambitions. As one newspaper put it:

> As a Dutchman one feels ashamed towards the natives to know that they are at the mercy of the terrorism of a bunch of escaped criminals. Secondly one feels ashamed as a Dutchman to know that even in the area of Batavia the poor have to offer their last pennies to robbers in order to free themselves from the fear of violence and murder—just because the police is everything except a police. In the third place one feels ashamed to hear the natives speak about the powers that are placed above them for their protection but that cannot guarantee the safety of their lives and possessions for one day, or even one hour.[56]

It is instructive to realize how many robbers were classified as "escaped criminals." Among the strongmen who were caught and put in jail, quite a number managed to escape either by force or by bribing the prison guards. Most of the strongmen, however, were never caught, not because their identity was not known, but precisely because of the fact that they were part of informal networks of alliance and self-interest which facilitated their predatory operations and guaranteed their safety.

Whereas in rural Java there was at least the formal appearance of a peaceful, imagined colonial order, open violence and unruliness were thought to be typical for the areas around Batavia and Bogor. Whether the origin of this violence ought to be attributed in colonial writings to the nature of native inhabitants, the vicious character of Chinese and Arab landlords or the bad habits of their *juragan* and *mandor* (overseers), the malfunctioning of local authorities, the absence of a decent colonial administration, or the continued use of the system of private estates became a subject of intense debate, although the violence was often seen as the consequence of all these factors in tandem.

Catching thieves and robbers had always been a problem on the private estates of West Java. Usually landowners made strategic deals with the most dangerous strongmen, just like village heads reached agreements with local *jago*. They paid them sums of money to leave them alone or hired them to enforce local peace keeping, opting for the strategy of "to catch thieves with thieves." But matters of law and order became more imperative when the colonial state wanted—or was expected—to expand its influence and control in the immediate surroundings of its own center.

If Si Gantang was in 1903 seen as the embodiment of criminality, it was on the other hand the Demang of Bekasi who personified the failure of local administrators to deal with this persistent problem. Although he was singled out as a scapegoat in

---

[56] *Bataviaasch Nieuwsblad,* November 19, 1903.

an official report,[57] the Demang was probably backed by his European superior, the Assistant Resident Meester Cornelis, who knew that the few indigenous officials he had at his disposal had to come to terms with local strongmen if they wanted to achieve anything. Moreover, the colonial government could hardly rely on the assistance of the overseers of the private estates. Although the overseers had to perform police tasks, they were on the payroll of the landowners who had other interests as well. Consequently, there was no clear distinction between spies, policemen, estate officials, thieves, and local strongmen. In such an atmosphere of elusive networks and an intimidating culture of prowess and *Selbsthilfe* (self-help), the ill-equipped colonial police had to try to come to terms with at least the most violent manifestations of the system.

It was in this context that a man like Adolf W. V. Hinne became the legendary adversary of Si Pitung.[58] Because of his success and his rather unorthodox methods of investigating criminal cases, Hinne became popular among the Europeans and respected among the Batavians. Numerous stories about Hinne emphasize his personal courage, his tough methods of interrogation, and his wide network of "indigenous detectives," and he displayed, no doubt, a good relationship with the Indische press. Hinne's career illustrates how "unprofessional" the Batavian police was at the time: before joining the police Hinne had been a clerk, a deputy forester, and a postmaster, and his success was not primarily based on any advanced police system or technology, but instead mainly on his personal *jago*-like qualities.

Complaints about the quality of the Batavian police were widespread among the Europeans in Batavia, and the shortage of money, means, and especially of white European officers was seen as the principal cause of this problem.[59] Salaries were on the whole low, and only retired members of the military were interested in the job, while corruption seems to have been quite normal and alcohol was used to help control one's nerves. As one newspaper put it, it could no longer be tolerated that

> . . . by strong cursing . . . and drinking plenty of gin, one could and tried to give oneself the image of being a courageous policeman. I remember some whose silver on their cap turned black simply because of the alcohol that had evaporated from their heads.[60]

When, however, the expansion of the colonial state was set in motion in the early part of the twentieth century, the building of a strong and modern police force was opposed by the established rulers of the colony because these civil administrators did not want to give up their monopolistic control over the domain of "peace and order." The colonial government only reluctantly started to reorganize its police force from 1905 onwards. One of the objectives was to increase the status of police officers and

---

[57] *Koloniaal Verslag* (Den Haag: Algemeene Landsdrukkerij, 1904), p. 5.

[58] See Van Till, "In Search of Si Pitung"; G. Termorshuizen, "A murder in Batavia or the ritual of power" in *Urban symbolism*, ed. P. Nas (Leiden: Brill, 1993), pp. 135-52.

[59] Bodemeijer, *Waaraan de achteruitgang van de bevolking in het district Bekasie*; De Veer, *Particuliere landerijen en de openbare veiligheid*.

[60] *Javabode*, February 7, 1903. See also accounts of the amount of alcohol drunk by the policeman Pangemanann in Pramoedya Ananta Toer, *Rumah kaca* (Jakarta: Hasta Mitra, 1988). Alcohol was, according to other European newspapers, seen by the population as a source of colonial power, for how could so few soldiers—who were often seen drunk in public places in town—otherwise control such a large colony. Personal communication, Cees van Dijk.

the "esprit de corps" among them by recruiting better educated candidates, establishing a police academy in Sukabumi, paying higher wages, supplying plain but neat uniforms, publishing a police magazine with information on technical, juridical, and even philosophical aspects of the profession, and housing policemen in barracks. One of the results of this process was the Europeanization of the colonial police force and the gradual disappearance of the old type of policeman who stood with one foot in the underworld. The new white policemen were respected counterparts of the civil administrators, and they knew much more about modern policing techniques, even if they lacked an adequate knowledge of the social world of the Batavian strongman. In 1916 the Resident of Batavia concluded that the newly arrived policemen from Holland were indeed better educated, but at the same time suffered from a lack of good connections with the local population. The Resident, however, was probably, all in all, not so displeased with the situation, because the inability of the modern police force to catch thieves demonstrated once more the importance of his own corps of civil administrators. The new police force also failed to gain support and sympathy among the wider European public. Despite various efforts to "modernize" the police force it remained a target of criticism.[61]

Since the activities of local strongmen could not be curbed by the police, the colonial government decided to introduce new forces in their war against the Batavian criminals. A military police corps, the *marechaussee*, was established in order to display a show of force and intimidate the invisible underworld enemy. The military only partially succeeded in catching thieves, but they did impress the population to such an extent that in popular memory this period is still referred to as the *zaman maresose* (the era or period of the *marechaussee*).[62] Nevertheless, despite increased military surveillance the area of Bogor and Batavia remained under the firm control of local strongmen until the end of colonial rule.[63]

A detailed discussion of colonial jurisdiction goes beyond the scope of this paper, but a few things merit mention in passing. Generally, the quality of colonial jurisprudence was judged by contemporary experts to be very low to mediocre. Until the early twentieth century there was no separate group of judges in Java, hence administration and jurisprudence were in the hands of the same ill-equipped officials. In particular, the jurisdiction of minor cases handled by one administrator, the so-called Politierol, was notorious for its arbitrary judgements. The Politierol was seen as an efficient instrument for disciplining the population with a minimum of juridical procedures. Especially in the days when cane punishment was an integral part of disciplining the population under the Cultivation System, the Politierol served as an instrument of repression and state violence.[64]

---

[61] ARA MvK MvO Resident Batavia Rijfsnijder (1916); I. Misset, "De politie in onze Indische maatschappij," *De Nederlandsch-Indische Politiegids*, 1,9 (1917): 10-11; see also P. Dekker, *De politie in Nederlandsch-Indië: hare beknopte geschiedenis, haar taak, bevoegdheid, organisatie en optreden* (Soekaboemi: Insulinde, 1938).

[62] Cribb, *Gangsters and Revolutionaries*, p. 31; Damardini, *Ceritra Si Pitung*, p. 150.

[63] "De onveiligheid op de particuliere landerijen in West-Java," *Indische Gids* 59,1 (1939): 532-7; *Inlandsch Persoverzicht* (1937), pp. 15-18.

[64] For an analysis of the Politierol and cane punishment in the period 1830-1870 see P. Consten, "Geweld in dienst van de koloniale discipline" (Unpubished paper, Vrije Universiteit Amsterdam, 1996). The extent of cane punishment was reflected in statistics as well. In 1862 ninety thousand Javanese appeared before a Politie judge and one-third of them received cane punishment.

More serious cases of theft and murder were brought to the Landraad or the Omgaand Gerecht. Yet another case demonstrates that it was often extremely difficult to gather reliable evidence, because witnesses often were not found or were unwilling to testify:

> Together with his five wives, two notorious sons, and a group of followers who did the actual stealing for him, Entong Tolo roamed around in Bekasi. He was caught in 1908 but the authorities had to release him due to lack of evidence. When he was captured again in 1910 the desperate Resident of Batavia asked the Governor General for special permission to exile the robber Entong Tolo from Bekasi without trial [thus on political grounds] because people were too afraid to testify.[65]

Due to changes in the judicial system in Holland, procedures and punishments in the Indies were also changing. As the formation of the Dutch nation-state proceeded and notions about civilized forms of punishment emerged, public flogging was abolished and a new type of prison was designed and developed in which the isolation of the individual criminal in his cell was emphasized.[66] As a result of the reforms in Holland, cane punishment in the Indies was abolished in 1864. But instead of being locked away in individual cells within "civilized" prisons, Javanese were convicted and sentenced to perform forced labor.[67] Prisons were not considered a suitable form of punishment for the Javanese, because individual confinement would lead them to madness and eventually suicide. This served as a nice cultural rationale for a policy of economic self-interest: the use of prisoners in projects of forced labor.

Summarizing the effects of both colonial policing and jurisprudence, it is not an exaggeration to argue that together they increased feelings of fear and notions of injustice among both the Dutch and the Javanese.

CREATING CRIMINALITY AND CRIMINALS

Crime, criminality, and criminals are not static terms, but are, rather, dynamic social categories which are closely connected in their meaning and deployment to processes of state formation.[68] Just as was the case in Europe, local problem solving in old Java involved a "normal" amount of violence, and in Europe this violence only

---

[65] *Laporan-laporan tentang gerakan protes di Jawa pada abad-XX* (Jakarta: Arsip Nasional Republik Indonesia, 1981), pp. 3-7.

[66] H. Franke, *De dood en het leven van alledag: Rouwadvertenties en openbare strafvoltrekking in Nederland* (Den Haag: Nijgh & Van Ditmar, 1985); *Twee eeuwen gevangen: Over de geschiedenis van het gevangeniswezen en het emancipatieproces van gevangenen vanaf het einde van de 18e eeuw tot heden* (Utrecht: Het Spectrum, 1990).

[67] In 1877, for instance, almost eighty thousand people were on the Politierol, fifty-seven thousand of whom were sentenced to forced labor. See Consten, "Geweld in dienst van de koloniale discipline."

[68] Compare the situation in British India as discussed in A. Yang, ed., *Crime and Criminality in British India* (Tucson: The University of Arizona Press, 1985).

gradually decreased as a consequence of stagnating state formation.[69] No doubt notions of potency in Java had changed by the early twentieth century. But many ideas were still relevant, and when in later times local strongmen in Java were compelled to inhabit the category of criminality by colonial officials, these strongmen entered a new domain in which they were transformed into violent entrepreneurs who turned against their own people.

The *jago* was not a bandit as defined by Hobsbawm.[70] He did not stand outside society but instead formed a crucial link within the political system. There was no transition from crime to rebellion, because the *jago* was part of the colonial power structure, and *jagos* did not desire a restoration of the good old traditional order because the colonial order offered them a great number of benefits. It makes, therefore, more sense to compare the *jago* with the Sicilian mafia—as the *Bataviaasch Nieuwsblad* had already done in 1903! The framework in which Anton Blok places the mafia corresponds with what happened in Java at about the same time: a process of "unfinished" or stagnating state formation enabled new groups of violent entrepreneurs to dominate the local order in alliance with, or under the patronage of, rural elites.[71] Like the mafia in Sicily, the *jagos* in Java did not strive for the renewal or the restoration of the old political order. They only tried, instead, to gain as much as possible from the current political order in which they had so much invested.

Although officially the *jago* was perceived as playing only a marginal role in colonial society, in actual practice he was vital to the perpetuation of colonial rule in rural Java. Only insofar as European interests were directly challenged or in places where bandits had more room to maneuver since their actions were less restricted by patron-client relationships, as was the case in the surroundings of Batavia, was the colonial state willing to act from time to time against the most notorious among the local strongmen. This implied that large areas of Javanese society were left under the unrestricted influence of *jagos*, which in turn led the population to the conclusion that the state was apparently run by crooks. Colonial state formation and criminality mutually constituted and reinforced each other, and once criminality emerged the colonial state could not, and often did not want to, control its own creation.

It was not only the European community on Java that lived in a permanent state of fear. The majority of the Javanese population felt threatened as well, as we have tried to illustrate at some length.[72] This may help to explain why new organizations like Sarekat Islam suddenly gained such mass support when they appeared on the political scene.[73] People longed for justice, but justice was not expected from either

---

[69] E. Johnson & E. Monkkonen, eds., *The Civilization of Crime: Violence in Town and Country since the Middle Ages* (Urbana/Chicago: University of Illinois Press, 1996), p. 13.

[70] E. Hobsbawm, *Bandits* (Harmondsworth: Penguin, 1972). In this respect also see Cheah Boon Keng, "Hobsbawm's Social Banditry, Myth and Historical Reality: A Case in the Malaysian State of Kedah, 1915-1920," *Bulletin of Concerned Asian Scholars* 17,4 (1985): 34-51.

[71] A. Blok, "The Peasant and the Brigand: Social Banditry Reconsidered," *Comparative Studies in Society and History* 14 (1972): 494-508; A. Blok, *The Mafia of a Sicilian Village 1860-1960: A Study of Violent Peasant Entrepreneurs* (New York: Harper & Row, 1974).

[72] For the kind of colonial Malay that was learned by freshmen, and which expresses distrust and fear, see Pieters, *Praktische Indische tolk*.

[73] *Sarekat Islam lokal* (Jakarta: Arsip Nasional Republik Indonesia, 1975, Penerbitan Sumber-Sumber Sejarah 7); *Laporan-laporan tentang gerakan protes di Jawa*; T. Shiraishi, *An Age in Motion: Popular Radicalism in Java, 1912-26* (Ithaca/London: Cornell University Press, 1990).

colonial authorities or local strongmen, although perhaps new organizations which had set new times and new hopes in motion could provide it.

THE USUAL SUSPECTS:
NARDONG PUTIK, DON PEPE OYSON,
AND ROBIN HOOD

John Sidel

Both scholarship and the culture industry in the Philippines have concurred on a view of "crime" as reflecting certain features of Philippine society. In particular, scholars and screenplay writers alike portray criminality in the archipelago as a form of societal "resistance" to injustices unpunished—or perpetrated—by predatory agents of capital and the state. Bandits and gangsters thus appear as authentic local heroes of the poor and downtrodden, "social bandits" in the sense popularized by Eric Hobsbawm.[1] Their success in evading "the law" is attributed to their Robin Hood-like popularity, to their intrinsic powers, *anting-anting* (magical amulets), and charisma, and to the "weakness" of the state. While numerous scholars, comic book writers, and movie producers have concurred in these depictions of "primitive rebellion" and "social banditry" in the Philippines, this paper offers a very different view of crime in the archipelago, one which takes as its essential point of departure an analysis of the Philippine state.

Compared to its counterparts elsewhere in Southeast Asia, the Philippine state is distinguished by its highly decentralized, politicized, and privatized administration of law enforcement, a legacy of the American colonial period. Since the first years of this century, elected municipal mayors in the Philippines have by law enjoyed considerable discretion over the appointment, transfer, payment, and removal of municipal policemen,[2] who thus, in the words of the Director of the Philippine Constabulary in 1908, have typically functioned as the "messengers, muchachos, and

---

[1] Eric Hobsbawm, *Bandits* (New York: Pantheon Books, 1981); Eric Hobsbawm, *Primitive Rebels: Studies in Archaic Forms of Social Movement in the Nineteenth and Twentieth Centuries* (New York: W. W. Norton & Company, 1959).

[2] See the "Brief History Of The Municipal Police," in Maj. Emmanuel A. Baja, *Philippine Police System and its Problems* (Manila: Pobre's Press, 1933), pp. 202-221.

servants" of the towns' chief executives.[3] Provincial governors, moreover, have long held the authority to appoint "special agents," security officers, and jail wardens, and have consistently intervened over the years in the appointment, promotion, transfer, and removal of provincial commanders of the Philippine Constabulary (PC).[4] In addition, congressmen and senators have, through the powerful Commission on Appointments, retained a measure of influence over the promotion and transfer of high-ranking Constabulary/Police officers, thus diluting the otherwise unimpeded discretion of the President in his control over the nation's primary law-enforcement agency. Long-time president Ferdinand Marcos worked to centralize and bureaucratize law enforcement through an Integrated National Police subordinated to the Philippine Constabulary (PC-INP) and the Armed Forces of the Philippines (AFP) in 1975. From 1975 through 1990, policemen throughout the archipelago served as members of the PC-INP/AFP, their assignments, promotions, and transfers determined by ranking PC/AFP officers instead of elected officials.[5] Today, however, due to legislation enacted in 1990, elected officials at municipal, city, provincial, and national levels have regained significant discretionary powers over the supervision and appointment of Philippine National Police (PNP) personnel.[6]

Viewed as a set of apparatuses geared for the maintenance of "order" and the administration of "justice," the decentralized, politicized, and personalized law-enforcement agencies of the Philippine state do constitute a structural "weakness" highly favorable to criminal activity. The limited capacities of national police agencies and the subordination of police forces to municipal and provincial elected officials allow criminals to exploit the parcellized jurisdictions of local law-enforcement authorities in the archipelago. As Eric Hobsbawm has noted:

> The ideal situation for robbery is one in which the local authorities are local men, operating in complex local situations, and where a few miles may put the robber beyond the reach or even the knowledge of one set of authorities and into the territory of another, which does not worry about what happens "abroad."[7]

Viewed alternatively, however, as predatory apparatuses geared not for the suppression of "crime" and the administration of "justice" but for the regulation and exploitation of illegal economies, these police forces appear less unsuccessful in stemming "lawlessness" and more successful in imposing "the law" upon Philippine society. After all, Philippine policemen have figured most prominently over the years not as the defenders of justice but as the protectors of bandits, car thieves, cattle rustlers, illegal loggers, *jueteng* (illegal lottery) operators, and smugglers, the

---

[3] "Report of Acting Director of Constabulary, Department of Commerce and Police, Bureau of Constabulary, Manila, P.I., August 8, 1908," in Bureau of Insular Affairs, War Department, *Report of the Philippine Commission to the Secretary of War, 1908, Part 2* (Washington, DC: Government Printing Office, 1909), p. 372.

[4] On this point, see Cicero C. Campos, "The Role Of The Police In The Philippines: A Case Study From The Third World," PhD dissertation, Michigan State University, 1983, pp. 205-206.

[5] Ibid., pp. 166-169, 211-230.

[6] See, in particular, Section 51 of Republic Act No. 6975, in Rod B. Gutang, *Pulisya: The Inside Story of the Demilitarization of the Law Enforcement System in the Philippines* (Quezon City: Daraga Press, 1991), pp. 164-165.

[7] Hobsbawm, *Bandits*, p. 21.

organizers of bank robberies and kidnappings, and the distributors of illegal firearms and narcotics. Through selective and discretionary enforcement of the law, the police have perhaps not so much failed to eradicate crime as they have managed to exact monopoly rents from the proceeds of illegal commerce. In their enforcement of the law, the police—and the elected officials to whom they are responsible—are thus quite successful *as racketeers*.

Reexamined against this backdrop, much of what has passed for "resistance," "primitive rebellion," or "social banditry" in the Philippines no longer appears so decisively in opposition to the state. "Outlaws," ironically perhaps, have often relied heavily upon "the law" and its selective enforcement. Bandits and gangsters have often depended for their survival not upon the popularity they enjoy among subaltern communities of peasants and the urban poor, but rather upon the informal franchise and protection they receive from the police and the elected officials to whom the police are responsible. As Anton Blok, a leading critic of Hobsbawm's "social bandit" formulation, notes: "This yields the following hypothesis, which may be tested against data bearing on all kinds of robbery: *The more successful a man is as a bandit, the more extensive the protection granted him.*"[8] Insofar as Filipino gangsters serve as the subcontracted agents of the state, they resemble not so much Hobsbawm's social bandits as what Blok calls *mafia*: entrepreneurs who use private, formally unlicensed violence as a means of social control and economic accumulation.[9] Through a monopoly of violence and provision of protection, *mafia* thus assume the position of police, even as police take on many features of *mafia*.

Against the backdrop of these revisionist arguments, the pages below revisit Cavite, a province long notorious for its bandits, cattle rustlers, carnappers, and smugglers.[10] Two case studies compare the most successful outlaws in the province during two successive periods: Leonardo Manecio alias Nardong Putik in the early post-war heyday of localized, civilian control over policing (1946-1972), and José "Don Pepe" Oyson in the era of centralization and military integration (1975-1990). The narrative situates Manecio and Oyson within evolving local landscapes of criminality and maps the shifting geography, organization, and social representation of crime in the province. Following Blok's example of close attention to criminals' connections to representatives of the state and of dominant social classes, the pages below chronicle the rise and fall of two outlaws more aptly seen as *mafia* bosses than as social bandits. A concluding section compares these two Caviteño criminals and then turns to a set of broader questions about the social representation of criminality in the Philippines.

I. CAVITE'S NOBLE ROBBER?: THE CASE OF NARDONG PUTIK

Throughout the early postwar period (1946-1972), a diverse geography of crime intersected with the complex circuitry of Cavite's evolving capitalist economy. Cattle

---

[8] Anton Blok, "The Peasant and the Brigand," *Comparative Studies in Society and History* 14,4 (September 1972): 498. Italics in the original.

[9] Anton Blok, *The Mafia of a Sicilian Village 1860-1960: A Study of Violent Peasant Entrepreneurs* (New York: Harper & Row, 1974), p. 6.

[10] See Carolyn I. Sobritchea, "Banditry in Cavite During the Post World War II Period," *Asian Studies*, volumes XXIII-IV (1984-1986), pp. 10-27.

rustlers preying upon rice-growing areas, highwaymen patrolling overland transit routes, smugglers claiming the coastal shores, and carnappers operating in suburban towns all responded to the growth of nearby Manila and the expansion of its markets for stolen or smuggled goods. By and large, these assorted *mafia* were firmly subordinated to the local law-enforcement authorities, their criminal monopolies sponsored and protected by town mayors and their flunky policemen, or, as in the case of smuggling, by provincial-level politicians and their protégés in the PC.[11] Tellingly, the careers of Cavite's cattle rustlers, highwaymen, and carnappers typically followed the rise and fall of their political patrons and police protectors. Against this backdrop, one notorious outlaw clearly stands out as the most successful, long-lasting *mafia* boss in Cavite in the pre-martial law postwar period: Leonardo Manecio alias "Nardong Putik."

In July 1972, Manila newspapers heralded the premier of the film "Nardong Putik (Kilabot Ng Cavite)" [Nardong Mud (Terror of Cavite)], starring Ramon Revilla. Establishing Revilla's reputation as an action-movie star, the film chronicled the life and times of the legendary Caviteño bandit Leonardo Manecio, alias Nardong Putik, whose exploits in the mid-1950s and late 1960s had, through banner headline newspaper stories and an earlier film, received more popular attention than any other outlaw figure in Philippine history. Following Manecio's death at the hands of National Bureau of Investigation (NBI) agents in October 1971 after an extensive manhunt, photographs of his bloodied and bullet-riddled corpse had graced the front pages of Manila dailies, and the promoters of the film took full advantage of the advance publicity. Newspaper advertisements promised that "AMULETS (*ANTING-ANTING*), GUNS, NEWSPAPER CLIPPINGS, DEATH PHOTOS and FATAL CAR H-81-31-CAVITE '71 used by NARDONG PUTIK (Courtesy of NBI) will be distributed in different Theaters and can be viewed by the public."[12]

The film etched in the popular memory a portrait of Nardong Putik as a charismatic, magically endowed Robin Hood figure, a "social bandit" par excellence. Aside from good looks and exceptional martial skills, he possesses an *anting-anting* which renders him virtually invulnerable to his enemies. Nardong Putik's outlaw career, moreover, begins with the death of his father at the hands of cattle rustlers, marking him as a victim of social injustice. Seeking revenge, he joins the town police force. As a film critic reviewing the film explained:

> Nardong Putik becomes a policeman, a terror of a policeman who delivers justice out of the barrel of his gun. Because of his merciless pursuit of justice, he is removed from the Cavite police force. Fast as lightning a series of events occur . . . Nardong Putik is accused of liquidating the town officials of Maragondon. A killing here, a killing there. Nardong Putik becomes The Terror of Cavite, defending himself against whoever challenges his bravery and putting away whoever acts conceited in his presence.

---

[11] See John Sidel, "Walking in the Shadow of the Big Man: Justiniano Montano and Failed Dynasty Building in Cavite, 1935-1972," in *An Anarchy of Families: State and Family in the Philippines*, ed. Alfred W. McCoy (Madison: University of Wisconsin Center for Southeast Asian Studies, 1993), pp. 140-142.

[12] Paid advertisement, *Manila Times*, July 13, 1972, p. 23.

In spite of all the killings, Nardong Putik still has a set of golden rules for his henchmen: don't steal carabao, don't rape, don't poison fishponds, don't steal cars. Whoever disregards these commandments is dead meat . . . [13]

Although the film has clouded popular memory, to the point where Ramon Revilla's Nardong Putik today overshadows the one chronicled in newspaper stories and local legend, it is still possible to establish several elements of correspondence between the two outlaw figures. Caviteños still impressed by Manecio's martial prowess and machismo describe him as *barako* (from the Spanish word *barraco* for boar), a term connoting manliness and potency. Photographs of Manecio alias Putik taken in the late 1950s reveal a strikingly handsome young man, whose good looks never fail to elicit admiration from Filipinas of all ages. In addition, some such photographs show Manecio's bare torso to be covered with numerous tattoos, including large letters spelling out KILABOT (The Terror) across his lower abdomen. Moreover, besides these magically endowed tattoos, Manecio supposedly possessed a stone amulet—shaped like a turtle entwined with a serpent—as well as a number of distinctly Masonic[14] charms which were believed to render him virtually invulnerable to harm.[15]

As in the film, Manecio enjoyed a reputation in Cavite as a kind of "noble robber"—a victim of injustice himself, a provider of local justice and protection, and a Robin Hood figure.[16] Indeed, Manecio's criminal career began with the death of his father, Juan "Putik" Manecio, at the hands of cattle rustlers in the town of Dasmariñas, Cavite, in October 1944.[17] Subsequently, according to Manecio's own claims in an exclusive interview with a newspaper correspondent in 1956, he faced continuing harassment from his father's killers, who attempted to murder him and later arranged for his arrest and conviction on trumped-up charges of "robbery in band." Imprisoned, Manecio escaped in 1951 after learning of the death of his brother at the hands of his enemies. Reincarcerated soon thereafter, he escaped again in 1955, allegedly incensed about cattle rustling in the barrios of Dasmariñas and two neighboring municipalities. Once freed, he is said to have assumed the role of a local Robin Hood. As one Cavite politician noted years later:

When there are thefts or highway robberies or hold-ups, the victims do not seek help from the government, since they do not expect any results from

---

[13] Clodualdo Del Mundo Jr., "'Nardong Putik': Makatotohanan?" in *The Urian Anthology 1970-1979*, ed. Nicanor Tiongson (Manila: Manuel L. Morato, 1983), pp. 148-149. Translation by the author.

[14] Cavite has traditionally been the most important locus of Masonic activity in the Philippines outside of Manila. See Teodoro M. Kalaw, *La Masonería Filipina* (Manila: Bureau of Printing, 1920), p. 195.

[15] Moises Timbang Saunar alias Esing Cavite, interview with the author, November 7, 1992, New Bilibid Prison, Muntinlupa.

[16] See Hobsbawm, *Bandits*, pp. 42-43.

[17] Church notarial records maintained at the Parish of the Immaculate Concepcion in the Poblacion of Dasmariñas, Cavite cite "Gun Shot" as the *causa mortis*.

that corner. The word on the street is that they take their complaints instead to Nardong Putik and immediately get the justice they are asking for.[18]

In its exclusive focus on the picaresque exploits of Manecio alias Putik, this narrative downplays the social, political, and economic circumstances that underlay his unparalleled longevity as a Cavite *mafia* boss. In fact, while Manecio's father was a small-time rice farmer, José Barzaga, the sponsor and godfather or *padrino* at Leonardo's baptism as an infant in 1925,[19] belonged to a wealthy Dasmariñas clan whose scions included prominent lawyers and politicians in the town.[20] Thus Juan "Putik" Manecio and, by extension, his son Leonardo claimed a long-standing affiliation with a major political faction in Dasmariñas that centered around the intermarried Carungcong, Mangubat, and Barzaga families.[21] By contrast, the cattle rustlers who killed Manecio's father in 1944, for example, were in fact members of a so-called guerrilla group whose members comprised the opposing political faction in the town. Throughout much of the Japanese Occupation period (1941-1945), this armed band competed with a rival group under Colonel Estanislao Carungcong (4th Infantry Unit) for control over "turf" in the town, whose residents were "taxed" in exchange for "protection."[22] While nominally deployed against the local Japanese garrisons, these "guerrilla groups" in fact spent their time rustling cattle. As one Dasmariñas resident later recalled:

> It was about three thirty in the morning when I heard our old clock strike which woke me up. Two gunshots were heard from a distance. After a little while many more shots were heard. I heard my wife who had been awakened at that time murmur, "Oh, those guerrillas. Some persons have been robbed of their carabaos."[23]

Drawn into local factional politics in Dasmariñas after the murder of his father, Manecio soon enlisted as a full-time armed retainer in the services of the Carungcongs, Mangubats, and Barzagas.[24] When pre-war Dasmariñas Mayor Felicisimo Carungcong was reappointed following Liberation in 1945, Manecio

---

[18] Rogelio L. Ordoñez, "Ang Kabite at Ang Mga Montano," *Asia-Philippines Leader* 1,4 (April 30, 1971): 47. Translation by the author.

[19] Baptismal Records of the Parish of the Immaculate Concepcion, Dasmariñas, Cavite, p. 192.

[20] See the references to Francisco Barzaga in "Historical Data of Dasmariñas" prepared by the Dasmariñas Elementary School Teachers, School Year 1952-1953 in *Historical Data Papers* (Manila: National Museum, 1953).

[21] While the Carungcongs predominated in politics and the Barzagas in the legal profession, the Mangubats owned over two hundred hectares of prime irrigated rice land and a major rice mill in Dasmariñas.

[22] See Melinda C. Tria, "The Resistance Movement in Cavite, 1942-1945" (MA thesis, University of the Philippines, 1966), pp. 21, 29-34.

[23] "A Memorable Incident During the Concentration of the People in the Town of Dasmariñas, Cavite by Japanese on December 17, 1944," in "Historical Data of Dasmariñas" in *Historical Data Papers*.

[24] As Hobsbawm notes: " . . . where landowning families fight and feud, make and break family alliances, dispute heritages with arms, the stronger accumulating wealth and influence over the broken bones of the weaker, the scope for bands of fighting men led by the disgruntled losers is naturally very large." Hobsbawm, *Bandits*, p. 95.

joined the town police force. In 1946, however, the newly appointed Governor of Cavite named a member of the anti-Carungcong faction as the new Dasmariñas Mayor. Dismissed from the town police force, Manecio reportedly found work as a bus driver but in 1947 was arrested by Philippine Constabulary officers and charged with kidnapping, murder, robbery in band, and illegal possession of firearms. Acquitted of all but the last charge, he served a six-month sentence in the national penitentiary in Muntinlupa. Returning to Cavite in 1948, he remained a target of harassment by remnants of the anti-Carungcong guerrilla group and their allies elsewhere in Cavite. After working briefly for the Mangubats on their fishing fleet in Manila Bay, Manecio returned to Cavite in 1950 to face charges of robbery in band, a crime of which he was convicted and sentenced to eighteen months in Muntinlupa. In September 1951, however, he again escaped from Muntinlupa and returned to Cavite.

During these early years, Manecio served as a mere *bata-bata* or henchman of the Carungcong and Mangubat clans in Dasmariñas. In Cavite during this period, elections were notoriously violent and local politicians deployed scores of armed retainers as bodyguards, campaigners, assassins, and election-day enforcers of vote-buying and fraud. Viewed against the backdrop of the local elections held in November of 1947 and 1951, the timing of Manecio's imprisonment in March 1947 and "escape" from Muntinlupa in September 1951 thus appears more the product of orchestration than of coincidence. If Manecio's enemies arranged for his arrest, conviction, and imprisonment to keep him out of Dasmariñas for the 1947 elections, so must the Carungcongs and Mangubats have helped to engineer his early departure from Muntinlupa in time for the 1951 campaign.

Provincial-level political developments in Cavite inaugurated the second phase in Manecio's outlaw career. Manecio's patrons, the Mangubats and Carungcongs, enjoyed close ties to Senator Justiniano Montano, Sr., and enlisted their henchman in his employ.[25] In September 1952, the mayor of Maragondon, a remote Cavite town, was kidnapped and stabbed to death along with the police chief and two municipal policemen. A preliminary investigation implicated Senator Montano, the Vice Mayor and two municipal councilors of Maragondon, and several Montano henchmen from elsewhere in Cavite, including Manecio.[26] PC officers loyal to then Governor Camerino (Montano's arch-rival) summarily arrested all the suspects, including the Senator. In the subsequent trial, witnesses claimed that a Montano flunky had brought Manecio to a meeting with the Senator where the so-called "Maragondon Massacre" was planned. Under considerable pressure, Manecio corroborated this account and confessed his guilt. In 1954, however, the election to the presidency of Ramon Magsaysay, Montano's close ally, and the sworn testimony on Montano's behalf of such political luminaries as Manila Mayor Arsenio Lacson, led to the dismissal of the case against the Senator. Left behind bars as the "fall guy" in the Maragondon case, Manecio had only Montano to thank for his fate.

---

[25] Over the years, Montano supported various Carungcongs in bids for municipal office in Dasmariñas and careers within the Philippine Constabulary. He likewise showed special consideration towards the Mangubats, whose construction company won numerous government contracts for public works projects.

[26] "Information," filed September 19, 1952 in Manila by Special Prosecutors Epitacio Panganiban and Felix Q. Antonio in People of the Philippines vs. Justiniano Montano, Magno Iruguin, Mariano de Raya, Leonardo Manecio alias Nardong Putik, alias Kilabot, et al. (Cavite City: Court of the First Instance of Cavite, 7th Judicial District, 1952).

Though abandoned by Montano, Manecio still had close ties to his long-time patrons in Dasmariñas as well as growing links to those most appreciative of his testimony against the Senator. In July 1955, Manecio "escaped" from the Constabulary's provincial stockade in Imus, aided by officers reporting to acting Governor Dominador Mangubat, Manecio's hometown benefactor.[27] Thus freed, he was available to assist the Mangubats and Carungcongs in the closely contested local elections in Dasmariñas four months later. However, the election in November 1955 of Delfin Montano, the Senator's son, as Cavite Provincial Governor removed Manecio from the protection of the provincial law-enforcement authorities.

It was in this context that Manecio first emerged as a *mafia* boss in his own right, an outlaw with a private criminal monopoly not reducible to the protection or sponsorship of any single law-enforcement authority. By early 1956, reports began to surface in the Manila newspapers about the activities of "Nardong Putik" in Cavite. Claiming as his bailiwick the neighboring towns of Dasmariñas, Gen. Trias, and Imus, Manecio was described as having eliminated cattle rustling and imposed a system of protection payments—collected in cash or kind—on landowners and tenant farmers alike. Residents of these towns interviewed by the author in 1991 and 1992 recall this "protection racket" as most favorable to the owners of rice mills and large landholdings in these towns. Tenant farmers lacking in influence with the local authorities, by contrast, are said to have borne the brunt of Manecio's exactions. Members of Manecio's *tropa* (gang), recruited from among his local network of relatives and criminal accomplices, dealt severely with farmers and local officials who were less than fully cooperative. The gang's occasional cattle rustling escapades in other nearby towns supplemented these regular "protection" remittances, as victims agreed to pay out "brokerage fees" to Manecio for "retrieving" and returning their stolen carabaos.

A confluence of economic and political circumstances combined to facilitate Manecio's effective monopoly over cattle rustling in the municipalities of Dasmariñas, Gen. Trias, and Imus. Comprising two friar estates during the Spanish era, these three contiguous towns had evolved into a rice-bowl zone of intensive *palay* (wet-rice) cultivation, with ten thousand hectares of irrigated paddy plowed and harrowed by some four thousand carabaos.[28] Tenant farmers cultivating small parcels tilled most of this land, owing half of their produce to landlords and delivering much of their remaining share to local rice millers, traders, and moneylenders. Living at the margins of subsistence and lacking in local political clout, the sharecroppers were highly vulnerable to cattle rustlers and thus paid Manecio out of their share of the harvest.

Moreover, unlike other rice-bowl towns in Cavite such as Naic and Tanza, the adjoining municipalities of Dasmariñas, Gen. Trias, and Imus comprised a zone in which Manecio enjoyed nearly complete political protection. In Gen. Trias and Imus, he won the backing of ex-governor and Montano foe Dominador Camerino, whose political career had long been supported by the two towns' most prominent landed families. While Camerino's protégés won re-election to the mayorships of Gen. Trias

---

[27] Documents presented by Manecio after his capture in 1958 included a PC identification card and authorization papers signed by a certain Lt. Fabian Ver (!).

[28] See *Census of the Philippines 1948, Volume II, Part I: Report by Province for Census of Agriculture: Abra to Cebu* (Manila: Bureau of Printing, 1953), pp. 535, 544; and *Census Of The Philippines 1960: Agriculture, Volume I - Report by Province: Cavite* (Manila: Bureau of the Census and Statistics, 1963), pp. 17-4, 17-18.

and Imus in 1955, Senator Montano's son defeated Camerino for the provincial governorship and thus assumed control over Cavite's constabulary command. Against these hostile provincial authorities, Camerino and his backers in Gen. Trias and Imus thus supported Manecio as a counterforce to insure protection from cattle rustlers and to keep the Montanos' supporters in these towns—including prominent landed families such as the Triases of Gen. Trias—on the defensive. Moreover, as newly elected Montano mayors in other towns worked for selective implementation of 1955 agrarian reform legislation against their landed opponents,[29] the large landowning families in Gen. Trias and Imus loyal to Camerino used Manecio's presence to discourage tenant farmers from pressing for more favorable tenancy conditions or expropriation proceedings now provided for by law.[30] Meanwhile, in Dasmariñas, the newly elected mayor, Remigio Carungcong, while a Montano protégé, belonged to the same clique of families that had backed Manecio since his father's death in 1944.

Following the elections of 1957, however, developments in provincial and national politics began to conspire against Manecio. Accused of attempting to assassinate Governor Montano in 1956 and blamed for the November 1957 election-day killing of the Cavite PC Commander, Manecio became the target of a vigorous manhunt. Demands for Manecio's capture took on a new sense of urgency following the ascension to the presidency in 1957 of Carlos Garcia, whose son-in-law belonged to a prominent Dasmariñas clan at odds with Manecio's sponsors, the Carungcongs and Mangubats. In May 1958, PC troops finally captured Manecio in a rice mill in Kawit. Despite the best efforts of his lawyer, Manecio returned to the penitentiary in Muntinlupa, sentenced to life imprisonment for his many crimes.

Manecio remained in Muntinlupa for over a decade, biding his time while the Montanos further entrenched themselves in power in Cavite.[31] Prison guards remember him as a well respected and feared prisoner, whose status was greatly enhanced by the frequent visits of prominent Cavite politicians to his cell. Indeed, Manecio won appointment first as the "mayor" of a special ward for mentally disturbed prisoners, and subsequently as the "mayor" of the ward for juvenile delinquents, a position in which he played a key role in supplying young boys to older prisoners and in quashing a number of prison riots. Following the election to the presidency in 1965 of Ferdinand Marcos, an arch enemy of the Montanos, Manecio gained additional privileges. Reclassified as a "living-out" prisoner, he slept outside the maximum security prison and was free to move around the prison grounds so long as he reported to his guards three times a day. According to one source, Manecio was even allowed to make supervised visits to Cavite while still nominally serving his life sentence.[32] In October 1969, weeks before the presidential and congressional elections, hearing rumors that the Montanos were plotting his

[29] Naic Mayor Macario Peña strictly enforced the newly legislated seventy-thirty share tenancy rule in favor of tenant farmers, while Carmona Mayor Cesar Casal engineered the expropriation of three large estates in his town.

[30] On Senator Montano's prominent role in the passage of this legislation, see Frances Lucille Starner, *Magsaysay and The Peasantry: The Agrarian Impact on Philippine Politics, 1953-1956* (Berkeley: University of California Press, 1961), pp. 136, 149-150, 181-184.

[31] See Sidel, "Walking in the Shadow of the Big Man," pp. 138-144.

[32] Inspector Diomedes Bador, interview with the author, November 7, 1992, New Bilibid Prison, Muntinlupa.

murder, Manecio "escaped," with the blessings of his political patrons and prison officials.[33]

Once at large, Manecio returned to his former bailiwick in the towns of Dasmariñas, Gen. Trias, and Imus. His long-time mentor, Mayor Carungcong, remained in office in Dasmariñas, a Camerino crony held the mayorship in Imus, and members of the Carungcong clan had risen to high-ranking positions in the Constabulary in Cavite. Mayors closely linked to Camerino also afforded Manecio protection in two other nearby municipalities. Moreover, while the Montanos still held the Cavite governorship and congressional seat, and, through their protégés, many municipal positions, President Marcos had launched an offensive against their political machine, sending loyalist Constabulary officers to Cavite. In his election-related and criminal activities, Manecio thus joined forces with a Palace-backed, province-wide effort to dislodge the Montanos.

While these political developments worked in Manecio's favor, economic change had begun to transform the geography of crime in his old bailiwick. On the one hand, cattle rustling was no longer the most lucrative racket in these municipalities. By the late 1960s, the towns of Dasmariñas, Gen. Trias, and Imus saw declining hectarage devoted to rice cultivation and a decreasing reliance by local farmers on carabaos (in favor of tractors, harvesting machines, and modern threshing equipment).[34] On the other hand, the proximity of these municipalities to the evolving national capital region presented increasingly attractive opportunities for criminal activities geared toward the Manila market. Beginning in the 1950s, these towns had begun to establish themselves (under Manecio's aegis) as a base for extensive carnapping operations: several "syndicates" maintained repair shops where jeepneys and cars stolen in Manila were overhauled for resale. By the late 1960s, these carnapping operations had grown more successful and more lucrative. Meanwhile, the proximity of the nation's premier metropolis encouraged the cultivation of marijuana in these towns for sale on the expanding urban market.[35]

As in the 1955-1958 period, Manecio assumed the role of the *mafia* boss in these towns. Banking on the privileged relations he enjoyed with the mayors and policemen of these municipalities (and with friendly elements in the provincial Constabulary) Manecio imposed his "protection" over the extensive illegal economies in his domain. Landowners and tenant farmers paid for "protection" from cattle rustlers, while car thieves and owners of marijuana plantations similarly submitted to his rule. Victims of carnappers and cattle rustlers likewise offered Manecio "brokerage fees" for arranging the retrieval of their purloined property.[36]

In some respects, however, Manecio's *mafia* personality had changed with the passing of time. One photograph of Manecio taken during this period reveals a garishly dressed gangster in his mid-forties, sporting a noticeable paunch, a large gold necklace, and carefully curled forelocks, the contrast with his 1950s image

---

[33] Former prison officials interviewed by the author in January and November 1992 readily admitted their collusion in Manecio's "escape."

[34] *1971 Census of Agriculture: Cavite, Volume I* (Manila: National Census and Statistics Office, 1975), pp. 4-50.

[35] National Bureau of Investigation, *Annual Report Fiscal Year 1970* (Manila: Department of Justice, 1970), p. 19.

[36] Justiniano S. Montano, Sr., Privilege Speech before the House of Representatives of the Republic of the Philippines, February 11, 1971.

strikingly reminiscent of Elvis Presley's transformation over the years. Reports of Manecio's activities following his 1969 escape also depict the outlaw as relying heavily on a group of M16-toting bodyguards, consorting frequently with prominent politicians and Constabulary officers, and owning a marijuana plantation and other properties in Cavite. Manecio's legendary charisma and Robin Hood reputation no longer appear as prominent elements of his power.[37]

As in 1958, a series of political developments led to Manecio's undoing in 1971. In February 1971, Manecio allegedly murdered two agents of the National Bureau of Investigation who were investigating reports of a marijuana plantation under his protection in Barrio Navarro, Gen. Trias.[38] A well-publicized NBI manhunt for Manecio ensued.[39] Meanwhile, shifting alignments in Cavite in anticipation of the November 1971 elections began to complicate Manecio's situation. Plotting to undermine the Montanos' grip on Cavite, Marcos had recruited notorious smuggler and former Montano crony Lino Bocalan to run as the Nacionalistas' candidate for the Cavite governorship, with Camerino as his running mate. Enormously wealthy and well connected from his illicit activities, Bocalan brought along with him key former Montano supporters—such as the Carungcongs of Dasmariñas—into the Nacionalista camp. While the scenario of an alliance between Bocalan, Camerino, and the Carungcongs against the Montanos promised an end to Manecio's divided loyalties, this scenario dashed the hopes of up-and-coming Imus-based politician Juanito "Johnny" Remulla, who, though also a Nacionalista, aspired to the Cavite governorship himself. Vying for a provincial board seat in the November 1971 elections, Remulla found himself at odds with Bocalan, the Carungcongs, and, by extension, Manecio, whose activities and influence in Imus intruded upon Remulla's home turf. With the assistance of his personal bodyguard, Demetrio "Metring" Villanueva, Remulla is said to have covertly assisted an NBI team in tracking Manecio down. In October 1971, less than a month before the local elections, an encounter allegedly took place between Manecio and members of an NBI team on the national road in Kawit, in which the famed outlaw was shot to death.[40] Knowledgeable sources, however, dispute the NBI's account of Manecio's death, claiming instead that the gangster was poisoned and knocked unconscious beforehand in a nearby resort and then propped up against the steering wheel of the car in which his bloodied corpse was subsequently found.[41]

Thus the famed Caviteño outlaw's career came to a close, as colorfully—and as violently—as it had begun. Revealingly, Manecio's death came not as a result of declining support but through a complex series of developments in factional politics at the local, provincial, and national levels. Tellingly, also, his career ended in the

---

[37] Moises "Esing Cavite" Timbang Saunar, interview with the author, November 7, 1992, New Bilibid Prison, Muntinlupa; Ligorio "Toting" Naval, interview with the author, November 19, 1992, Alima, Bacoor, Cavite.

[38] By some accounts, the NBI investigation and visit to Cavite occasioned extortionate demands for "protection" that Manecio violently rebuffed.

[39] National Bureau of Investigation Director Epimaco A. Velasco, interview with the author, October 28, 1992, NBI Headquarters, Taft Avenue, Manila.

[40] Special Agent Epimaco A. Velasco, "Leonardo Manecio y Malihan @ "NARDONG PUTIK"," Report of October 10, 1971 Re: Killing of two (2) NBI Agents (Manila: National Bureau of Investigation, 1971).

[41] These sources include former close associates of Manecio, a long-time Cavite-based newspaper reporter, and a former police chief of a Cavite municipality.

heat of an election campaign, at the hands of law-enforcement officials, and in a dispute over the "protection" and control of "turf" in the lowland towns of Cavite. Overall, thirteen Caviteños lost their lives in the course of the 1971 local election campaign, and three Cavite mayors fell to assassins' bullets the following year. In this context, Manecio's death appeared not as the tragic end of a popular Robin Hood, but as merely another casualty of intensified factionalism in a province of political gangsters and gangster politicians.

II. CAVITE'S GODFATHER?: JOSE "DON PEPE" OYSON

Followed shortly thereafter by President Marcos' declaration of martial law in September 1972, Manecio's death marked the end of an era for criminality in Cavite. By the 1970s, cattle rustling had fallen by the wayside, as tractors replaced carabaos and industrial estates and residential subdivisions supplanted rice fields as the mainstays of Cavite's suburban northern towns. Moreover, with the construction of the Coastal Road, Gen. Aguinaldo Highway, and South Expressway, passenger traffic became less vulnerable to highwaymen on remote Cavite roads. In addition, after the closing of the US naval station at Sangley Point, Cavite City no longer played host to a lively illegal economy centered around gun-running, luxury contraband smuggling, and prostitution. Meanwhile, the creation of an Integrated National Police subordinated to the Philippine Constabulary in 1975 and the subsequent creation of regional PC/AFP commands removed law enforcement from the hands of local elected officials and effectively centralized policing powers in the hands of top Manila-based PC and AFP officers. In subsequent years, such rackets as carnapping on the outskirts of Metro Manila and smuggling in Manila Bay fell largely under the discretion of PC colonels and generals rather than Cavite mayors and governors.

Even as these developments drew control over criminal rackets away from the hands of Cavite-based *mafia* bosses, the economic transformation of Metro Manila and neighboring provinces offered new opportunities for criminal activities in Cavite. With the closer integration of the Philippines into a regional economy in the 1970s and 1980s, the province fell into the orbit of big-time criminal elements operating in Manila and linked to international syndicates in Hong Kong and Japan. Thus, even as protection for criminal activities in Cavite was effectively "nationalized" with the centralization of law-enforcement, a rapid internationalization occurred in the production and distribution of illegal goods in the province. This trend has perhaps been most evident in the "illegal recruiting" of overseas contract workers, cases of which today fill court dockets in Cavite much as cattle rustling did thirty years ago. Yet while scores of fly-by-night illegal recruitment agencies have preyed upon unsuspecting Cavite residents in recent years, none has established a monopolistic position in the industry. In the international drug trade, by contrast, one well known *mafia* boss—José "Don Pepe" Oyson—imposed his rule over Cavite.

Like "Nardong Putik" before him, Oyson was the subject of a posthumous film biography, "Don Pepe Oyson: The Rise and Fall of a Drug Lord," which was filmed and released in 1990, less than a year after his death at the hands of a Manila policeman detailed with the NBI. Unlike the Ramon Revilla classic of 1972, however, this action movie, starring the lesser known John Regala, was noteworthy neither as a commercial success nor as a memorable pathbreaker in the genre. In fact, the melodramatic "Don Pepe Oyson" presents the famed drug lord not as a popular Caviteño folk hero armed with supernatural powers, charisma, and Robin Hood appeal, but rather as an ordinary Manileño driven by desperation and opportunism to criminal entrepreneurship in the illegal narcotics trade.

As the film opens, Pepe Oyson appears as a lower-class Manileño struggling to stay alive, provide for his family, and maintain his male pride in the face of constant dangers, hardships, and humiliations. Poorly armed and poorly paid, Pepe works as a warehouse security guard, daily defending himself against thieves and against the complaints of his materialistic wife, who soon leaves him (and their daughter) for a richer man. A burly but cuddly bear of a man, Pepe is fearsome in combat but sweetly affectionate with his daughter and protective of his sister, whose lodging and schooling he supports with his meager salary. Concerned for his family, Pepe engages in violence only when provoked—by local drunkards in the squatter settlement where he lives, or by his sister's boyfriend, a policeman who mocks Pepe's low status and subjects his sister to pre-marital sexual intercourse and, after a shotgun wedding at Oyson's insistence, wife battering.

Desperate for money to pay for his ailing daughter's hospital bills, Oyson accepts a friend's invitation to work as a *bata-bata* of the drug lord Don Ochoa. First tasked as the driver for dangerous exchanges of drugs and cash, Oyson soon earns a promotion with an assignment to kill Ochoa's arch rival. Though successful in this task, Oyson loses his nerve when a journalist marked for assassination by Ochoa begs for mercy, appealing to him as a fellow family man and father. Reprimanded by Ochoa for this lapse, Oyson threatens the startled "drug lord" and stalks away, starting his own rival gang with former members of Ochoa's entourage. By killing off Ochoa's couriers and establishing his own network of dealers, Oyson earns the ire of his former boss. A victim of his own success, "Don Pepe" devolves into an obese, garishly dressed, decadent, and emotionally distant version of his former self. Gunfights claim the lives of Oyson's sister, daughter, and closest henchmen. In the last scene, he mounts a desperate solo attack on Ochoa's mansion, armed with a machine gun and wearing a white suit. Predictably, the film closes with Oyson's wife sobbing and wailing "Pepe, Pepe . . . " over his blood-spattered corpse.

Considerably less idealized than the film version of Leonardo Manecio alias Nardong Putik's life, "Don Pepe Oyson: The Rise and Fall of a Drug Lord" portrays the slain *mafia* boss as a tragic hero, whose fall from grace recalls Michael Corleone (Al Pacino) in the later Godfather movies. Originally an honest, hard-working family man, Pepe is driven by desperation and disillusionment into a life of violence and crime. Demonstrably impressive with a pistol or his bare hands, he gradually loses his martial prowess and increasingly relies on henchmen and high-powered firearms to defend himself and intimidate his enemies. Once modest in his income and personal style, he slips into a haughty and garish "godfather" role modelled after "Don" Ochoa. Lacking in charisma, amulets, and Robin Hood appeal, Oyson winds up not as a primitive rebel but as a crude and mean-spirited gangster-entrepreneur, a *mafia* Don.

In its exclusive focus on the tragic fate of José "Don Pepe" Oyson, the film relegates to virtual obscurity the social milieu of his criminal career. For example, the film neglects to provide key details about Oyson's illegal activities: the illegal drugs he is selling, his sources, customers, and market. Similarly, Oyson's geographical whereabouts are somewhat obscure: most of the film takes place somewhere in

Metro Manila, yet occasional shots depict an Oyson compound in a distinctly rural, bucolic setting. The law-enforcement agencies of the Philippine state, moreover, are completely peripheral, appearing in only a few scenes, and then as weak, ineffectual, and easily neutralized or corrupted. In one scene, a police colonel is shown to accept an envelope stuffed with pesos from Oyson; in another, junior police officers claim that the drug lord is "untouchable." "How can we catch him?," they grumble. "No one provides information, no one files complaints, no one talks." As in the legend of Nardong Putik, the law-enforcement agencies of the Philippine state appear chronically weak in the face of "rampant," unchecked criminality.

In contrast with Leonardo Manecio alias Nardong Putik, José "Don Pepe" Oyson, as the film version of his life suggests, was neither a native of Cavite nor a fugitive from the law. Born in 1934 in Binondo, Manila's Chinatown, Oyson was a tall, athletic youth whose physical prowess allowed him to rise above his family's modest means. Finishing high school in 1956, he won a college basketball scholarship offered by Roberto Oca, the waterfront labor leader and politician.[42] Working part-time for Oca to help pay for his tuition, Oyson also became a star basketball player on the team that won the intercollegiate championship in 1959. While Oyson evidently never graduated from college, basketball stardom allowed him to mix with the likes of Oca, well-connected sports journalists, and other prominent figures active in off-court betting (and game-rigging). Through these associates, Oyson evidently gained access to businessmen, politicians, and law-enforcement officials involved in smuggling activities in Manila Bay. By most accounts, Oyson spent the better part of the 1960s providing muscle for smuggling operations along the coastal shores of the city.

By the 1970s, moreover, Oyson's involvement in this illegal commerce had drawn him southwards to the shores of Cavite. He had taken as his common-law wife Erlinda Figueroa, whose family hailed from Tanza, a Cavite town best known as the base for the smuggling of foreign ("blue-seal") cigarettes. Newspaper reports list Oyson among members of Cavite-based smuggling syndicates arrested in 1976 and 1979 by Constabulary officers for the "ship-side" smuggling of contraband cigarettes. In these ventures Oyson appears to have joined remnants of a syndicate once run by Lino Bocalan, the avowed "fisherman" from Tanza who served briefly as Governor of Cavite (1971-72) before being suspended and imprisoned by Marcos following the declaration of martial law. By some accounts, Oyson also engaged in ship-side smuggling of textiles and electronic goods on behalf of other syndicates based in Metro Manila.[43]

In the early 1980s, moreover, a confluence of fortuitous circumstances provided Oyson with the ingredients of further commercial success. First of all, a Constabulary colonel related to Oyson's common-law wife evidently became a close aide of Defense Minister Juan Ponce Enrile. Meanwhile, one of Oyson's smuggling partners and financiers, the Binondo-based merchant Benito Tan alias Go Pok alias "Manok" (Chicken), had won the protection of AFP Chief of Staff Fabian Ver in his illegal

---

[42] For details of Oca's labor racketeering activities on the waterfront in Manila's South Harbor, see Johnny C. Tan, "The Waterfront Controversy and Our Civil Liberties," letter of January 11, 1963 to Joaquin M. Roces, General Manager, Manila Times Publishing Company, found in the "Oca, Roberto" file in the Lopez Museum library, BenPres Building, Pasig, Metro Manila.

[43] Commander Guillermo Paraida, interview with the author, January 1992, Economic Intelligence and Investigation Bureau (EIIB) Headquarters, Camp Aguinaldo, Quezon City. Paraida served as the Chief of the Bureau of Customs' Intelligence Division from 1981 to 1986.

currency transactions ("dollar salting") and other criminal activities.[44] Moreover, Oyson himself, as the owner of a prominent nightclub on Roxas Boulevard and the proprietor of one of the largest cockpits in the Las Piñas/Parañaque area of Metro Manila (just north of Cavite), had "entertained" and befriended numerous policemen from various municipalities in the national capital region, especially Las Piñas, Parañaque, and Pasay City. Finally, by the early 1980s, perhaps through the Hong Kong business partners of his Binondo-based financier, Oyson had brought in shipments of an illegal and highly addictive drug previously unavailable in the Philippines, "shabu" or methamphetamine hydrochloride, the East Asian version of what is known today in the United States as "crack." Within a few years, this drug had gained an expanding and enduring market in the densely populated national capital region.

Enjoying these multiple commercial advantages, Oyson had by the mid-1980s emerged as the godfather of a multi-million peso criminal empire that spanned Manila Bay from Cavite to Bataan. With municipal and provincial law-enforcement personnel and other officials on his payroll,[45] Oyson was free to smuggle in—and to distribute—"shabu"[46] and other contraband almost anywhere along Manila Bay.[47] In 1985, an exposé published by a Bataan-based newspaper described in great detail Oyson's smuggling and drug trafficking operations in Bataan, Cavite, and Metro Manila as well as the collusion of local civilian and police officials in these localities.[48] Soon thereafter, the author of this newspaper exposé disappeared after he was abducted by armed men. A subsequent investigation revealed that he had been stabbed to death, his remains burned. placed in a plastic bag, and dumped in the sea off the coast of Cavite.[49] This investigation led to the arrest and trial—for kidnapping and murder—of Oyson and three other men, including a hired killer (allegedly paid fifty thousand pesos for his part in the deed), Oyson's cock handler, and a Philippine Constabulary Narcotics Command (PC-NARCOM) agent so beholden to the "drug lord" that he had the name "Don Pepe Oyson" tattooed on his body.[50] Two PC sergeants, described as a close friend and a *compadre* (baptismal co-parent) of Oyson, faced related charges in military court.

[44] On the connections between Benito Tan and AFP Chief of Staff General Fabian Ver, see PC/AFP Colonel Gerardo N. Flores, "Affidavit" of August 27, 1987, Annex "B" of Civil Case No. 0063, Go Pok alias Benito Tan, Petitioner, versus The Presidential Commission on Good Government and The People of the Philippines, Respondents (Manila: Sandiganbayan, Second Division).

[45] Knowledgeable Caviteños claim that Oyson included the mayors and police chiefs of several coastal towns in Cavite on his payroll, and that he gained the cooperation of the security aide of the provincial governor in distributing *shabu* in the province.

[46] Oyson also reportedly set up "laboratories" in Cavite, Las Piñas, and Parañaque for the "recooking" of the drug.

[47] Ligorio "Toting" Naval, interview with the author, November 11, 1992, Alima, Bacoor, Cavite.

[48] Timoteo Olivares, "Untouchable Smugglers Exposed, Bataan politician linked as brains," *Luzon Tribune*, January 13-19, 1985.

[49] See the various documents included in Criminal Case No. 20507, People of the Philippines versus Jose Santos Oyson @ "Don Pepe," Raymundo Bagtas y Caparas @ "Reddie," Herminio Catan, and Napoleon Ibañez (Makati: Regional Trial Court, National Capital Judicial Region, Branch 144, 1985).

[50] "Opposition to the Motion to Bail Filed by Accused Oyson, Bagtas, Cruto, and San Miguel," filed by Vicente D. Millora, Private Prosecutor, January 4, 1986, pp. 2-3; and "Transcript" of

The trial revealed Oyson's extensive network of friends and accomplices among various law-enforcement agencies.[51] Moreover, during the course of the trial, Oyson was first allowed to reside in the Makati Medical Center and later released on bail, while his accomplices, supposedly held without bail in the Makati jail, spent evenings at Oyson's nightclub on Roxas Boulevard in the company of the Makati jail warden and slept in the air-conditioned office of the Makati police chief. Unsurprisingly, Oyson and the other suspects were acquitted on a technicality in 1988.

Despite the inconvenience and negative publicity caused by this case, Oyson retained firm control over his criminal empire. From a strategically located base in the southern Metro Manila municipalities of Las Piñas and Parañaque, his illegal activities evidently expanded into *jueteng* operations in Cavite and professional basketball game fixing. Moreover, Oyson evidently had a hand in facilitating the transshipment of heroin flown into Manila's international airport (conveniently located in Parañaque) and bound for the US market.[52] By 1989, Oyson's group ranked as one of the three major drug syndicates operating in the country.[53] Numerous high-ranking military and law-enforcement officials, and members of the police forces of several Metro Manila and Cavite municipalities, were still said to be on his payroll.[54]

In the Las Piñas Narcotics section, Major Gonzalo Gonzales and several of his subordinates are said to comprise the largest membership of policemen in the drug cartel belonging to Don Pepe. The top henchman of this cartel is a certain Atong, who operates in the Las Piñas, Parañaque, and Cavite areas. This Atong is said to be untouchable because of his connections with police authorities. The NBI estimated that 40 percent of policemen are connected with the drug cartel.[55]

In this period of political uncertainty and rapid change in the military and law-enforcement hierarchies, Oyson had to work hard to maintain his multiple forms of protection. The escalating tensions between Defense Minister Enrile and AFP Chief Ver, for example, may well have played a role in Oyson's arrest and indictment in 1985 for the Bataan-based newspaper reporter's kidnap-murder, as suggested by the persistent involvement of Justice Minister Estelito Mendoza, an Enrile ally, in the

---

Hearing, held December 22, 1986, before Hon. Candido P. Villanueva, Presiding Judge of this Court, p. 17, found among the documents relating to Criminal Case No. 20507.

[51] See "Sworn Statement of Mr. Jose Oyson y Santos Given to INV AGT [Investigating Agent] I Virgilio T. Publico in the Presence of ILT [Investigating Team Leader] Gil C. Meneses, Here at the Office of the Chief, Special Investigation Branch National Capital District, Criminal Investigation Service, Philippine Constabulary Headquarters, Camp Crame, Quezon City, This 13th Day of May 1985."

[52] US Drug Enforcement Administration (DEA) officials claim that Manila became a major transshipment point in the international heroin trade in the early 1980s. William C. Bish, Narcotics Attaché, US Embassy, interview with the author, January 21, 1994, US DEA office, Ramon V. Magsaysay Building, Roxas Boulevard, Malate, Manila.

[53] Senator Ernesto F. Herrera, "A Just War Against Drugs," Privilege Speech delivered on September 21, 1989, in *Speeches of the Senators: A Collection of Speeches by the Senators of the Philippines* (Manila: Senate, 1990), p. 168.

[54] Former EIIB and Customs intelligence officials told the author in January 1992 that the United States Drug Enforcement Administration has in its possession a videotape of high-ranking law-enforcement officials dancing with Oyson at his nightclub on Roxas Boulevard.

[55] Senator Ernesto F. Herrera, "A Just War Against Drugs," Privilege Speech delivered on October 12, 1989, in *Speeches of the Senators*, p. 175.

case. After the ouster of Marcos in 1986, moreover, Oyson had to hedge his bets more than ever. Foreseeing the restored Congress's discretion over law enforcement, he bankrolled the successful 1987 campaign of one candidate for the Parañaque seat in the House and maintained personal ties with a key member of the Senate. In addition, against the backdrop of numerous military coup attempts, he provided financial support to the Reform the Armed Forces Movement and allegedly assisted in the escape of renegade Lt. Col. Gregorio Honasan from a Navy prison ship in Manila Bay in April 1988. Meanwhile, through his nightclub, cockpit, supply of "shabu," and enormous wealth, Oyson remained the patron of ranking Constabulary officers and local policemen from Bataan, Cavite, and the southern municipalities of Metro Manila.

Ultimately, however, Oyson ran up against the Philippines' most ambitious law enforcer, Police General Alfredo Lim, whose appointment as Director of the National Bureau of Investigation in December 1989 led to Oyson's demise in early 1990. A much decorated officer in the Manila Police Department in the years before martial law, Lim was first relegated to a desk job and eventually banished to the Northern Police District in the 1970s and 1980s due to his alleged political loyalties to opponents of President Marcos.[56] Appointed as Superintendent of the Western Police District (WPD) following Marcos's ouster in 1986, Brigadier General Lim assumed control over law enforcement in such key areas as Binondo, Manila's Chinatown, and the port area. Having proved his allegiance through his heroic defense of the Aquino regime during several coup attempts, and cemented it by establishing warm relations with José "Peping" Cojuangco, the President's brother, Lim was personally promoted by Aquino in 1989 to the rank of Major General and the WPD was removed from the supervision of the Metropolitan Police Force and the Capital Command (CAPCOM). Aquino's move, which left Lim only nominally responsible to the PC/INP Chief, generated considerable resentment among the officers of the Constabulary, who had enjoyed more than a decade of PC/AFP domination over career policemen.

Lim's appointment, moreover, came in the midst of a brewing controversy over the prominent role of law-enforcement officers in the illegal narcotics trade. Senate hearings in the autumn of 1989 had led to published reports about three international drug syndicates operating in the Philippines—Oyson's group and two Binondo-based Chinese gangs—and to public allegations against ranking Constabulary officers reportedly involved in the drug trade, including the commanding officer of the PC Narcotics Command. Over the next few months, a number of the seventy drug traffickers who had been identified in the Senate hearings died in "shoot-outs" with law-enforcement agents. The most prominent victims were members of the Binondo-based Chinese gangs and their killers were mostly NARCOM personnel. The godfather of the Hong Kong-based "14-K Gang," moreover, was variously described as having died in a similar episode or as having left the country, escorted to the airport by an unidentified police general.

Enjoying the President's favor and importing numerous WPD protégés, Lim assumed the directorship of the National Bureau of Investigation in January 1990 and immediately launched a campaign to expand the NBI's role in the enforcement of

---

[56] See, for example, Miguel Deala Paruñgao, *The Manila Police Story* (Manila: Regal Printing Company, 1976), pp. 96-100, 171; and Miguel Deala Paruñgao, *The Lawmen And The Lawless* (Manila: Regal Printing Company, 1977), pp. 134-149.

"the law" in the illegal drug trade. In March 1990, WPD patrolmen detailed with the NBI accosted Oyson at a billiards tournament in Cubao, Quezon City, and "invited" him to the NBI headquarters in Manila for questioning. Alone with three NBI/WPD patrolmen in a police van while his bodyguards rode in a separate car, Oyson was shot dead, supposedly after attempting to grab the gun of one of the policemen. In subsequent months, other members of Oyson's syndicate likewise fell victim to an intensified law-enforcement campaign.

Since Oyson's demise in 1990, the drug trade has remained a highly profitable, and hotly contested, industry in Metro Manila and neighboring provinces such as Cavite. Rivalry between Lim's NBI and the PC's NARCOM over heroin transshipment, for example, led to a series of armed confrontations between agents of the two law-enforcement bodies in the summer of 1990. With the abolition of the Philippine Constabulary and the subordination of the newly created Philippine National Police to elected officials in 1990, moreover, the illegal drug trade has become more decentralized. In Las Piñas, Parañaque, Pasay City, and Cavite, elected municipal officials—and law-enforcement agents subordinate to them—have assumed control over the distribution of "shabu." With local police forces responsible to local elected officials rather than a centralized military hierarchy, the powers of law-enforcement authorities at the national level are quite limited and the possibilities for centrally protected criminal monopolies severely circumscribed. As in the 1980s, the coastal Cavite towns today remain among the primary points of entry for the ship-side smuggling of shabu, yet the re-localization of law enforcement appears to have prevented a new "drug lord" from claiming Manila Bay for himself in the style of "Don Pepe."

III. CRIME IN CAVITE: GEOGRAPHY, ORGANIZATION, REPRESENTATION

As the case studies of Leonardo Manecio alias "Nardong Putik" and José "Don Pepe" Oyson have made clear, Cavite's most successful outlaws have been essentially predatory and conservative, their coercive resources deployed in pursuit of economic accumulation and in support of political domination. Whether in the service of gangster politicians or in league with kleptocratic Constabulary officers, these criminals have exacted "monopoly rents" and "predatory incomes," first by reproducing and enforcing conditions of economic insecurity and limited access to scarce resources upon a captive population of rural and urban poor, and then by selling "protection" and illegal goods and services to this same captive population.

Moreover, as the two case studies have suggested, the rise and fall of Cavite's most successful outlaws, and the longevity and scale of their criminal empires, have depended heavily upon privileged access to politicians and agents of the state's law-enforcement apparatuses. Emerging where illegal economies of scale spanned multiple and/or overlapping police jurisdictions, these outlaws' empires and monopolies on violence achieved a measure of autonomy irreducible to the protection of a single politician or law-enforcement agency. Ultimately, however, Cavite's criminals rose and fell, flourished and faded, lived and died, at the sufferance of those controlling the coercive levers of the Philippine state, its court rooms and prisons, its enforcers and executioners. Imposing not "lawlessness" but rather "the law" upon society, criminals in this notoriously bandit-ridden province have served essentially as sub-contracted law-enforcement agents, their successes bearing witness not to the state's supposed "weakness" but in fact to its "strength."

Viewed comparatively, the case studies of Leonardo Manecio alias Nardong Putik and José "Don Pepe" Oyson underscore the shifting geography, organization, and social representation of *mafia* activity in Cavite. In terms of geography, Manecio's construction of a cattle rustling empire in the 1950s in the northern towns of Cavite reflected a distinctive social terrain, characterized not by large landed estates but rather by share-cropping, scattered landholdings, wet-rice cultivation based on animal traction, economic insecurity among an impoverished class of share tenants, and proximity to metropolitan markets for stolen cattle.[57] Located "between wholesale markets of the city and the rural latifundia," Cavite's rice-bowl towns provided a "fertile field" for criminal predation and "protection" from both rampant cattle thievery and potential class conflict. [58]

By the 1980s, socioeconomic change in Cavite had drastically altered the setting for criminal activity in the province. The mechanization of agriculture, the construction of paved highways, and the replacement of rice paddies with residential subdivisions and industrial estates reduced the attractions of cattle rustling and carnapping in Cavite. Meanwhile, the continuing availability of coastal towns as strategically located entry points for smuggled goods combined with urbanization, rising population density, and closer integration with Metro Manila (thanks to the Coastal Road, the Gen. Aguinaldo Highway, and the South Expressway) to make the province a key site for the import, marketing, and consumption of illegal narcotics, most notably "shabu."

In terms of organization, moreover, the cases of Manecio and Oyson further highlight the changing nature of criminal activity in Cavite. In the pre-martial law period, Cavite's most enduring and successful outlaw operated as the political *lider* and hired assassin of local politicians and as the protector and enforcer of large landowners in the province. Enmeshed in small-town networks of family and faction, he relied for his survival and success upon the maintenance of close personal relationships with both the members of his *tropa* and the other local power brokers in his bailiwick. In this context, the personal projection of physical prowess was essential for creating and sustaining a local monopoly on violence and "protection." In the 1970s and 1980s, by contrast, the most successful criminal figure in Cavite served as the sub-contracted agent of Binondo-based financiers, the partner of Hong Kong-based syndicates, and the accomplice and patron of high-ranking Manila-based PC/AFP officers. Embedded in a cash economy, he operated essentially as a businessman, making multi-million-peso deals and maintaining a large retinue of full-time employees, a chain of legal business establishments, and an elaborate

---

[57] Similar conditions prevailed in those regions of Italy where mafia achieved the greatest prominence and power. On this point, see Pino Arlacchi, *Mafia, Peasants, and Great Estates: Society in Traditional Calabria* (Cambridge: Cambridge University Press, 1983). See also Diego Gambetta, *The Sicilian Mafia: The Business of Private Protection* (Cambridge, MA: Harvard University Press, 1993), pp. 83-89.

[58] Diego Gambetta describes western Sicily as a similar area "in which the structure of property was such that it allowed greater autonomy to the protector: whereas on large estates several men looked after one property, here, where properties were smaller, one man looked after several fields for different customers. The price of the protection was therefore higher, since the independence of the protector was greater relative to the protectee." Gambetta, *The Sicilian Mafia*, pp. 87-88.

network for the marketing and distribution of "shabu." In this context, the cooperation of PC officers, NARCOM agents, and Cavite policemen, as well as the availability of hired killers, provided the coercive resources necessary for the imposition and maintenance of an effective criminal monopoly spanning numerous municipalities and law-enforcement jurisdictions. In short, growing economies of scale, internationalization of illegal commerce, centralization of law-enforcement, and the suburbanization of Cavite transformed the organizational basis of criminal activity in the predictable direction of monetization and rationalization, trends only partially reversed by the resubordination of the police to local elected officials after 1990.

Finally, the cases of Manecio and Oyson highlight the changing social representation of local *mafia* domination in Cavite, as amply illustrated by the contrasting film biographies and popular personae of the two *mafia* bosses. In the case of Leonardo Manecio alias Nardong Putik, the Cavite bandit's good looks, possession of *anting-anting*, and supposed Robin Hood-like popularity served to identify him as a latter-day "man of prowess," buttressing the coercive power which underlay his monopoly on "protection" in the northern towns of the province. As one scholar of *mafia* has noted:

> a reputation for credible protection and protection itself tend to be one and the same thing. The more robust the reputation . . . , the less the need to have recourse to the resources which support that reputation.[59]

In the case of José "Don Pepe" Oyson, by contrast, the Manila-based smuggler and drug trafficker reached the height of his career when he was in his forties and fifties, sporting spectacles and a beer belly. As his nickname, "Don Pepe," suggests, Oyson adopted the public personality of the godfather or *padron*, entertaining Constabulary officers, policemen, journalists, and politicians in his nightclub and cockpit, plying them with wine, women, song, gambling tips, money, and "shabu." Despite his declining physical prowess, Oyson in this sense remained to the end a "big man," amassing and dispensing his "fund of power" to "a coterie of loyal, lesser men" in sports arenas, pool halls, nightclubs, and cockpits.[60] Perhaps the role of tattoos in the two case studies best captures the changing personae of Cavite's criminals: Nardong Putik proudly sported tattoos as emblems of his prowess; Oyson's underling, by contrast, tattooed the drug lord's name on his body to signify his personal allegiance and subordination to the "big man" himself.[61]

In their contrasting portraits of Cavite's most successful mafia bosses, the film biographies of Leonardo Manecio and José Oyson highlight the changing portrait of "the outlaw" in the Philippine popular imagination. In the first instance, the Nardong Putik of the 1972 film represents the quintessential "noble robber," whose

---

[59] See Diego Gambetta, *The Sicilian Mafia: The Business of Private Protection* (Cambridge: Harvard University Press, 1993), p. 44.

[60] Marshall D. Sahlins, "Poor Man, Rich Man, Big-Man, Chief: Political Types in Melanesia and Polynesia," *Comparative Studies in Society and History* 5,3 (April 1963): 289, 292.

[61] On the role of tattoos in signifying relations of dependence in pre-colonial Southeast Asia, see Michael Aung-Thwin, "*Athi, Kyun-Taw, Hpayà-Kyun*: Varieties of Commendation and Dependence in Pre-Colonial Burma," pp. 78, 84, and B. J. Terwiel, "Bondage and Slavery in Early Nineteenth-Century Siam," pp. 124, 135, both in *Slavery, Bondage and Dependency in Southeast Asia*, ed. Anthony Reid (St. Lucia: University of Queensland Press, 1983).

picaresque exploits, charismatic features, and Robin Hood-like services in a bucolic setting counterpose themselves against the capitalist transformation of rural society and the predatory apparatuses of the state, thus offering some hope for resistance against social injustice and political oppression. In the second instance, the Don Pepe of the 1990 film appears as a tragic figure, whose response to the hardships and humiliations of urban poverty lies in criminal and violent entrepreneurship which serves only as a form of social mobility and self-enrichment.

In emphasizing the colorful personalities of Cavite's most successful outlaws, these films obscure the economic and political bases of their success, their role in capitalist exploitation, and their links to and dependence on the law-enforcement agencies of the state. Viewed sequentially, the films present a shift from the romanticization of the *picaro* (adventerous rogue), waging a desperate, rear-guard battle against the capitalist transformation of rural society, to the melodrama of the *mafioso*, escaping urban poverty through entrepreneurship in violence and crime. As products of the Philippine movie industry taken from two different historical junctures, these films may reflect changes both in popular culture and in underlying societal conditions, as suggested above. With Nardong Putik's passing, it appears, Cavite has witnessed the disappearance of the "noble robber," the victim of injustice who, like Robin Hood, rights social wrongs, enjoys the admiration and support of the poor, is essentially "invisible and invulnerable," kills only in self-defense or just revenge, and "dies invariably and only through treason, since no decent member of the community would help the authorities against him."[62] In his stead, less honorable avengers have taken center stage:

> They are heroes not in spite of the fear and horror their actions inspire, but in some ways because of them. They are not so much men who right wrongs, but avengers, and exerters of power; their appeal is not that of the agents of justice, but of men who prove that even the poor and weak can be terrible.[63]

IV. AUTHOR'S CONFESSION: THE ROBIN HOOD PUZZLE

So far, so clear: revelations of the gap between "myth" and "reality," and a detailed examination of changes in the organization, geography, and social representation of criminality in Cavite. Yet in the case of Cavite's Nardong Putik, the author must confess to continuing puzzlement. Unfinished sentences on the doorsteps of widow's homes in Dasmariñas, furtive glances in the *carinderias* (road-side food stalls) of Gen. Trias, and drunken, Masonic threats from a shotgun-toting amputee in a shack on the edge of Muntinlupa's prison grounds: such were the traces of Nardong Putik which could be found among the industrial estates, residential subdivisions, and golf courses that have come to replace the rice fields of his former bailiwick. No one who knew the man appeared too eager to reminisce about his exploits, to share a laugh about his foibles, or to shed a tear for his passing. Even Nardo's former fellow carnapper and inmate in Muntinlupa seemed infinitely more interested in recounting the history of Masonic amulets in the Philippines than in revelling in the old gang's misdeeds in the badlands of pre-martial law Cavite.

[62] Hobsbawm, *Bandits*, pp. 42-43.
[63] Hobsbawm, *Bandits*, p. 58.

Meanwhile, the most forceful proponents of the Nardong Putik myth were found among those who could easily be described as his worst enemies. For example, the flattering comments quoted above were spoken in April 1971 by none other than Juanito "Johnny" Remulla, the Cavite politician who, several months later, plotted Nardo's murder. Remulla's description of Nardong Putik is perhaps worth quoting again in full:

> When there are thefts or highway robberies or hold-ups, the victims do not seek help from the government, since they do not expect any results from that corner. The word on the street is that they take their complaints instead to Nardong Putik and immediately get the justice they are asking for.[64]

A similar paradox is apparent in the essentially sympathetic film biography which action movie star Ramon Revilla, Sr. produced, directed, and starred in. The film is scrupulously faithful to the "real-life story" of Leonardo Manecio alias Nardong Putik, as Revilla proudly recounted to the author over lunch in Manila in 1995. Even the ending is essentially "true-to-life," as Revilla explained, thanks to consultations with his long-time cockfighting chum (and, until recently, political ally) Johnny Remulla. Indeed, the last segment of the film does introduce Remulla (played by the famous actor Rudy Fernandez) and depicts him as masterminding Nardo's murder. In memory and in myth, it seems, Nardong Putik's enemies honored him well.

What, then, is the logic of the legend of Nardong Putik in Cavite? Neither the yearnings of subalterns nor the efforts of state propagandists can be seen as the driving force of this legend, which seems to have circulated via word of mouth, newspaper articles, radio commentary, *komiks*, and film. At least as much as anyone else, Nardong Putik's own mortal enemies appear to have promoted the outlaw's reputation as a Robin Hood-like figure, as a charismatic man who enjoyed considerable respect and popularity in a society characterized by great injustice and inequality. But why would Johnny Remulla—who, as Provincial Governor of Cavite (1979-86, 1988-95), earned great notoriety for union-busting, violent land eviction schemes, and accumulation of vast wealth and landholdings—speak of Nardong Putik in the language of Eric Hobsbawm? Why would Remulla give his blessings to his pal's film hagiography of the very man he arranged to be murdered?

In the legend of Nardong Putik, the Cavite outlaw's luster and legitimacy depend, to a great extent, upon the projection of his intrinsic personal power, as expressed through references to his martial prowess and possession of magically potent *anting-anting*. Nardong Putik, like other successful outlaws, constructs his reputation through acts of violence that establish his personal visibility, his singularity, and his bravery and willingness to risk his life in combat. Paradoxically, in Nardong Putik's case, the outlaw's singularity involves magical powers of polymorphism—the ability to change his form. In addition, the charismatic outlaw's appeal and authority rest on his courageous and violent opposition to the predatory forces of the state. Commenting on Ramon Revilla's "Nardong Putik" and other films in the same genre, one scholar has noted:

> Revilla's themes do not vary: a man with his back against the wall has no choice but to fight those he perceives to be the perpetrators of injustice. This

---

[64] Ordoñez, "Ang Kabite at Ang Mga Montano," p. 47. Translation by the author.

is the reason why all the heroes in Revilla's films turn their back on society to lead the life of a fugitive, killing policemen and other government agents with impunity.[65]

Thus, against the backdrop of Nardong Putik's long "outlaw" career, the mythology surrounding his life can be seen as working not only to romanticize his activities, but also to obscure the essential origins of his power. Depictions of this bandit as a provider of protection and material rewards to grateful peasants masks his role as a predatory extortionist who imposed his will by violence. Cast as a subaltern champion of primitive rebellion and everyday forms of resistance, Nardong Putik is seemingly uninvolved in "primitive" capitalist accumulation and everyday forms of oppression and domination. In short, Nardong Putik appears not as a local *mafia* boss, but as a charismatic and popular Robin Hood-like figure.

In this context, the impulse of men like Remulla and Revilla to protect and promote the reputation of Cavite's most famous gangster makes most sense, perhaps, if we consider how much *of themselves* these gangster-politicians recognized in Nardong Putik. Even as Provincial Governor of Cavite, Johnny Remulla was—like his predecessors—known to surround himself with a coterie of bodyguards and hangers-on notorious for their involvement in illegal activities. Among the town mayors most loyal to Johnny were a handful whose sponsorship of local criminal rackets—smuggling, carnapping, contract killing, and illegal gambling—was well established in Cavite, while five mayors who unwisely opposed or betrayed Johnny wound up losing their lives to assassins' bullets. Winning elections through vote-buying, fraud, and intimidation, Remulla also won loans and public works contracts for his companies, vast landholdings for his family, and countless millions through kickbacks, bribes, and percentages, all through his hold over state office in Cavite. Much like Nardong Putik, Johnny Remulla was a first-class gangster, but one who, thanks to local family wealth and connections, a University of the Philippines law degree, and Upsilon fraternity connections, could move further up the gangster food chain, feasting more liberally on the biggest racket of all: the state.[66]

Like Nardong Putik and other gangsters, Johnny Remulla, Ramon Revilla, and other gangster-politicians of their ilk share a common self-image and a common style and logic of self-legitimation. Success in attracting women and prodigious numbers of offspring, for example, are valorized as a sign of a local politician's intrinsic powers. A reputation as an enthusiastic and successful *sabungero* (cockfighting aficionado) and sponsor of cockfighting tournaments (often followed by lavish feasts) is also important, as seen in the case of Ramon Revilla, Sr., owner of the biggest *sabungan* (cockpit) in Cavite. The victories of the local *politico*'s fighting cock vividly reflect his personal prowess and potency, while the selective sharing of some of the bounty—a practice known as *balato*—binds supporters closely to him.[67]

---

[65] Soledad Reyes, "The Outlaw and the Prostitute: Images of Otherness in Popular Culture," in *The Romance Mode in Philippine Popular Literature and Other Essays* (Manila: De La Salle University Press, 1991), p. 293.

[66] See Sheila S. Coronel, "Cavite: The Killing Fields of Commerce," in *Boss: 5 Case Studies of Local Politics in the Philippines*, ed. José F. Lacaba (Pasig City: Philippine Center for Investigative Journalism, 1995), pp. 1-29.

[67] Filomeno V. Aguilar, Jr., "Of Cocks and Bets: Gambling, Class Structuring, and State Formation in the Philippines," in *Patterns of Power and Politics in the Philippines: Implications for*

Moreover, much as the outlaw relies on Church paraphernalia for *anting-anting*, the local politician affirms his privileged access to the spiritual world through identification with the institutions of organized religion, sponsoring baptisms, weddings, funerals, and Holy Week processions, liminal moments in which common feasting reaffirms both small-town "communitas" and the potency of the sponsor. Finally, as with the provision of spiritual resources, the local politician poses as the source of material welfare as well. Public resources, funds, and prerogatives are passed off as flowing from the local politician's personal powers and magnanimity. Thus various public works projects are portrayed as evidence of generosity towards constituents: bridges, public markets, *barangay* (smallest administrative unit of a village) basketball courts, funds for fishermen's cooperatives, repairs of public school buildings, all flow forth as the gifts of the *politico*. Cavite's recently completed highway, "Governor's Drive," is only one of many examples.[68]

As with the legend of Nardong Putik and other supposedly Robin Hood-like Philippine gangsters, the myths propagated by and about local politicians in provinces like Cavite work to claim that power is not simply reducible to money and state office. The *anting-anting* of Nardong Putik, the weddings and town *fiestas* sponsored by Governor Remulla, the movie-star looks and cockfighting victories of Senator Revilla—all locate the source of power in the intrinsic personal qualities of these aspiring powerbrokers. These various mechanisms thus represent claims that power—unlike money and electoral office—does not circulate and that the "big man" is essentially irreplaceable and indispensable.

Moreover, legitimation along these lines also obscures the derivative nature of power, its origin in the predatory state, and its role in the process of capital accumulation. Through Nardong Putik's Robin Hood escapades, Governor Remulla's funeral donations, and Senator Revilla's public works projects, power is equated with personal benevolence even as its source in the state apparatus and the cash economy remains conveniently hidden. Big man/little people, public/private, monopoly/common property: such distinctions thus fade from view. Extracting monopoly rents from various state-based rackets, exploiting low-wage labor, and expropriating the country's scarce natural resources, these predators pose as the providers of land, employment, and sustenance. As in the myth of Robin Hood, there is always a malevolent Sheriff of Nottingham lurking in the background as a less promising alternative to the local predator. But, as in the case of Robin Hood, the victory of the Cavite gangster is ultimately a victory for the status quo:

> The Iustice and the scherreve bothe honged drye,
> To weyven with the ropes and with the winde drye.

Development, ed. James F. Eder and Robert L. Youngblood (Tempe: Arizona State University Program for Southeast Asian Studies, 1994), pp. 147-196.

[68] These paragraphs borrow heavily from John T. Sidel, "The Philippines: The Languages of Legitimation," in *Political Legitimacy in Southeast Asia: The Quest for Moral Authority*, ed. Muthiah Alagappa (Stanford: Stanford University Press, 1995), pp. 136-169, especially pp. 156-161.

Then "finally," as one scholar of Robin Hood has noted, "he makes his peace with the King and is appointed Chief Justice of the Forest."[69] Such is the logic of the Robin Hood legend, not only in bygone times in Nottinghamshire, but in recent Cavite history as well.

---

[69] J. C. Holt, "The Origins and Audience of the Ballads of Robin Hood," *Past & Present*, 18 (November 1960): 99.

SURVEILLANCE AND TERRITORIALITY IN BANDUNG

Joshua Barker

BACKGROUND

Bandung is a densely populated city, with a population of over two million squeezed into an area of just 16,662 hectares. In fact, it is said to be home to the most densely populated neighborhood in the world.[1] Despite this crowding, Bandung is considered to be a relatively safe city, and in 1990 was even listed in a *Time* magazine survey as "the safest city in the world." While the statistics upon which this survey was based are highly questionable, the characterization of Bandung as safe is probably not unjustified. Certainly Bandungers, although frequently worried about crime, feel themselves to be living in a far safer environment than Jakarta, Surabaya, or New York City. Nonetheless, it is difficult to find someone who has not been the victim of a crime in the past few years, and when asked, everyone has a crime story to tell.

In this paper, I examine one of the institutions that makes Bandung a safe city, the so-called *siskamling* or *sistem keamanan lingkungan* (literally: surroundings security system).[2] This term was coined by the head of the Indonesian police in the early 1980s to describe what is, in fact, an extremely old social institution: the policing of buildings and neighborhoods by the community, or by someone directly responsible to the community, rather than by the state. In Bandung, as in most of Java, *siskamling* currently takes three different forms: the SATPAM (*Satuan Pengamanan*, or Security Guard), the so-called HANSIP, and the much older *ronda* (night guard).[3] In general,

---

[1] The population density for the whole city is 10,775 square kilometers.

[2] Among the police it is also frequently called the *sistem swakarsa*.

[3] While technically called KAMRA (*Keamanan Rakyat*, or Peoples' Defense), these guards are generally referred to as "hansip." HANSIP (*pertahanan sipil*) is the name of a civil defense force that was very active in supporting the government during the 1950s and 1960s when Islamic rebels with millenial tendencies controlled most rural areas in West Java. Whereas HANSIP guards are civilians organized to deal with emergency situations (war, natural disasters), KAMRA guards are civilians working in a more routine fashion to help police enforce the laws.

SATPAM guards are responsible for protecting commercial and public buildings and spaces, while HANSIP and *ronda* guards patrol residential neighborhoods. In cities like Bandung, where social reproduction is almost entirely mediated by the cash economy, the *ronda* has become less common than the HANSIP and the SATPAM, as the SATPAM and HANSIP guards are low-paid workers, while the *ronda* is made up of volunteers providing a non-paid, obligatory community service. Insofar as the *ronda* persists, it is to be found in neighborhoods where household heads find it easier to perform the service occasionally rather than pay a monthly fee of three or four dollars toward employing someone.

While this paper is ostensibly about *siskamling*, it is only in the last section that *siskamling* itself receives explicit consideration. The bulk of the paper is rather spent developing a distinction between two concepts of security that will allow us to assess the import of the apparently minor event of *siskamling*'s introduction. These concepts are elaborated through an historical and ethnographic examination of forms of security prevalent in neighborhoods and commercial spaces "before" they were enframed by *siskamling*. It is argued that although much of what defines security in Bandung can be attributed to a concept of security rooted in practices of *surveillance*, there is another set of practices that obey a quite different logic of *territoriality*. While the former are apparent in state operations that penetrate neighborhoods, the latter can be seen in institutions like the *ronda* and in the actions of the local tough or *preman*.[4]

NEIGHBORHOOD SECURITY AND THE RONDA

The *ronda* is a night watch, or guard, that patrols the environs of a village or neighborhood. The term *ronda* in Indonesian is a loan word from Portuguese, a fact that indicates just how old the practice is.[5] The *ronda* is typically performed by male heads of households (or their sons) from each neighborhood. These individuals take turns participating in the watch, which means that each person has to perform the service anywhere from once a week to once a month. The number of guards on duty on any one night may range from just a few to over a dozen.

On Java, the *ronda* is typically organized at the level of the smallest administrative unit. In urban centers now it is inevitably organized by a member of

---

[4] I ought to mention that the advent of *siskamling* in the early 1980s is not the only event I have in mind when I develop the distinction between territoriality and surveillance. Two other events that occurred contemporaneously with *siskamling*'s introduction also figure prominently in my thoughts; these are the introduction of a new code of criminal procedure that significantly reduced the legal powers of the police, and the state-sanctioned "mysterious killings" (PETRUS) of thousands of ex-convicts or *preman*. Taken together, these three events had the potential completely to remake the culture of crime and security in Indonesia, from one of territoriality into one of surveillance.

[5] It is possible that the *ronda* is a precolonial institution. Its central instrument, the *kentongan*, is certainly precolonial in origin. This having been said, the basic idea of the *ronda* is not peculiar to Indonesia. In Peru, for example, the so-called *ronda campesinos* of the 1980s had an important role to play in resisting the efforts of both the Sendero Luminoso and the Peruvian military to force villagers to take sides in the civil war. These guard units, originally formed by members of local communities for defence against thieves and rustlers, evolved into an armed civil defense force that rejected encroachments by both the military and Sendero Luminoso.

the *Rukun Tetangga* (RT) or the *Rukun Warga* (RW)[6]; usually this person is either the head of the RT (*kepala* RT), the head of the RW (*kepala* RW), or a person designated by such an authority to be in charge of neighborhood security.[7] The heads of the RT and RW are often locally respected people, either by virtue of being the oldest residents of the area, by having been to Mecca on the *haj*, or because of their status in the government bureaucracy. They are generally not, however, the key informal leaders of an area. Administering the *ronda* involves keeping a roster of heads of households and the days that they have agreed to fulfill their obligation to participate.[8] It can also involve other responsibilities: keeping track of an inventory of tools, making sure the guard post is maintained, and establishing rules for the frequency of patrols and for their routes.

There are two technologies that define the *ronda*: the *pos ronda* (now the *pos kamling*) and the *kentongan* or *tong-tong*. The *pos ronda*—also called the *gardu*—is the post where members of the *ronda* gather when they are not out patrolling. It takes a variety of forms, depending on the amount of money or work community members are willing to invest. In its minimal form, very common in rural areas, it is a small building made from wood planks, lengths of bamboo, and a bamboo roof. It measures about three by two meters, and it is often elevated about a meter off the ground. Usually it is closed at the back and partially open on the ends and the front. The front has a doorway to climb into, and inside there might be a bench to sit on. Otherwise one just sits on the floor. In cities, the *pos ronda* is often a more permanent structure. Sometimes it is made of brick, sits on the ground, and has old sofas and chairs inside or laid out beside it.

The *kentongan* is an instrument that hangs in the doorway of the *pos ronda*, and like the *pos ronda*, it frequently appears in photographic and textual representations of village and neighborhood life. It is made from a hollowed-out tree branch with a slit down the middle. The slit is about a fifth of the diameter of the branch, runs lengthwise, and stops short of the ends of the instrument. *Kentongan* range in size from the length of a hand to a size greater than a man's body. To produce a sound it is struck with a wood stick. Some of the examples of *kentongan* one sees are actually carved in the shape of an armless and legless man. Thus, at the top of the instrument, a head is carved with eyes and a nose. The body of the instrument is thus the man's trunk. At the bottom of the instrument a hole is drilled where the stick is inserted such that it protrudes as an erect phallus.

In Bandung, residential neighborhoods are arranged so that there is one main access point to a thoroughfare and several minor access points to more distant thoroughfares. When one is given directions, it is not in terms of an abstract grid but

---

[6] *Rukun*: harmonious; *tetangga*: neighbor; *warga*: member/citizen. The RT and RW are neighborhood associations. Each RT consists of several dozen households (*rumah tangga*), while each RW consists of a handful of RTs. This administrative system was formalized and made compulsory during the Japanese occupation and is largely based on the Tonari Gumi model used in Japan. See N. Niessen, "Indonesian Municipalities under Japanese Rules" in *Issues in Urban Development*, ed. Peter J. M. Nas (Leiden: Research School, CNWS, 1995), pp. 125-127.

[7] More often than not, the person designated is a member or retiree of the armed forces.

[8] In the late nineteenth century, before the penetration of the bureaucratic state, this roster was often memorized using oral poetry. An example of one of these poetic *ronda* rosters (written on palm leaf), taken from a West Javanese village, is said to reside in Snouck Hurgronje's private library collection.

in terms of this main access point, the primary location for entering a neighborhood. It is through this access point that almost all traffic flows, and consequently there is inevitably an orderly crowd of *becak* (rickshaw or pedicab) and *ojek* (motorcycles with jockeys) waiting here for passengers and goods in need of transport. The *pos ronda* is generally located at this mouth, or at a location from which one can see a couple of different points of entry into the neighborhood. In special cases, it may be located somewhere else. In one neighborhood in which I stayed, for example, it was explained to me that thieves tended to come from the poor *kampung* (neighborhood/quarter) across the river. Thus, the *pos kamling* was built along that border rather than at one of the four locations where one could enter the neighborhood in a car. To guard against robbery, a gate was also built to block vehicle access from the main thoroughfare at night and "sleeping policemen" (speed-bumps) were installed to slow traffic.

From the *pos ronda,* the guards on duty keep an eye on the traffic that passes within their line of sight: hawkers, people returning home, cars driving by. With the aid of the speed-bumps and gates, traffic is slowed and re-routed to facilitate inspection. The guards have an impressive ability to recognize details that indicate a threat. They may notice a person because he or she is a stranger to the neighborhood (*orang asing, orang tidak kenal*), that is, someone who is neither a resident nor a regular night-time visitor (and this they know, despite what is sometimes a fair amount of traffic). The same observation is made of cars. But more frequently the threat is described in terms of movements that give cause for suspicion (*gerak-gerik yang mencurigakan*). It is the way someone walks or the way a car pauses that draws the guards' attention. One also finds this theme in police reports by citizens who have caught a thief red-handed: that which aroused their suspicion in the first place was someone's peculiar movements.

The guards extend this way of seeing beyond the *pos ronda* when they patrol. As they walk or cycle around, they check the streets and each of the houses in their territory, looking to see that everything is in its place. Usually this means making sure things are not left outside a house's fence, gates and doors are closed and locked, curtains are closed, and there are no strangers skulking about. On these outings guards bring along a portable version of the *kentongan*, striking it as they go. The hollow sound it produces is one of the few sounds to be heard in the city's neighborhoods at night.

SYSTEMS OF LIGHT AND SYSTEMS OF LANGUAGE

Given the above description, it is tempting to argue that the *ronda* is essentially a system of surveillance. After all, the *ronda* routinely and systematically brings an eye to bear on the neighborhood, both through the *pos ronda* and through the patrols that extend its view. But the *ronda*'s concern with the visual is not reason enough to characterize it as an instrument of surveillance. To show why not, it is necessary to compare the *ronda* with two other institutions of neighborhood security, institutions that originate in the state rather than the local neighborhood. The first of these is a set of rules and regulations, often passed down by the municipal government, that must be enforced by the *kepala* RT and RW. While some of these pertain to the administration of the *ronda*, others do not, focusing instead on the collection of data about residents and visitors. The second institutional form is an apparatus of *operasi* (operations), performed by the police, the health department, and other authorities. Such *operasi* penetrate the neighborhood, bringing with them a form of organization and an image of order quite different from that developed in the *ronda*. How these two apparatuses function and compare to one another will be described later. First, however, a few words on what "surveillance" means in the context of this analysis.

Surveillance is usually understood to concern the question of visibility. Bentham's prison panopticon, as the instrument of surveillance *par excellence*, is a technology that allows for prison guards to see without being seen. That is, it aligns prisoners and their cells in a series on an open prison yard to facilitate their inspection by guards who are invisible in their watchtower. In such a system, the prisoners and their cells are constituted as *visibilities* (i.e. segmented units of a visible world) by a central power. Yet according to Foucault, the panopticon is more than just a system of light and seeing: "It is a type of location of bodies in space, of distribution of individuals in relation to one another, of hierarchical organization . . . "[9] In this conception, surveillance relates to more than just prisons and other technologies of seeing. As Deleuze puts it, the "abstract formula" of the panopticon is not so much to see without being seen as "to impose a particular conduct on a particular human multiplicity."[10] Surveillance in this broader sense is not restricted to the control of visibilities, for although it may employ a system of light that "forms or organizes matter," it also employs a system of language that "forms or finalizes functions and gives them aims."[11] The two systems of light and language must be conceived of separately before their interactions are examined. For although the two systems might have the same abstract formula, "the fact remains that [they] are heterogeneous, even though they may overlap: [between them] there is no correspondence or isomorphism, no direct causality or symbolization."[12] It would thus be a mistake, for example, to presume that prisons and legal codes are enforcing surveillance on the same object; prisons distribute, organize, and hierarchize prisoners (formed matter) while legal codes distribute, organize, and hierarchize illegalities (formalized functions).

The residential neighborhood also interweaves systems of light with systems of language. In the first place, it interweaves state operations with regulations, and in the second place, it interweaves *ronda* patrols with *ronda* stories and gossip. How these four "systems" compare, and whether they can all be characterized as apparatuses of surveillance, will be examined below.

Regulations and Operations

During the late-colonial period Bandung had a reputation for being an exemplary modern colonial city. With the highest concentration of Dutch residents in the Indies and as the site of its only technical university, it was home to many respected architects and urban planners. These architects and planners played an important role in developing the layout of the city and drafting legislation that embodied the ideals of a modern, pluralist colony. In these ideals, the notion of the city figured prominently, with neighborhoods viewed as components that ought to

---

[9] M. Foucault, *Discipline and Punish: The Birth of the Prison* (New York:Vintage, 1995), p. 205.

[10] G. Deleuze, *Foucault* (Minneapolis: University of Minnesota Press, 1988), p. 34.

[11] Ibid., p. 33.

[12] Ibid., p. 31.

suit the larger whole. The result was a city divided into north and south, with the Dutch living on the hill in the north and Indonesians living in sometimes ethnically divided *kampungs* in the south. In between these two zones lived the Chinese and a few Arabs, who together dominated the commercial traffic that surrounded the main square and train station. Since independence, however, the ideal of a pluralist city has collapsed, and no new totalizing vision has replaced it. Dutch municipal legislation has remained largely unchanged, and the logic of urban transformation has become very ad hoc, usually reacting to the pressures of urbanization rather than setting out a vision for the city's future. One consequence of this has been that the neighborhood has achieved a new prominence in recent times, as it (and increasingly the household), rather than the city, is now the level at which residential ideals are played out. The city itself has become little more than a sprawl of different neighborhoods, interspersed with commercial, military, and government complexes, and tied together by traffic-jammed thoroughfares.

To fully understand how the Bandung neighborhood has taken the form it has, it would be necessary to examine the complex historical interplay between systems of language and systems of light that have taken components of the neighborhood as their object. For the neighborhood, the system of language has consisted of municipal codes, government regulations, *adat* rules, and educational booklets, whereas the system of light has consisted of short-term operations that compose and recompose visibilities. While an in-depth analysis of the interplay of these two systems is beyond the scope of this paper, a few illustrations of how they function are provided below.[13]

The system of language has given shape to concepts like *kampung, rumah tangga* (household), *keluarga* (family), *pekarangan* (yard in which a house is placed), and individual *identitas* (identity papers). Many of these concepts were developed during the Dutch colonial period. Popular books, for example, were published in Sundanese about how to keep a good yard by planting certain types of plants and trees or laying it out in a particular way; government regulations were enforced concerning the administrative separation of races and the collection of census data; municipal regulations were imposed concerning the materials to be used in house construction, the height of fences, the positioning of ditches, and the location of hearths; and *adat* rules were applied to issues such as the clothing that different classes and ethnicities ought to wear or what gestures one had to perform if one met royalty on the street, for example.

In the postcolonial period, many of the regulations and books have fallen into disuse, but the concepts developed in them are often still important. Some, like *keluarga, rumah tangga,* and *identitas,* have been refined and developed to meet the needs of a new urban and consumer society. The former two concepts are particularly important in marketing campaigns that emphasize a new, nuclear family lifestyle. *Identitas* is a concept used by the state that underlies a substantial portion of the daily work performed by heads of the RT and RW. It provides a good example of how the system of language works.

The use of *identitas* for certain segments of the population began during the colonial period, but with the end of the colonial administrative separation of races, it

---

[13] Rudolf Mrázek's paper in this volume provides a wonderfully detailed analysis of the technologies of seeing that, during the colonial period, gave form to the types of visibilities I describe below.

has become increasingly important as a means to monitor and control populations. The central technology for this monitoring is the identity card or KTP (*Kartu Tanda Penduduk*) that people are obligated to carry with them at all times. Information on this card includes religion, name, address, place of birth, age, nationality, sex, and identity number.[14] If one is "stamped" (*dicap*) as a former member of the outlawed communist party (*eks*-PKI [Indonesia Communist Party]) this fact is also included on the card.[15] Recently this individual identity card has been supplemented with a Family Card which each household head is obligated to hold. This card lists all the individuals who reside at a particular address (which implicitly ought to be a "family"). It includes all the information from their identity cards, but also includes new categories of information such as level of education, employment, relation to household head, names of parents, type of family-planning used, and a category for "special deviances" (handicaps). Such information is administered by the *kecamatan* (district) but is collected through the heads of the RT or RW, just as is census and voter registration data. The sectoral police station often collates this information and creates lists and tables that represent the concentration of the various categories in particular neighborhoods, with special attention paid to political party affiliation as well as the number of *residivis* (ex-convicts) and *eks*-PKI.

As a form of surveillance, the system of language at the level of the RT and RW thus takes *identitas* as its object. As the lowest level in the administrative hierarchy, the RT and RW is often used for the collection and verification of this data but is rarely in a position to put it to use. For the RT and RW administration such data collection is a burden that does not have the clear benefits associated with their other tasks like administering the *ronda*, helping with flood control, and keeping alleys clean. Those who carry the cards express surprisingly little anxiety about how the information might be used by the state. Even those who are "stamped" *residivis* or *eks*-PKI do not fear their categorization so much as feel it to be a very real blockage to getting work. In relation to *identitas*, the stories people tell are not conspiracy theories but stories about the special channels one used to get one's card. A relative in the police made it faster or cheaper than usual to get the card, or the use of a *calo* (unofficial middle-man) made it unnecessary actually to go to the government office to do the paperwork. The other stories people tell relate to other, more exclusive forms of identification people might carry: a Military Police sticker on a car, an official's name card in one's wallet, a Harley-Davidson club ID card. These stories all center around how when someone was stopped by the police, the *identitas* in question facilitated safe passage. Someone who carries such tokens, they say, is "*kebal*" (invulnerable) to hassle by the lowly police on the street.

In conversations with older residents about Bandung's history, however, the question of regulations and *identitas* rarely arises on its own. Far more memorable to these people is the history of visibilities. The detail with which people remember the arrival of something new to the neighborhood, be it a bicycle, a car, or a new police

---

[14] Until the early 1980s information about ethnicity was also included (specifically to monitor ethnic Chinese). Some believe it is still there, but now hidden in the identity number. The identity card is only one of a number of such technologies of surveillance. Another important one is the *Surat Kelakuan Baik* (Letter of Good Behavior) that is issued by the police and that must be attached to all job applications. This letter marks ex-convicts.

[15] *Eks*-PKI are divided into three categories, A, B, and C, depending on the degree to which they are thought to have been involved in the communist party.

uniform, is often surprising. When I asked one man about what houses in south Bandung were like in the old days, he replied more or less as follows:

> In the Dutch period the houses were off the ground. The floors were made of wood, and the sides and top of *bilik* [bamboo]. At first the walls had two layers with a space in between, and the *atap* [roof] was made with whole pieces of bamboo, open at the end. The problem with this was disease, because *kutu busuk* [bedbugs] would come from the chickens underneath the house (when they had a new chick). But then the problem became the 'pest' of rats in the walls and the bamboo. So the walls were made with only one layer and the roof bamboo lengths were closed off. If a family experienced a death they would be taken away and *dibarak* [placed in barracks] with other families of victims to prevent it from *mengular* [spreading]. They would then place a police guard on the house to prevent theft and the spread of the lice. The kids at school would have to line up to receive their *suntikan* [injections], which in those days were given in the chest, not in the arm. It would leave a red mark.

His reply is typical in that it describes a history of visibilities and in doing so pays particular attention to origins. Origins of the new visibilities are always of interest, and they are the subject of much discussion both at the time of their first appearance as well as subsequently. In the case above, the visibilities of the house are remembered as originating in the Dutch public health operations against pestilence. Indeed, if one sets aside the question of the penetration of consumer goods, *operasi* (as they are now called) like the anti-pestilence drive loom very large as the source of new visibilities in the neighborhood.

Such *operasi* are unmistakable in that without exception they create images of the house, *kampung*, and other objects as they existed "before" and "after" the intervention. As the old man explained, sanitation and disease control under the Dutch were instrumental in the decomposition and recomposition of Sundanese houses. There were also highly organized efforts at *kampung-verbetering* (neighborhood improvement) which consolidated hamlets and aligned houses, fences, and ditches in a Euclidean space, sometimes forcing this aesthetic on the local population.[16] Both of these projects were represented in government publications through the use of "before" and "after" photographs. In the postcolonial period there

---

[16] In the early part of the twentieth century, a colonial official described the situation in Serang as follows: "A *kampong* has fifteen houses, disorderly and close together which is detrimental to the health of the inhabitants. Twelve of the inhabitants place their houses such that they are in the middle of their respective compounds with the front facing the roads, while the distance from one house to another is not less than three Rhineland birches. The three other inhabitants nevertheless categorically refuse to change the stance of their houses in their plots because their present stance has provided them with with luck and will continue to do so . . . In the territory of belief, the Inlanders in general are holding very fast . . . So it is with the three people mentioned above that it happened that one by one they were physically taken by a strong *oppasser* [policeman] to a dark corner and given the necessary kicks. To that the underdistrict-head made up a *process-verbaal* [written report] in which it was stated that the *kampong-verbetering* shall, according to the rules, be brought through the friendly deliberation of all those concerned." See "Bantam" in *Het Recht en de Politie,* from the series *Onderzoek Naar de Mindere Welvaart der Inlandsche Bevolking op Java en Madoera* (Weltevreden: F. B. Smits, 1907), p. 11.

has been a number of such operations, the most far-reaching of which has been the family-planning program with its nurses and officials, military personnel, diagrams, condoms, injections, and representative data on the birth rate "before" and "after."

Nowadays in Bandung, there are two bodies that regularly perform operations on the city streets: the police and the so-called TIBUM (*Penertiban Umum*: Public Order). While the police target drugs, alcohol, and people without *identitas*, the TIBUM aim to increase *disiplin* by clearing *pedagang kaki lima* (pushcart traders), *becak*, and *bangunan liar* (wild buildings) out of particular streets. The TIBUM is a police-like body of officers, but unlike the police, it is under the control of the metropolitan government rather than the military. While the police *operasi* tend to use roadblocks, the TIBUM descend upon an area *en masse*, wearing vests with the name of the particular operation on the back (e.g., GDN for *Gerakan Disiplin Nasional*, or the National Discipline Movement). In a very short time they are able to remove any eyesores from the zone they are targeting. In Bandung, as in other cities in Indonesia, the TIBUM operations do not happen just anytime but usually precede the visit of an important official. In anticipation of such visits, trucks and bulldozers are brought around and unfortunate victims watch as their sources of livelihood are destroyed or carted away. Then the street curbs are painted with their white and black checks and everything looks "clean." It is rumored that in Jakarta the entire route to President Suharto's favorite golf course was cleared of street vendors, "after" he expressed anger upon seeing them on one occasion.

What happens to all the moonshine, *becak*, unlicensed public transport vans, false Levis, weapons, drugs, and so forth that get carted away? This is a question that people frequently ask in the letters column of newspapers. The police say they are destroyed and to prove this they stage rather bizarre spectacles in which such things are burned or crushed by bulldozers and steamrollers. These displays are broadcast on television, where shots of the destruction are intercut with shots of uniformed police officials and their wives, seated in rows, clapping as the spectacle unfolds before them. It may be that the aim of such shows is to establish in the television viewer an identification with the ruler's eye, such that they appreciate the elimination of these eyesores. But this is not what happens. In my experience, viewers tend rather to consider it a waste to destroy perfectly usable commodities. More importantly, and almost without exception, they note cynically that the goods being destroyed are only a small part of what was confiscated, or that the crates being burned are empty and that the remainder—those things not destroyed—are being sold by the police for profit. Thus, although the police may see the spectacle only as a demonstration of the power of surveillance, what viewers see is the generation and appropriation of a surplus. They see a performance in which the state's power (of surveillance) is converted into personal wealth.

In these spectacles, and in the operations that preceded them, the ruler's eye thus plays a central role. Just as the spectacle of destruction takes place for the pleasure of the police officials' eyes, so too is an official eye invoked before an operation is launched, with the TIBUM imagining how the visiting official will gaze upon the roads he or she uses on the way from the airport to the hotel, or from home to the golf course. The operation is then planned, organized, and executed with this imagined official perception in mind. What defines the "before" and "after," therefore, is precisely the intervention of the ruler's eye.

Ronda Eyes and Tales

As the *ronda* guards putter through their patrols, they too see things in a particular way. Unlike the officials involved in the operations described above, however, they have no interest in classifying, isolating, and eliminating visibilities. Rather, they are checking things, making sure everything is as it should be. As we have noted, this means doors and gates are closed and locked, valuables are put away, and no strangers are prowling about. As there is no public streetlighting, it usually also means that each house has an outside light switched on. But although the *ronda* creates visibilities, it differs in two important respects from the operations described above. First, the definition of these visibilities is not exclusively in the hands of a class of guards, police, or functionaries, but is divided amongst the members of the community. The identification of visibilities is thus fragmented, rather than centralized through a single administrative gaze. The rotational nature of the night *ronda*, combined with the tendency of *pembantus* (domestic workers) and household mothers to monitor daytime activities, insures this. Second, there is no spectacle of destruction in the *ronda*. The fragmented eyes of the neighborhood community do not appropriate visibilities, but evaluate them. Their focus on strangers and unrecognized vehicles thus does not seek to classify, block access to, or destroy these individuals and items so much as to examine their movements in the hope of determining what relation they have to neighborhood residents.

Between the surveillance of visibilities in operations and the examination of visibilities in the *ronda*, therefore, there is an almost complete discontinuity. We do not even find a cooperative relationship by means of which operations constitute neighborhood visibilities and the *ronda* monitors them (as would be the case, for instance, with prison architecture and prison guards). Thus, when guards were needed to protect and quarantine disease victims' homes, it was the police and not the *ronda* association that supplied personnel. What we find is rather a discontinuity between an apparatus of seeing that operates on the basis of the logic of the panopticon, and one that does not. The panopticon actively produces relations between visibilities through its very functioning, while the *roonda* just "waits and sees" what relations will emerge.

This is not to say that the *ronda* is independent of systems of surveillance. Its interactions, however, take place with surveillance's system of language rather than with the system of light evident in operations. Consider, for example, the case of *residivis*. Nowadays these individuals are monitored primarily through the system of language: names and addresses of *residivis* appear on a list in the hands of the police and, perhaps, the *kepala* RW. But in the old days such shadowy characters were subject to surveillance by the *ronda* by means of an obligation to carry torches whenever they went out at night so that they could not disappear under the cover of darkness.[17] Hence, in Cirebon they became known colloquially as *koenang-koenang*

---

[17] In some periods, this practice was extended to the whole population, as the following indicates: "In no town or village of Java are the natives allowed to walk after seven in the evening without a light. Some make their rambles with torches of small thin split bamboo, made up into bundles, and lit at the end. Others carry about a tumbler filled half-way or two-thirds with water, and the rest with oil, upon the surface of which floats a wick made of pith, and pierced with a couple of sticks having corks at the end. I saw many carrying these tumblers in white pocket handkerchiefs, through which the light shone. How they kept them from lighting was always a mystery to me, unless it be that the handkerchief has been previously dipped in some incombustible solution. Some natives carry torches of damar and

(fireflies).[18] Here a category defined by the state's system of language is fed into the *ronda*'s system of light. We see the way in which one system might provide the content for another. In the process, however, a metamorphosis takes place: a *residivis* becomes a firefly. While a *residivis* is a category for statisticians, psychologists, and criminologists, a firefly is an insect that might fly away unnoticed if it is not induced to stay alight.

Another example of how the systems interact is found in the law that dictates that anyone who stays in a neighborhood for more than twenty-four hours must report his or her presence to the *kepala* RW (*1X24 jam wajib lapor*, [must report once every twenty-four hours] as stated by the hand-painted sign at the entrance to a RW) and provide notification when he or she leaves.[19] In a poor suburb of Bandung where I lived with a *kepala* RW, this monitoring of arrivals and departures constituted a large portion of his work. But the system that this reporting feeds into may vary in different settings. In urban areas the important thing about this reporting is that the visitor's identity is recorded in a book. Whether one does this oneself or by proxy is not overly important. But in a small town I visited, the man I reported to did not even make a note of it. He asked, instead, the usual questions a guest is asked, such as where I was from or how I came to know the family I was staying with. When I asked whether he should make a note of my *identitas*, he said that it was not necessary. The important thing was that I had visited him, so that if I was seen around, I would be known. The recording of identity card numbers and other information, he said, is something they do in the cities (in a tone suggesting that they do not understand the essence of the reporting procedure). Here a state regulation to control *identitas* was translated into a different system altogether, one

---

rosin, the extract of some indigenous plant, or sticks of wood tied in a bundle and rubbed over with ignitable compounds, which generally give the most glaring but least durable lights." See W. B. D'Almeida, *Life in Java with Sketches of the Javanese, Vol. I* (London: Hurst and Blackett, 1864), p. 271.

[18] "Cheribon" in *Het Recht en de Politie*, from the series *Onderzoek Naar de Mindere Welvaart der Inlandsche Bevolking op Java en Madoera* (Weltevreden: F. B. Smits, 1907), p. 20.

[19] This is a colonial law that has never been taken off the books and which seems to be enforced rather systematically, especially for foreigners. The terms in which this law was first communicated to the local population were as follows:

"Rules of Police Punishments for the Public. A fine of one to fifteen rupiah for: No. 1. He who moves from a kampoeng to another kampoeng and does not let the head of the first kampoeng know.

"No. 2. He who moves to a kampoeng and does not let the head of the kampoeng know his name, work, and place of origin within 24 hours of arriving in the kampoeng.

"No. 3. He who within twenty-four hours does not let the head of the kampoeng know that someone not from the kampoeng is staying over in his house, that is, by telling the kampoeng head the name of the person, his work, and place of origin. And he who does not tell the kampoeng head upon the departure of this person.

"Because in each and every region [*negri*] it is appropriate for the heads, or persons in charge, who are responsible for defending public security [*kaslamettanja orang banjak*], to be informed when people are coming and going. It is included in these regulations that breaking the rules results in punishment, so that no-one will be reckless enough to leave his place or bring another person into his place without informing the area's leaders or their police. It is also to make searching for evildoers or others easier."

See L. Th. Mayer, *Peratoeran Hoekoeman Policie jang oemoem atas orang bangsa Jawa dan sebrang di Tanah Hindia-Nederland* (Samarang: G. C. T. van Dorp, 18—).

that addressed me like the *ronda* might address me, not as a bureaucratic category but as a guest. In this process of translation, my *identitas* went missing.

Thus, even when it interacts with the state's system of language, the *ronda's* system of light operates discontinuously with the rules and regulations passed down through the RT and RW. In fact, the *ronda* itself is not overly concerned with rules and regulations that do not pertain to its own functioning. If one does not report within twenty-four hours, it will not be a *ronda* guard who reminds one to do so, but rather the head of the RT. Similarly, it is not the *ronda* that performs censuses and voter registration but the RT and RW administration. Insofar as the *ronda* is embedded in a system of language, it is embedded as one of the language's objects, not as one of its instruments.

This discontinuity between the *ronda* and surveillance is even more pronounced if one considers the *ronda's* own "system" of language. The *ronda's* "system" of language is very informal, consisting of gossip, stories, and conversation. The *gardu* in particular is where men gather and chat (*ngarumpi*). The Sundanese author Mohammad Ambri captured this aspect of the *ronda* beautifully in his 1932 story entitled "Munjung."[20] This story follows the discussion between men at a guard post as they come and go from their turns patrolling. It is dreamy conversation, following associations, drifting from story to story, from speaker to speaker. The chat in this case, however, all centers around the same theme: how so-and-so got rich or beautiful by making a pact with a spirit.[21] In other words, it is talk about the way in which things invisible to the normal eye (spirits, people-as-animals) explain the appearance and disappearance of visibilities (money, beauty, wealth).[22] One of the tales, for example, tells of two men, Istam and Suta, who go off in search of a *keramat* (sacred spot) where it is said one can marry a spirit and become rich. Upon arrival they meet with the *keramat's jurukunci* (gatekeeper) who takes them through the forest to the site of the *keramat*:

> When they arrived at a large stone, the *jurukunci* stopped and said, "Here is Sanghiang Lawang [the name of the *keramat*]. We must first burn incense here while scattering offerings of money, as much as you want, one or two cents if you wish. While I burn the incense the two of you must close your eyes."
>
> "Alright," they both replied. Istam really closed his eyes, as the *jurukunci* had ordered. But Pak Suta did not. Rather, he gazed upward, watching two sparrows hopping together as if in love. When the *jurukunci* invited them to walk onward, Istam opened his eyes. His view had changed.

---

[20] Translated into Indonesian by Ajip Rosidi with the title *Memuja Siluman*. *Memuja* means "to worship" while *siluman* means both "invisible" and "a human who has taken the appearance of an animal." See M. Ambri, *Memuja Siluman* (Jakarta: Pustaka Jaya, 1977).

[21] For example: the neighbor who turns into a pig that goes and steals loose change from nearby houses; the spirit that provides money that when spent will be returned as double the value that is spent; the man who is given money by a person so tiny that he can pass through any hole that a ray of light can pass through, allowing him to break into houses to steal money.

[22] Theories of inner power (*tenaga dalam*) emphasize that it can affect the physical world but not the reverse.

What was called Sanghiang Lawang was a huge gate, with a straight wide road leading to an immense palace . . . [23]

The two enter but only Istam is received by the spirit for marriage. When they leave,

Istam is very pleased, because he had got what he wanted, he would be rich. When they had passed out of Sanghiang Lawang, he looked back, but all that was visible now was a thick forest, the straight wide road to the palace could be seen no longer. All that could be seen in the direction of the palace was a pointed, rocky mountain. As for Pak Suta, he just shivered, saying nothing to Istam or to the *jurukunci*. Since leaving, what he saw had not changed; on the way there and on the way back it was just the same. At Sanghiang Lawang he had not seen the wide straight road . . . [24]

In this story it is emphasized that the normal eye will be unable to see the powers that generate visibilities. So as the *ronda* guards patrol their neighborhood, creating and evaluating visibilities, they supplement this activity with talk that points to a world that cannot be grasped by their activity.

Not all *ronda* stories deal with the supernatural. In my experience, the *ronda* is also a favored place to exchange stories about thefts and attempted thefts in the neighborhood and its surrounding area. Such stories describe the appearance of suspicious characters, the event of the crime, and the response of the community. Usually they circulate not only among the *ronda* but among household mothers and *pembantu*. Like the stories about spirits, this idle chatter is not concerned with ordering and disciplining populations so much as with accounting for appearances and disappearances. It does not attempt surveillance but describes what is beyond surveillance.[25]

In sum, we have distinguished four apparatuses that pertain to security in the Bandung neighborhood. The first is an apparatus of operations in which authorities suddenly descend upon the neighborhood to recompose its visibilities so that they conform to some idealized image. These operations are oriented around the eye of the ruler, and may provide the occasion for spectacles that convert state power into personal wealth. The second is an apparatus of rules and regulations that operates through government administration, utilizing the RT and RW to realize its objectives. This apparatus serves to monitor and control categories of persons (*identitas*). The third apparatus works through the *pos ronda* and the eyes of community members; it monitors and controls visibilities in a fragmented and routine way, evaluating them and taking a particular interest in their relationships. Finally, there is the *ronda's* system of language, a system that provides oral accounts of events and appearances that escape those apparatuses previously described. While the former two apparatuses are aptly called systems of surveillance, the latter are not.

---

[23] M. Ambri, *Memuja Siluman*, pp. 21-22.

[24] Ibid., p. 23.

[25] Perhaps it is precisely these types of stories that the Dutch colonists are "deaf" to when they come to depend solely on their technologies of seeing (see Mrázek in this volume).

TERRITORIALITY

Comparing the *ronda* to systems of surveillance is a useful way to establish how it differs from these systems, but such a comparison is only of limited value in trying to unravel the character of *ronda* security itself. A robust understanding of *ronda* security can only be achieved by analyzing another form of power, one that functions quite differently than that of surveillance. To unearth this power it is necessary to examine the characteristics of that other icon of the *ronda*: the *kentongan*. My own interest in the *kentongan* came about as a result of irritation. In a middle-class neighborhood in which I lived, every night as I was drifting off to sleep the *hansip* would pass by and strike the metal electricity pole just outside my window, producing a loud clanging noise that would jolt me out of my sleep with a real start. For a time, this nightly occurrence came to stand for all my frustrations at living in an environment where peace of mind was so hard to come by. Then I began to wonder what function this practice could possibly have. As I questioned people, the first thing that became clear was that the electricity poles were standing in for the *kentongan* which guards sometimes carry around at night and strike, producing a jarring, loud sound.[26] The second thing that became clear was that there was no single answer as to my question of what purpose this practice served. The replies I received were as follows:

1. It is music that the guard plays "just for fun" (*iseng*).
2. It is to warn off potential thieves and robbers by indicating to them that the neighborhood is being patrolled.
3. It is to insure no one sleeps too deeply by periodically waking them up.
4. It is to communicate back to the *pos ronda* that the patrolling watchman is still there.
5. It is a call to the owner of a house who is then supposed to reply with a shout, and then perhaps give the watchman something to drink.
6. It is a way to mark the passage of time.

Music And Warnings

The *kentongan*, like so many other tools and arts (e.g. *pencat silat* or the *kris*) in Indonesia, blurs the line between functionality and expression. The *kentongan* may be found both in pragmatic circumstances such as the *pos ronda* and in artistic circumstances such as Sundanese musical band performances (*calung*). But using the *kentongan* to make music during the long *ronda* nights is not unheard of. Unlike during a *calung*, however, it is done "just for fun," as an elderly gentleman with fond memories of the *ronda's* music once put it.

The *ronda's* music, although just for fun, is nonetheless important. At night, when the sounds of work disappear and visibilities retreat into shadow, the sounds of the *kentongan* appear as a song, a song that keeps the darkness at bay. The song is little more than a gathering together of sounds into a rhythm since the *kentongan* does not produce many tones. Yet this gathering of sounds creates an ephemeral

---

[26] Other substitutes for the *kentongan* I have seen hanging in the *pos kamling* are a car wheel rim and an empty WWII rocket shell.

order, a tempo in the night. The player of the music traverses the neighborhood, giving coherence not just to a temporality but to a milieu in which all the nearby dwellings are drawn together. This milieu is not yet a territory, just a loose clumping of households held together by the sounds they share. The *ronda*'s milieu only becomes "territorialized" when the sound becomes a mark, a mark that stakes out a territory.[27] It might be, for example, that the song or the musical beat takes on a particular character, a character specific or exclusive (*khas*) to that place.[28] In doing so it creates a boundary separating inner from outer, member from non-member. For anyone with a desire to intrude, the beats signal a territorial claim. It is in this sense that the sound of the *kentongan* is heard as a warning signal telling thieves and robbers that the neighborhood is guarded.

Constituting and Challenging Territoriality

However, the beating of the *kentongan* is not primarily about marking a territory in relation to threats from the outside. Thieves might, in fact, be helped by the sounds of the *kentongan* since they would know exactly where the patrolling guard is and thus would not have to worry about being caught unawares while breaking into a house. The *kentongan* finds its key territorial function, rather, in being an activator: it activates territorializing forces and keeps them alive. It does this by preventing people from sleeping too deeply and, therefore, keeping them alert and attentive.[29] In relation to this function, when one hears the *kentongan* at night, one does not feel relief that the neighborhood is being guarded but rather a fear that an impending threat is nearby; one thus thinks about whether all the doors are closed and locked as they should be or whether anything has been left outside by mistake. As the *ronda* guard passes through the neighborhood striking the *kentongan*, thus, he wakes up or activates a whole series of territorial relationships that might otherwise have slipped away into disuse.

What does it mean to activate territorial relationships? In Bandung one can identify two examples of contexts in which territorial relationships are fully activated: the *keramat* and the *kebal* body. The *keramat* is a place, usually off in a forest

---

[27] The distinction between the milieu and the territory is elaborated in G. Deleuze and F. Guatarri, *A Thousand Plateaus: Capitalism & Schizophrenia* (Minneapolis: University of Minnesota Press, 1991), pp. 311-322.

[28] The song is *khas* in the same sense that a regional food or clothing is *khas*: it gives expression to an exclusive constellation of qualities. Food that is *khas* Sunda, for example, is made from local products and cooked using local implements.

[29] "[I]t is almost entirely prevalent that patrouilles traverse the *desas* [villages] at night, making people vigilant or waking them up with all sorts of hub-bub, and making certain that all is in order. Frequently such wakefulness is the occasion for the discovery of a digging-under and theft; one time the ronde trapped a thief busy digging a hole. Also, suspected persons receive a search from the patrol in the middle of the night in order to see if they are home or off on some obscure adventure." See "Cheribon" in *Het Recht en de Politie*, from the series *Onderzoek Naar de Mindere Welvaart der Inlandsche Bevolking op Java en Madoera* (Weltevreden: F. B. Smits, 1907), p. 16.

If dreams are what prevent people from waking up, the *kentongan* is what prevents them from sleeping. But even when they do sleep and dream, people are not always free of the *kentongan*. I say this because the only dreams people ever mentioned to me were dreams about theft. It is almost as if in letting go and sleeping deeply, a feeling of fear is generated which produces a dream about the loss effected by letting go.

or in a cemetery, where a spirit resides. As we have seen above, the *keramat* is not visible to ordinary people. Nonetheless, it can exert its powers over anyone who passes by its locale. To avoid inadvertently being possessed by a spirit, therefore, people recommend that any trip to the forest or cemetery should be preceded by a request for permission to enter (one uses the same terms for this that one uses daily upon entering someone else's house: *"punten"* or *"permisi"*). Otherwise one's entry will be interpreted as a challenge (*tantangan*) to the power of the spirit. Moreover, one should never urinate in these places because that draws the ire of the spirit. The *keramat* is watched over not only by a spirit but by a *jurukunci*. This person lives nearby and is the one who takes care of the *keramat*. It is he who holds the "key" to the *keramat*, so visitors who come in search of special powers must ask him what offerings need to be made to the spirit and what requisite actions performed in order to have their wishes fulfilled.

While the *keramat* is a territory by virtue of being occupied, the *kebal* (invulnerable) body is a territory by virtue of being protected by an *ilmu* (magical science). Like the *keramat*, the *kebal* body describes an interiority, an interiority which by definition is unmarkable or impenetrable by foreign objects. One becomes *kebal* in one of three ways: by being made so by a powerful person like a *dukun* (shaman); by going through a series of rites like reciting mantra, fasting, and submerging oneself in water; or by carrying or wearing a *jimat* (talisman), which might take the form of a magical piece of writing, a tattoo, or a piece of clothing that has been invested with supernatural Power.[30] The result is that if one is shot, stabbed, chopped, or struck, no mark will be made, no penetration of the skin will occur, or sometimes, no pain will be felt. A young lawyer, for example, told me of how when he was in high school he went to a *dukun* in Tasikmalaya to be made *kebal*. The *dukun* recited a mantra and touched his body. When this was done he took a *golok* (machete) blade and cut a piece of paper with it to demonstrate that it was sharp. He then chopped and sawed at the lawyer's arms and chest which caused pain but left no mark at all.

Like the *keramat*, one of the characteristics of the *kebal* body is that it can be penetrated if one can only figure out the proper technique. Police and criminals alike talk in terms of finding the weakness (*mencari kelemahannya*) of the invulnerability. A policeman I talked to, for example, told of how he had once tried to beat up a robber with a metal pipe but that it had had no effect whatsoever. The policeman then searched for information on what art of invulnerability the man was using. When he got the information he consulted a *dukun* who could tell him what the *kelemahan* (weakness) of that art was. He then returned to beat up the robber, but this time used the twig of a palm leaf. The robber fell and writhed in pain, later claiming that each touch of the twig had brought a horrible burning sensation.

In the magical realm, if one wants to constitute, enter, or find the weakness of a territory, one will inevitably require the aid of a specialist. Such specialists can create effects like those associated with a *keramat* or make spaces *kebal*. A *dukun*, for example, can be asked to perform rites for one's household territory to keep it secure. One such rite makes a house invisible to anyone intent on breaking in. Another rite makes the thief confused after he enters the house, causing him to wander around in

---

[30] The notion of "Power" as a substantial force that invests people and things has been elaborated by Benedict Anderson in his essay entitled "The Idea of Power in Javanese Culture" in *Language and Power: Exploring Political Cultures in Indonesia* (Ithaca: Cornell University Press, 1990). In terms of this analysis, Power could be defined as "the capability of territorializing." *Ilmu* provides a theory or map of particular territories.

circles until the owner returns and releases him. Thieves also use such specialist knowledge (*ilmu*) to determine what day and time they should strike, where they should enter from, and in which direction they should make their escape.[31] There are also some thieves known to be able to cast spells on houses that cause all the occupants to fall into a deep sleep (*sirep*), making the removal of valuables much easier.

Self-defense courses often emphasize the development of a sixth sense which will make it possible for the practitioner to either perceive any object or space that is "filled" (*diisi*) or to fill them oneself. This is similar to having an eye or a nose for territoriality. One guru demonstrated this sixth sense to me by having a friend of mine, who was his student, "fill" one of two spoons. Out of site of the guru, the student concentrated his energy on one of the spoons. The guru was then given the spoons and by passing his hand over them and using his sixth sense, he could identify which of the two was "filled." He explained that the practitioner of this art must be careful because others can sense this power, and if one strays into someone else's territory, it may be taken as a challenge. In such circumstances, one should utter the name of one's guru to avoid problems.[32]

In sum, the territory is described as something that is capable of being inhabited or occupied. The key relation that must be maintained is thus between the inhabitor and the inhabited, or perhaps, between the occupier and the occupied. The territorial mark expresses an active relation between inhabitor and inhabited, as does the inability of an outsider to mark or to penetrate the territory (at least, without being subjected to the territorial power). Such an active relation is perceptible to those who utilize their sixth sense. There are three possible orientations toward such an active territoriality: one may submit to it (*punten*), one may challenge it, or one may search for its fatal weakness. As each territory has its own particular characteristics, any of these orientations may require special knowledge.

When a territorial relation is not fully activated, it invites challenges. The term frequently used for such a state of affairs is *kelengahan* or inattentiveness. It is a condition that thieves and tricksters prey upon. Daydreaming is one of the most common expressions of *kelengahan*. As an elderly gentleman described it, when a woman daydreams (*melamun*) her body is empty of thoughts (*kosong*), "like a car left with its engine running but without a driver." Such emptiness is dangerous because, like the car left running, it invites occupation by another. Possession of someone's body by another spirit is described as an accidental or unintentional entry (*kemasukan*). To prevent this spirit possession, a person who is daydreaming will almost always be chastised for it in a tone of voice that calls them back: *"Eh, jangan ngelamun!"* (Eh, stop daydreaming!) or just *"Ei!"* and a clap of the hands. The territory of a house too may be *kemasukan*, for example by a thief. But the thief will not succeed at breaking in if the house is already fully occupied. The following story, told to me by an engineering student, illustrates the relation between inhabitation—or what I would call *presence*—and security:

---

[31] For an analysis of a *primbon* (divination manual) used by thieves for this purpose, see G. Quinn, "The Javanese Science of Burglary," *Review of Indonesian and Malayan Affairs* 9,1 (1975): 33-55.

[32] Students are marked by their gurus, just as a neighborhood is flagged by the *kentongan*. Students display this mark, a sign of the care of their guru, by being disciplined in following his orders and advice.

Last night Ujog stopped by. He and Titik got to talking about ghosts. Ujog told a story about how the house he has in Kopo has a ghost that watches over the house. When he bought the house the former owner explained that the house was guarded [*dijaga*] by a *makhluk halus* [supernatural creature] so even if it was left empty and unlocked, it would be safe. Last week a thief broke in [*maling masuk*] but was caught because the house was protected.

In Ujog's neighborhood they have a *ronda*, which is done on a rotational basis. That night two of Ujog's friends were taking their turn at the ronda. One would stay at the post and the other would patrol around, striking the *kentongan* as he went. When he passed Ujog's house the first time he didn't see anything unusual but when he came back he saw his friend, who was meant to be on duty at the post, outside the house. He asked why the guard had left the post and the guard answered that there was a *maling* [thief] in the house, and told him to get the people [*masyarakat*] to surround the house. So he ran back to the post to gather people together but when he arrived was shocked to see his friend waiting at the post.

"How did you get here?," he asked his friend. His friend said that he hadn't gone anywhere, that he had been there at the post the whole time. The first guard then figured that it must have been someone else who had warned him. They then got people out and circled the house, and some went in and caught the thief. The thief was then beaten by the people. When he would try to get up someone would come over and say "You're a thief, ya?" and then hit him again. By the end of it the thief's face was completely wrecked [*hancur*]. After all this the guy on the ronda started wondering who it was that warned him, since there was nobody else on the ronda that night, and he was sure he had recognized his friend at the time. They realized that it must have been the *makhluk halus* who had taken the form of his friend to warn him so that he wouldn't be scared. After the thief had been handed over to the person in charge of "keamanan," a man from ABRI [Angkatan Bersenjata Republik Indonesia], the thief too described how he had gone in with the desire [*niat*] to steal but that after he had gone in he got confused. He had entered through the roof, but once he was in he couldn't figure out how to get out again as the door was locked. And then he got really tired and wanted to go to sleep. Finally, when he was about to try to leave he looked out and saw that the house was surrounded, although at this time, says Ujog, the people hadn't yet arrived. It was the *machluk halus* again. (Ujog says that the maling knew how to get in because he was actually a friend of Ujog's who lived a few blocks over and had helped him put up the antennae on the roof. So it seems that while he was helping he was also taking note of how to get in. Then when he knew Ujog was out of town for a week, he broke in).

In this interesting story, Ujog explains that his house is secure when he is not living there precisely because it is not really empty, but is inhabited by a presence that guards (*ada yang jaga*). The presence was strong enough that the thief became confused and sleepy.

The *kentongan* thus does the same for the house that the "*jangan ngelamun*" does for the body: it calls forth the possessor, pulling it back and making it fully occupy its territory. Hence, when the guards make their rounds, people wake up and think about their house, or sometimes, ghost-guards appear and express their awareness of a thief.

What is a bit unusual about this process is the incredible impermanence of the territories activated. That is, territorial claims do not "take" very well on inanimate objects, tending instead to fade away if not repeatedly renewed. This can be seen in a number of very different circumstances. Take, for example, the case of moveable possessions. Although laws of private property provide for ownership until the good has been legally transferred, there is a strong non-legal tradition that goods not attended to may justifiably change hands. It is not unlike the swidden fields of old when one's possession of the field depended upon keeping it cleared. If one left it fallow and plants began to grow wildly within it, someone else might come along and take possession of it. Similarly, if one takes insufficient care of one's things, leaving them out in the living room, for instance, rather than keeping them hidden in a cupboard in one's room, they may well go missing. And one can only blame oneself for being careless. Also, if one lends something to someone, one cannot expect that it will be returned. It could well be that it receives great care from the borrower and ends up *de facto* becoming hers (I know of many cases in which goods as large and as valuable as cars have changed hands in this way).

To sum up: the primary territorial relationship can be described as one of *presence*. This presence may be rendered in natural or supernatural terms, but the underlying principle remains the same. On a day-to-day basis, this presence makes itself felt through qualities that evidence a care of, or attentiveness to, one's surroundings: responsive eyes, a well-groomed garden, "things in their place," for example. If these qualities, these territorial marks, are not maintained on a regular basis, presence dissipates and the territory loses its consistency. The *kentongan*, in preventing deep sleep, functions to prevent this loss of consistency.

Interpolation, Communication, and the State

There are times, however, when the *kentongan* not only activates relations of territoriality but demands a response. That is, as the *ronda* guard passes in the night, the inhabitant of the house ought to reply with a shout *("jaga")* to indicate that he or she is awake and on guard. Sometimes the *ronda* guards also hope to be provided with some coffee and snacks. In some cases, this practice is attributable to strategies of surveillance. For instance, ex-convicts used to be subjected to special monitoring by the *ronda* to make sure they were in their houses and not out making trouble. This monitoring was done first of all by placing a special black mark on the ex-convict's house to distinguish it from the other houses. Secondly, each time the *ronda* passed by making a ruckus, a reply from the occupant would be noted by placing a token on a board by the house to indicate that the house had been checked and that the occupant was home. Village regulations would dictate how many times the *ronda* had to pass by the house each night and the village head would check the tokens in the morning to make sure the job had been done. But in other cases, the reply is not so much part of an effort to subject the occupants of the house (or the *ronda* guards) to surveillance as it is the expression of a supra-household territoriality. That is, as long as the *ronda* only served to activate territorial ties but did not demand a response, the neighborhood had the characteristics of a milieu rather than a territory; it was nothing more than a clumping together of household territories (like when the *ronda* music was just for fun, and had not yet become a *khas* song). But when the *kentongan* demands a response, the households are made to signify their belonging to a larger territory. The response indicates that the household, as a quality of the neighborhood, is being cared for (just like the trimmed lawn indicates that the household is cared for). In this new configuration of relations, the household does not so much lose its territoriality, but is, rather, subordinated to the territorial power of the neighborhood, which (like the household) is watched over by the *ronda*.

The subordination of the household territory to the neighborhood territory is expressed by a debt relation. The *ronda* is not the primary mechanism for extracting this debt, but it does play some part. As we have seen, for example, the call of the *kentongan* demands a response from occupants of the household. The response may be in the form of a shout or in the form of a provision of coffee. On special occasions, the call may demand more, such as cooperation in refurbishing the *pos ronda*, paving a street, or dredging a canal. Indeed, the way the *kentongan* has been used to call forth the population has sometimes been extremely elaborate. A particular pattern of *kentongan* beats might bring people out with particular tools, or it might indicate the presence of a specific threat which the people ought to prepare for. It is said that in some areas of Java (e.g. Kediri), the pattern of codes is extremely sophisticated, such that there is a particular signal for every imaginable danger, including a danger that can be sensed but whose form is not yet apparent. The greater the specificity of the warning, the more the *kentongan* takes on the function of an instrument of communication rather than an activator of territorial relations. As a wake up call, the *kentongan* merely activates relations, leaving the determination of threats and the mode of response up to the discretion of individual households. As an instrument for conveying warnings and orders, however, the *kentongan* is capable of calling forth very particular forms of collective action.

Moreover, the employment of the *kentongan* as a means of collective communication in general, and warnings in particular, has not historically been restricted to use within a single neighborhood. Long before the introduction of clocks into peoples' homes, for example, villages and neighborhoods throughout Java were using the *kentongan* to beat out the passing of an abstract and universal time. Also, long before the advent of the telephone, news of a fire could be carried almost instantaneously across long distances by using the *kentongan* to relay messages from village to village, neighborhood to neighborhood. The importance of such communication should not be underestimated. At the turn of the century, for instance, a Dutch official found the *kentongan* a most effective way to catch *kerbau-* (water buffalo) rustlers for within a very short time of the theft being reported as many as ten thousand people could be mobilized to catch the thieves.

One should be careful, however, about jumping to the conclusion that the *kentongan* has inevitably evolved from an instrument of local character into an instrument of state power. Schulte Nordholt provides an interesting example of a contrary tendency in the nineteenth century, when the *kentongan* was used by *desa* (village) heads to warn the population that government officials or police were coming to search for stolen goods.[33] From the pattern of the signal, the population would know which goods ought to be hidden away to avoid being confiscated. In

---

[33] H. Schulte Nordholt, "The *jago* in the shadow: crime and "order" in the colonial state in Java," *Review of Indonesian and Malaysian Affairs* 25,1 (Winter 1991): 84.

this case, the *kentongan* protected local thieves by warning them of the danger of the colonial state.

When the *kentongan* becomes an instrument of communication rather than a territorial mark or an activator of territoriality, it enters into a whole new series of relations. One can compare, for example, the two extremes of the *kentongan*'s design: the first being a small instrument that the *ronda* guards carry around on their patrols (Sundanese: *koprek*), the second being a body-sized instrument with a phallus that hangs in the guard post or in front of the *desa* head's house (Sundanese: *kohkol*). The former might be used to scare away thieves by flagging the territory or to activate multiple territorialities by bringing them into a rhythmic relation to one another (without creating a center). In contrast, the latter functions both as a center that interpolates the zone around it (a kind of erogenous zone) and as an instrument of relay and distribution, allowing for the grouping of zones adjacent to one another. The latter instrument is no more territorial for being fixed and immobile, but rather is "deterritorialized" in the sense that it has ceased to be a flag and has become a conveyor of language.[34] As a conveyor of language it no longer expresses territoriality in itself but acts as a vehicle for a more abstract form of territoriality, that of the state, and perhaps even, of the nation.[35] This is clear, for example, in the cases when the *kentongan* is used as a clock that beats out the passing of a universal time. The *kentongan*'s ability to function as an interpolator is expressed by its fusion with a body of phallic Power. The result of this fusion is an instrument capable not only of relaying and distributing messages, but of using a language of Power to consolidate and distribute masses of people. Between these two extremes stands a middle function in which the *kentongan* neither occupies the territory nor constitutes a component in the territory occupied, but instead brings the occupier and territorial components into relation with one another. That is, it keeps people awake and incites them to take care of themselves and their possessions, but it does not bring them out of their houses.

THIEVES

The call that brings people out of their houses at a run is a beat on the *kentongan* that means a thief has been spotted, or more often, the sound of someone shouting "*maling*." The thief is the most talked about criminal at the neighborhood level, and it is the protection against thieves that provides the *ronda* with its *raison d'être*. Indeed, thieves are the most despised of creatures. According to inmates at Bandung's prison, it is easier to return to one's community after serving time for murder than it is after serving time for petty theft.

---

[34] There are areas of Indonesia where the messages beaten out on percussion instruments (gongs as well as *kentongan*) are said to form a language in which particular combinations of beats form neither messages nor words, but rather syllables. These syllables are partly a representation of an oral language and partly a prearranged code.

[35] The Sarikat Islam used the *kentongan* to call people out to rallies and to convey messages. Could we not see in the *kentongan* a kind of proto-newspaper (universal time, news, calls to rallies), and in the "imagined community" a kind of large-scale territoriality that uses the great orator, Sukarno, as a *kentongan*? On "imagined community" see B. Anderson, *Imagined Communities: Reflections on the Origin and Spread of Nationalism* (London: Verso, 1983). On the comparison of Sukarno's voice to a cow-bell, see Siegel's paper in this volume.

Theft is a crime against the territory.[36] What thieves do is enter into a territory unnoticed and uninvited, remove some of its elements, and leave. In the old days (through the 1970s), according to a pensioned police officer, Bandung's thieves were organized into gangs. If a theft took place the police would know that its perpetrator must be a member of a specific gang because each gang had a particular technique of entering and leaving. Some would enter through a window and leave through the front door. Others would operate only at night, entering by digging under the exterior fence and coming up under the house (when houses were built on stilts). Still others would enter through the roof and always defecate on the roof as they left.[37] In some cases, as we have seen, the *modus operandi* might be informed by an *ilmu* that gave very specific instructions about how and when to enter and leave, depending on a whole series of calculations. But whether he used magic or not, what defined the thief was that he entered an interiority (a house, a yard) without permission, left a mark (the absence of property, defecation), and exited again. What identified him among his peers, and among the police, was his method of thievery.

When people hear the shout "*maling*" and come rushing out of their houses, they are not interested in who the thief is or in his methods (in Ujog's story it is only at the very end that he mentions as an aside that the *maling* he had been talking about was a friend of his!). What they are interested in first of all is catching the rascal ("*bangsat*"). What might have been an ordinary day with people going about their own business is suddenly transformed into a swirl of activity. People run after the thief, get in their cars and give chase, or if he has already disappeared, set off to search nearby hiding places, like fields and ditches. In the last century the *ronda* might have been the primary apparatus for this capture, as it had a whole kit of tools whose special purpose was to stop a fleeing thief.[38] But nowadays the pursuers

---

[36] Theft in Indonesia is thus unlike kidnapping in the Philippines, as described by Carol Hau in this volume. As Hau pointedly shows, kidnapping presupposes that the object of "theft" is commodifiable, a fact victims must recognize when the demand for ransom is made. With ordinary theft, no such demand for ransom is made, so victims are free to interpret the event as they wish. In Indonesia, victims tend to tell stories not about the value of the thing lost, but about how thieves got in and out.

[37] As the police often knew which *modus operandi* was particular to which gang, they could immediately reduce their list of suspects to a couple of dozen people. As many of these as possible would then be hauled in to the police station and forced to reveal who was responsible.

[38] "The three implements which are seemingly indispensable for constabular use are the *bunday*, the *kumkum*, and the *toyah*. The first is a short pole, about four feet in length, upon the top of which are tied two pieces of wood, so placed as to meet in an acute angle, and open towards the ends, like the distended jaws of an alligator; the resemblance being made greater by the addition of dried stems of sharp thorns, tied on the two pieces of wood, and looking somewhat like rows of teeth. These effectually serve the purpose of detaining any runaway around who neck they are fixed, lacerating the flesh to a terrible extent should he offer the slightest resistance.

"The man into whose keeping the *bunday* is confided is called upon to act on the escape of the prisoner. In pursuing him he runs at full speed, endeavouring to fix the instrument round the neck waist, arm, or leg of the pursued, who, as soon as he feels the sharp thorns encircling his body, generally comes to a full stop. Should he prove, however, one of those determined ruffians who are dead to all feelings of pain, another instrument, the *kumkum*, is brought into play. This heavy-looking weapon, which is of a very formidable aspect, consists of a bar of iron in the shape of a small sword, attached to the top of a stave some five feet long. The third of these singular instruments is the *toyah*, which is as simple in its construction as the use to which it is put is novel. It is in the shape of a pitchfork, the points of which are purposely

include anyone who happens to be around to hear the shout. Once the thief has been captured, he is *dikeroyok* (swarmed), *digebuki* (pummeled), or in ex-convict slang, *digulung* (literally: defeated, eradicated). As Siegel has pointed out, what is important about this is that the thief's face or body show the marks of the beating.[39] The bruises and swelling are always mentioned in the stories told afterward. This marking is done not vicariously but directly by each person. As Ujog described it in the case presented above:

> When he would try to get up someone would come over and say "You're a thief, ya?" and then hit him again. By the end of it the thief's face was completely wrecked [*hancur*]. Everyone needs to get in a punch. In one neighborhood I lived, the treatment did not end there. The thief was then stripped and given a sign to wear that said "*saya maling*" [I'm a thief], and was paraded around the neighborhood for everyone to see.

What is the order restored by this beating? Siegel's book has already provided an extremely interesting response to this question. The Solo neighborhood's sense of "community," he argues, is expressed not through ties of kinship nor through shared economic interests, but through a shared concern with security. What people say distinguishes their neighborhood from others is that it is "a safe neighborhood, one that thieves are afraid to enter."[40] For residents, especially *ronda* guards, the figure of the thief thus provides a name for that which stands "outside" the neighborhood, for that which threatens the community. In beating the thief, the residents enact a way of relating to this outside world, a way of addressing it. Siegel compares the beating to a kind of language: whereas it is proper to speak low Javanese to one's neighbors and high Javanese to one's superiors, "it is proper to beat a thief."[41] In Solo then, what defines both security and neighborhood identity is adherence to the proper order, an order that is at once linguistic and hierarchical. By speaking to the thief in the proper way, the Solonese seek to restore the hierarchy that the thief had offended. The success of this restoration is achieved when the thief behaves in a way that in Javanese society indicates respect: he feels something (pain) that terror and respect make him hold back (he remains silent during the beating). He has, as they say, been "taught his lesson" (*kapok*).

In Bandung, a similar process is at work, but there is an important difference. Whereas in Solo, security is defined by adherence to a linguistic hierarchy, in Bandung it is defined by submission to territorial power. One can distinguish two

---

made blunt. This is certainly the most humane-looking of the three, and it is to be hoped therefore the one first tried against the delinquent. The object for which it is used is that of bringing the pursued down on his knees, and thus effectually stopping his further progress. This is accomplished by thrusting the open space between the prongs against the knee-joint— from the back of course—and so compelling the man by the force and suddenness of the attack, to make a genuflexion; the result of which is, that he becomes an easy prey to the pursuer. In the interior of some guardos there are some other weapons, or *sunjata*, such as the *tomba*, or long spear, but none of them so ludicrously novel as those I have just described." See D'Almeida, *Life in Java*, pp. 22-24.

[39] J. Siegel, *Solo in the New Order: Language and Hierarchy in an Indonesian City* (Princeton: Princeton University Press, 1986), p. 43.

[40] Ibid., p. 39.

[41] Ibid., p. 48.

moments in the act of beating. In the first moment, the naming of the thief is followed immediately by a punch. The thief is subjected to the word-punch. The purpose of this punch does not differ greatly from the purpose of striking the *kentongan* or clapping to startle someone who is daydreaming. It territorializes the thief, using pain to pull him back from a place outside normative sociality. In the second moment, the reaction of the body to the word-punch is evaluated by a spectator's eye that "jumps" back and forth between the bruise and the body and between the sign and the face.[42] The "success" of the word-punch at territorializing the body is evidenced by the bruised face, for the bruised face shows that the body can be marked. (It is, in fact, this mark-body relation, sensed by the jumping eye, that defines a territorial visibility).[43] What is "eliminated" in this beating is a body upon which a territorial mark did not take hold, in essence the possibility of failure in establishing a territorial relation. Replacing this feared non-territorial body is a body that is fully territorialized in two senses: it is fully occupied and it is marked by a territorial power (in being beaten and not cared for it is marked as coming from "outside"). Thus, as Siegel has shown, the beating of the thief is a gesture that simultaneously identifies the threat the thief represents and expels him from the community. But the "hierarchy" that is established in this process is not necessarily a hierarchy of speech levels. In Bandung, where neighborhoods are often linguistically heterogeneous, neighborhood security and identity are not synonymous with the maintenance of a distinction between speech levels. In linguistic terms, the most we could say is that the beating of the thief restores the possibility of language, for it emphasizes that the mark has significance.[44] What gives it significance is not language but territorial power. The beating of the thief is a demonstration of this power.

There are, consequently, fundamental differences between the spectacle of the thief's beating and the spectacle of surveillance described earlier. First, the capture of the thief is not a planned operation in anticipation of an official's visit but a rather spontaneous reaction to a disturbance. Second, the "elimination" of the thief is performed not for the eye of the ruler nor in front of an identifying or cynical public, but by the public itself. Each person gets his or her kick in and peers at the results. The social order constituted in this process is not a state defined order in which the creation of visibilities is mediated by the ruler, but is, rather, an order of mass participation. Finally, the relation of the two spectacles with regards to their respective threats is very different. The spectacle of surveillance presumes an image of order from the beginning, treating visible discrepancies from this order not as threats so much as eyesores. In doing so, however, surveillance hides the possibility

---

[42] On the the jumping eye, see G. Deleuze and F. Guatarri, *Anti-Oedipus: Capitalism and Schizophrenia* (London: The Athlone Press, 1984), p. 204.

[43] In this sense, it may have been a misnomer to call the visibilities created in the context of the *ronda* a mechanism of surveillance. For the eye of the *ronda* is a territorial eye: it differs in nature from the eye of state surveillance. The fragmented visibilities of the neighborhood pertain to territoriality not to surveillance.

[44] From the standpoint of my analysis, the hierarchy of speech levels would necessarily be a secondary elaboration of a territorially based hierarchy. Language can only begin where territoriality leaves off. Territoriality is the power that brings into relation a mark and a body. Language then uproots the mark and embeds it in a system of abstract differences, just as the *kentongan*'s music that was "just for fun" was uprooted and embedded in a system of signification.

that mediation will fail, that signs will be treated as empty of meaning (the empty crates). In a word, it hides territoriality. It does so because territoriality de-naturalizes the mediation the ruler's power depends on, always treating it as open to challenge. The territorial spectacle, in contrast, hides nothing. What it does is to eliminate the possibility of a body on which territoriality cannot express itself.[45]

JAWARA

If the thief exemplifies a figure that searches for the weakness of a territory, the figure that exemplifies a challenge to the territory is what the press, public, and police in Bandung refer to as the *preman*, and what inmates from the local prison call the *jawara*.[46] As the inmates describe it, the *jawara* is someone who originates in provincial villages and towns (*daerah*), making a name for himself there before moving into the big city. He can be young or old, large or small, but he frequently sports tattoos ("*otat* ")[47] and is said to be *kebal*. Upon arrival in Bandung the *jawara* picks a site to "plant his flag" (*mendirikan benderanya*), usually the *alun-alun* (central square), a bus terminal, the train station, a market, or some other location with lots of commercial traffic. He finds out which *jawara* controls that area already and then challenges him to a duel (*jantan*). The duel usually involves the use of hand weapons, such as *golok* ("*ulak goman*" [machete]), samurai swords, knives ("*sikim*"), and *clurit*

---

[45] From the standpoint of many thieves and some police officers, however, the association of the *maling* with a non-territorial body is not justified. For in fact, the act of theft is precisely an expression of the thief's form of territoriality. It is just that this territoriality is not defined in terms of a plot of land, but instead in terms of technique. One of Bandung's celebrated cases of theft illustrates this point. During the colonial period someone would periodically break into the most secure houses, banks, and vaults in the city, usually taking nothing, but leaving behind a chisel. At that time, Bandung had its first *pribumi* ("native") police commissioner. None of the Dutch police could make headway in determining who was responsible for these embarrassing acts. But the commissioner realized that the thefts were taking place only on a particular day of the Javanese calendar and by consulting a divination manual he determined when the thief would strike next. On the night in question he set up roadblocks in the city and succeeded in catching the man responsible. Upon interrogation, the man explained that he performed these thefts not in order to take anything but because he had inherited *ilmu* from his father that had to be put to use on particular days or it would be lost forever. The *ilmu* just happened to be that used for breaking in and out of secure buildings. Thus, in this case the territorial relation is not defined in terms of a spirit and a body, or an owner and a plot of land, but between a technique and a line of descent. Only by caring for this relation, by regularly putting into use the inheritance from his father, could misfortune be avoided. Perhaps understanding this dilemma, the police commisioner arranged to have the man's son sent to be schooled outside of Java, far from his father's influences. As it turned out, however, the boy and his parents died shortly after. This case is described in H. Kunto, *Semerbak Bunga di Bandung Raya* (Bandung: Granesia, 1986), pp. 353-358; and S. Kolopaking, *Tjoret-tjoretan Pengalaman Sepandjang Masa* (Jogjakarta: Balai Pembinaan Administrasi, 1969), pp. 29-41.
  Unlike this thief and the police commissioner who understood him, however, the neighborhood community as such cannot recognize this other form of territorial relation. For the community the thief represents only a non-territorial body, the ultimate threat. To address this threat the community territorializes thieves and labels them outsiders.

[46] The term *preman* is sometimes used to refer to any ex-convict or criminal, or to mean civilian, but these are not the senses in which I use it here.

[47] The terms enclosed in inverted commas are those used by the inmates. They are *basa okem*, or *preman* language.

("*CR*" [sickle]). The name of the winner of the duel circulates so people know who it is that "owns that area" (*punya daerah situ*), who it is that must be respected (*disegani*).

In owning an area, the *jawara* establishes or takes over the right to collect on the debt that people have simply by virtue of living or doing business there. This debt is resolved by paying to the *jawara* a percentage of any commercial activity that takes place in his territory. People who operate businesses in the area pay protection money, transportation vehicles pay a fee for the use of the roads, parking attendants pay a portion of their income, street vendors pay a rent. Even pickpockets who successfully extract a wallet from passersby through the area feel obliged to pay the *jawara* a tenth of their take, even though the *jawara* is not their boss. The money that is collected is called tribute (*upeti*) or "*japrem*" (*jatah preman*: *preman*'s allotment) and is generally collected not by the *jawara* himself, but by his underlings (*anak buah* or "*kronco*"). Indeed, tribute is the right name for it: it is the fee paid under duress for the right to live or do business in the *jawara's* domain.

The people most frequently targeted for this fee are people deemed to be foreign in some sense. As they are not considered "natives" of the land, their debt to the territory is all the greater. This is especially so for the "Chinese," as they are both outsiders and deeply dependent on local business. But *pribumi* ("native") too can be considered foreign to a territory. The following story, drawn from statements to the police by both a mugging victim and a suspect, provide an impression of how basic this orientation is, especially for small time *preman*:

> At first me and Dani went out for a ride on a motorcycle. When we were finished we headed home by way of Veteran street but were caught in the rain. So we stopped and took shelter at the scene of the crime, and as we were sheltering there at the side of the road, a person called Idang showed up and asked us something and stood by our motorcycle. Then he disappeared and returned shortly with Ewit who asked Dani, "What are you up to?," to which we replied we were taking shelter. They then introduced themselves and asked where we were from, and "Do you like to use drugs or not?," to which we answered no, and then they offered us cigarettes but we said we had some. Then they advised us not to take shelter there because it is dangerous with lots of drunk people so you could be taxed. They advised us to move the motorcycle into the alley, at which point we became suspicious and Dani immediately started the motorcycle and invited me to go but I couldn't cause Ewit already had me in a strangle hold. [His wallet is then stolen.]

Ewit describes what Idang does after first seeing the two guys:

> Idang came to my house and invited me to go out and explained that there were two strangers [*orang asing*] taking shelter on Veteran street. Then he suggested we tax them, saying: "Urang pajek we" [Sundanese: Let's just tax them], so with that intention I grabbed my Carter knife, and we went out . . .[48]

---

[48] POLRI, Polsek Lengkong police report number LP41iii1994 (Bandung: unpublished, 1994), p. 2x.

Like the *ronda* guards, these *preman* take a special interest in strangers. For the *preman*, however, strangers are not so much a threat as an opportunity; in this case an opportunity to collect rent (on the shelter, as it were). This despite the fact that the "strangers" in the above case are *pribumi* who live just a kilometer away from where they were mugged.

For the *jawara*, the territory is defined very much in terms of land. One might think then that his power would be limited to things like "taking shelter" and so forth. But what is impressive about the *jawara* is his ability to territorialize any activity that passes through his domain. No matter how deterritorialized the activity is, he always manages to find the points at which it must locate itself within his domain, and he uses these moments as his leverage for extracting tribute. Even forms of commerce that are "national" in character, or are in the hands of multinationals, cannot avoid dealing with him. For example, the expansion of the telephone system, an activity that obeys a logic of blueprints, capital, and bureaucratic power, and which treats territories only as nodes in a web of relays, is territorialized by the *jawara* at two points: public phones and cable installation. When the man comes to collect coins from the pay phone, he is charged a "parking fee" that amounts to a significant percentage of the income from the phone. Similarly, when Telkom wants to lay down cables in an area, these cables will be tampered with if a fee is not paid.

While the *jawara* is a territorial power in a spatial sense (i.e., the aspect of land transactions that involved a new resident actually moving in rather than simply the legal transfer of a title), he is also territorial in the more general sense described above. That is, he occupies his territory, developing relationships with its elements and taking care of them. If one of his underlings is detained by the police, it is the *jawara* who pays the bribe to spring him. If one of the businesses he extracts tribute from is bothered by someone, it is the *jawara* who comes forward to offer protection. This is why the public's relation to him is always somewhat ambivalent. On the one hand, the *jawara* is resented for the extra economic burden he places on people, but on the other hand, there is always an attempt to keep up good relations with him.[49]

In sum, the *jawara* takes over a territory by challenging it. Like the large-bodied *kentongan*, he subordinates households and businesses to his encompassing domain of authority and presence. Because he "owns" the area, anyone who passes through, lives, or does business in it is forced to acknowledge his presence, often by paying a rent. This rent is all the higher for people deemed not to be natives of the area.

One of the few jobs open to *jawara* after they have served time in prison is as security guards, often for Chinese businessmen. Yet even as hired hands they retain a certain independence from their boss. One land baron I visited used *preman* for guards. When I arrived they blocked my path, looked me up and down, and barked "*Yu mau ke siapa?*" (Who do you think you're coming to see?), followed by some questions about my business there. They then escorted me into their boss's house,

---

[49] The following comments by *pedagang kaki lima* (pushcart trader) about *preman* in Tanah Abang, Jakarta, are typical: "To sell here you really have to be good at dealing with *preman*. If they already know you, they don't ask for too much, and not every day. And there is an advantage to having them around. Now no pickpockets have the guts to operate here." Or, "If we are good to them, they don't hassle us. People say that they used to be quite tough. They used to order one of their underlings to collect protection money. If it wasn't given then the seller would be called or taken to the back of the market and be beaten up." See A. Purwanto and M. Subroto, "Kalau Preman yang Dituding," *Detektif & Romantika* 25/28 (Febuary 8, 1997), p. 34.

always staying close and emphasizing how much space they took up. As I frequently visited the house, I found it useful to spend time getting to know them. While it was possible to become "friends" with them, it was an odd kind of friendship, punctuated by occasional challenges and threats. With their boss it was clear that when it came to questions of territory (i.e. the physical side of land transactions rather than the legal one), it was they who told him what to do. Also, if they felt a guest was acting unreasonably toward their boss, they would shout at the guest without taking note of whether or not their boss had been offended. Their boss was their territory, and any threat to him was a threat to them.

For all his independence, however, the *jawara* is not necessarily a free man (*prijman*). Precisely because he is so good at keeping a grip on an area and extracting tribute, he is often a necessary component in the maintenance of state power and the collection of taxes.[50] In recent years, the relation of *preman* to the state has usually been expressed as one of *"bekking "* or *"dekking"* (backing), which refers to the way in which *preman* receive protection from members of the Armed Forces in return for regular payments of rent (*setoran*).[51] There are some *preman* who have such *bekking*, and others who do not. Thus, like the *ronda-kentongan*, the *jawara* or *preman* may tend toward independence from the state or may be "deterritorialized" and put into the service of the state.

SISTEM KEAMANAN LINGKUNGAN

Until the late 1970s, the *ronda* and the *preman* (or *preman*-like security guards) were the central forms of local security in Bandung. On the surface at least, the advent of *siskamling* appears to have changed this. The *ronda* is now much less common than the HANSIP, and almost all government and commercial buildings are kept secure by SATPAM.[52] Indeed, in less than twenty years, both HANSIP and SATPAM guards have become central characters in urban culture, both in everyday life and in television shows set in the city.

The economic backdrop for this change was the wave of industrialization and commercial growth that swept Indonesia in the 1970s. On the one hand, this meant a deepening penetration of the cash economy, making the non-paid *ronda* a bit of an anachronism. On the other hand, banks, factories, malls, chain restaurants, and housing complexes sprouted up everywhere, squeezing out old *kampungs* and local businesses. Accompanying the emergence of these new commercial spaces was a

---

[50] The history of the *jago* in the context of the colonial state and monopoly capitalism has been treated beautifully by J. Rush, *Opium to Java: Revenue Farming and Chinese Enterprise in Colonial Indonesia, 1860-1910* (Ithaca: Cornell University Press, 1990). See also the insightful analyses of Schulte Nordholt, "The *jago* in the shadow," and Onghokham, "The Inscrutable and the Paranoid: An Investigation into the Sources of the Brotodiningrat Affair," in *Southeast Asian Transitions: Approaches Through Social History*, ed. Ruth T. McVey (New Haven: Yale University Press, 1978), pp. 112-157.

[51] Superficially, this relation seems to replicate the *preman*'s relation to businesses in his area. But it is not so simple. The military brings into play a whole other power, that of Office/Rank, which differs from both territoriality and surveillance. An analysis of this relation is thus beyond the scope of this paper.

[52] To give some idea of the numbers involved: In the police district I studied there was a population of seventy-one people. They had eighty-three *pos kamling*, 240 SATPAM, and eighty HANSIP. The police sector itself had just fifty-two officers.

growth in private security services which often used military and *preman*-type characters for personnel, a development that caused the government some concern. Moreover, the increase in commercial activity provided *preman* with new sources of income and increased power.[53]

The introduction of *siskamling* was an attempt by the New Order government to impose state control over local security practices. It was an off-shoot of a larger government program, called KOPKAMTIB (Operations Command for the Return of Security and Order, or Komando Pemulihan Keamanan dan Ketertiban), which aimed to increase military control over local populations.[54] Unlike KOPKAMTIB, however, *siskamling* was not targeting political opponents so much as *preman* power. As the founder of *siskamling*, Awaloedin Djamin, described it, "We definitely did not want to have the same thing happen in Indonesia that happened in other countries. In Japan, for example, the Yakuza forced protection on business people. Such a situation can give rise to excesses that are difficult to overcome. The same was true in the early days of the mafia in the United States."[55] Preventing the growth of non-state security services entailed two strategies: efforts to subject security guards to surveillance, and efforts to make surveillance, rather than territoriality, the principle of urban security. Such strategies were not new, as state surveillance had long been trying to find a way to subvert and dominate territoriality. But the case of *siskamling* provides an unusually clear example of just what the limits of surveillance are when it comes up against a tradition of territoriality.

The first thing *siskamling* did was to provide a new framework for thinking about urban security.[56] Within this framework, the security of commercial and public buildings was made comparable to the security of neighborhoods. The basis for the comparability was the similarity between the SATPAM and the HANSIP, both of

---

[53] In public consciousness, at least, the late 1970s and early 1980s are remembered as the peak of *preman* power.

[54] KOPKAMTIB was a product of the 1965 failed coup. It was an operation first headed by Soeharto, and later by Soemitro and Sudomo, the aim of which was to eliminate the communist threat and to return national security and order. It was known for its abuses of power. Soeharto disbanded KOPKAMTIB in 1988.

[55] A. Djamin, *Pengalaman Seorang Perwira POLRI* (Jakarta: Pustaka Sinar Harapan, 1995), p. 240.

[56] The key word in *sistem keamanan lingkungan* is *aman*, the Indonesian term for secure. *Aman*, however, has a slightly different set of connotations than does the equivalent English term. It is used to refer to a state of affairs in which a thing, place, or person is untouchable rather than fixed in place. It is thus often better translated as safe. For example, building a high fence that prevents people from constantly visiting one's house makes one feel *aman*. The opposite of a neighborhood that is *aman* is one that is *rawan*. *Rawan* means both an unsafe area and a state of affairs in which emotions are easily touched or disturbed. The opposite of feeling secure is feeling *takut* or fearful. Like the English term "secure," *aman* thus has both a physical and a psychological frame of reference. Unlike the English term, however, *aman* cannot refer to economic or social security.

That *aman* refers to a state of untouchability is even clearer when the root is transformed into a transitive verb: *mengamankan*. This term is used most frequently by the police and the military to describe the act of making secure, in the sense that something or someone has been removed or separated from its former setting. A criminal or an inciter of a riot, for example, has been made secure when he or she has been captured and placed in a cell. Liquor and illegal weapons are also made secure (confiscated) by the police. *Keamanan*, or safety/security, is used both as a qualifier for agents of security and as a noun in its own right. "Call security," for example, is *"Panggil keamanan"* (*sekuriti* is also used in this sense).

which are salaried and uniformed guards. The *ronda*, a far older institution, entered into this *sistem* as just another way of organizing neighborhood *sekuriti*, with the same functions as the HANSIP.

What makes *siskamling* differ from prior attempts to subject local security to a regime of surveillance is that the model originated with the police, rather than from local government. Consequently, its systems of language and light unfold not through the administrative structure of the RT and RW, so much as through the division of the police responsible for the "Guidance of Society" (*Bimbingan Masyarakat*, or BIMMAS).[57] These systems take a variety of forms. The *pos kamling* are now counted, inspected, and classified according to their facilities. It is noted, for example, what building type the *pos* has, and whether it has weapons, maps, flashlights, or beds, for instance. Based on this information, the police then work together with HANSIP and *ronda* guards to improve the facilities by making recommendations to the heads of RTs and RWs (it is they who must find a way to pay for improvements, salaries, and other responsibilities). In some *pos kamling* one now finds maps of the area, lists of important residents, lists of *residivis*, and rules for the patrols. These visual cues and guidelines mimic those found at the local police station. Similarly, the *pos keamanan* that is usually to be found in the parking lot or lobby of commercial establishments is subject to similar monitoring, and recommendations are made to SATPAM employers if facilities are found to be lacking in any essential respects.

It is not just facilities that are subject to surveillance. SATPAM and HANSIP guards are also counted and classified according to the education and training they have received. Frequently they receive training directly from BIMMAS. There are three month and one month training courses provided for SATPAM by the police, and more than half of SATPAM guards in Bandung have attended these. Such courses amount mostly to military training, combined with some advice about how to make reports to the police and what procedure to follow when one catches a thief. While the HANSIP does not have such a specialized training course, in principle its members gather with those of the SATPAM once a week at the police station for training (in practice not so often). Moreover, both sets of salaried guards are "controlled" on a regular basis by members of BIMMAS at their posts. On these informal occasions, the police gather information about threats for their intelligence reports and give advice to the SATPAM and HANSIP guards.

To distinguish them from ordinary civilians, SATPAM and HANSIP guards wear standardized uniforms and carry identification issued by the police. The SATPAM's uniform consists of black pants and a smart white shirt with logos on the arms and a label on the front saying "SATPAM," while the HANSIP uniform is comparable but army green in color. Such paraphernalia are objects of pride for the guards. When I visited the home of one *satpam* who lived in a village an hour and half from his Bandung office, I noticed that his certificate of graduation from the one month SATPAM course was prominently displayed on his wall. When I pointed it out, he took it down and proudly showed me the photo of himself on it and the signature of the supervising police official.

For HANSIP guards, the question of official recognition is most apparent during the provincial competitions for best *pos kamling*. These competitions are spectacles in

---

[57] In addition to its work with *siskamling*, BIMMAS is also involved in training and working with youth groups.

which police brass inspect the posts, rank them, and provide prizes to the most exemplary posts. In one neighborhood in which I lived, the *hansip* talked about this for a couple of weeks before the event. The year before they had won only second prize, which they attributed to the fact that the *pos* was complete except that it still had no toilet. To prepare for the upcoming inspection the *pos* was repainted and cleaned up, and banners extolling *siskamling* were hung out. On the day of the visit the guards wore smart uniforms and shiny boots. On this particular occasion the officials did not end up coming, to the great disappointment of the *hansip*. After a little while, the banners were taken down and things returned to normal.

Thus, local security is itself one of the primary targets of state surveillance under the *siskamling*. The *pos kamling* and its guards are categorized and entered into a whole system of tables, charts, and regulations. In addition, they are entered into a system of light in which the *pos kamling* and the guards' uniforms appear in all their cleanliness before the eye of the visiting official. This spectacle, however, is not one of elimination, as it was with the steamrolling of *becak* and pushcarts, but of recognition. The prize in this case goes to the best image of "after."

The *ronda* is only exposed to these forces indirectly. Although it is entered into the *sistem* (by being noted in the police data books), BIMMAS usually does not examine the guards directly, but focuses instead on the RT or RW official in charge of the *ronda*'s organization. This official is provided with guidance about how best to administer the *ronda*, what equipment should be provided, and so forth. The rotational character of personnel participation in the *ronda* makes any more direct involvement with the guards too difficult.

In addition to making local security an object of state surveillance, the *siskamling* takes a number of steps toward making surveillance the basis for practices of local security. Unlike the *ronda*, for example, the *hansip* and the *satpam* are permanent, salaried workers. The *hansip*'s salary is paid by the residents of the area he patrols, whereas the *satpam*'s salary is paid by his or her business's boss. In both cases the guards usually live outside the area they patrol, coming in only for nightly or daily shifts. In principle, such an organization of neighborhood security could lead to the HANSIP becoming a kind of police force, with control over visibilities being separated from the community and concentrated in the eyes of guards trained and certified by the state. And indeed one can identify a tendency in this direction. HANSIP guards can often be heard complaining about residents' lack of discipline in locking up or keeping gates closed in a way that *ronda* guards would not be heard complaining. Also, HANSIP guards treat strangers in much the same way as police officers would. But unlike the police they never give orders to residents or institute operations on local visibilities. In large part, this is because they are employed directly by the community members. Each month they are painfully reminded of their dependency as they must themselves knock on each door in the neighborhood, soliciting contributions to their salary. In this regard they differ fundamentally from the police.

For the *satpam*, the situation is different. *Satpam* are hired by a boss to monitor the comings and goings of strangers (customers, guests, etc.) and to monitor other employees. They are never placed in a position in which they have to ask for money from the people under surveillance. Consequently, *satpam* often have a very different stance toward the public than do *hansip*. In factories, for instance, they frequently take the liberty of body-searching workers as they leave, in order to insure nobody is stealing materials or products. In some government and corporate buildings all people who enter must write their identity in a book along with the time they enter and leave. Sometimes they are made to wear a badge that identifies them and the floor they are going to. In these respects, *satpam* are far more likely to create and appropriate identities and visibilities than are *hansip*.

If on a formal level *siskamling* has functioned to segment and categorize urban spaces, to assign them particular types of security personnel, and to bring them under the control of the police, on an informal level territoriality persists to a striking degree. We have already seen a number of examples of this: the power of *kebal identitas*, like a Harley Davidson club membership, to withstand the police's demand to see a state identity card; the tendency of people to interpret the category of *eks-PKI* not as an abstract identity but as a brand or *cap*; the prevalence of self-defense schools that emphasize territorial power and perception rather than purely "physical" fighting skills; the failure of spectacles of surveillance to establish the public's identification with the eye of the ruler. Other examples of persisting territorializing forces are found in the day-to-day interactions people have with their local *satpam* or *hansip*. Employees at banks, for example, are careful to acknowledge the *satpam* when they enter the office each day, exchanging a few words even if they do not have to "report." Students at the Bandung Institute of Technology go further, establishing relations of debt with their *satpam* by providing him with training in computers in return for being allowed to stay in college buildings through the night, an activity that is in violation of campus rules. In doing so, they show their *satpam* the same type of respect they would a *preman*, and they expect the same protection in return.

In all these examples, what distinguishes practices of surveillance from those of territoriality is the role played by mediation. With surveillance, mediation always occurs in advance of an encounter, predefining the terms in which the encounter will take place. Exactly what form the mediation takes varies; it may be that people are expected to see spectacles through the eye of the ruler, that they are expected to pay security guards through the intermediary of the state, or that they are expected to recognize individual identities through systems of meaning established in police files. Whatever form mediation takes, however, surveillance always locates it ouside the sphere of encounter and naturalizes its power to define the terms under which encounters take place. Territoriality, in contrast, knows nothing of externally defined power relations. Power is only meaningful insofar as it is directly present in the encounter. Its legitmacy is not derived from some outside authority but is based on evidence of force. There is thus a kind of immediacy in territorial practices that practices of surveillance lack: the immediacy of a power that challenges as opposed to one that presents power relations as natural and always already achieved.

* * *

If there is anything that could be called a culture of security in late New Order Bandung, it is the constant battle between surveillance and territoriality. Surveillance works on territoriality by hiding it and segmenting it. It boxes territoriality in, creating smaller and smaller domains within which it is allowed to operate. As with the deterritorialized *kentongan*, it then seeks to establish mechanisms for bringing these discrete domains into a larger *sistem*, thus making them of service to the state in the process. Territoriality, in contrast, always seeks the moments at which surveillance must touch down, the moments at which mediation can be short-circuited and power localized. It treats *eks*-PKI not as a category but as a *cap*, and the thief not as a criminal but as something less than human. In doing so, it denaturalizes the power of surveillance, challenging the ruler to do battle in territorial terms.

In large part, it is this battle that makes living in late New Order Bandung so interesting and so oppressive. For just as surveillance has caused instruments and representatives of the state to appear in almost every setting, so too has territoriality made these appearances feel unnatural, like something of an intrusion. The result is a world where power can never be forgotten, where it is always "in your face." For agents of the state, such a situation poses a dilemma, for it is never nice to be thought of as an intrusion. Nowhere is this dilemma clearer than in the *hansip*, the figure of neighborhood security who wears a uniform required by the police, but who must ask the community for the money to pay for those very same uniforms.

In early December 1996, just before a series of anti-Chinese and anti-government riots broke out in West Java, I happened to be home when the local *hansip* came to collect his dues. As usual, he came with his clipboard, which had a letter from the head of the RT verifying that the request for money was legitimate. He could have asked me to read the letter, or pointed to the authorizing signature of the *kepala* RT, as he sometimes did. Instead, when I opened the gate, he pushed the clipboard at me, pointing to the sum I owed. When I invited him into the yard to have a seat while I found the money, he just stood there rigidly on his side of the gate. When I returned with the money, I passed it to him with a bow of my head, which he acknowledged with a nod. He then turned around and, without saying anything, went on to the next house. The *hansip* and I, in this case, defined neighborhood security not as surveillance but as territoriality. The payment was not a salary but the payment of a debt, like the *japrem* paid to a *preman*. As in Ujog's story, the territorial ghost had made its appearance, and when it did, it took the form of a *hansip*. For Ujog, this appearance was reassuring, because it meant his house was secure from thieves. For me, however, as a foreigner in the neighborhood, it was more than a little disconcerting.

"WHO WILL SAVE US FROM THE 'LAW'?": THE CRIMINAL STATE AND THE ILLEGAL ALIEN IN POST-1986 PHILIPPINES[1]

Caroline S. Hau

In the December 1995 issue of the Chinese Filipino news digest *Tulay* (literally, "bridge"), Jacqueline Co related the following anecdote: "Two years ago [i.e., in 1993]," she wrote, "I asked a University of the Philippines [UP] graduate student if she was bothered by the spate of kidnapping in the country. Her response was, 'No, because I am not Chinese and I am not rich.'"[2] The UP student's response is a disturbing, albeit relatively mild, version of what is by now a truism about the economic prominence and visibility of the Chinese in the Philippines, a truism that seems to be empirically validated by media coverage since the late eighties of the more spectacular cases of kidnap-for-ransom.

These cases come to our attention already mediated by a narrative that features such well-worn storyline conventions as the exchange of huge sums of ransom money, a rogue's gallery of cops and military personnel, shootouts between government forces and kidnap gangs, and the accidental or deliberate killing of kidnap victims. The UP student's unassailable belief that the Chinese are rich and are therefore the "proper" victims of kidnapping appears to partake of the same general distancing move that characterizes the media reportage of the events themselves, with its clearcut demarcations of "us and them," spectator and spectacle, subject and object, Chinese and Filipino. This demarcation is perhaps most forcefully exemplified by yet another truistic attribute of the Chinese, that of its relative cohesiveness as a

[1] I lifted the quote in this title from the title of an editorial on the theme "*Quies custodiet custodies* [Who will guard the guardians]?" which appeared in the *Philippines Free Press*, September 5, 1992, pp. 1-2.

I thank Pheng Cheah and Professors Benedict Anderson, Daniel Lev, Rudolf Mrázek, Vicente Rafael, John Sidel, and James Siegel for their comments on earlier drafts of this paper. The shortcomings of this essay are my responsibility alone.

[2] Jacqueline Co, "'Democracy' At Work in Crime," *Tulay*, December 4, 1995, p. 7.

social body, the state within the state that *is* the Chinese community.[3] In the last ten years, however, the enclave has seemingly broken out of its internal borders (to use Fichte's term) and taken over the *fin de siècle* urbanscape. A report in the *New York Times* explains the connection between space, visibility, and extortion: "[t]he highly visible role of the Chinese in Philippine economic growth—the Chinese-owned shopping malls and high rises that are transforming Manila—have made them obvious targets of extraction."[4]

The tenacity of deeply held beliefs about "Chinese capital" largely determines the kind of responses available to ethnic Chinese like Co when they deal publicly with the kidnapping issue. One strategy has been to emphasize the fact that the Chinese are not the only victims of kidnap-for-ransom, the goal being to disentangle the identification of "Chinese" ethnicity with the capitalist class. Co goes on in the rest of her article, for example, to argue that the kidnappers, instead of preying exclusively on the members of the ethnic Chinese community, *as is universally believed*, are now more "democratic" in their choice of victims. This is supposedly evident in the fact that recent demographics of kidnap victims appear to have cut across class, racial, and geographic lines. Co's argument implicitly stresses that kidnapping is no longer a "Chinese" problem because it has become, indeed *should* be considered, "everybody's problem."[5]

In this paper, I present some preliminary observations concerning the nature of a specific type of response that "Chinese Filipinos" such as Jacqueline Co have formulated to address the kidnap-for-ransom of ethnic Chinese in the Philippines. Kidnapping, of course, remains a timely and persistent issue in Philippine politics, in light of statistics that indicate a record high for kidnapping incidents in 1996. In his *Ulat sa Bayan* (State of the Nation Report) early in 1997, in fact, Fidel Ramos acknowledged for the umpteenth time his administration's failure to curb the rampant criminality that has "lacerated Philippine civil society" and pledged to devote the last eighteen months of his incumbency to solving the problem.[6] Co's arguments about the democratization of crime notwithstanding, a large number of the most successful and spectacular cases of kidnapping, both in terms of the amount

---

[3] The metaphor of a Chinese state within the state can clearly be seen in a series of articles on the internal politics of the Federation of Filipino-Chinese Chambers of Commerce and Industry, Inc., written by Robert C. Villanueva at the height of the kidnapping crisis. See his "Big Trouble in Little China," *Philippines Free Press*, May 8, 1993, pp. 14-15, 47; "The Chinese (Near) Exodus," *Philippines Free Press*, July 3, 1993, pp. 38-39; and "Secrets of the Federation," *Philippines Free Press*, January 8, 1994, pp. 23-24.

[4] Seth Mydans, "Kidnapping of Ethnic Chinese Rises in the Philippines," *The New York Times*, March 17, 1996, p. 3.

[5] "The exclusive club the kidnap and other crime victims belong to has been democratized by sheer numbers. Few people will still think that kidnapping is a Chinese community problem if they read the latest statistics." Co, "'Democracy' At Work in Crime," p. 7.

[6] Carlito Pablo, "Kidnapping worst in '96; 241 abducted," *Philippine Daily Inquirer*, January 7, 1997, pp. 1, 7. The report also noted that twenty-nine people were kidnapped (about one victim a day) in November 1996, the same month that the Philippines hosted the Asia-Pacific Economic Cooperation summit in Subic. The figures are based on reports by two civic groups, the Movement for the Restoration of Peace and Order and Citizens Action Against Crime. The total amount of ransom money that year has been conservatively pegged at ninety-nine million pesos. The statistics were provided by the Movement for the Restoration of Peace and Order and the Citizens Action Against Crime in their joint press conference on October 31, 1996.

of ransom paid and the death of the victims, have involved, and continue to involve, the ethnic Chinese.[7] This paper, then, attempts to look into the ways in which kidnapping historically articulates the specific conflation of ethnicity and class that casts the Chinese as "obvious" and "proper" targets of extraction. It also aims to examine the assumptions that inform the specific responses of the ethnic Chinese to kidnapping. My main intention is to highlight the implications that these assumptions have for our ability to think beyond our commonsensical notions of the state, nation, and economy.

What interests me about Co's article is not whether her argument about democratic victimization is valid, but whether Co was really saying something else when she made the argument. I shall thus begin by analyzing the language in which ethnic[8] Chinese like Co have framed their responses to kidnapping.

Co's implicit message that kidnapping is no longer a "Chinese community problem" has two intended audiences: the Filipino public and the Philippine state. Her message tries to engage the public and the state in an interlocutory relation. The content of this dialogue between the Chinese and the Filipino public and state draws substantially, at least on the part of the Chinese, on the discourse of citizenship and rights. If kidnapping constitutes a kind of resistance to the juridically defined notion that citizens are equally subject to the same law,[9] it does not come as a surprise that attempts on the part of the Chinese to formulate a position against kidnapping have built the force and logic of their argument on the invocation of citizenship and rights which kidnapping abrogates (the right to freedom, equality, security, and property, for example). Co's argument that kidnapping is and should be treated as "everybody's problem," for instance, imagines the possibility that every Filipino, and not just every Chinese, is a potential victim of the kidnap-for-ransom crimes. The argument urges all Filipinos to seek a solution to the problem and ultimately expects the proper response from the state. This kind of generalization widens the political scope of responsibility to include all Filipinos and thereby "depoliticizes" the issue by unraveling the identification of kidnapping with the Chinese. But such a depoliticizing generalization also creates, paradoxically, a venue for politicizing *specific* rights-claims, in this case, the rights-claims of Chinese Filipinos. In other words, the point at which kidnapping becomes everybody's problem serves at one and the same time to call attention to the way in which kidnapping has abrogated the specific rights to freedom and equality of the Chinese Filipinos. This paradox also underlies the contradictions of most public responses to kidnapping, which oscillate

---

[7] To give an example: in August 1996, realtor and construction magnate Benito Co Uy-Gam was released by his kidnappers after his family paid the ransom money, believed to be at least thirty million pesos. The most well-known cases include high school student Charlene Mayne Sy, who died in a shootout between her abductors and government forces at the EDSA-Quezon Boulevard junction in January 1993, and college students Kenneth Go and Myron Uy Ramos, who were tortured and killed by their captors in September 1992. Since 1991, more than fifty-eight people have died in the hands of their abductors, or in shootouts between the kidnap gangs and government forces.

[8] I am using the term "ethnic Chinese" in an inclusive way to refer to residents of the Philippines who identify themselves as Chinese or as Chinese Filipino, regardless of their citizenship.

[9] The link between kidnapping and citizenship was first suggested to me by Vicente Rafael when he discussed a paper about political representation and the formation of the Chinese community in the Philippines which I had presented at the Association for Asian Studies Conference in Honolulu, Hawaii in April, 1996.

between claiming that kidnapping is an "equal-opportunity menace"[10] and noting "a form of nationalism" at work in the kidnapping of the Chinese.[11]

The timing of the Chinese responses is a crucial element in accounting for these responses. It is no coincidence that the Chinese Filipinos began "speaking out" as individuals and, more importantly, as a community on the issue of kidnapping at about the same time that the media began carrying reports about the "entry" of the ethnic Chinese into politics.[12] To be sure, this is not the first time that the Chinese have involved themselves in politics. Fifty years ago in the presidential election campaign of 1946, for example, nearly one thousand Chinese led by Huang Jie and Li Yongxiao, noted leftist resistance leaders, participated in a mass demonstration on September 23, 1945 against Manuel Roxas, whom they denounced as a collaborator. The political action of the Chinese, however, was regarded by some Filipino politicians as "unwarranted interference in the internal affairs of the Philippines."[13] As the editorial of *The Manila Post* put it: "The Chinese can advance no justification for butting into the Philippine collaborationism question, or into any of our domestic affairs, for that matter. In passing judgment on our congress, the Chinese have stepped over the heads of the Filipino people who had elected their people to congress, the Filipino people who are the only legitimate critics of the officials they have willed into office."[14]

What makes the present situation of the Chinese different from that of the leftists in 1945 is that the Chinese criticism of the Philippine government today can no longer be seen to warrant the same kind of dismissive response from the Filipino politician. In claiming citizenship[15] and the right to politics, the present Chinese are saying that they are no longer speaking to the state as Chinese, but as Chinese Filipinos, *both* Chinese and Filipino. For these second-, third-, and fourth-generation "Tsinoys" (from *Tsino* and *Pinoy*, Tagalog words for Chinese and Filipino, respectively), speaking out, sometimes critically, is part of the universal right to politics to which they are entitled as citizens of the Philippines.

The terminological shift from Chinese to Chinese Filipino, however, is telling in another sense, since it indicates an attempt on the part of self-identified Chinese Filipinos to distance themselves both temporally and conceptually from the politics of the 1945 Chinese. The claim to citizenship is a claim *against* a certain kind of "Chinese," a Chinese who can identify with the Filipinos without being one of them, a Chinese who is *neither* one nor the other, a Chineseness that admits the possibility of contamination and demands that we rethink our commonsensical notions of borders and boundaries, our experience of home and of nation, of the economy and

---

[10] J. P. Saspa, "Welcome to Kidnap Town—Again," *Philippines Free Press*, September 9, 1995, p. 10.

[11] "Why Chinese Only?," *Philippines Free Press*, October 3, 1992, p. 20.

[12] Joaquin Sy, "Tsinoy sa Pulitika," *Tulay*, June 5, 1995, pp. 10-11. See also Evelyn Cullamar's discussion of Ephraim Areno's paper on ethnic Chinese political participation in Iloilo in her "Hua Qiao's Long Road to Being Filipinos," *Tulay*, November 20, 1995, p. 9.

[13] Antonio Tan, *The Chinese in the Philippines During the Japanese Occupation, 1942-1945* (Quezon City: University of the Philippines Press, 1981), pp. 113-114.

[14] Quoted in Yuk-wai Yung Li, *The Huaqiao Warriors: Chinese Resistance Movement in the Philippines, 1942-1945* (Quezon City: Ateneo de Manila University Press, 1996), p. 170.

[15] This claim to citizenship was made historically possible by the mass naturalization of the Chinese under the Marcos regime in 1975.

of politics, on the eve of Philippine "independence."[16] This Chinese exceeds the juridical bounds of a *jus sanguinis* citizenship that tries to neutralize or domesticate the (often secret) immigrant, either by criminalizing him or her as an illegal alien or—and this amounts to the same thing—by "naturalizing" him or her as a citizen. This Chinese exposes the fact that the extremes of rejection and absorption both imply a refusal of difference as well as a denial of the necessary violence of institutional exclusion that founds any political community. I will return to this point in the concluding section of the paper.

In claiming membership in the body of citizens, the Chinese Filipinos are in effect attempting to exorcise a concept of the political by reducing it to a matter of politics within the accepted juridical parameters. This move into politics often appears as a counterpoising of the body of citizens to the state. It is not a coincidence that terms like civic consciousness and duty, social justice and moral recovery are now being bandied about in public and official forums,[17] with the post-EDSA period[18] witnessing the proliferation of non-government organizations (NGO's) and the "resurgence of civil society" debates.[19] This appears to be a time when the state

---

[16] To push this point farther, the question of the "Chinese" in the Philippines demands an examination of the affiliations between ontological and historically specific sociopolitical sites of analysis and critique. Inasmuch as the question of the Chinese within Southeast Asia is co-extensive with questions of nationalism, colonialism, imperialism, orientalism, racism and sexism, it is deeply implicated in the question of Occidental modernity and its (uneven) planetary scope. For a general theorizing of such affiliations, see Jacques Derrida, *Specters of Marx: The State of the Debt, the Work of Mourning, and the New International*, trans. Peggy Kamuf (New York and London: Routledge, 1994).

[17] This kind of vocabulary has also been used by the Federation of Filipino-Chinese Chambers of Commerce and Industry, the official spokesman organization of the Chinese community. In celebration of *Tulay*'s eighth anniversary in 1995, the congratulatory ad of the Federation describes the Federation as "an association serving the Filipino people and committed to promote commerce and industry, foster national unity, and in every way uphold the torch of true friendship, brotherhood and understanding among all peoples of whatever race, religion or political belief, under the ideals of peace, freedom, democracy and social justice." *Tulay*, June 19, 1995, p. 16.

[18] EDSA (Epifanio delos Santos Avenue) was the site of the so-called "People Power Revolution" that drove Ferdinand Marcos into exile and paved the way for the ascension to presidency of Corazon Aquino, widow of assassinated Marcos opponent Benigno Aquino, in February 1986.

[19] The current articulation of the discourse of citizenship owes its provenance to the events that led to the so-called "People's Power Revolution" at EDSA and the toppling of the Marcos administration. The general opposition to the Marcos dictatorship in the early 1980's addressed itself to two adversaries: absolutism, which represented a negation of freedom, and privilege, which represented a negation of equality. The events at EDSA brought the two terms of equality and liberty together in public discourse. This conjoining of terms would later be appropriated by the Chinese Filipinos in their deployment of the general discourse of citizenship and rights. Since the proposition of "equaliberty" was first historically articulated during the French revolution of 1789, and since the EDSA event has often been represented as a "revolution" reminiscent of 1789, I decided to use Etienne Balibar's close reading of the *Declaration of the Rights of Man and the Citizen of 1789* as a reference for my argument. See Etienne Balibar, "'Rights of Man' and 'Rights of the Citizen': The Modern Dialectic of Freedom and Equality," in *Masses, Classes, Ideas: Studies on Politics and Philosophy Before and After Marx*, trans. James Swenson (New York and London: Routledge, 1994), pp. 39-59.

itself has explicitly organized its separation from society.[20] In fact, public criticism of government economic policies has focused not only on the government's overemphasis on showcasing the democratic features of the Philippine political system, but also on its inadequate intervention in the economy through the organization of the private sector.[21]

In truth, however, the state continues to act in both public and private spheres, and it does so precisely because political and economic stability are linked in an indissoluble yet conflicted manner. Aggressively pursuing a policy of attracting foreign investments, Ramos has logged more mileage points than any other Filipino president in history. At the same time, however, state efforts to secure investments by showcasing the attractions of the Philippine democratic system are undermined by an often empirically violent flouting of the law by the very people who are tasked to enforce it.[22] Moreover, the formal recognition of equality in law—that is, the very condition of property and rights—that the state is supposed to secure is constitutively undermined by the reality of economic inequality in the Philippines. This distinction between formal political equality and actual economic inequality has important implications for the state's attitude toward the Chinese as well as for the kind of responses that are available to the Chinese. The problem is further complicated by the fact that the real and potential antagonisms created by this distinction cannot be glossed over, *contra* Hegel's *Philosophy of Right*, by expelling violence as a non-civil phenomenon from the social whole. For the state concretizes the recognition of the original violence of property and commerce that constitutes the "non-violent" life of civil society, not by going to war against other nations (although the Spratley Islands dispute with China has generated some military brandishings on both sides in the region), but by turning this violence on the nation-state itself. In other words, the state itself brings its own military strength to bear on the inhabitants within its boundaries. Violence, then, is something that cannot be consigned to the outer limits of the individual's domain. The irony of the "separation" of state and society is that it comes at a time when the concept of both civil society and the state as terrains that putatively mediate and recuperate social antagonisms is at its most tenuous. The anxiety which attends the everyday threat of violence or every rumor of martial law, constitutional change, and overstaying presidents has done more to underscore the fragility of civil society itself than to highlight the dream of consensus within Philippine society.

In analyzing the Chinese responses, we appear to be dealing with a demand for political representation on the part of the Chinese, but in truth, as I will argue, it is a politicized representation that lacks a solid foundation in society. This lack would normally have been filled by the state's construction of a substitute for the dynamics of civil society. While the Philippines' information culture and communicative

---

[20] See Fidel V. Ramos, "Inaugural Address: To Win the Future," *Philippines Free Press*, July 11, 1992, pp. 10, 36-37; "The State of the Nation," *Philippines Free Press*, August 7, 1993, pp. 8-9, 32, 47.

[21] James P. Saspa, "Mastermind or Fall Guy?," *Philippines Free Press*, January 13, 1996, p. 6.

[22] This is complicated by the existence of non-reformist liberation movements such as the Communist New People's Army and the Moro Islamic Liberation Front, for which armed struggle (basically a justification of violence in the name of a social subject, "the people") is the main principle of political action. One interesting question would be: to what extent does the ontologizing of violence as the principle of political action serve to highlight the necessary relation between the law and violence?

processes have contributed to this end—and this explains why I have chosen to work on the media output of Kaisa, a new civic organization of young Chinese Filipinos—they cannot paper over the state's failure to secure, in the words of Antonio Negri and Michael Hardt, the normative production of the social, in other words, the state's failure to maintain the illusion of a civil society.[23] There are a number of reasons why this is so, but I have decided to concentrate on examining the contradictions within the discourse of politicized representation itself, contradictions that make it both possible and impossible for the self-avowed elements of civil society to depend on the discourse of citizenship and rights to secure political solutions to the social antagonisms which they act out within the nation-state.

Co's article and the Chinese Filipinos' entry into politics attest to the fact that the ethnic Chinese began using the discourse of citizenship, the affirmation of the universal right to politics extended to "all" Chinese, in order to address the stereotypical conflation of ethnicity and class that the phenomenon of kidnapping reinforces. I shall devote the first part of the paper to examining the way in which kidnapping historically articulates this conflation. I go on to argue, following Etienne Balibar's close reading of the French Declaration of the Rights of Man and the Citizen, that while much of the rhetorical force and political charge of the call for public inscription of the "right" to be Chinese Filipino arises from its indeterminacy and its lack of specificity regarding particular rights to, say, freedom and security, it is this same indeterminacy inherent in the discourse of citizenship and rights that accounts for the practical weakness of the Chinese Filipinos' deployment of the discourse.

In other words, I argue that the Tsinoy's decision to use a discourse of citizenship, a discourse of equality and liberty, constitutes a problematic attempt to disentangle the conflation of ethnicity and class that the kidnapping phenomenon highlights because the discourse comes up against the contingencies of the Tsinoy's problematic relationship with the Philippine state and nation, as well as the Philippine nation-state's equally problematic relationship with global capitalism. I shall attempt to elaborate these points through an analysis of one specific Tsinoy response: Kaisa Para sa Kaunlaran (Unity toward Progress), a civic organization of young Chinese Filipinos that has emerged as the unofficial spokesman organization of the Chinese community in light of the rampant kidnapping incidents in the early 1990's.

BOOMING BUSINESS, SPECTRAL BODIES

I begin with a brief reconstruction of the kidnap-for-ransom phenomenon before I proceed to an analysis of the conflating logic of kidnapping. The first incidents of kidnapping during the Aquino regime were not reported in Manila, where more than 50 percent of the Chinese in the Philippines reside,[24] but in Central Mindanao, specifically Cotabato City. The kidnapping-for-ransom of Chinese Filipino

---

[23] See Antonio Negri and Michael Hardt, *Labor of Dionysus: A Critique of the State Form* (Minneapolis: University of Minnesota Press, 1994), especially pp. 259-260, 269, 271, 295, 304-307.

[24] Teresita Ang-See, "The Many Faces of the Ethnic Chinese," *The Manila Chronicle*, November 19, 1995, p. 5.

businessmen broke into the headlines in late 1989.[25] By late April, 1991, the Chinese Filipino news digest *Tulay* reported seventeen "rumored" cases of kidnapping in Manila, none of which had been officially reported to the police.[26]

Several theories have been advanced to account for the upsurge of kidnapping cases in Cotabato: kidnapping-for-ransom was quick and easy money for common criminals, the Aquino government had failed to pay the rebel returnees (to the government fold) their regular monthly stipend of 1,500 pesos, kidnapping helped to fill the coffers of the Moro National Liberation Front and the New People's Army (NPA), and the tolerance of the kidnapping by government officials pointed to a "secret agenda" on the part of the state (the creation of civilian armed units, the undermining of the leadership credibility of the Autonomous Region of Moslem Mindanao, and the much-rumored reimposition of Martial Law).[27] The more suggestive link between the spate of kidnapping and the upcoming national elections in 1992, while unestablished, appears to be a more credible explanation, especially in the case of the Manila kidnappings. The veracity of the above theories can only be tested against the indubitable evidence of the membership of police and military officers and personnel in the kidnap gangs.[28]

Two civic organizations formed in the wake of the early wave of kidnapping, the Citizens Action Against Crime and the Movement for the Restoration of Peace and Order, have kept track of the cases, whether reported or not, involving kidnap-for-ransom. They reported 179 kidnap victims in 1993, 286 victims in 1994, 119 in 1995, and 241 in 1996, mostly from Luzon and the Visayas.[29] In 1995 alone, the total amount of ransom money that was disbursed to the kidnap gangs stood at almost

---

[25] Articles on kidnapping began appearing in *Tulay* during the last quarter of 1989.

[26] Jacqueline Co, "Kidnap-for-Ransom Leaves Trail of Terror," *Tulay*, April 21, 1991, p. 7.

[27] Ibid. See also Mydans, "Kidnapping of Ethnic Chinese Rises in the Philippines," p. 3.

[28] "Order of Battle: Kidnap-for-Ransom Gang Members Wanted," *Tulay*, November 8, 1992, pp. 6-7, lists the names and affiliations of arrested suspects. The Philippine police and military seem to be very well represented, with PNP (Philippine National Police) officers in the Red Scorpion Gang, marines in the Tinsay-Espejo Gang, Philippine army officers in the eight "Hoodlums in Uniform" Gang, BID (Bureau of Immigration and Deportation) and NBI (National Bureau of Investigation) people in Atayde's Gang, CPD (Central Police District) personnel in the Omar Ring, WPD (Western Police District) members in the Eddie Chang Group, the AFP (RAM) (Armed Forces of the Philippines/Rebolusyondryong Alyansang Makabayan, Revolutionary Nationalist Alliance) in the Morales Group, and PNP-NARCOM (Philippine National Police-Narcotics Command) personnel in the "Wang-Wang" Group. Most recently, in 1995, a former police officer, Col. Reynaldo Berroya—who headed an anti-kidnapping task force under the Presidential Anti-Crime Commission as a replacement for two previous task force chiefs who were accused of involvement in the kidnap-for-ransom cases that they themselves were investigating (José Pring and Timoteo Zarcal)—was convicted of involvement in the kidnapping of a Taiwanese businessman and sentenced to life imprisonment. See also Edward R. Kiunisala, "Kidnap-for-Ransom: A Big Business (Part III)," *Philippines Free Press*, October 24, 1992, pp. 10-11, 31. Last year, the *Shijie Ribao* (*World News*) carried an editorial commenting on the hosting of the APEC Conference by the Philippines. The editorial voiced (in an understandably circuitous manner) the Chinese community's general belief that Fidel Ramos himself is implicated in the kidnappings either through indirect participation or tacit sanction. See "Yataijinghefenghui yu Bangjia," *Shijie Ribao*, November 11, 1996, p. 1. See also "Kidnap ransom is source of politicians' campaign funds, says Crime Watch," *Philippine News*, April 9-15, 1997, pp. A1, A10.

[29] "The Losing War Against Crime," *The Sunday Chronicle*, October 22, 1995, p. 4; and *Tulay*, January 8, 1996, p. 4. The figures for 1994 include Fr. Cirilo Nacorda and the seventy-eight teachers abducted by the Abu Sayaff in Mindanao in June 8, 1994.

112 million pesos. This figure only covers known payments; in many cases, the exact sum of ransom money remains unknown. A good number of these cases involved the abduction of capitalists themselves, while the rest involved the abduction of their relatives and immediate family members.

Kidnapping has been called a "growth industry" and a "booming business,"[30] and to a certain extent it does employ the kind of systematic labor, large personnel, and capital outlays (in the form of weapons and vehicles) that characterizes an industry explicitly geared to profit-making. The difference, however, is that kidnapping foregrounds aspects of commodity relations specific to capitalism in a spectacular way. Like any industry, kidnapping is premised on the power of a commodity to command other commodities in exchange, a power of exchangeability that Karl Marx calls value.[31] In this case, the commodity happens to be a body, the body of the capitalist or of someone related to the capitalist. The act of kidnapping transforms the body of the victim into an object of exchange, thereby instituting a logic of commodification which treats the commodity, whether capitalist or kindred, as qualitatively equal but quantitatively differential: All kidnap victims are alike except in terms of the amount of value that they "contain." Value here is determined by the victim's net worth, that is, by the victim's access to accumulated capital in the form of money. Kidnapping transforms the body of the capitalist into a commodity, the value of which is based on the capitalist's possession of money, which, in turn, comprises the accumulation of unpaid surplus labor of the past that is appropriated by the capitalist in the present. The capitalist's body is thus a commodity the value of which is a calibration of the capitalist's accumulation of unpaid surplus labor.

There is a certain irony, then, in the fact that kidnapping does to the capitalist what capitalism does to the laborer.[32] If capitalism institutes a circuit in which the capitalist buys the labor power that the laborer sells for a price, the wage, kidnapping institutes a circuit in which the capitalist buys himself back for a price, a fraction of his total net worth, which, it must be remembered, represents his accumulation in the present of unpaid surplus labor in the past. Kidnapping, therefore, imagines and realizes a subjectivity—often experienced as a *loss* of subjectivity[33]—that inexorably links the objective movement of capital and the subjective purpose of the capitalist. That is, kidnapping makes the capitalist an almost *literal* personification of capital, in the same sense that capitalism makes the laborer the personification of his own labor power. In kidnapping, both the kidnapper and the kidnap victim are constituted by—and both realize—social relations that mimic capitalist relations. Perhaps the real irony lies in the fact that, by making the capitalist its primary source of extraction, kidnapping trains the lens of inequality inherent in the capitalist relation onto those who control the means to sustain this inequality.

The peculiarity of the kidnap-for-ransom phenomenon in the Philippines, however, consists of its victimization of ethnic Chinese in public spaces.[34] By

---

[30] See, for example, Mydans, "Kidnapping of Ethnic Chinese Rises in the Philippines," p. 3; Michael Dueñas, "The Kidnapping 'Industry,'" *Philippines Free Press*, March 21, 1992, pp. 34-36; and "Kidnapping—the Growth Industry," *Philippines Free Press*, February 27, 1993, p. 20.

[31] See Karl Marx, *Capital* I, Chapter I, 3C, 1.

[32] The seeds of this insight belong to Vicente Rafael.

[33] I am indebted to Marx's discussion of the capitalist as "capital personified" in *Capital* I, Chapter VIII, I (English editions, Chapter X, 1).

[34] Charlene Mayne Sy was snatched on her way to school, while Kenneth Go and Myron Uy Ramos were abducted on their way home from a party. Kidnappings have also been reported

publicly subjecting the capitalists and their relatives to the forces of capital, kidnapping seemingly erases the subjective and human qualities of the victim, and imputes to the victims no other motives than that of being instruments of capital. Kidnapping is, therefore, as much a signifying act as a social relation, because the kidnapping phenomenon invites and fulfills a certain public demand for knowledge of existing social relations. I argue that the knowledge that kidnapping "proffers" is condensed into the term "Chinese." It is this condensation, rather than the mere fact of the personification of capital as a social relation by the capitalist, that evokes strong emotional reactions. By making the Chinese an almost literal personification of capital, kidnapping calls attention to the ways in which the bodies of the Chinese exist as codifications of a complex, shifting network of material and cultural forces that constitute, among other things, nation-ness, neocolonialism, and globalization.

What distinguishes the kidnappings of this decade from those of the past is the degree to which these kidnappings have become highly technicized. That is, their success depends on the speed of communication, negotiation, and exchange, which is made possible to a great extent by mobile phones, ATM machines, and computerized banking. But this technology foregrounds a certain notion of "pure" capitalist relations in that kidnap victims and their relatives are treated as atomized individuals who are warned, for obvious reasons, not to "talk" to the state. In targeting the Chinese as "obvious" sources of extraction, kidnapping frames the issue not in terms of the fact that the capitalists who were kidnapped happened to be Chinese, but that those who were kidnapped *were* Chinese capitalists. That is, kidnapping highlights the ontologization of commodity relations in an unprecedentedly technically dominated world. It seems to give a new twist to Marx's observation that "commodities cannot go to market by themselves and perform exchanges in their own right," and that the possessors of these commodities need to "place themselves in relation to one another as persons whose will [*Willen*] resides [*haust*] in these objects and must behave in such a way that each does not appropriate the commodity of the other, and alienate his own, except through an act in which both parties consent."[35] Although Marx's observation elucidates a general theory of the juridical form of the contract, his observation also makes a compelling point about how the absolute abstraction of the individual as "legal" personality is posited alongside the abstraction of possession into property.

Yet by reflecting on this observation within the context of kidnapping, we are forced to consider a more disturbing issue: In a situation where the kidnap victim's will inhabits the commodity (that is, the kidnap victim himself or herself), how do we begin to draw the line between the effect of commodification and the effect of personification?[36] Kidnapping forces us to consider the process of the spectralization

---

in malls and outside school compounds. In July of 1997, the Chinese-language daily *Shijie Ribao* began carrying readers' letters and reports concerning abductions of "Chinese-looking" people by armed motorcycle riders along Banawe Street, Quezon City. See "Duzhelaisin zhonggao bannaweijie huaren," *Shijie Ribao,* July 13, 1997, p. 1.

[35] Marx, *Capital* I, Ch. 1, 4. In Ben Fowkes's translation (New York: Vintage Books, 1977), see p. 178.

[36] See Jacques Derrida's discussion of the phantomalization of the social bond in his *Specters of Marx*, p. 158: "Persons are personified by letting themselves be haunted by the very effect of objective haunting, so to speak, that they produce by inhabiting the thing. Persons (guardians or possessors of the thing) are haunted in return, and constitutively, by the haunting they produce in the thing by lodging there their speech and their will like inhabitants."

of the Chinese through which an "idea or spiritual form is incarnated or given a prosthetic body, which is then (mis)taken by the subject as his or her own corporeal body. The subject's real body thus becomes spectral when it incorporates this prosthetic body."[37] This intimate compound of bodies and meaning that *is* the Chinese appears to blur the distinction between matter and idea.

In this context, "Chinese" has perforce to take on, literally, the attributes of "capital." Kidnapping creates situations wherein the Chinese victims, in order to survive, actively/passively take on stereotypical codifications of "Chinese capital" as a "second nature," thereby enacting their bodies' susceptibility to particular oppressive forms such as racism and commodity-fetishism. The lives of these victims are prolonged only insofar as they are commodities that are "worth" something, even if this commodification renders them equally vulnerable to racist slurs, torture, and rape. In the moment of kidnapping, some form of codification of "Chinese capital" takes place whereby the victims actively/passively take on the stereotypes of Chineseness, in fact *live* these stereotypes as though they were co-extensive with their own bodies and consciousness. More than just a signifier, "Chinese," with all its attendant associations, assumes the character of a referent, a something *there*, something finite that "takes on and is trapped by specters of what it is not."[38] Since there is no space in the present essay for me to develop this point, I will leave off with the observation that the spectral character of the Chinese as a conflation of class and ethnicity extends (or ought to extend) the argument beyond the question of the constitution of the subject as citizen and into the question*ing* of the nature/culture, active/passive, and form/matter divide in our theorizing of such a constitution. In its distinctive way, kidnapping provides an account of the persistence of the truism about the Chinese as "material men" (to use James Rush's term) whose virtual nationality within the Philippine neocolonial nation-state remains a politically charged and contested issue, even in the face of critiques that expose the contingent and non-natural character of Chinese identity.

SPEAKING TO/ABOUT THE NATION-STATE

Let me now look at how the indeterminacies of the codification of citizenship become articulated historically. I have mentioned that kidnapping is as much a signifying act as it is a social relation because it invites and fulfills a certain public demand for knowledge of social relations. At least two main narratives about "the Chinese" are at work in the responses to the conflation of ethnicity and class through the practice of kidnapping. On the one hand, the Chinese are an object of class resentment because, as those who have benefited economically from the system as a group, they come to stand in for the evils of the present social system. On the other hand, the Chinese are an object of nationalist distrust because they represent, by virtue of the history of their highly symbiotic relation with the colonial and

---

[37] See Pheng Cheah's excellent discussion of Derrida in the context of feminist theorizing of the body in his "Mattering," *Diacritics* 26,1 (1996): 108-39.

[38] Rather than being a unique case, the spectralization of the Chinese points to the unavoidability of spectralization for all finite beings. For a discussion of the latter point and its implications for the analysis of historical forms of power and transformative agency, see Cheah, "Mattering," pp. 129-137, especially 134.

neocolonial state, the living, "foreign" trace of the colonial history—itself seen as foreign and external—of the Philippine state and nation.[39]

These two narratives have their origins in the intimate and often conflict-ridden relationship between nation, state, and capitalism. On the one hand, a "developing" country like the Philippines places an official premium on its citizens' entrepreneurial skills and activities. The truisms regarding Chinese business acuity and resilience establish the Chinese as exemplary citizens of a new regime of economic liberalization and political stability, an ideal to which the post-Marcos governments aspire.[40] The identification of "Chinese" with money ironically allows the Chinese to be dissociated from money. The Chinese Filipinos' rhetoric of citizenship depends on the multilayered associations surrounding money itself, not least of which is its ability to command exchange and desire. Chineseness is therefore inflected by its double-edged association with modernity (the idea of "development") and with the consumption of goods (the idea of a "middle class"). In particular, Chineseness soaks up the positive connotations of a "nationalist" entrepreneurship that effects the circulation of money within the space of the nation-state. I have heard a number of Chinese argue against the fear of Chinese capital flight by insisting that most of the Chinese stood by the Philippines during its most troubled times (that is, in the mid-eighties) instead of funneling their money abroad, "like the Ayalas did." This kind of argument sets up a contrast between the "old money" Spanish mestizo families and the "new money" Chinese.[41]

---

[39] The most influential twining of these two narratives in historiographical form is Renato Constantino and Letizia R. Constantino's *The Philippines: The Past Revisited* (Quezon City: Foundation for Nationalist Studies, 1975).

[40] See, for example, Lito B. Zulueta, "Pinoy Taipans: The Secret of Their Success," *The Sunday Chronicle*, November 19, 1995, pp. 1, 4. Relying heavily on the ideas of business journalist James Clad, the article blames the Marcos administration for distorting and truncating the "entrepreneurial attitude," and concludes that "Chinese-Filipinos and non-Chinese Filipinos can best excel in a business regime where there are transparent rules consistently and fairly applied and where government paternalism is restrained." Zulueta, "Pinoy Taipans," p. 4.

[41] The fortunes of the five taipans--Henry Sy, Lucio Tan, John Gokongwei, Andrew Gotianum and George Ty—were all made and consolidated after World War Two. Ibid., p. 4.

The opposition between Spanish mestizo (mixed blood) and Chinese is interesting because it casts light on the disappearance of the Chinese mestizo from contemporary consciousness. Nowadays, when referring to mestizo, people automatically think of white (European or American) ancestry. Chinese is therefore defined in either-or terms—one is either "pure" Chinese or one is a Filipino (quantification of Chinese blood, as in "I am one-fourth Chinese" or "my grandmother was Chinese," comes up only in situations where alluding to Chinese ancestry allows one to appropriate the positive connotations of "Chinese" entrepreneurial skills). The history of Binondo, now synonymous with Chinatown in the Philippines, testifies to the vicissitudes of changing definitions of Chineseness. From its inception, Binondo, like the Parian (or Chinese quarter), was tied up with Spanish regulation of the Chinese who played an indispensable role in the colonial economic establishment of the colonial city of Manila. But Binondo differed from the Parian because its production as space was originally grounded in the notion of conversion. Binondo was purchased from its *encomemderos* (beneficiaries of royal grants who were entitled to collect taxes from inhabitants covered by the land grant) by the Spanish Governor Gomez Perez Dasmariñas, who made a formal land grant of Binondo to a group of *sangley* ("Chinese" is a somewhat anachronistic term for *sangley*, which does not have a fixed national denotation and literally means "merchant") merchants and artisans. With a population of about five hundred Christianized *sangleys* and their mestizo offspring (who were physically separated from the Parian-housed unconverted *sangleyes infieles* or infidel "Chinese") in the 1620's, Binondo was supposed to be the site for what was hoped to be an eventual all-mestizo community. In theory, the *sangley*

On the other hand, given the ambivalent cast of nationalist formulations on capitalism (a consequence of the Philippine's position in the current international division of labor, which puts the nation-state in a position of acceptance as well as rejection with regard to capitalism) and the fact that the national question in Third World countries is indissolubly linked with the issue of the country's specific colonial past as embodied by the state, it is not surprising that the term Chinese also comes to stand for all that is "alien" and alienating within the body politic. That the issue of the "alien" Chinese often shades into the issue of "alienating" capital is no doubt a consequence of the ambivalent relation between the nation, the state, and capitalism. But it also seems doubly ironic in light of the fact that it is "kidnapped"

---

would have eventually disappeared from Binondo. But the continuing influx of married converts resulted in the creation of separate spheres for each of the legal categories of *sangley* and *sangley mestizos*.

A comparison of Spanish and Dutch policies regarding the Chinese is instructive here because it sheds light on the relationship between Chinese self-definitions and the colonial state. The Spaniards, like the Dutch, saw the Chinese as merchant or artisanal communities which could and had to be inserted into the colonial state without threatening the mode of production (in this case, the galleon trade) operating in the colonies. This insertion, however, did not take the form of subordination of the Chinese to European authority, at least in the early years of colonization, since the method of insertion resembled alliance more than filiation. The Dutch, for example, appointed as officers of the Chinese community those who had economic dealings with the Dutch. These appointments strengthened the prestige of the officers among the Chinese, but the appointments were by no means filiative, in the sense that the authority that was conferred upon the officers did not highlight the power of the colonial administration as a source of beneficence. Rather, the authority conferred merely affirmed the fact of the administration having dealings with the Chinese who had access to it. This explains Leonard Blussé's observation that the Dutch Governor Camphuys "had the installation of the new Chinese captain coincide with his own, thus symbolically sharing authority with him." See Leonard Blussé, *Strange Company: Chinese Settlers, Mestizo Women, and the Dutch in VOC Batavia* (Leiden: Koninklijk Instituut voor Taal-, Land- en Volkenkinds, 1986), p. 87. One consequence of an alliance-based insertion is that the Chinese officers often lost their authority vis-à-vis the Chinese, who would bypass their own officers in the settlement of disputes among themselves. Only from the nineteenth century onward, when relations between the Chinese and the colonial state became filiative, did the spokesman authority of the Chinese officers become cemented to the prestige of the office they held. Edgar Wickberg has noted the same phenomenon in his study of the capitan (captain) system in the Philippines. See Edgar Wickberg, *The Chinese in Philippine Life, 1850-1898* (New Haven: Yale University Press, 1965), pp. 194-202. In colonial Manila, with the levelling of the Parian and the building of a new *Alcaiceria* (silk market) in San Fernando in the latter half of the eighteenth century, Binondo absorbed both the converted and unconverted *sangleys*.

The legal distinction between the Chinese and the Chinese mestizo had an impact on the economy. Following the last expulsion of the Chinese, the Chinese mestizos took over the retail trade. But when the Chinese were allowed back into the Philippines in the 1850's, they wrested the retail trade from the mestizos, who shifted to agriculture and landholding. These Chinese mestizos formed the base of a Hispanized class that sought to dissociate itself from its Chinese ancestry. Although the mestizo's articulation of Filipino nationalism flexibly opened itself to all the inhabitants of the Philippines, whether creole or native, we get a sense of an emergent ethnic consciousness in the case of José Rizal, who was legally a Chinese mestizo but who was said to have objected strenuously to his being called a Chinese mestizo, declaring that he was "'pure' Filipino." This incident—which, albeit of doubtful authenticity, is indicative of how later generations of self-identified "Filipinos" viewed nationality in the either-or terms discussed above—is recounted in Leon Ma. Guerrero's biography of José Rizal, *The First Filipino* (Manila: National Historical Institute, 1971), p. 473.

Chinese money that has helped underwrite the cost of carrying out the political programs of groups or factions that work within or against the state.[42]

As should be obvious by now, no discussion of the Chinese in the Philippines can afford to ignore the constitutive role played by the state in framing the Chinese question.[43] As a form of social relation, kidnapping owes its historical provenance and success to, first, the long and often troubled relationship between the Chinese and the state, second, the economic role of the Chinese as middlemen and capitalists within the nation-state, third, the immigration history of the Chinese and the pernicious effects of the neocolonial state's exploitation of this history, and lastly, the perceived "cultural difference" and alienation of the Chinese from the body politic.[44] The most immediate and visible effect of this relationship has been the creation of the Chinese as a "perfect victim," which is reflected in the perennial uneasiness and distrust with which the Chinese have dealings with government officials, their reliance on forging symbiotic "alliances" with government officials, and their relative readiness to pay kidnapping ransoms.

This kind of behavior on the part of the Chinese has often been criticized by the media and by the law enforcers themselves, but rather than blame the victims, I argue that the only way to understand the way in which the Chinese have chosen to "respond" to the state is to look into the way in which the state has chosen to speak to the Chinese. I argue that kidnapping allows us that one telling glimpse of the interlocutory relation between the Chinese and the state.

It is not an exaggeration to say that the present state has an interest, as reflected in the case of kidnapping, in conflating race with class because it has historically benefited from such an arrangement. I would argue, however, that this conflation is not a mere effect of state practice and policy, but is instead constitutive of the post-colonial state as such. That is, the post-colonial nation-state necessarily constitutes itself in terms of a formal repudiation of both economic and political inequality and the colonial past. These two positions, in fact, are conjoined in the state's periodic attempts to deal with the problem of the legal status of the Chinese as well as safeguard the economic and political interests of the Filipinos against the "virtual

---

[42] The Federation of Filipino-Chinese Chambers of Commerce and Industry established a "war chest" for campaign contributions, arguing in 1954 that channeling campaign contributions through the Federation would create a buffer between the politicians and the rich Chinese, as well as increase the political leverage of the community as a whole. See James R. Blaker, "The Chinese in the Philippines: A Study of Power and Change," PhD dissertation, Ohio State University, 1970, p. 225.

[43] It should be added that the Chinese played a constitutive role in the formation of the colonial state under the Spanish and the American regimes. I explore these issues in "Reading Binondo: Mapping the Chinese Community in Manila," paper delivered at the Association of Asian Studies Conference, April 1996.

[44] See Edgar Wickberg, *The Chinese in Philippine Life, 1850-1898*; Antonio Tan, *The Chinese in the Philippines: A Study of Their National Awakening* (Quezon City: Garcia Publications, 1972); Remigio Agpalo, *The Political Process and the Nationalization of the Retail Trade in the Philippines* (Quezon City: Office of the Coordinator of Research, University of the Philippines, 1962); Alfonso Felix, Jr., ed., *The Chinese in the Philippines*, 2 vols. (Manila: Solidaridad Publishing House, 1966); Schubert Liao, *Chinese Participation in Philippine Culture and Economy* (Manila: The Author, 1964); and for recent materials, publications by the Philippine Association for Chinese Studies. Chinese-language histories of the Philippine Chinese include: Huang Zisheng and He Sibing, *Feilubin Huaqiao Shi* (Guangzhou: Guangdong Gaodeng Jiaoyu Chubanshe, 1987); Liu Zhitian, *Zhong-Fei Guanxi Shi* (Taibei: Zhengzhong Shuju, 1969); and Huang Mingde, *Feilubin Huaqiao Jinji* (Taibei: Haiwai Chubanshe, 1956).

nationality" of the Chinese. The uniqueness of the present state policies on the Chinese, however, consists of their similarity to kidnapping-for-ransom: even though the policies continue to operate on a extractive logic vis-à-vis the Chinese as they had done during the colonial and post-war periods,[45] the main difference is that they now operate in a terrain wherein the overlapping of membership in kidnap gangs and state apparatuses has rendered the legal/criminal distinction inoperative. It becomes very difficult to determine whether the state is acting like a criminal, or if the criminals act like the state. We need not go any farther than the recent enactment of the Alien Social Integration Act (ASIA) of 1995 to obtain some insights into the blurring of the legal/criminal distinction in the Aquino and Ramos administrations' policies toward the Chinese. Immigration Commissioner Leandro Verceles explained that the Act was necessitated by the state's intention of bringing "illegal aliens into the mainstream, and [thus] mak[ing] them active participants in [the country's] development." Active participation here is interpreted in strictly monetary terms— two hundred thousand pesos per Chinese, fifty thousand for spouses and twenty-five thousand for dependents. The government expects to earn forty billion pesos from the Chinese, and has strengthened its persecution of illegal aliens in order to drum up more participants.[46] Lest it be thought that this Act will have an impact only on illegal aliens, we need to remember that Chinese with Filipino citizenship are not safe from state harassment and official inquiry into the history of their immigration and naturalization (the investigation of "Plastics King" William Gatchalian being the most celebrated case).[47] The state has made it easy for Taiwanese and other foreign investors to secure their permanent residency in the Philippines, while rendering the situation of Philippine-born Chinese problematic by virtue of the threat of *jus sanguinis* illegality which continues to shadow their status as well as that of their progeny.

---

[45] The Chinese provided one of the major sources of revenues for the colonial state during the Spanish period, mainly in the form of taxes and contract farming. James Blaker argues that American policies toward the Chinese appeared to be contradictory, laying the legal foundations for, on the one hand, depriving the Chinese of the means of political participation and, on the other hand, encouraging Chinese economic activities. See Blaker, "The Chinese in the Philippines" Legal and economic nationalism before and after the Second World War has made it difficult for the Chinese to acquire citizenship, while encouraging an entire industry of corruption based on bribery and forgery.

[46] "BI [Bureau of Immigration] Now Accepting Applications from Illegal Aliens," *The Manila Chronicle*, June 1, 1995, p. 3. The Verceles quote appeared in a related article in the June 2, 1995 issue of *The Manila Chronicle*, p. 2. For Chinese reaction to ASIA, see "Act with Integrity," *Tulay*, April 1, 1996, p. 3. ASIA grants permanent residency status to the aliens, who will be eligible for citizenship after five years. For an account of the most recent harassment of "illegal aliens," see "BID 'Raids' Tutuban Center," *Tulay*, July 4, 1994, pp. 6, 13. Witnesses to the Tutuban raid claimed that BID agents used the criterion of "Chinese looks" to arrest people. Moreover, some raiders demanded twenty to thirty thousand pesos from the arrested in exchange for their freedom. Of the eighteen people taken to the Immigration offices, eleven were released immediately for lack of evidence, and six of the remaining seven were freed after presenting proper documentation. The sole foreigner whose status remained in doubt was an Indian. The rather inflated figures that the government expects to earn have since been scaled down to a more modest sum of one billion pesos. See "P 1-B Immigration Revenue Eyed," *Manila Bulletin*, September 4, 1996, p. 19.

[47] For an account of the Gathchalian case, see Salvador T. Hernandez, "The Man Who Fought to be Called a Filipino," *Philippines Free Press*, July 6, 1991, pp. 2, 13-14, 30.

If there is one thing that kidnapping tells us, it is that the extractive logic that used to be identified with the colonial and neocolonial state vis-à-vis the Chinese has become generalized and diffused throughout society. This generalization of criminality is the phenomenal expression of the *violent* "objective reality" of neocolonialism in the Philippines, that is, of the persistence of the imbalance of unequal development, not only within the nation-state, but between *this* nation-state and other nation-states in the world capitalist system. Unequal development translates into an active pursuit of transnational capital, in the name of "global competitiveness," at the cost of the super-exploitation and outward movement of the Filipino labor force.[48] In marrying "national interest" with neoclassical economics, the Philippine state, like most Third World countries, finds itself dealing with its attempts to "apply" the seemingly universal economic laws of capitalist development to its territories, and to rationalize its repeated failure to follow the path of the industrialized countries. The notion of criminality can be considered a form of rationalizing for this failure in the state application of the "universal" law of value within its own territorial borders; thus, criminals like the kidnappers have been blamed for undermining political stability and therefore driving away foreign investments.

Yet, what cements criminality to the state is precisely the state's identification with the world capitalist system, and, consequently, its identification with the injurious consequences of its incorporation into the center-periphery system of unequal development. The state is criticized as much for its deployment of an extractive violence against which it claims to safeguard its citizens, as for its inability to guarantee its citizens' rights (to freedom, security, equality) both within and beyond its borders. Like Filipino domestic worker Flor Contemplacion's hanging, which called forth a veritable outpouring of national grief and anger directed as much against the ineffectual Philippine state as against the offending Singaporean state, kidnapping constitutes the most visible sign of the instability—a perennial flickering—of the hyphen between nation and state within the context of neocolonialism.

The kidnapping of the Chinese highlights the way in which the state is itself implicated in the ontologization of commodity relations. This means that, as in the kidnappings, the Chinese find themselves in a position whereby their lives are actually in the hands of a racist state that can only be spoken to and made to listen if the Chinese speak *as* capitalists, that is, if the Chinese define themselves through their everyday economic activities as though this abstraction of the economic were what "Chinese" and "Chineseness" *is*. The relationship of the Chinese with the state is a deeply conflictive one of dependence and distrust, yet this relation is also, ironically, an indispensable component of Chinese "nationalism" (whether oriented toward China or the Philippines), because the fact of the matter is that the Chinese are historically dependent on the state's ability to secure their continued existence within the Philippines and must perforce deal with the consequences of this

---

[48] For an exposition of unequal development in the context of center-periphery relations within the world capitalist system, especially as it is articulated in the Third World, see the works of Samir Amin, in particular, *Delinking: Towards a Polycentric World*, trans. Michael Wolfers (London and New Jersey: Zed Books, 1990).

dependency.[49] The concepts of home and nation take shape in the language and practice of "Chineseness" as a memory of—or anxiety about—displacement.[50]

In similar terms, the political efficacy and contradictions of both Chinese and Filipino responses to kidnapping emerge in the very ambiguity of the relation between nation, state, and capitalism. Kidnapping appears to provide the public with a handy account of both the political and economic alienation of society in general, and, at the same time, the state's mediation of inequality in both national and global terms.[51] Put another way, kidnapping highlights in the most visible and audible way the primary mode in which the state *speaks*. The language that kidnapping and the state speak is that of inequality, and the term "Chinese" is a signifier of the givenness of this practical inequality, an inequality that the state can neither master nor abjure, anymore than the Chinese can repudiate or accept the state.

WHO/WHAT IS A CITIZEN?

In the rest of this paper, I will deal with the way in which the Chinese community produces itself, and I will examine the effect that the community's history of dialogue with the Philippine state has on its self-representation. Here I discuss the activities of Kaisa Para sa Kaunlaran. I argue that Kaisa seeks to intervene in the contestation over the construction of the "Chinese" by interrogating the state's constitutive conflation of ethnicity and class. It does so by invoking, in however sketchy a fashion, the discourse of citizenship and of rights to equality and liberty as an antidote to the state's identification of the Chinese with capital. In effect, Kaisa may be considered an historical articulation of the constitutional coding of citizenship. The kidnapping crisis is central to its attempts to (re)define the Chinese within the parameters of citizenship, since kidnapping brought things to a head, so to speak, by serving as the latest manifestation and practical realization of this conflation, but more important, as the site of the contestation over this conflation.

[49] It is, perhaps, no accident that one of the stereotypical attributes of the Chinese in the Philippines involves their litigiousness or legal-mindedness (depending on the attitude of the beholder). See Victor Purcell, "The Chinese in the Philippines," in *The Chinese in Southeast Asia,* Second Edition (Oxford: Oxford University Press, 1965), pp. 493-564.

[50] See Derrida, *Specters of Marx*, p. 83.

[51] See Etienne Balibar's discussion of the Jew as scapegoat in "'Class Racism',"in Etienne Balibar and Immanuel Wallerstein, *Race, Nation, Class: Ambiguous Identities,* trans. Chris Turner (London and New York: Verso, 1991), p. 206. The classic text on the relationship between property and civil rights is Karl Marx's "On the Jewish Question," in *The Marx-Engels Reader,* ed. Robert C. Tucker (New York: W. W. Norton and Co., Inc., 1972), pp. 24-51. Although the analogy between the Chinese in Southeast Asia and the Jews in Europe enjoys some currency in popular and academic discourse, this analogy has for the most part been made with only the most general comparisons in mind, and with immigration/diaspora, persecution in the host nation, cultural and religious difference, and economic visibility as categories of comparison. The crucial difference between the Jewish question and the Chinese question is that the former is mainly posed in terms of the religious opposition between Christianity and Judaism, often as a question of the Jew's virtual nationality within a Christian state, while the latter is posed in terms of the political opposition between the national and the colonial, often as a question of the Chinese's virtual nationality within the neocolonial state. In this sense, the analogy between the Jews and the Chinese should be investigated with more than simple empirical parallels in mind.

For Kaisa, the kidnapping crisis had the unforeseen effect of providing the crucial impetus that allowed the organization to take on the function of community spokesman, establishing itself as a rival of the erstwhile spokesman organization of the Chinese community, the Federation of Filipino-Chinese Chambers of Commerce and Industry. I want to examine in some detail the claims that underlie Kaisa's invocation of citizenship and rights.

Kaisa intervenes in the representation of the Chinese as a collective subject by attempting to reorient the stereotypical identification of the Chinese with capital. Since the early nineties, it has emerged as the unofficial spokesman for the Chinese community. The word "unofficial" is important because the existence and success of Kaisa is based on its avowed difference from the official spokesman organization of the Chinese community, the Siongzong (Hokkien abbreviation for the Federation of Filipino-Chinese Chambers of Commerce and Industry). It is important to stress that Kaisa sees itself as an organization of young businessmen and professionals, and that this organization has declared itself to have civic rather than economic goals. To wit, Kaisa has concentrated on research and publications, public relations, and social work. Its research and publications include the monthly and now biweekly English and Tagalog-language news digest *Tulay*, the first issue of which, not incidentally, appeared on June 12, 1987 (June 12 being Independence Day), and the monthly Chinese-language column *Ronghe* (literally, "fuse" or "merge")[52] which appears in *Shijie Ribao*, or *World News*, the Chinese daily with the largest circulation in the Philippines. Public relations have centered on achieving representative status with the Office of the President, Congress, the Department of Justice, and others on issues affecting the Philippine Chinese. Kaisa's social work includes weekly Philippine General Hospital Medicine-Assistance programs, the Alay Puso feeding Center in Del Pan and Tayuman, and the Tatalon Free Clinic and Immunization projects. Until funds ran out, Kaisa also coordinated with the Batibot Children's program to produce "Pin-pin," a "Sesame Street" for Chinese Filipino kids.

Kaisa's credo establishes its integrationist stance quite clearly: "The Philippines is our country,/it is the land of our birth,/the home of our people./Our blood may be Chinese,/but our roots grow deep in Filipino soil,/our bonds are with the Filipino people./We are proud of the many cultures,/which have made us what we are,/it is our desire, our hope and aspiration—/that with the rest of our people,/we shall find our rightful place/in the Philippine sun."[53] The fact that this credo is written in English points to an important difference between Kaisa and the much older and rival spokesman organization, the Federation of Filipino-Chinese Chambers of Commerce and Industry. Kaisa's use of English and Tagalog in both its internal and external communications represents the first break within this century between the spokesman function and its "native" medium of communication. If Chineseness used to be tied to linguistic nationalism (here, Chinese encompassed Hokkien and *putonghua*), Kaisa represents a new appropriation of Chineseness, a Chineseness no longer tied to language, but linked instead to a more abstract "anthropological" and "cultural" difference within the givenness of the nation-state.

Compared to the Federation, Kaisa has been vocal in its criticism of the government, focusing on the government's failure to "maintain law and order" in the

---

[52] It may be worth observing at this point, as a preview of a later argument, that the *he* in *ronghe* is also the *he* in *hetong*, which means contract.

[53] *Tulay*, June 12, 1987, p. 1.

face of rampant kidnapping and its exploitation of the Chinese community (its treatment of the Chinese primarily as "sources of relief funds and campaign contributions" and a "convenient scapegoat for economic ills").[54] Teresita Ang-See, one of the founders of Kaisa, has said in an interview: "When I start to speak up about the peace and order situation, I did so conscious of the fact that as a Filipino, it is not just my right to do so, it is my responsibility, too."[55] This kind of statement not only constitutes a subjective recasting of rights (most evident in the term "Chinese Filipino" and the hybrid neologism "Tsinoy" popularized by Kaisa), but an affirmation of the universal right to politics. The claim that the Chinese are Filipinos is both a cultural and a political claim, because it not only reiterates the demand for citizenship, but also for what Etienne Balibar has called the "*public* inscription of freedom and equality."[56]

More importantly, the credo suggests that the acquisition of full political rights redefines the Chinese in terms of their historical belonging to the Philippine nation-state. This claim to rootedness, then, contrasts with the "flexible citizenship"[57] of the Chinese business family, which has often translated rather conveniently, by virtue of the conflation of ethnicity and class, into capital flight.

Kaisa's credo also explains the provenance, as well as function, of a news digest like *Tulay*. The demand for public recognition, *in writing*, of the Tsinoy's right to freedom and equality antes up the stakes in talking successfully to the state. Kaisa has criticized the government for its inability to forge a comprehensive, cohesive, and responsive policy on the Chinese in the Philippines.[58]

Kaisa's demand for the public inscription of freedom and equality through its deployment of the discourse of rights and citizenship, however, must contend with the fact that both the discourse and the demand are institutionally unstable. This means that while the very force of such statements comes from their indeterminacy, such an indeterminacy is also the source of the practical weakness of the act of enunciation. More precisely, the practical weakness of the statement consists of the fact that (quoting Balibar) "the consequences of the statements are themselves indeterminate because they are entirely dependent on 'power relations' and the evolution of a conjuncture in which it will be necessary in practice to construct individual and collective referents for equaliberty."[59] In other words, Kaisa must

---

[54] "Tsinoys: Responding to Change and Challenge," *Tulay*, June 6, 1994, p. 13. This article was first published in the June 10, 1994 issue of *Philippine Graphic Magazine*.

[55] Ang-See, "The Many Faces of the Ethnic Chinese," p. 5.

[56] Balibar, "'Rights of Man' and 'Rights of the Citizen'," p. 49.

[57] This term comes from Aihwa Ong's "On the Edge of Empires: Flexible Citizenship Among Chinese in Diaspora," *Positions* 1,3 (1993): 746-778. Ong's notion of flexible citizenship is based on her assumption regarding the location of overseas Chinese elites "on the edge of empires" (p. 747) in relation to countries and capitalisms. Although Ong limits her essay to a general discussion of hegemonic notions of "being Chinese" and focuses on the way the Chinese themselves have selectively intervened in Orientalist constructions of Chineseness, her argument does not go beyond interrogating the Orientalist logic endemic to scholarship on Chinese societies. Research into the exact nature of the Chinese's negotiation of "different terrains in the world economy" is needed, if only to begin a critique of the "edge of empire" location of the Chinese that Ong takes for granted.

[58] "Tsinoys: Responding to Change and Challenge," p. 13.

[59] Balibar, "'Rights of Man' and 'Rights of the Citizen,'" pp. 49-50. Balibar uses the portmanteau word "equaliberty" to signify that "equality is identical to freedom, is *equal to freedom*, and vice versa."

contend with the fact that the success of its statements about citizenship and rights is dependent on the existing power structures and on the existence of situations that call for Kaisa's ability to tell us who the Tsinoy is and what the ethnic Chinese community is. The kidnapping phenomenon is one such conjuncture.

Kaisa "constructs" a referent for the term "Chinese" by using an integrationist stance, which basically uses a discourse of citizenship that explicitly calls attention to its own overdetermination by anthropological and cultural difference. Kaisa's credo is oriented toward the transformation of the idea of citizenship as inclusive of *all* people (including the Chinese) by its insistence that the Chinese have a "rightful place in the Philippine sun" and are among the many peoples who are also finding *their* rightful places in the Philippine sun. But at the same time, Kaisa sees its integrationist agenda as distinct from the state's domestication of "cultural difference" as a "foreign," "alien" source of revenue (as discussed in the first half of this paper). While Kaisa insists on the inclusiveness of the idea of citizenship and its ability to accommodate cultural difference (the "Chinese heritage"), it denies with equal fervor the naturalization of Chineseness by the state. In so doing, Kaisa finds itself dealing simultaneously with the problem of cultural difference and with the state. The difficulty for Kaisa, as I see it, lies in constructing a practical conduct on both these levels—how to talk to the Chinese and how to talk to the state—without synthesizing or collapsing them both into "Chinese interests." For previous spokesman organizations like the Philippine Chinese General Chamber of Commerce and the Federation of Filipino-Chinese Chambers of Commerce and Industry, conflating, on the one hand, the state's naturalization of Chineseness as foreign, with, on the other hand, the idea of "Chinese" cultural difference, had not been a problem, since it was precisely this conflated identification that allowed them to speak on behalf of "alien" Chinese interests to the state.[60] Kaisa, however, works within the context of its avowed goal of securing democratic representation for "all Chinese" and its production of the Chinese as "national" constituents.

WHO/WHAT IS CHINESE?

But who are the constituents? The invocation of citizenship and rights to liberty and equality can only be guaranteed a degree of institutional stability by requiring the mediation of terms like "fraternity" and "property." Kaisa, as I have argued, ostensibly uses the concept of fraternity (the Chinese community) to mediate its invocation of citizenship and rights. Kaisa commits itself to an idea of nation that is not a mere set of all citizens, for as the first stanza of its credo makes clear, it is the claim to historical belonging that guarantees the citizenship rights of the Chinese.

---

[60] For a history of the Philippine Chinese General Chamber of Commerce (PCGCC), which acted as spokesman for the Chinese during the American and the Commonwealth period, see *Feilubin Minnila Zhonghuashanghui Sanshizhounian Jiniankan* (Manila: Manila Press, Inc. for the PCGCC, 1936). See also Li Qichang, ed., *Feilubin Huaqiao Shanju Gongsuo Jiushizhounian Jiniankan* (Manila: Philippine Chinese Charitable Association, Inc., 1968). For a history of the Federation, organized in 1954 at the height of the anti-Communist drive with Magsaysay's blessings, see Gao Qingyun, "Shangzong de Dansheng yu Zhuangda," in *Shangzong Niannian: Feihua Shanglian Zhonghui Changli Ershizhounian Jiniantekan* (Manila: Federation of Filipino-Chinese Chambers of Commerce, Inc., 1974). See also Deng Yingda's *Wo Zai Shangzong Sanshinian* (Manila: The Author, 1988).

This idea of the nation, however, remains centered on the state, and nowhere is this clearer than in the incident that I shall relate.

On the occasion of the Chinese New Year in 1995, the Alex Boncayao Brigade (ABB), a breakaway faction of the Communist New People's Army, faxed a letter to the media, a letter addressed specifically to the Chinese Filipinos and urging them never again to allow themselves to be the "milking cows" of corrupt government officials. The ABB also threatened to execute more "corrupt police officers involved in kidnapping," and vowed to "hunt down . . . officials and other notorious elements in the bureaucracy who victimize the Chinese community." The ABB said that it was not against economic development as long as it "benefits our country and people." As long as the workers' welfare is assured, the ABB promised to "foster industrial peace." Finally, the ABB stated that the Chinese Filipinos were "integral parts of the nation who should not be treated as second-class citizens," and declared that "there can be unity of purpose despite the cultural diversity."[61]

When Teresita Ang-See of Kaisa was asked to comment on the ABB statement, she gave a very interesting response. She expressed surprise and comfort in the fact that "the leftist group seem[ed] to be stretching out its hand to the Chinese Filipino community." At the same time, however, she noted that it was a big shame that such statements had to come from the ABB. "It would have been better, and we would have been happier," she said, "had such statements come from the government itself."[62]

The ABB's assertion of the discourse of rights and citizenship would seem to echo in an uncanny way the position that Kaisa takes—its insistence that the Chinese should not be treated as second-class citizens, for example, as well as its emphasis on the coexistence of unity of purpose and cultural diversity. Ang-See's statement, however, reflects Kaisa's strong reliance on addressing the state, a distinct but not unusual feature of Chinese spokesman positions from the capitan de chino (captain of the Chinese) office to the Chamber of Commerce and the Federation. Because of its dependence on state interlocution, Kaisa's production of the Chinese as a collective referent is necessarily dependent on the terms on which dialogue can be conducted with the state. Seeing how the state persists in employing an extractive logic in its dealings with the Chinese, Kaisa does not totally escape its own adoption of the very definition of its constituents made by the state, despite its criticism of such a stance. One example is Kaisa's cooperation with Miriam Defensor Santiago's Alien Legalization Program (ALP), which had originally set the pattern for "buying" citizenship.[63]

The mediating term "fraternity" is thus necessarily a split term, an aporetic term, precisely because it comes up against the additional mediating term of "property."

---

[61] "ABB Expresses Brotherhood with Tsinoys," *Tulay*, February 6, 1995, p. 8. The NPA (New People's Army) itself has disavowed kidnapping-for-ransom as a source of funds on ideological grounds. See Edward R. Kiunisala, "Ka Hector: Rebel or Common Criminal?," *Philippines Free Press*, March 27, 1993, p. 3.

[62] Ibid.

[63] On March 27, 1996, Immigration Commissioner Leandro Verceles announced that aliens who had applied for permanent residency under the ALP had to re-apply under the ASIA and pay the new and increased fee of two hundred thousand pesos, up from the original fifty thousand pesos. Although this statement was later rescinded when Fidel Ramos signed ASIA into law, it remains a fitting example of the cupidity characteristic of state policies toward the Chinese.

Because Kaisa pins its main hope for achieving its goals on successfully establishing a dialogue with the state, its notion of the people is necessarily circumscribed by the terms of the referent that the state "sees." In other words, the moment Kaisa's concept of the nation becomes centered on the state, a certain notion of the "masses" is generated and marginalized by this identification. Although Kaisa acknowledges the existence of poor Chinese, it is unable to gauge the extent to which ethnic Chinese live below the poverty line. Historian Edgar Wickberg's estimate that more than 20 percent of the Chinese live below the poverty line seems necessarily speculative, given the lack of available statistics.[64] Where the middle- and upper-class Chinese can integrate into the so-called mainstream of society, the rest of the Chinese, that is, the poor Chinese, can only disappear into the masses. The point at which one becomes or does not become Chinese, the point at which one *appears* as Chinese on the social map, turns out to be a question as much of property as of fraternity. The main implication of my argument is that Kaisa's production of a collective referent called the Chinese community is implicated in the general ideological form of the class struggle.

But, most importantly, even the term "fraternity" itself is not as self-evident as it appears to be. For Kaisa's insistence on revaluing the heritage of "Chinese culture" comes at a time when public space itself has been emptied of the Chinese. Chineseness is marked visibly in temples, cemeteries, and TV programs, but these "Chinese" spaces do not bear the imprint of the "lived experience" of Chineseness.[65] The traditional day-long Chinese celebration of All Soul's Day disappeared after Chinese community officials banned parking inside the cemeteries. TV programs run Hong Kong and Taiwanese soap operas that the younger generation can no longer understand, thanks to the decrepit Chinese-language curriculum of "Chinese" schools. Opera troupes are manned by Chinese-mestizo actors who learn their lines phonetically, and attendance is feeble. The much touted Chinese "traditional rituals" which attend engagement and wedding ceremonies are often remembered only by Filipino cameramen who videotape (in fact, orchestrate) the ceremonies. Who and what is Chinese, then?

CONCLUSION

Let me summarize, in brief, some of the points I made about kidnapping. I argued that media coverage of the kidnap-for ransom cases since the late eighties appears to lend fresh credence to the truism about the economic prominence and visibility of the Chinese in the Philippines, a truism which casts the Chinese as "obvious" and "proper" targets of extortion. Kidnapping, however, adds a new dimension to this truism because, by treating the *body* of the Chinese as a commodity, it makes the Chinese an almost literal personification of capital. Kidnapping, therefore, calls attention to the ways in which the bodies of the Chinese Filipinos exist as codifications of a complex, shifting network of material and cultural

---

[64] Edgar Wickberg, "Notes on Contemporary Social Organizations in Manila Chinese Society," in *China, Across the Seas/The Chinese as Filipinos*, ed. Aileen S. P. Baviera and Teresita Ang-See (Quezon City: Philippine Association for Chinese Studies, 1992), pp. 59-64.

[65] Instead, the Chinese have taken over "Filipino" spaces like Luneta Park for morning exercises, and they appear in "politically neutral" spaces like the malls.

forces that constitute, but also destabilize, nation-ness and neocolonial globalization. But, more than that, kidnapping highlights a situation wherein the Chinese victims, in order to survive, actively/passively take on these codifications as a "second nature," and enact their bodies' susceptibility to particular oppressive social relations such as racism and commodity-fetishism. In its distinctive way, kidnapping provides an account of the persistence of the truism about the Chinese as alien, "material men" whose virtual nationality within the Philippine neocolonial state remains a politically charged and contested issue, despite the existence of critiques such as those advanced by Kaisa that expose the contingent and non-natural character of these claims.

In this paper I examined not only the specific ways in which the kidnappings historically conflate Chinese and capital, but also the ways in which the Chinese themselves have used the specific historical occasion of the kidnappings in order to publicly interrogate such a conflation. My inquiry took, as its starting point, the interlocutory relation between the Chinese and the Philippine state and looked into the changing relations between the Chinese and the state during the post-EDSA period. These relations primarily express themselves, on the one hand, in terms of the Chinese demand for political representation and their deployment of a discourse of citizenship and rights that counterpoises the body of citizens to the state. On the other hand, these relations express themselves in terms of the state's own explicit organization of its separation from "civil" society and its intensified deployment of an extractive policy toward the Chinese with regards to the issue of permanent residency and citizenship.

In my analysis of the activities of Kaisa Para sa Kaunlaran, I have argued that its cultural/political solution to the conflation of Chinese and capital highlighted by kidnapping reveal, in its turn, the conflictual and contradictory aspects of the discourse on citizenship. Balibar has argued that these repressed contradictions haunt modern politics.[66] My main concern is not merely to point out that the issue of kidnapping and the response of the Chinese community trains the spotlight on these contradictions. I am more concerned about the implications that must be drawn from this kind of analysis. What remains central to any invocation of rights is not only the history of naming and the creation of individual and collective referents that seek to grant any such claim a degree of enunciative and practical stability. What remains central to any invocation of citizenship and rights, as Balibar has noted, is the question of power relations, the issue of inequalities, and "the foundations (equality, liberty, property, fraternity) that are constantly invoked in order to institute inequalities and thereby limit or annul the freedom of an entire 'class' of humanity." As Balibar writes: "[B]ehind these inequalities, there is a kind of difference that cannot be overcome by the institution of equality. This does not mean that equality is not the formal condition of liberation. It only means that it remains purely external, that is, there can be no 'political solution' purely in terms of equaliberty."[67]

"Chinese" must be seen as a term, following Balibar, that is inscribed in a relation of collective inequality which is "reproduced, exercised and verified as a personal relation, which is to say that instituted state power does not subject the same individuals, nor the same class of individuals, by the same means, even though

---

[66] Balibar, "'Rights of Man' and 'Rights of the Citizen,'" p. 55.

[67] Ibid.

it does not stop adding to itself in the process."[68] In resisting the juridically defined notion of citizenship that subjects everybody equally to the law, kidnapping is only the generalized form of the way that the state has chosen to speak to the Chinese. The danger lies in the Chinese community allowing itself to be defined by this kind of state interpellation, and by the meaning of history that this interpellation entails.

But while it is necessary to challenge the ways in which the Philippine state has constrained the discourse of citizenship, we would do well to think of the lessons from Kaisa, to wit, that the discourse of citizenship presupposes the existence of a state and that therefore citizenship cannot be conceptualized outside of state interpellation. The Chinese recourse to citizenship as a matter of strategy is determined by the specific characteristics of the Philippine colonial and neocolonial state, even as it is indicative of the historical negotiations in which the Chinese have engaged in order to secure a space for themselves within the bounds, perhaps even within the teleology, of the nation. But given the contradictory articulations of Chinese belonging to the Philippine nation-state, the Chinese attempt since the post-EDSA period to counterpoise themselves as a body of citizens against the state appears to be an ineffectual political solution to the kidnapping crisis, especially because this solution cannot by itself bring about changes in the attitude of the state, nor curtail the violence that the state is capable of bringing to bear on the Chinese.

We need, instead, to change the state, partly through a rearticulation of the meaning of citizenship in a way that opens up the possibility of justice, a justice that is not a matter of calculable distribution nor restitution, but a justice open to the call for emancipatory transformation. For Chinese Filipinos, heeding the call for justice entails listening to the call of other voices, the call of the other across time, and undoing the fifty years of neocolonial amnesia. We cannot re-imagine a "Chinese in the Philippines" without questioning borders, without rethinking and re-experiencing a new state, economy, home, and nation. Can we, in fact, begin to think of the secret immigrant who lives and moves amongst us as one who is not one of "us" but whom we cannot kick out of "our" country? Can we begin to think of historical belonging not in terms of blood or birth, but in terms of shared experience and struggle? Can we rethink the ethnic Chinese's place in Philippine history? If our present ambivalence about the Chinese is part of a larger effort to make sense of our (neo)colonial history, what implications would this have for our ability to deal with the essential contingency of the Chinese which the nation-state can neither embrace nor repudiate, especially if by embracing or repudiating the Chinese the Philippine nation-state hopes to exorcise what is, in fact, constitutive of its existence and to which the Chinese bear witness by their very presence and what they signify? And what of the essential contingency of the nation-state itself that the Chinese can neither embrace nor repudiate? Kidnapping teaches us that dealing with our ambivalence as Tsinoys cannot be a matter of noting the irresolution of the contradictions within our lived experience, but of understanding that this irresolution is that which forces us to decide and act. This may be a way of acknowledging that it is precisely in the sense that a political community is formed through the violence of exclusion and struggle that it *must* always be made and unmade.

---

[68] Ibid.

THE HISTORY OF THE MODERN PRISON AND THE CASE OF INDOCHINA

Peter Zinoman

During the 1930s, the colonial prison system in French Indochina played a critical role in nurturing the development of the Vietnamese Revolution. After the massive arrests and convictions that followed the repression of the Yên Báy Uprising and Nghệ-Tĩnh Soviets in 1930-1931, the prison system provided a curiously stable environment for the reconstitution and expansion of the radical anti-colonial movement.[1] By the end of the 1930s, the claim that colonial prisons served as revolutionary schools had become a commonplace in both colonial and anti-colonial circles.[2] In addition to functioning as clandestine centers for revolutionary recruitment and training, colonial prisons offered a vulnerable target for the legal anti-colonial press.[3] Beginning around 1934, radical journalists in the colony

---

[1] For western-language histories of these movements, see Martin Bernal, "The Nghệ Tĩnh Soviet Movement," *Past and Present* 92 (August 1981): 148-168; Hỷ Văn Lương, "Agrarian Unrest from an Anthropological Perspective: The Case of Vietnam," *Comparative Politics* 17,2 (January 1985): 153-174; Pierre Brocheux, "L'implantation du mouvement communiste en Indochine française: le cas du Nghệ-Tĩnh (1930-1931)," *Revue d'Histoire Moderne et Contemporaine* 24 (January-March, 1977): 49-74; Ngô Vĩnh Long, "The Indochinese Communist Party and Peasant Rebellion in Central Vietnam, 1930-31," *Bulletin of Concerned Asian Scholars* 10,4 (1978): 15-36. For accounts of the French repression, see Patrice Morlat, *La repression coloniale au Vietnam, (1908-1940)* (Paris: L'Harmattan, 1990) and Daniel Hémery, *Révolutionnaires vietnamiens et pouvoir colonial en Indochine: communistes, trotskystes, nationalistes à Saigon de 1932 à 1937* (Paris: Maspéro, 1975).

[2] From the early 1930s, the Sûreté consistently described colonial prisons as revolutionary schools. The following remark from a 1932 report is exemplary: "After a certain period in detention, prisoners who had been utterly ignorant of communism are thoroughly indoctrinated and become perfectly capable of carrying out propaganda themselves." Dépôt d'Archives d'Outre Mer, Aix-en-Provence, Service de Liaison des Originaires des Territoires Français d'Outre Mer (hereafter AOM-AP, SLOTFOM), Series 3, Carton 52 (AAPCI) 1/1932. The earliest Vietnamese anti-colonial activist to promote the transformation of colonial prisons into revolutionary schools was the great scholar-patriot Phan Châu Trinh. Huỳnh Thúc Kháng recounts in his Côn Đảo prison memoir how, in 1908, Phan encouraged him to imagine the penitentiary as "a natural school" [trường học thiên nhiên]. Huỳnh Thúc Kháng, *Thi Tù Tùng Thoại* [Prison Verse] (Huế: Tiếng Dân, 1939), p. 42.

[3] For the most comprehensive treatment of the radical press in Indochina, see Nguyễn Thanh, *Báo Chí Cách Mạng Việt Nam: 1925-1945* [Vietnamese Revolutionary Newspapers] (Hanoi: Khoa

launched a high-profile press campaign, harshly critical of the colonial prison system. The campaign provoked a series of outside investigations which promoted reforms and ameliorated temporarily the system's more egregious abuses. It also pressured the colonial state to issue amnesties and sentence reductions for numerous political prisoners.[4] Following their release, newly hardened ex-political prisoners returned to and reinvigorated the revolutionary movement, eventually coming to dominate its leadership.[5] Throughout the anti-French resistance (1946-54), the American conflict (1960-75), and the post-war era, colonial imprisonment remained an important credential for advancement into the upper echelons of the communist party.[6] Clearly, any explanation for the success of the Vietnamese revolution must account for the important role assumed by the colonial prison system.

While an examination of the prison system in French Indochina illuminates important areas within the social and political history of Vietnam, it also promises to contribute to a broader field of historical enquiry. Over the past several decades, significant research has been carried out on the history of the modern prison. However, although the explosive growth of prisons and juridical imprisonment during the nineteenth century was a global phenomenon, most research on the topic focuses on the Euro-American experience. Indeed, the editors of *The Oxford History of the Prison*, a recent attempt to survey comprehensively the most important

---

Học Xã Hội, 1984). Also instructive is Trần Huy Liệu's brief essay on the radicial press from 1936-1939, "Những Tờ Báo Mở Màn Của Phong Trào Mặt Trận Dân Chủ" [Newspapers opened during the period of the Democratic Front] in *Trần Huy Liệu: Hồi Ký* [Trần Huy Liệu: Memoirs] (Hanoi: Khoa Học Xã Hội, 1991), pp. 168-176.

[4] For the only secondary source which examines the Indochinese amnesty movement during the 1930s, see Đinh Xuân Lâm and Phạm Xanh, "Đảng Cộng Sản Pháp Với Vấn Đề Tù Nhân Chính Trị Ở Việt Nam Vào Những Năm 30 Của Thế Kỷ" [The French Communist Party and the Problem of Political Prisoners in Vietnam during the 1930s] in *Tình Đoàn Kết Chiến Đấu Vô Sản Việt-Pháp* [The Spirit of Unified Struggle of the Franco-Vietnamese Proletariat] (Hanoi: Thông Tin Lý Luận, 1986), pp. 305-323.

[5] From 1951 to 1976, members of the Political Bureau of the Communist Party Central Committee had spent an average of six and a half years in colonial jails. Consider, for example, the colonial prison experience of Politburo members named at the fourth Party Congress in 1976: Phạm Hùng: fifteen years; Lê Đức Thọ: thirteen years; Lê Văn Lương: thirteen years; Lê Duẩn: eleven years; Nguyễn Duy Trinh: eleven years; Lê Thanh Nghị: eleven years; Nguyễn Văn Linh: eleven years; Trường Chinh: seven years; Phạm Văn Đồng: seven years; Văn Tiến Dũng: six years; Đỗ Mười: five years; Trần Quốc Hoàn: four years; Tố Hữu: four years; Võ Nguyên Giáp: three years. No information is available on the three remaining members: Võ Chí Công, Chu Huy Mân, and Võ Văn Kiệt.

[6] Bùi Tín argued recently that colonial imprisonment has been a necessary credential for advancement in the party. In the memoir he produced after defecting to France in 1990, the former North Vietnamese colonel and editor of *Nhân Dân* [The People] described how prison credentials helped shape the outcome of a leadership struggle following the failed land-reform in the late 1950s. "Still the question remained who would replace Trường Chinh as Party General Secretary. Several cadres close to Hồ Chí Minh at the time said that he had two people in mind. They were Võ Nguyên Giáp and Lê Duẩn, but Hồ was inclined to favor the former with whom he had worked closely for many years. However, Lê Duẩn, was appointed because of the criteria then prevailing. He had spent two long periods in prison amounting to almost ten years in all. This was a significant qualification for rising to the top of the party, since it was considered that the more one had been put to the test, the more trustworthy one was. In fact, imprisonment was regarded as the university of politics and here General Giáp did not qualify because his degree in law resulted from a conventional education." Bùi Tín, *Following Ho Chi Minh: Memoirs of a North Vietnamese Colonel*, trans. Judith Stowe (Honolulu: University of Hawaii Press, 1995), p. 32.

contributions within the field, limit their attention to Western countries exclusively.[7]

This essay represents an attempt to explore the extent to which evidence about the history of the prison in Indochina dovetails with or departs from recent scholarship on the history of the modern Euro-American prison. Two distinct approaches from the Euro-American literature will be examined. The first is associated with the work of David Rothman, Michael Ignatieff, and Patricia O'Brian and is known as the Revisionist School.[8] The second is a tradition that grew out of Michel Foucault's seminal study of the French penal tradition: *Discipline and Punish: The Birth of the Prison*.[9] A consideration of these two bodies of scholarship allows us to integrate the rise of the Indochinese prison into the history of the modern prison more generally and to isolate what was specifically colonial about the system in Indochina.

I argue that the major questions posed by the Revisionist School—questions concerning the conditions necessary for the institutional emergence of the modern prison and the degree to which humanitarian ideals animated nineteenth-century penal reformers—yield meager analytical returns for the history of the prison in Indochina and point to significant differences between colonial and metropolitan institutional arrangements. I also contend that the approach adopted by Foucault— an approach which entails mapping the gradual infiltration and hegemony of disciplinary practices within modern punishment—runs up against the fact that the transformative potential of discipline was of little interest to penal officials in the colony. Indeed, the evidence from Indochina undermines arguments, prevalent within recent Foucaultian scholarship on colonialism, that European imperialism triggered abruptly the global expansion of disciplinary power. Rather, it suggests that technologies of power in Indochina—such as the prison system—were composed of diverse, countervailing elements which derived from the peculiarities of the colonial project and the enduring influence of pre-colonial traditions.

THE REVISIONIST HISTORY OF IMPRISONMENT AND THE INDOCHINESE CASE

The revisionist history of imprisonment emerged in the 1970s as a reaction against so-called narratives of reform which had long dominated conventional accounts of the rise of the prison in Europe and the United States.[10] In narratives of

---

[7] Norval Morris and David Rothman, eds., *The Oxford History of the Prison: The Practice of Punishment in Western Societies* (Oxford: Oxford University Press, 1995).

[8] David Rothman, *The Discovery of the Asylum: Social Order and Disorder in the New Republic* (Boston: Little Brown, 1971); Michael Ignatieff, *A Just Measure of Pain: The Penitentiary in the Industrial Revolution, 1750-1850* (New York: Pantheon, 1978); Patricia O'Brian, *The Promise of Punishment: Prisons in Nineteenth Century France* (Princeton: Princeton University Press, 1982).

[9] Michel Foucault, *Discipline and Punish: The Birth of the Prison*, trans. Alan Sheridan (New York: Pantheon, 1978).

[10] Useful accounts of the narrative of reform literature can can be found in Michael Ignatieff, "State, Civil Society and Total Institutions: A Critique of Recent Social Histories of Punishment" in *Social Control and the State*, ed. Stanley Cohen and Andrew Scull (Oxford: Martin Robertson, 1983), pp. 75-76, and Peter Tyor and Jamil Zainaldin, "Asylum and Society: An Approach to Institutional Change," *Journal of Social History* 13,1 (1979): 23-25, 44-45.

reform, the consciences of enlightened reformers drive institutional change. The rehabilitation of social deviants and law-breakers—the principle justification offered for the modern prison—is lauded as a noble, if imperfectly realized, objective. And the penitentiary, despite its unfortunate shortcomings, is favorably contrasted with the brutal tortures, beatings, and public executions it displaced. Narratives of reform, in other words, assimilate the birth of the prison to a glorious history of human progress.

A characteristic feature of the revisionist history, embodied in the work of Rothman, Ignatieff, and O'Brian, is a rejection of such unalloyed whiggishness. Dismissing any link between the birth of the prison and the growth of a new spirit of humanitarianism, the revisionists advanced radically skeptical arguments about the intentions of reformers and the consequences of their efforts. The new punishment, so they argued, marked the rise and entrenchment of more effective modes of discipline and tighter forms of social control. Instead of lauding them as kinder, gentler forms of punishment, the revisionists exposed prisons as paradigmatic of an insidious and pervasive unfreedom characteristic of modern society.

As should be apparent, the appeal of the revisionist approach derives, in part, from its compelling attempt to turn on its head the conventional account of the prison's emergence. This tactic, described by Rothman as a "reversal of interpretation," lends a characteristically combative tone to revisionist works.[11] Indeed, revisionist arguments attempt to unmask the humanitarian pretensions of generations of penal reformers and the naiveté of historians who celebrate their efforts uncritically. In a colonial environment, however, a similarly revisionist approach to the history of incarceration runs up against a scarcity of material to revise. Other than several article-length studies, little research has been undertaken on the social or institutional histories of colonial systems of judicial incarceration.[12] More striking in the Indochina case is the relative absence of a contemporaneous theoretical or programmatic French discourse on colonial imprisonment. Despite its crucial role in colonial society, the prison system in French Indochina produced no towering figures on the order of John Howard, Jeremy Bentham, or Charles Lucas.[13] Nor does the archival record for Indochina yield a dense body of social scientific literature on the theory or practice of colonial penology.[14] When high-profile

---

[11] David Rothman, "Social Control: The Uses and Abuses of the Concept in the History of Incarceration" in *Social Control and the State,* ed. Stanley Cohen and Andrew Scull (Oxford: Martin Robertson, 1983), p. 106.

[12] Anand Yang, "Disciplining 'Native': Prisons and Prisoners in Early Nineteenth Century India," *South Asia* 10,2 (1987): 29-45; David Arnold, "The Colonial Prison: Power, Knowledge and Penology in Nineteenth-Century India" in *Subaltern Studies VIII, Essays in Honour of Ranajit Guha,* ed. David Arnold and David Hardiman (Oxford: Oxford University Press, 1994), pp. 148-188; Michael Salman, "Nothing Without Labor: Penology, Discipline and Independence in the Philippines under United States Rule," in *Discrepant Histories: Translocal Essays on Filipino Cultures,* ed. Vicente Rafael (Philadelphia: Temple University Press, 1995), pp. 113-132.

[13] For the significance of Bentham and Howard, see Michael Ignatieff, *A Just Measure of Pain,* pp. 47-59, 65-76. For Lucas, see Patricia O'Brian, *The Promise of Punishment,* pp. 30-33.

[14] While several exceptional texts may be identified, only in the strained imagination of the historian can they take on the character of a coherent discourse. See for example: L. Lorion, *Criminalité et médicine judiciare en Cochinchine* (Lyon: A. Stork, 1887), and J. C. Demariaux, *Les secrets des iles Poulo-Condore: le grande bagne Indochinois* (Paris: J. Perronnet, 1956). Neither Lorion nor Demariaux discusses prison administration or reform.

Indochinese officials such as Hubert Lyautey, Paul Doumer, or Albert Sarraut recounted their professional achievements in memoirs, promotional portfolios, or at colonial exhibitions, they seldom pointed to accomplishments in prison administration.[15]

Bereft of pioneering crusaders or zealous reformers, the archive of colonial penal discourse is dominated by the accounts of practicing bureaucrats and administrators—wardens, doctors, inspectors, and guards. Such figures rarely expressed the theoretical concerns of nineteenth-century metropolitan penal reformers or the utopian ideals which Paul Rabinow associates with the "specific intellectuals" who spearheaded the development of French colonial urbanism.[16] Rather, what absorbed Indochinese penal officials was the daily maintenance of an unwieldy and under-funded administrative system. In fact, the colonial state's stubborn disinterest in reform, despite the perpetual disorder and counter-productivity of its prison system, remains one of the most remarkable and enigmatic aspects of the history of imprisonment in French Indochina.

The absence in French Indochina of an idealistic cohort of penal innovators renders irrelevant the revisionist penchant for debunking the prison system's humanitarian pretensions. Unlike its metropolitan counterpart, the colonial prison system did not evolve from the utopian fantasies of social and religious activists. In place of a reformist enthusiasm over the "promise of punishment," the archive of colonial penology discloses a mundane preoccupation with institutional security and the profitable employment of penal labor. Hence, far from endeavoring to discern the real motives behind or consequences of an avowedly humanitarian project, a history of the Indochinese prison must account for the failure of its founders and managers to legitimate their efforts by appeals to a discourse of humanitarianism.

Another important feature of the revisionist history is its attempt to identify the conditions which facilitated the emergence of the nineteenth-century prison. This focus draws attention to those factors which allowed the modern prison to be conceived intellectually and eventually to dislodge and replace earlier modes of punishment. Unlike older approaches which highlighted administrative innovations and the heroic efforts of reformers, the revisionist history encourages scholars to venture beyond the walls of the prison itself and to consider connections between the birth of the prison and a broad range of social, political, economic, and intellectual developments.[17]

For example, in *The Discovery of the Asylum*, Rothman traces the prison's emergence in Jacksonian America to a pervasive social anxiety that economic and demographic changes were threatening to generate disorder and political turmoil. This anxiety dovetailed, so Rothman argues, with a new environmental

---

[15] Hubert Lyautey, *Lettres du Tonkin et Madagscar, 1894-1899* (Paris: Armand Colin, 1921); Paul Doumer, *L'Indochine française: souvenirs* (Paris: Buibert et Nony, 1903); Albert Sarraut, *La Mise en valeur des colonies français* (Paris: Payot, 1923).

[16] Paul Rabinow, *French Modern: Norms and Forms of the Social Environment* (Chicago: University of Chicago Press, 1989), pp. 16, 251, 260-70. Rabinow takes the concept of the "specific intellectual" from Michel Foucault. Michel Foucault, "Truth and Power," in *Power/Knowledge: Selected Interviews and Other Writings, 1972-1977*, ed. Colin Gordon (New York: Pantheon, 1980), pp. 126-33.

[17] In a brief essay on the revisionist history, Patricia O'Brian made an explicit call for an extra-institutional approach to the history of imprisonment. Patricia O'Brian, "Crime and Punishment as Historical Problem," *Journal of Social History* 11,4 (1978): 518.

understanding of human disorder which facilitated social acceptance of the penitentiary as a logical antidote.[18] For Michael Ignatieff, expanding interest in Nonconformism and Materialist Psychology during the eighteenth century only partially explains the birth of the prison in England.[19] In *A Just Measure of Pain* he contends that the penitentiary emerged in response to rising crime rates and an increasing unruliness in crowd behavior, economic changes connected with the industrial revolution, and the disruption of penal transportation caused by war in the American colonies. For France, Patricia O'Brian argues in *The Promise of Punishment* that "the changing structure of the prison was most basically a response to changes created in the transition from traditional to modern society."[20] In addition to highlighting "long term trends towards greater bureaucratization" and the gradual entry of the bourgeoisie "in the process of punishment," she persuasively links institutional innovations to political watersheds in 1789, 1830, 1848, and 1871.[21]

While their arguments diverge in many respects, it is their shared commitment to extra-institutional explanations which make the accounts of Rothman, Ignatieff, and O'Brian such rich and compelling social history. By endeavoring to shed light on the conditions of institutional emergence, these historians illuminate an array of economic, intellectual, social, cultural, and political changes, which arguably prepared the terrain for the birth of the prison. Whether particular developments were formative or merely incidental to the prison's ultimate ascendance, we come away from each account with insight into numerous important areas of social historical enquiry.

In a colonial context, however, the revisionist preoccupation with the prison's conditions of emergence proves less rewarding. The main problem is that rather than emerging more or less organically, prison systems in the colonized world were imposed externally.[22] Hence, the abrupt appearance of a superficially modern prison system in nineteenth-century Vietnam (as opposed to in France or Japan) reveals little about the ascendancy of new ideas and social groups or changes in domestic political or economic life. This is not to deny that internal transformations were occurring in late nineteenth-century Vietnamese society, for they certainly were. It is only to point out the limited capacity of the history of the colonial prison to serve as a barometer for these changes.

On the other hand, while the sudden growth of juridical imprisonment in southern Vietnam during the 1860s cannot be tied analytically to social, economic, political, or epistemic shifts within the society of the colonized, it does raise questions about the capabilities and motivations of the colonizers. Why in 1862, upon

---

[18] Rothman provides a succinct summary of his argument in "Perfecting the Prison: United States, 1789-1865" in *The Oxford History of the Prison*, pp. 111-130.

[19] Michael Ignatieff, *A Just Measure of Pain.* See especially chapter three: "Cords of Love, Fetters of Iron: The Ideological Origins of the Penitentiary," pp. 44-80.

[20] Patricia O'Brian, *The Promise of Punishment*, p. 20.

[21] Ibid., pp. 20-29.

[22] This is not to argue that the nineteenth-century penitentiary movement in Europe did not have a significant international dimension. For example, Jacques-Guy Petit has demonstrated the profound influence of American, Dutch, and British penology on French developments. The point, rather, is that the first Euro-American penitentiaries were built by Euro-American states in response to complex domestic reform movements. Such was not the case in the colonies. Jacques-Guy Petit, *Ces Peines Obscures: La prison pénale en France (1780-1875)* (Paris: Fayard, 1990), pp. 61-67.

seizing territory along the southern Vietnamese coast, did French naval officers immediately construct camps of confinement? Why, by 1865, had they already built elaborate penitentiaries in Saigon and on Côn Đảo Island? And why, twenty years later, as French power expanded over Laos, Cambodia, and northern Vietnam, did colonial officials promptly erect prison networks in each new administrative unit they created?

Intimating that the answers to such questions are self-evident, the brilliant scholar of comparative colonialism in Southeast Asia, J. S. Furnivall, wrote:

> The rule of Leviathan is the rule of law. He expects his subjects to be normal men and to act in a normal manner; if they are abnormal or act abnormally, he claps them into jail or a lunatic asylum—not out of ill-will, but in the sequence of cause and effect which is the law of his being.[23]

Whether all modern Leviathans—colonial or otherwise—are as inherently predisposed to build prisons as Furnivall suggests, efforts to identify conditions for the emergence of the prison in Indochina draws our attention to the nature of the infant colonial state and, in Furnivall's words, to "the law of [its] being." To accord primacy to such problems, however, raises old questions, long central to studies of the non-Western world, about the appropriateness of a scholarly preoccupation with European strategies and practices.[24] My point here is not to call for an elimination of the French from the history of imprisonment in Indochina, rather it is to suggest how a characteristically revisionist emphasis on institutional emergence tips the analytic balance away from arguably more important considerations, such as the impact of the colonial prison system on Vietnamese society, culture, and politics. Rather than simply extending our understanding of European history, the study of colonial prisons, I maintain, should help illuminate the internal dynamics of colonized societies.

DISCIPLINE'S COLONIAL CAREER

Foucault's Discipline and Punish

A history of colonial imprisonment in Indochina might also seek methodological guidance and a comparative perspective in *Discipline and Punish*, Michel Foucault's brilliant and influential examination of disciplinary power in eighteenth- and nineteenth-century France. Because of its historical scope, skepticism toward humanist reform, and misleading subtitle—*The Birth of the Prison*—commentators frequently lump the book alongside those of Rothman, Ignatieff, and O'Brian as a

---

[23] Furnivall was writing with specific reference to British Burma. J. S. Furnivall, "The Fashioning of Leviathan: The Beginnings of British Rule in Burma," *The Journal of the Burma Research Society*, 29,1 (April 1939): 3.

[24] In Southeast Asian Studies, this concern goes back at least to J. C. Van Leur's writings in the 1930s and 1940s and received increasing attention in response to John Smail's influential call for an "autonomous history" in the early 1960s. J. C. Van Leur, *Indonesian Trade and Society: Essays in Asian Social and Economic History* (The Hague: W. van Hoeve, 1955); John Smail, "On the Possibility of an Autonomous History of Modern Southeast Asia," *Journal of Southeast Asian History* 2,2 (July 1961): 72-102.

work within the Revisionist school.[25] However, as Foucault himself acknowledged, the emergence and history of the prison is not the real subject of *Discipline and Punish*.[26] More accurately, Foucault's project here can best be described as a "recounting of the growth of disciplinary power."[27] For Foucault, the significance of the regimented nineteenth-century prison, idealized in Jeremy Bentham's panopticon, is that it serves as a paradigmatic example of what he calls a "disciplinary technology." His central concern is the expansive employment of disciplinary technologies in various modern institutions—the prison, the factory, the school, the lunatic asylum, the barracks—and eventually, their pervasive dissemination throughout the social body.[28] The prison is only accorded primacy in Foucault's account because it happens to be the "privileged locus of realization" (the clearest embodiment, in other words) for the deployment of disciplinary power.[29]

As described by Foucault, the main features of disciplinary power are, by now, familiar.[30] First, because it aspires to maintain a radically continuous "hierarchical observation" or surveillance, discipline employs an architecture which distributes individuals in space so as to increase their visibility. Second, it attempts to transform individual behavior or character (the soul, in Foucault's words) through the regimentation of activity and mandatory labor. Third, it introduces "normalizing judgments" which set standards for the tiniest aspects of everyday life through a system of "micro-penalties" covering time, activity, behavior, speech, the body, and

---

[25] For examples, see Franklin Zimring and Gordon Hawkins, *The Scale of Imprisonment*, (Chicago: University of Chicago Press, 1991), pp. 38-60; Stanley Cohen, *Visions of Social Control: Crime, Punishment and Classification* (Cambridge: Polity Press, 1985), pp. 13-39.

[26] "There can be no question here of writing the history of the different disciplinary institutions, with all their individual differences. I simply intend to map on a series of examples some of the essential techniques that most easily spread from one to another." Michel Foucault, *Discipline and Punish*, p. 139. Also, see Foucault's explanation of his project in Michelle Perrot, ed., *L'Impossible Prison: Recherche sur le système pénitentiare au XIXe siècle* (Paris: Editions du Seuil, 1980). "What is at issue in the 'birth of the prison'? French society in a given period? No. Delinquency in the eighteenth and nineteenth centuries? No. Prisons in France between 1760 and 1840? Not even. Rather something more tenuous: the reflected intentions, the type of calculation, the 'ratio' which was put in place in prison reform when it was decided to introduce in a new form the old practice of incarceration. In sum, I am writing a chapter in the history of 'punitive reason.'" *L'Impossible Prison*, p. 33.

[27] Hubert Dreyfus and Paul Rabinow, *Michel Foucault: Beyond Structuralism and Hermeneutics* (Chicago: University of Chicago Press, 1982), p. 143. Dreyfus and Rabinow also argue that Foucault is not primarily interested in institutional history. "The institution of the hospital or the school is not really Foucault's target, no more than the prison was. Rather he is interested in the disciplinary procedures themselves." *Michel Foucault*, p. 153.

[28] "The panoptic schema, without disappearing as such or losing any of its properties, was destined to spread throughout the social body; its vocation was to become a generalized function." Michel Foucault, *Discipline and Punish*, p. 207.

[29] Ibid., p. 249. Foucault argues that Bentham himself saw the penitentiary as simply the "prime example" of the use to which panopticism could be put because "it has many different functions to fulfill—safe custody, confinement, solitude, forced labor and instruction." Ibid., p. 206.

[30] In drastically schematizing Foucault's account of discipline, I am attempting to bring together common features highlighted repetitively in his depictions of panopticism and prisons as well as his own descriptive outline of the phenomenon in Part Three of *Discipline and Punish*.

sexuality.[31] And fourth, it gives rise to systems of "penal accountancy," manifest in examinations, reports, files, and dossiers, which provide raw material for the formation of bodies of knowledge about specific individuals and eventually for the creation of new pseudo-scientific disciplines about social groups. In *Discipline and Punish*, it is the gradual intrusion of these methods, since the seventeenth century, into institutions and eventually into every aspect of human existence—the creation of a "disciplinary society"—which forms the topic of Foucault's research.[32]

How did Foucault arrive at this specific group of features? In an instructive footnote, he claims to have culled them from empirical investigations into the detailed practices of pre-nineteenth-century military, medical, educational, and industrial institutions.[33] However, he remarks casually that "other examples might have been taken from colonization, slavery, and child rearing."[34] Foucault was to return to child rearing in his subsequent studies of sexuality, but the task of identifying the disciplinary technologies characteristic of colonialism has fallen to others.[35] Before turning to consider the relevance of Foucault's conclusions to the history of imprisonment in Indochina, it may be useful to consider how other scholars within colonial studies have employed Foucault's concepts in their work.

The Colonies: Laboratories of Modernity?

Following Foucault, scholars of colonialism have attempted to unearth the deployment of disciplinary power in the colonies. And in most cases, they have discovered what they set out to find. Emblematic is David Arnold's study of state medicine in British India, in which he asserts that, "bodies were being counted and categorized, they were being disciplined, discoursed upon, and dissected, in India much as they were in Britain, France, or the United States."[36] Taking the American Philippines as an example, Michael Salman argues that "it is in the colonies of the late nineteenth and early twentieth centuries that we might find the most complete examples of the 'carceral continuum,' the concept Foucault introduced to represent the circulation of disciplinary techniques throughout societal institutions and the

---

[31] "The work shop, the school, the army were subject to a whole micro-penalty of time (lateness, absences, interruptions), of inactivity (inattention, negligence, lack of zeal), of behavior (impoliteness, disobedience), speech (idle chatter, insolence), of the body (incorrect attitudes, irregular gestures, lack of cleanliness), of sexuality (impurity, indecency). Ibid., p. 178.

[32] "One can speak of the formation of a disciplinary society in this movement that stretches from the enclosed disciplines, a sort of social 'quarantine,' to an indefinitely generalizable mechanism of 'panopticism.' Not because the disciplinary modality of power has replaced all the others; but because it has infiltrated the others, sometimes undermining them, but serving as an intermediary between them, linking them together, extending them and above all making it possible to bring the effects of power to the most minute and distant elements." Ibid., p. 216

[33] Ibid., p. 314, n.1.

[34] Ibid.

[35] Michel Foucault, *The History of Sexuality. Volume I: An Introduction*, trans. Robert Hurley (New York: Vintage/Random House, 1980).

[36] David Arnold, *Colonizing the Body: State Medicine and Epidemic Disease in Nineteenth-Century India* (Berkeley: University of California Press, 1993), p. 9.

human sciences."[37] Timothy Mitchell's variant of this approach, with reference to colonial Egypt, contends that not only were disciplinary technologies employed extensively in the colonies, but that they were employed there first.

> Foucault's analyses are focused on France and Northern Europe. Perhaps this focus has tended to obscure the colonizing nature of disciplinary power. Yet the panopticon, the model institution whose geometric order and generalized surveillance serve as a motif for this kind of power, was *a colonial invention*. The panoptic principle was devised on Europe's colonial frontier with the Ottoman Empire, and examples of the panopticon were built for the most part not in northern Europe, but in places like colonial India. The same can be said for the monitorial method of schooling, also discussed by Foucault . . . [38]

In their explicitly Foucaultian studies of French colonial urbanism, Paul Rabinow and Gwendolyn Wright attempt to explain why the disciplinary technologies embodied in modern architecture and urban planning (i.e. "the planned city as a regulator of modern society") might have originated in the colonies.[39] They claim that, freed from the cumbersome political constraints of the metropole, colonial officials perceived the colonies as "laboratories" for testing new techniques of welfare and social control. "The colonies," Rabinow argues, "constituted a laboratory of experimentation for new arts of government capable of bringing a modern and healthy society into being."[40] Wright and Rabinow find substantial evidence for their thesis in the prominence accorded images of the "colonial laboratory" in the discourse produced by a wide range of French architects and urbanists.[41]

Turning to the prison system in French Indochina, a very different kind of colonial institution comes into view. Among the most remarkable aspects of the system is the relatively small role assumed by disciplinary power. If we accept that disciplinary power maintains order through spatial structures which isolate, individualize, and enhance visibility, what should we make of the crude communal architecture typical of Indochinese prisons?[42] If disciplinary power, following

---

[37] Michael Salman, "'Nothing Without Labor,'" p. 115.

[38] Timothy Mitchell, *Colonizing Egypt* (Berkeley: University of California Press, 1988), p. 35.

[39] Rabinow, *French Modern*; Gwendolyn Wright, *The Politics of Design in French Colonial Urbanism* (Chicago: University of Chicago Press, 1991). The quote is from Rabinow, *French Modern*, p. 12.

[40] Ibid., p. 289.

[41] For example, Wright highlights the significance of Joseph Chailley-Bert's depiction of the colonies as "experiments, in whatever sense, whether laboratory or greenhouse on a small scale." Wright, *The Politics of Design in French Colonial Urbanism*, p. 72.

[42] "The Hai Duong provincial prison is very old and although large, its arrangement does not permit the efficient use of its space. It is composed of one room, large enough to hold two-hundred convicts, a smaller room reserved for defendants, several cells, an infirmary and a small room for women which can hold fifteen comfortably." AOM-H-RST 81831: "Prisons and Pénitentiaires, 1917-18." The communal room type set up was characteristic of Indochina's larger penitentiaries as well: "Convicts on Con Dao are not divided into categories based on sentence. Instead they are mixed pell-mell so that those sentenced to relegation or to short terms of forced labor mingle freely with those condemned for life. It must be pointed out that material inadequacies have prevented adherence to legal prescriptions." AOM-AP-NF GG 4260 "Inspection de Poulo Condore, September 23, 1916," p. 3.

Foucault, entails "the technical transformation of individuals," what conclusions can be drawn from the meagerness of a discourse in Indochina on penal rehabilitation, behavioral modification, or the reformative effects of mandatory labor?[43] If "character" or "the soul" represents the primary target of disciplinary power, why do all accounts confirm that a brutal regime of corporal punishment figured ubiquitously behind the walls of Indochinese prisons?[44] And how do we square Foucault's description of the dialectical relationship between the workings of disciplinary power and the production of instrumental knowledge with the insignificance of colonial penal science, the virtual absence of technical experts, and the dominant role played by that supreme administrative generalist—the Provincial Resident—in the management of colonial punishment?[45]

The contrast between the modernist laboratories of Indochinese urban design and the archaic chamber of horrors of Indochinese punishment suggests how power could function differently in different colonial institutions. Such inconsistency squares poorly with Foucault's depiction of a "carceral society" in which discipline becomes "naturalized" by virtue of its ubiquitous operation throughout the social body. On the contrary, in Indochina, instead of Foucault's seamless "carceral continuum," we find the simultaneous operation of different modes of power, often within the same institutional setting.[46]

The prison system is a case in point. While I have been suggesting that disciplinary power never dominated the workings of the colonial prison system, it would be an overstatement to deny its existence there altogether. Like their metropolitan counterparts, colonial wardens devised daily schedules, set standards for inmate conduct, attempted to monitor behavior, punished petty infractions, maintained individual dossiers, and tabulated statistics. Still, we should be wary of the fact that such disciplinary technologies reveal themselves today at the site most accessible to historians: the archive of penal directives and regulations. These institutional blueprints and decrees were typically imported directly from the metropole, modified (more or less) for colonial conditions, and eventually published in annual collections of administrative documents. Consequently, historians have little difficulty finding Indochinese analogues to those metropolitan texts which Foucault cites as evidence for discipline's abrupt ascendance in European penology.[47]

However, as colonial officials pointed out repeatedly, the gulf between prison policy and practice could be vast. "At this moment," remarked one colonial inspector

---

[43] Even the handful of Criminal Anthropological studies on Indochina devoted little attention to penological questions. See for example, Lorion, *Criminalities et médicine judiciaire en Cochin Chine*.

[44] "The word 'prison' conjures immediately two images: rotten food and beatings." Phan Văn Hùm, *Ngồi Tù Khám Lớn* [Sitting in the Big Jail] (Saigon: Dân Tộc, 1957 [1929]), p. 78.

[45] Provincial prisons, which contained roughly 75 percent of Indochina's inmate population, were managed directly by Residents, the highest-ranking administrative official in each province. This is borne out by the extensive correspondence on prison administration between the Résident Supérieure du Tonkin and Provincial Residents found in Le Fonds de la Résidence Supérieure du Tonkin at the National Archive I, Hanoi.

[46] See the final chapter of *Discipline and Punish* entitled "The carceral."

[47] An example appears early in *Discipline and Punish* where Foucault contrasts Léon Faucher's rules for "the House of young prisoners in Paris" with the torture and execution of the regicide, Damiens. Ibid., p. 6.

in 1932, "the prisons of Tonkin reveal so much overcrowding and promiscuity, and such a melange of different categories of condemned of all sorts that I am led to the conclusion that there is no longer any observation of legal texts."[48] A report on the Con Dao Penitentiary expressed a similar view:

> Indochina possesses decrees and local texts which constitute an imposing arsenal of penalties: prison, reclusion, detention, deportation, forced labor, banishment etc . . . which are ill-adapted to the conditions of the colony. On Con Dao, the bagne receives convicts of all categories and sensibly subjects them to an identical regime.[49]

While the distance between colonial penal policy and practice poses problems for historians, the discrepancy itself can be interpreted as embodying the very disorder of the system. The failure of colonial prison administration to conform to written regulations reflected deeper problems: badly kept records, incompetent management, disobedient personnel, and the general failure of the colonial prison to meet metropolitan standards. A report on the Saigon Central Prison in 1932 raised the possibility of complete administrative break-down.

> The detailed observations formulated by M. Le Gregam are applicable in other penitential establishments: a chronic disorder in bookkeeping, an ignorance or disregard of the most elementary administrative rules, the confinement together of detainees from all categories, minors included, without any observation of legal prescriptions for each order of penalty. Given the extent of such practices, the regulations are little more than a facade.[50]

Despite the absence of sustained scholarly research on colonial prisons in other contexts, anecdotal evidence suggests that the Indochinese system was not unique. Discussing a notorious East Sumatran multiple murder case in 1876, Ann Laura Stoler cites the example of a newly appointed Dutch Assistant-Resident who found "prison ledgers in such disarray that he can neither find records of the number of people in the prison nor dossiers detailing the length of their sentences nor even their crimes."[51] In British Indian penal documents, Anand Yang reports finding neither a

---

[48] AOM-AP-NF Indochine, AF POL 1728. "Rapport fait par M. Chastend de Gery, Inspecteur de Colonies concernant l'organization du Régime Pénitentiaire au Tonkin, April 26, 1932," p. 12.

[49] AOM-AP-NF Indochine, AF POL 1728 "Observations de M. l'Inspecteur des Colonies Demongin, April 23, 1932." The term "bagne" originally referred to shore-based naval prisons that used hard labor to maintain port facilities and arsenals. It eventually came to denote any penal institution for hard-labor convicts.

[50] AOM-AP-NF Indochine AF POL 1728 "Rapport fait par M. Le Gregam, Inspecteur des Colonies sur la Maison Centrale de Saigon, January 30, 1932," p. 1.

[51] Ann Laura Stoler, "'In Cold Blood': Hierarchies of Credibility and the Politics of Colonial Narratives," *Representations* 37 (Winter 1992): 178. Stoler continues that Assistant-Resident Valck's predecessor "may have never kept a register, but neither did Valck take it upon himself to start one. Faber reported that among the few dossiers he found was one for a prisoner who had been interned for over eleven months for a four month sentence."

"voice of humanitarianism" nor a discourse "about reformation or rehabilitation."[52] In British Burma, Furnivall remarked that "the jails were continually being enlarged and continually overcrowded," that "whipping is freely used," and that "a prisoner could have anything he wanted except women; some said he could even have women."[53] Seen in the light of the prison system in Indochina, the images conjured by Stoler, Yang, and Furnivall suggest that despite the historical convergence of high imperialism and the birth of disciplined penal institutions in Europe, colonial prisons rarely employed or embodied modern disciplinary technologies.

Why might this be the case?

THE LIMITS OF COLONIAL DISCIPLINE

Discipline and Racism

Here, perhaps, aspects of the revisionist argument may prove instructive. Several revisionist scholars point out that the distinctively modern commitment to behavioral modification through incarceration—a key pillar of disciplinary power according to Foucault—declined where ethnic or racial differences separated the keepers from the kept. By the 1860s, so Rothman argues, the Jacksonian faith in rehabilitation through discipline and regimentation had given way to a strictly custodial mode of incarceration "characterized by overcrowding, brutality, and disorder."[54] He links this transformation to the fact that, as the nineteenth century progressed, "an increasing number of prison inmates were drawn from new immigrant groups, specifically the Irish."[55] Michael Hindus's comparative history of penal systems in nineteenth-century Massachusetts and South Carolina also suggests how the ethnic composition of the inmate population could shape the penal regime.[56] According to Hindus, whites who ran the criminal justice system in South Carolina resisted the introduction of a rehabilitative prison regime because the inmate population was made up of black slaves.

> Rather than wishing to inculcate middle-class virtues in the criminal, dangerous and laboring classes, as was the goal in Massachusetts, South Carolinians conceived of their dangerous and criminal classes as one which by its innate inferiority could not be salvaged. This meant, of course, that no reformatory sentence was ever contemplated for South Carolina slaves.[57]

This attitude of white South Carolinians towards the state's largely black inmate population may help shed light on the idiosyncratic character of colonial prison administration.

---

[52] Anand Yang, "Disciplining 'Natives'," p. 30.

[53] J. S. Furnivall, *Colonial Policy and Practice*, pp. 137, 173, 268.

[54] David Rothman, "Perfecting the Prison," p. 126.

[55] Ibid.

[56] Michael Hindus, *Prison and Plantation: Crime, Justice, and Authority in Massachusetts and South Carolina, 1767-1878* (Chapel Hill: The University of North Caroline Press, 1980).

[57] Ibid., p. xxvi.

Like their counterparts in the American South, colonial officials were not unaware of the reformist currents which had transformed Euro-American institutional life in the late eighteenth and early nineteenth century. However, in both cases, the profoundly racist structure of the societies in which they lived discouraged the introduction of state-of-the-art institutional practices.[58] For the French in Indochina, romantic notions of an "unchanging Orient" and racist convictions in the innate inferiority of the indigenous populations tempered their oft-noted commitment to a civilizing mission. These powerful prejudices discouraged a belief that modern technologies (disciplinary or otherwise) could effect fundamental changes in the nature of colonial subjects. How could one expect significant "improvements" in a people considered to be, in the words of one Governor-General, "mentally retarded, more or less asleep?"[59] Even avowedly anti-colonial French observers such as Roland Dorgeles tended to see in the "yellow races" an essential cultural incorrigibility.

> Some people believe that European inventions are going to produce a revolution in the old World. This is a great mistake. The old world adopts, but is not astonished. Give the yellow race the telegraph and they send telegrams; the phonograph, and they listen to songs; the railway and they buy tickets. But *they do not change fundamentally* for these trifles. As a matter of fact, it is the machine and not they, that is metamorphosed.[60]

French racism partially explains the contrast between the modernist ambitions of Indochinese urban design and the crude brutality of Indochinese punishment. Because the racial composition of the colonial prison population differed significantly from that of the colonial urban population, French officials conceptualized penal and urban policy in radically different terms. Not only were status-obsessed colonial courts loath to incarcerate Europeans, but long-term French convicts in Indochina were always transported to the metropole for execution of sentence.[61] Since colonial inmates were drawn almost exclusively from native populations, officials showed little faith in the capacity of disciplinary techniques to reform prisoners and rarely imagined that their work would be judged by metropolitan standards. Conversely, colonial cities were to be peopled not only by colonized subjects but by Europeans as well. For colonial urban designers, the presence of large, long-term French communities and the growth of European

---

[58] See Albert Sarraut's memoirs for particularly articulate examples of the profound contempt even reputedly enlightened French administrators held for Indochinese populations: "Without us, without our intervention. . . these indigenous populations would still be abandoned to misery and abjection; epidemics, massive endemic diseases, and famines would continue to decimate them; infant mortality would still wipe out half their offspring; petty kings and corrupt chiefs would still sacrifice them to vicious caprice; their minds would be degraded by the practice of base superstition and barbarous custom; and they would perish from misery in the midst of unexploited wealth." Albert Sarraut, *Grandeur et Servitude Coloniales* (Paris: Sagittaire, 1931), p. 117.

[59] Speech of Governor-General Martial Merlin, *Conseil de Gouvernement de l'Indochine, Session Ordinaire de 1923* (Hanoi: Imprimerie de l'Extrême-Orient, 1923), p. 13.

[60] Roland Dorgeles, *Sur la route mandarine* (Paris: Jean Budry et Cie, 1925), p. 47. My emphasis.

[61] J. De Galembert, *Les Administrations et les Services Publics Indochinois* (Hanoi: Imprimerie Mac Dinh Tu, 1931), p. 902.

tourism generated a desire to "win favor in the eyes of metropolitan colleagues."[62] Since they imagined their efforts targeting the expectations and working on the bodies of a European audience, colonial urban planners were motivated to experiment with the most modern disciplinary practices.

Discipline and The Weight of the Past

Like colonial racism, the lingering influence of pre-colonial penal traditions prevented the Indochinese prison system from approximating its metropolitan counterpart. Such traditions weighed heaviest in Annam, where the royal court and the decaying imperial bureaucracy continued to control much of the prison system until the end of the colonial era.[63] Other than the penitentiaries at Lao Bao and Ban Me Thout which were run by French officials directly, the protectorate's smaller prisons were managed by court-appointed mandarins.[64] Given their limited role there, French officials imagined that prison administration in Annam owed more to paternalistic Vietnamese traditions than scientific European penology.

> Political and common-law prisoners in Annam enjoy a treatment founded on the natural generosity which flows from the essence of the Annamese political system. Here, the Sovereign is known as the "father and mother of the people" and the more scientific penal methods employed in our other territories are never applied.[65]

While inmates may have recognized the precolonial character of the prison regime in colonial Annam, their efforts to avoid serving sentences there suggest that the "natural generosity" of the old system impressed them less than its chronic brutality, randomness, and squalor.[66]

Although imprisonment was never one of the five major forms of punishment in traditional Sino-Vietnamese jurisprudence (i.e. light flogging, heavy flogging, penal servitude, exile, and death), prisons are mentioned in Vietnamese chronicles as early as the eleventh century.[67] Evidence for the existence of a premodern prison system in

---

[62] Wright, *The Politics of Design in French Colonial Urbanism*, p. 55.

[63] Throughout the 1930s, prisoners in Annam could only receive amnesties and sentence reductions directly from Emperor Bảo Đại. See the article "Ở Trung kỳ cũng có nhiều chính trị phạm và thường phạm được tha cùng được giảm tội" [In Annam, many political prisoners and common-law prisoners receive amnesties or sentence reductions] in *Đông Pháp*, June 19, 1936.

[64] Tỉnh Ủy Dak Lak and Viện Lịch Sử Đảng, *Lịch Sử Nhà Đày Buôn Ma Thuột (1930-1945)* [History of Buon Ma Thuot Penitentiary] (Hanoi: Sự Thật, 1991); Lê Kim Quế, "Tìm Hiểu Về Nhà Tù Lao Bảo."

[65] AOM-AP-NF Indochine AF POL "Détenus politiques, January 5, 1935."

[66] In his prison memoir, Tôn Quang Phiệt describes his efforts to avoid being transported to an "Annamese" prison. Tôn Quang Phiệt, *Một Ngày Ngàn Thu (Lần Thứ Nhất Ở Nhà Ngục)* [The Eternal Day (My First Time in Prison)] (Huế: Phúc Long, 1935), p. 32.

[67] According to the fifteenth-century Vietnamese annals, King Lê Thánh Tông instructed his court officials to distribute blankets, mats, and rice to prisoners during the harsh winter of 1055. "Living in the palaces heated with coal stoves and wearing plenty of warm clothing, I still feel this cold. I am quite concerned about the prisoners [*người tù*] in jails [*ngục*] who are miserably locked up in stocks and manacles [*gông cùm*], without enough food to eat and without clothes to warm their bodies, or even some undeserving dying before their guilt or

Vietnam can also be found in the fifteenth-century Le code which includes roughly a dozen regulations on prison administration.[68] As in early modern Europe, prisons in traditional Vietnam were mainly used to hold defendants awaiting adjudication of their cases.[69] However, premodern legal texts suggest that, by at least the early nineteenth century, imperial magistrates could employ long-term imprisonment as punishment.[70]

A picture of the daily workings of pre-colonial Vietnamese prisons can be found in the writings of colonial scholars, descriptions left by nineteenth-century European inmates, and Vietnamese literature. While such accounts must be used cautiously, several recurring features are worthy of note. One was the ubiquity in prison of corporal punishment. Consider, for example, the following excerpt from English seaman Edward Brown's account of his incarceration in Cochinchina during the late 1850s.

> The warden of the prison was a Canton man by birth. It appears, that the Cochinchinese government generally choose these men to fill situations where severity is required, and truly this man was severe, and even brutal, for he kept the rattan going on the unfortunate prisoners' hides from sunrise to sunset, and for the most trivial of offenses . . . He used to sit on a couch, in the middle of the cottage floor, and there award the daily punishment to the poor prisoners of whom there were more than two hundred. About twenty of them were flogged daily on average.[71]

Catholic missionary M. Miche echoed Brown in his observation that the training of Cochinchinese soldiers for guard duty "was confined to a single practice—the use of the rattan—so as to lay it on with dexterity." Miche described the training he witnessed in the prison compound in Hue:

> A stuffed figure was placed in the midst of the courtyard and one after the other, the soldiers took their turn in elaborately thrashing it. The great art was to administer the blows so that they left a single wheal. He who hit best

innocence has been determined. I feel a deep compassion for them." Ngô Sĩ Liên, comp., *Đại Việt Sử Ký Toàn Thư, Tập I* [The Complete Book of the Historical Records of Great Viet] (Hanoi: Khoa Học Xã Hội, 1972), p. 284.

[68] Nguyễn Ngọc Huy and Tạ Văn Tài, *The Le Code: Law In Traditional Vietnam: A Comparative Sino-Vietnamese Legal Study with Historical-Juridical Analysis and Annotations*, vol. I (Athens: Ohio University Press, 1987). See articles 650, 651, 658, 659, 660, 661, 663, 664, 695, 707, 717.

[69] "Only those detained pending judicial trial remained in jail." Tạ Văn Tài, *The Vietnamese Tradition of Human Rights* (Berkeley: Institute of East Asian Studies, University of California, Indochina Research Monograph, 1988), p. 68.

[70] In addition to the five penalties of Sino-Vietnamese law, the following seven punishments are frequently alluded to in official decrees and supplementary commentaries: military servitude, the cangue, the whip, branding, fines, public display, and the prison. Alfred Schreiner, *Les Institutions annamites en Basse-Cochinchine avant la conquête fraçaise*, vol. I (Saigon: Claude et Cie, 1990), pp. 145-148.

[71] Edward Brown, *Cochin-China, and my experience of it; a seaman's narrative of his adventures and sufferings during a captivity among Chinese pirates on the coast of Cochin-China, and afterwards during a journey on foot across that country, in the years 1857-8, by Edward Brown* (originally 1861, republished Taipei: Ch'eng Wen, 1971), p. 186.

in this manner carried off the prize of skill . . . In Cochinchina, indeed, the rattan is the universal remedy and the soldier feels it as often as he uses it.[72]

The extensive flogging of the confined suggests that unlike in Europe, imprisonment in Vietnam functioned to facilitate, rather than to substitute for, more corporal forms of punishment. This can also be seen in the widespread use of chains, fetters, and cangues on prisoners.[73] A French doctor studying jails in colonial Annam in the late nineteenth century expressed dismay at the repeated sight of "inmates with purulent wounds or skin ulcerations at places where they wore cangues or stocks."[74]

Another important feature of the pre-colonial prison was the way its loosely structured spatial order allowed for the indiscriminate mixing of different kinds of prisoners. The simple architecture of pre-colonial prisons comprised a walled court-yard, known as the *ngục thất*, or outer jail, and a fortified hard-wood chamber within the courtyard called the *trại lá*, or inner jail.[75] The *trại lá* was to contain serious offenders and inmates awaiting the execution of capital sentences.[76] All other prisoners—the accused and the convicted, adults and juveniles, men and women— lived and worked much as they pleased within the *ngục thất*. Edward Brown was struck by the freedom of movement and activity which prisoners enjoyed there:

> The prisoners had free access to every part of the outer jail. They were allowed to follow their trade, which was chiefly making baskets, or other fancy wicker-work, of bamboo or rattan. The bamboo was supplied to them gratuitously, but the rattan they had to purchase for themselves; and each was allowed to dispose of his own work as he saw fit, in small bazaar within

---

[72] John Rutherford Shortland, *A History of Christianity in Cochinchina and Tonking* (London: Burns and Oates, 1875), p. 256. The widespread use of corporal punishment in precolonial prisons is further evidenced by the fact that the authors of the Le Code felt compelled to introduce strict penalties, not found in parent Chinese codes, for officials who beat prisoners unjustly. Article 707 of the Code reads: "Jail officers who mistreat or strike prisoners and inflict injury on them without reason shall be punished." Nguyễn Ngọc Huy and Tạ Văn Tài, *The Le Code: Law in Traditional Vietnam*, p. 290.

[73] The practice is described by Brown in some detail. "Words cannot express my feelings, when I saw numbers of men fettered with strong irons, jingling about their bodies. A chain is fastened to a large ring, riveted on their necks, and extending down to their waist, where there is a small ring, with two branches of chain, reaching their ankles, where it is linked to other rings, riveted to those joints. The whole weighs about ten pounds, and is very clumsily made. The weight of it, upon the upper ring causes it to cut into the flesh at the back of the neck and form dreadful sores on that part as well as at the ankles; I saw many prisoners suffering in this manner." Brown, *Cochin-China, and my experience of it*, p. 183.

[74] Tạ Văn Tài, *The Vietnamese Tradition of Human Rights*, p. 73.

[75] Maurice M. Durand and Nguyen Tran Huan, *Connaissance du Vietnam* (Paris: Imprimeries Nationale, 1954), pp. 111-112. See also, Schreiner, *Les Institutions annamites en Basse-Cochinchine*, p. 148. "In Annamite prisons, there exists that which can be called an interior prison; it is a kind of dark dungeon, composed of a compartment constructed with hardwood. This prison is reserved for the serious criminals and sequestration in this prison is called 'incarceration.' The simple 'detention' in the external part or openings of the prison does not constitute 'incarceration.'"

[76] This picture conforms roughly to Michael Dutton's understanding of pre-twentieth century Chinese prisons. Michael Dutton, *Policing and Punishment in China: From Patriarchy to the 'People'* (Cambridge: Cambridge University Press, 1992), pp. 97-140.

the precincts of the jail . . . A few of them made fans, umbrellas or embroidery.[77]

The lively randomness of pre-colonial prison life was enhanced by the fact that the institution made no provisions for food, clothing, or medicine. Instead, prisoners were to be supplied by friends or family who enjoyed wide access to the *ngục thất*. About pre-colonial jails, Alfred Schreiner remarked that most prisoners "are not sealed off and can communicate easily with and are supplied food by those on the outside."[78] Given the porousness of prison walls, it is not surprising that guards acted as middlemen between prisoners and their families and frequently extracted extortionate fees in return for petty privileges, services, and protection.[79]

While the unbroken continuity of prison administration in Annam helps explain the continuation there of traditional penal practices, their persistence in Tonkin and Cochinchina reflects the endurance of older cultural expectations about the nature of judicial confinement. Heirs to an ancient penal tradition in which the flogging of prisoners was the norm, locally recruited guards simply carried on with the practice in colonial prisons. Such cultural conventions could be passed down through depictions of crime and punishment in popular culture. For example, a satirical prison scene of considerable brutality figures prominently in an early nineteenth-century version of, what must have been, a much older Vietnamese verse-fable: "The Catfish and the Toad." In the story, a toad's bogus lawsuit against a catfish lands the latter in jail. There, he is chained and beaten repeatedly by his abusive keepers:

> "Well, let the Toad go home," the prefect said
> "For further hearings bolt the Catfish in!"
> The zealous bailiffs did as they were told
> and promptly clapped the Catfish into jail.
> Alas, they kept him under lock and key—
> ten men closed in on one to bleed him white.
> From mandarin to bailiffs orders flowed:
> they cangued his neck by day and chained his legs
> by night, they cut his hide to rags and shreds,
> plying a twin-lash whip with diligence.[80]

Cultural representations linking judicial confinement and corporal punishment were sustained and deepened by the routine brutality French penal officials directed at prisoners and native guards alike. Episodes featuring the flogging of both

---

[77] Brown, *Cochin-China, and my experience of it*, p. 187.

[78] Schreiner, *Les Institutions annamites en Basse-Cochinchine avant la conquête française*, p. 148.

[79] The Le Code set strict limits on the amount guards could charge prisoners for specific services and stipulated punishments for bribes. See, for example, Article 717: "Jail officers and judicial clerks who compel payment of a lamp-light fee (*đăng hỏa tiền*) or a paper fee (*chỉ tiền*) in an amount of five (*mạch*) or more over the official rate shall receive fifty strokes of the light stick and a one grade demotion," and Article 664: "A guard who takes bribes from detainees in order to advise them about changing their statements or to communicate what other people say about their case . . . shall be punished." Nguyễn Ngọc Huy and Tạ Văn Tài, *The Le Code: Law in Traditional Vietnam*, pp. 292, 278.

[80] Huỳnh Sanh Thông, trans.,"The Catfish and the Toad" in *The Heritage of Vietnamese Poetry: An Anthology* (New Haven: Yale University Press, 1979), p. 61.

prisoners and "native" guards occur regularly in colonial-era prison memoirs and appear repeatedly in internal reports.[81] It is not surprising that victimized guards tended to take out their frustrations on vulnerable prisoners, creating an institutional culture of extreme violence and terror. "Beatings in Côn Đảo follow a prearranged plan," ex-prisoner Huỳnh Thúc Kháng observed in 1908, "The French beat the guards, the guards beat the caplans, and the caplans beat the prisoners."[82] Here, colonial racism and the persistence of pre-colonial penal practices coalesced to create a prison system which functioned not through the subtle technologies of disciplinary power but through the dramatic deployment of terror, deprivation, and violence.

In rare cases, habitual abuse could generate revolts in which desperate prisoners and disgruntled guards joined forces against the administration, an event all but unknown in the history of the modern French prison.[83] The Thái Nguyên Rebellion of 1917, in which prisoners and guards torched the provincial prison, executed the French staff, seized the town, and raised the flag of revolt against the colonial state provides a particularly dramatic example.[84] Indiscriminate French hostility towards the keepers and the kept could also produce more subtle allegiances between the two groups, manifested in a high frequency of escape attempts and in widespread collusive smuggling and gambling. Accounts of collusion, real or imagined, appeared regularly in internal reports.

> The indigenous surveillants have shown themselves to be such incorrigible idlers that three convicts assigned corvée under their care were found yesterday morning gambling for large sums of money in the living quarters of one of their wives . . . I call your attention to the demoralized state of the guards. These agents, a large percentage of whom are drunkards and opium addicts, are, with rare exceptions, involved in pimping and collusion with the detainees. The degree of corruption is so extensive and the staff so

---

[81] For examples, consult: Phan Văn Hùm, *Ngồi Tù Khám Lớn*, p. 79, 80; Hoàng Đầu Minh, *Cái Thân Tù Tội* [My life as a prisoner] (Saigon: Xủa Nay, 1932), p. 7; Lê Văn Hiến, *Ngục Kontum* [Kontum Prison] (Hanoi: Nhà Văn, 1958 [1937]), p. 47. For a graphic official account of the routinization of beating in prison, see the confidential report prepared in 1918 on the sadistically violent behavior of M. Darles, the Director of the Thái Nguyên Penitentiary. AOM-AP-NF 7F51 "Affaire de Thai Nguyen: Rapport Confidential 2547, December 24, 1918."

[82] Huỳnh Thúc Kháng, *Thi Tù Tùng Thoại*, p. 68. "Caplans" were prisoners who enjoyed special treatment for assisting guards with their surveillance duties.

[83] Perrot points out that the archive of the prison in France discloses little on collective violence of any kind. "There is also the matter of collective revolt, but we know little about it. The inventory of series F16 [in the National Archives] mentions a considerable number of petitions, protests by prison inmates and foiled conspiracies during the Restoration. ...But we hear nothing that would qualify as an 'event'; rather, it is all a vague background noise, a muted, far-away rumbling that may have died before it came to fruition." Michelle Perrot, "Delinquency and the Penitentiary System in Nineteenth-Century France" in *Deviants and the Abandoned in French Society: Selections from the Annales: Economies, Sociétés, Civilisations Vol. IV*, ed. Robert Forster and Orest Ranum (Baltimore: Johns Hopkins University Press, 1978), p. 217.

[84] Accounts of the rebellion can be found in: Trần Huy Liệu, *Loạn Thái Nguyên* [The Thai Nguyen Uprising] (Hanoi: Bảo Ngọc, 1935) and Đào Trinh Nhất, *Lương Ngọc Quyến và Cuộc Khởi Nghĩa Thái Nguyên* [Lương Ngọc Quyến and the Thái Nguyên Rebellion] (Saigon: Tân Việt, 1957).

debauched that it seems foolish to even attempt a moral and material reorganization of the penitentiary.[85]

While inmate-guard relations of a similar nature were not unknown in Europe or the United States, the distinctive racial apartheid practiced in Indochinese prisons muddied the line between inmates and staff, giving rise to a much less stable institutional environment.[86]

RESISTANCE: STORMING THE COLONIAL BASTILLE

My argument, that colonial racism and the enduring legacies of pre-colonial Vietnamese punishment prevented disciplinary technologies from dominating the Indochinese prison system, supports Partha Chatterjee's generalized characterization of, what he calls, "regimes of power" in colonial and post-colonial societies. For Chatterjee, such regimes are marked by a simultaneous "combination of different modes of power." He goes on to say:

> When one looks at the regimes of power in the so-called backward countries of the world today, not only does the dominance of the characteristically "modern" modes of exercise of power seem limited and qualified by the persistence of older modes, but by the fact of their combination in a particular state formation, it seems to open up at the same time an entirely new range of possibilities for the ruling classes to exercise their domination.[87]

While the Indochinese prison system sustains Chatterjee's description of the internal complexity of colonial power, it does not support his pessimistic lament that regimes based on a "combination of different modes of power" always exercise domination in new, more effective ways. On the contrary, the radical Indochinese prison movements of the 1930s suggest how the colonial system's simultaneous deployment of discipline together with "older modes" of power could generate abundant opportunities for resistance.

For example, communal architecture, one of the colonial prison system's most outdated attributes, enabled inmates to launch coordinated protests, hunger strikes, and work stoppages. The indiscriminate mixing of different categories of prisoners, another of the system's more conspicuous pre-disciplinary features, facilitated the mutual exchange of revolutionary sentiments and criminal practices between political and common-law offenders. Other anachronistic elements—the ubiquity of corporal punishment, the spectacle of forced labor, and the absence of reformative

---

[85] AOM-AP-NF 7F51 "Affaire de Con Dao, February 21, 1910."

[86] Such institutional apartheid was manifest in the rule that French prison officers could never assume positions subordinate to their "indigenous" counterparts and in the vast discrepancy between the salaries of these two groups. In 1899, the lowliest French employee in the Hanoi Central Prison made roughly fifteen times as much as the highest ranking "indigenous" employee. AOM-H-MH 3925: "Maison Centrale - Correspondances diverses, 1899."

[87] Partha Chatterjee, "More on Modes of Power and the Peasantry," in *Selected Subaltern Studies*, ed. Ranajit Guha and Gayatri Chakravorty Spivak (New York: Oxford University Press, 1988), p. 390.

regimes, for example—created political issues which the anti-colonial press was quick to exploit.

On the other hand, when disciplinary technologies were deployed, prisoners proved adept at appropriating them as models for their own resistance strategies. For example, just as wardens kept dossiers on individual inmates, so networks of political prisoners produced secret reports and maintained clandestine written records on the prison staff. A remarkable thirty-page document recovered from political prisoners in Lao Bảo Penitentiary in 1934 included detailed assessments of the corruptibility of individual guards, the political sympathies of common-law prisoners, and the popularity and administrative skill of the warden.[88] A similar example of appropriation can be seen in the systems which political prisoners devised to evaluate and process new inmates. During the 1930s, those entering colonial prisons were often interrogated and assessed twice, initially by the administration and afterward by the prisoners themselves. As a Sûreté informant in the Hanoi Central Prison reported in 1934: "Upon arrival, new prisoners are questioned by members of the party-cell about their political opinions. Based on their knowledge, they are then assigned to one of several training courses held nightly."[89]

Finally, the coexistence within the Indochinese prison system of disciplinary and non-disciplinary power brought into bold relief France's refusal to introduce truly "modern" institutions into the colony. For many opponents of the system, the incomplete and irregular deployment of discipline symbolized the failure of France to bring "civilization" [văn minh] to Indochina.[90] Critics exploited this failure by highlighting the contradiction between the disciplinary ideals inscribed in prison regulations and the chaotic and disorderly realities of institutional practice. However, instead of linking the anachronisms of colonial penal administration to pre-colonial Vietnamese punishment, they found it more effective politically to liken them disparagingly to images out of France's pre-modern past. Hence, journalist Nguyễn Văn Nguyên compared the wretched food provided Côn Đảo prisoners to the diet of "medieval French peasants."[91] More popular, still, were comparisons with the Bastille. In a 1936 editorial, a group of ex-prisoners invoked the Bastille to denounce the conditions on Côn Đảo: "Six years behind us. Six years locked in the colonial Bastille. Six years during which we have had to endure the notorious atrocities of a hateful and terrible regime."[92] The language of Saigon's *La Lutte* was more emphatic: "This hellish regime is unbearable!!" bellowed a front-page letter, also in 1936. "Down with the bagne and its regime of death! Down with all colonial

---

[88] AOM-AP SLOTFOM, Series 3, Carton 53, 1st Trimester 1934: "Annexe à la lettre #1099-SG de 10-4-1934: Traduction de Documents Saisis au Penitenticier de Lao Bao."

[89] AOM-AP SLOTFOM, Series 3, Carton 52, 1st Trimester, 1934, p. 3.

[90] Such was the thrust of "The Civilized Prisons of the United States," an editorial published in *Tiếng Dân* in 1939, which contrasted the custodial prisons of Indochina with the reformative regime employed at the Pennsylvania State Penitentiary for Women. "Nhà ngục văn minh ở Mỹ," *Tiếng Dân*, August 10, 1939, p. 1.

[91] Nguyễn Văn Nguyên, "Poulo Condore: le terre des damnés," *Le Travail*, December 20, 1936, p. 2.

[92] "Une lettre ouverte des libérés politiques à M. la Ministre des colonies," *Le Travail*, November 11, 1936, p. 1.

Bastilles!"[93] While the comparison with the Bastille was made to yield short-term political gains, it also draws attention to real parallels between colonial prisons and pre-modern European jails.[94] Such similarities underline the fact that Indochinese prisons were never mere copies of contemporary metropolitan models but embodied features characteristic of the penal systems of pre-colonial Vietnam and pre-modern Europe as well.

CONCLUSION

Critics of the colonial prison system frequently punctuated their attacks by demanding stricter regimes of classification and segregation so that political prisoners would be isolated from the general inmate population and enjoy better conditions.[95] Such a strategy aimed to protect political prisoners from predatory criminals and exempt them from forced labor. Alternatively, it can also be interpreted as an inadvertent effort by the colonized to promote their own subjugation to disciplinary power. One of the ironies of the colonial state's failure to consistently deploy discipline in Indochinese institutions is that, in the minds of middle-class Vietnamese activists, disciplinary technologies came to be associated with a modernity that the colonial project had failed to deliver. As a result, critics of colonialism frequently wrote approvingly of the very practices Foucault vilifies as prototypically disciplinary. For example, although Huỳnh Thúc Kháng's prison memoir persistently bemoans the squalid and brutal aspects of life on Côn Đảo, his description of the penitentiary's more regimented features conveys a tone of awed respect.

> One virtue of Europeans is that whenever they have any task, large or small, they follow strict rules which remain stable over long periods of time. They don't procrastinate carelessly or work diligently only at first and lazily thereafter like orientals and especially like the people of our southern country. Even in the middle of the ocean on an island for criminals like Côn Đảo, the method of distributing and ordering penal labor follows strict and consistent regulations. Everyday for over ten years, everything is done precisely and in exactly the same way. This is really true! I will give you an example of how this works in practice. At 5:30 each morning, prisoners from each cell-block enter the yard and line up according to the kind of labor they have been ordered to do. Those sentenced to "fixed labor," are grouped according to their worksites. The other prisoners wait to be sent out on "diverse corvée." The Guardian Chief gives the guards and *matas* their

---

[93] "Appel des condamnés politiques de Poulo-Condore à la Ministre des Colonies pour l'amnistie immédiate et intégrale de tous les condamnés politiques indochinois," *La Lutte*, June 10, 1936, p. 1.

[94] See, for example, John Bender's depiction of the "heterogeneous interiors," "slight administrative structure," "rudimentary classification of prisoners," and "easy traffic of visitors" characteristic of eighteenth-century English prisons. John Bender, *Imagining the Penitentiary: Fiction and the Architecture of Mind in Eighteenth-Century England* (Chicago: University of Chicago Press, 1987), pp. 14, 17, 29.

[95] For example, see *La Lutte*'s eight part series: "Pour l'Application du Régime Politique," August 24, 1935 to October 26, 1935.

assignments and they in turn lead the prisoners in their charge off to work. Before they leave, the Guardian Chief counts the prisoners and a *mata* records their I.D. numbers in a notebook. A guard responsible for cell-block security also records which prisoners go where in a separate notebook. Thus both the Guardian Chief and another guard maintain a record of which prisoners go where. When the prisoners reach the worksites, the guards, *cais*, *dois*, and *matas*, in charge must record in a notebook how many have arrived and the I.D. number of each one. The process of repeatedly counting the prisoners and recording their numbers in numerous notebooks as they are distributed to different worksites brings great advantages.[96]

Kháng continues, describing several more instances during which prisoners are enumerated. He then concludes with the following commentary:

During the half day, from the morning till the afternoon, prisoners leave the bagne, go to work, return for lunch and re-enter the bagne. They are counted over seven times. During the second half of the workday, from 2:00 to 5:00, the same thing occurs. Thus, each day prisoners are counted fourteen times and often if the numbers do not add up, then the guards must count and recount. The process of distributing work and counting prisoners occurs everyday of every year except holidays. After a while, it becomes a habit; never missed or neglected. This is something in which our oriental people are very weak. Orientals do not possess the character to work consistently and strictly in this way.[97]

It is instructive that Kháng does not criticize the process of near constant enumeration and surveillance to which he and his fellow-inmates are subjected. Instead he points out the "advantages" created by these disciplinary mechanisms and chides his countrymen for their inability to work in the same way, "strictly" and "consistently."

Although he never joined the communist movement and died shortly after assuming a position in Hồ Chí Minh's first independent administration in 1946, Kháng's admiration toward disciplinary technologies on Côn Đảo foreshadowed a virtual cult of discipline introduced by the Communist Party after coming to power in 1954. If the colonial state deployed disciplinary technologies only haltingly and sporadically, the post-colonial state adopted them with great enthusiasm. As Charles Armstrong has recently pointed out, communist institutional innovations such as reeducation camps and rituals of self-criticism embody modern (self)disciplinary power more perfectly "than anything Foucault writes about in Western history."[98] Perhaps it is no surprise that the scope and intensity of the disciplinary power deployed by the colonial state paled beside that of the movement which eventually dislodged and replaced it.

---

[96] Huỳnh Thúc Kháng, *Thi Tù Tùng Thoại*, pp. 157-158. *Matas* were Vietnamese prison guards, *dois* were local militiamen who were frequently employed to guard hard-labor convicts while they worked, and *cais* were caplans. See note 82 above.

[97] Ibid.

[98] Charles Armstrong, "Surveillance and Punishment in Postliberation North Korea" *Positions: East Asia Cultures Critique* 3,3 (Winter 1995): 714.

THE CRIMINAL REGIME:
CRIMINAL PROCESS IN INDONESIA

Daniel S. Lev

If nature pondered a means of keeping assorted intellectuals, philosophers, lawyers, social scientists, and reformers off the streets, it could not do better than to give them criminality to think about. There is not much about crime on which students of it agree. Is it eternal, caused by a never ending supply of evil people, do otherwise good people make bad mistakes, or are we all victims of our economic and social conditions? Is it fundamentally a matter of cultural construction, or social construction, or elite construction; religious tenet, moral consensus, political will, economic interest?[1]

If criminality is a quagmire, criminal law, one dimension of which this paper examines, is not much better. Everywhere its pretense of precision, clarity, absoluteness, and universality rests on a foundation of contestable fuzziness, uncertainty, and discrimination. All law depends in some measure on a mystique of confident consistency and fairness, but this is particularly so in the case of criminal law, whose patent failure of full enforcement—not all violators are ever caught, let alone punished—places criminal law institutions persistently in question.[2]

Identifiable patterns or trends nevertheless exist everywhere in the conception and treatment of crime. They are not necessarily determined by or even evident in substantive law, however, as one might expect; the preconception that they are rings true only if one dismisses all the provisions that are ignored, suppressed, unenforced, or reinterpreted. Criminal codes, moreover, cannot keep up with the criminalizing obsessions of religious sources, changes in economic concerns, political

---

[1] For various perspectives on the problem, see Mark Kelman, "The Origins of Crime and Criminal Violence," in *The Politics of Law: A Progressive Critique*, ed. David Kairys (New York: Pantheon, 1982), pp. 214-230; and Leon Radzinowicz, *Ideology and Crime: A Study of Crime in its Social and Historical Context* (New York: Columbia University Press, 1966). For a single-minded view, this one Marxist, see for example Richard Quinney, *Class, State and Crime* (New York: Longman, 1977).

[2] Thurmond Arnold, *The Symbols of Government* (New York: Harcourt, Brace, 1962 [1935]) remains one of the most subtle and useful approaches to the problem, not only with respect to criminal law. More than other areas of law in the modern state, criminal law is substantially symbolic. What it symbolizes is worth exploring, of course, though without much more hope of resolving conceptual disagreements than is the case with the criminality which it defines.

worries, or momentary rages of public opinion. Consistency, such as it is in the management of crime, comes less from the law than from legal process, understood not only as formal rules of procedure but also as the commitments, inclinations, and habits of criminal law institutions and their satellites—police, prosecutors, courts, counsel, intelligence agencies, security apparatuses, officially or politically connected underworld forces, prisons, and other related organizations that cohere more or less systematically. Here, more than in the substantive law, one is likely to find compelling classifications of crime, punishment, and defense.

Observing procedure in this sense helps to clear away the fog laid down by formal law around criminality and the reactions to it, which themselves may be formally (or ethically) criminal. Criminal procedure may be more or less professionally detached, fair, brutal, oppressive, exploitative, or responsive to disparate values and interests, including those of the criminally charged. In the messy institutions of criminal law, rather than the pristine codes, one discovers when murder and rape are neither, when criticism is slander or a political crime, when assault is merely a street fight, when embezzlement is a clerical error or misjudgment but anyway less reprehensible than theft, depending on who does it, and when rehabilitation is exactly the opposite. These ambiguities tend to frustrate formulaic approaches to criminal law, just as empirical research into crime discredits pat answers about the sources and meaning of criminality.

The principal argument here is that law is as law does, and what law does depends on legal process.[3] When it works passably well, however, or enough so for most groups that nothing seems amiss, procedure tends to be taken for granted, its peculiarities left to insiders. It is hidden, often subtle, as invisible as the actual sources of law, until the practice of it becomes so successfully ameliorative, hopelessly ineffective, or shockingly abusive that interested observers cannot help but shift focus. There are many examples: the *parlements* of pre-revolutionary France, the police and prosecution of modern Italy, the courts of Argentina, the police of New York City, and the entire judicial regime in Indonesia, to name a few.

COLONIAL BASICS

The Indonesian case demonstrates this argument better than most because the degeneration of its legal institutions, and its causes and consequences, can be traced clearly.

The structure of Indonesian law, essentially the skeleton of the modern state, came ready-made from the Netherlands-Indies, whose legal arrangements were no less discriminatory than in other colonies but were peculiarly honest about it. As in many colonies, there was only one criminal code (still in effect), which awkwardly implied the equality of all population groups, a principle never countenanced in fact. The English solution imposed a unified procedural regime, relying on English or

---

[3] Even as concepts of criminality change, they are initially reflected less in statutory form than in the work of police, prosecutors, courts, or their informal surrogates, which participate actively in defining criminality. The same is true whether the cause of change is an elite interest or a popular temper. Powerful interests may inject their concerns directly into police and judicial establishments without mediation by legislative authority. Reform lawyers and related interests opposed to or in favor of a criminalization may first make their cases in the press and the courts.

English-trained judges to discriminate sensibly. In contrast, the Dutch developed separate procedural codes (both criminal and civil) for Europeans and natives under the charge of distinct judicial instances with final appeal to the Indies Supreme Court. The two codes of criminal procedure accurately reflected cleavages in the colony's political economy, largely though not entirely following racial boundaries.[4] For Europeans, the code of criminal procedure (*strafvordering*), modeled on the Dutch code, provided a standard Continental menu of judicially enforceable rights and protections, reinforced by a requirement of professional counsel. The code for Indonesians (HIR[5]) combined administrative and judicial rules, with less rigorous guarantees and without provision for counsel—accused persons could hire a lawyer or not. Given the logic of colonial political structure, however, ethnicity alone could not define the jurisdiction of the codes. The alliance between the Dutch administration and local aristocracies brought the latter, and certain high administrative and military officials of ethnic Indonesian origin, under the purview of the European procedural code.[6] In effect, Indonesian commoners, those most vulnerable to exploitation and most likely eventually to object to it, were subject to more relaxed rules governing arrest and prosecution. A few backup provisions endowed the administration with extraordinary authority unfettered by judicial process, to impose exile for example.

Colonial criminal law institutions rushed to modernity in this century, mainly in pursuit of Indonesian nationalism. As repressive machinery evolved to keep up with unwelcome political activity, the police force was expanded, reorganized, and diversified.[7] An internal intelligence organization was added in the 1920s that was as inclined to stretch its responsibilities as intelligence agencies usually are. It predictably widened the penumbra of borderline criminal activity—attending, even as bystander, suspicious gatherings, meeting with suspected persons, and the like, for example—even, occasionally, over outraged Dutch personnel.[8]

---

[4] A concise social-legal history of the century and a half from 1840-1990 is available in the recent study by Soetandyo Wignjosoebroto, *Dari Hukum Kolonial ke Hukum Nasional* [From Colonial Law to National Law] (Jakarta: RajaGrafindo Persada, 1994). See also Daniel S. Lev, "Colonial Law and the Genesis of the Indonesian State," *Indonesia* 40 (October 1985).

[5] Originally the IR, Inlandse Reglement (Native Regulation), and later the Herziene Indonesische Reglement (Revised Indonesian Regulation).

[6] As a consequence, Soekarno was tried during the late 1920s in the Bandung court for Indonesians (*Landraad*) according to HIR rules, but he was defended by his fellow founder of the Indonesian National Party (PNI), Sartono, who could not be arrested on the same grounds because, with high aristocratic rank from the principality of Solo, he was subject to the procedural rules for Europeans.

Similarly, while the economic importance of ethnic Chinese merited coverage by the European commercial code and related procedural rules, for criminal purposes they were subject to the HIR. Unlike ethnic Chinese, however, Japanese were not Foreign Orientals to whom the rules of criminal procedure for natives applied, but rather at the turn of the century were recognized as Europeans. Power obviously counted in the legal definition of ethnicity. After this blessing was conferred on Japanese, ethnic Chinese, with some outspoken exceptions, demanded European status too; lacking a navy, they were denied.

[7] Very little research has been done on the police. One of the few works, though now much outdated, is M. Oudang, *Perkembangan Kepolisian di Indonesia* (Jakarta: Mahabarata, 1952).

[8] The political intelligence service (PID) is dealt with in a book on which Takashi Shiraishi is now working.

To say that independent Indonesia inherited its repressive inclinations from colonial history is a tautology. The colonial administration had merely established, or recapitulated, all the machinery of control common to the modern state. It differed from the basic model only in that the Netherlands-Indies contained the makings of two states, evident in its administrative and judicial organization: one for all Europeans, the other for most Indonesians.[9] Independent Indonesia's political elite had some choices in the matter. What they chose to inherit was the most repressive side of colonial legal structure.

Exactly why is not all that obvious. During the revolution (1945-1950) legal reform was hardly a priority, but neither did it become so afterwards, despite demands that "national" law replace "colonial" law. There were serious ideological differences over what kind of law was most appropriate, which also meant what kind of state. Much of the political elite, however, including most lawyers among them, evidently believed the legal system worked well enough, or in any case could not imagine how to change it fundamentally. Only one or two participants in the constitutional debates of mid-1945 had remarkable ideas about legal reform.[10] Almost all of the corpus of colonial law was retained without significant amendment; and a respectable proportion of it remains in force now, including the criminal code.

A few significant institutional changes did occur, however. Early in the revolution, republican leadership ratified Japanese occupation reforms that had eliminated the courts for Europeans, unifying the judiciary on the basis of the former courts for Indonesians, the *Landraden*. Despite the misgivings of professional advocates, the government also adopted the HIR rather than the more rigorous procedural codes for Europeans. The HIR, ironically, had rather more nationalist cachet than the European codes, but the major justification for retaining it was that Indonesian judges had little experience with the European codes. More to the point, neither did prosecutors, descended as they were from the untrained, subordinate pre-war *jaksa* (prosecutors) attached to the *Landraden* or migrated into the new parquet from the regional administrative corps, the *pamong praja*.[11]

---

[9] See my "Colonial Law and the Genesis of the Indonesian State." One can argue that in some measure all states are dual, as Disraeli complained of nineteenth-century England, but the Dutch colonial administration made the duality explicit.

[10] The most outspoken and imaginative reformer was Muhammad Yamin, who proposed remodelling the judiciary on the American pattern, with a powerful supreme court fully equipped with powers of judicial review. He won little support. See Muhammad Yamin, *Naskah-Persiapan Undang-Undang Dasar 1945* [Preparatory Documents of the 1945 Constitution] (Jakarta: Prapantja, 1959), pp. 330-337.

[11] Among the consequences of adopting the HIR was that *jaksa*, following *landraad* practice, now sat on the bench next to the judge, which often confused accused persons in court. Only in the early New Order period did resentful judges here and there force *jaksa* to descend to a position of equality with defense counsel. More seriously, *jaksa* were not fully responsible for their own indictments, which were subject to review and amendment by the judge; this held true until a new law on the prosecution was promulgated in 1961. On this point see A. Karim Nasution, *Masaalah Surat Tuduhan dalam Proses Pidana* [The Problem of the Indictment in Criminal Procedure] (Jakarta: Percetakan Negara, 1972).

THE PARLIAMENTARY REGIME

Adopting the HIR meant keeping the colonial administrative and judicial apparatus for "natives" intact. Yet, for a time it was not particularly repressive or notoriously inept. Looking back on the parliamentary period of the 1950s from the New Order 1990s, it is striking that the same legal institutions now filled with corruption and abuse then worked reasonably well, despite serious difficulties. The judiciary's problems were still enormous: too few trained judges, even fewer trained prosecutors, meager budgets, neglect by state leaders, and myriad uncertainties about legal integration in the new state.

The legal system also had some advantages, however. Supreme Court and appellate judges, the Chief Public Prosecutor, Soeprapto, and the national police commandant, Soekanto Tjokrodiatmadjo, were all well educated in the law, professionally committed to their institutions, widely respected, intimately part of the national elite, and disinclined to take much guff from peers who happened to exercise political authority.[12] Despite bureaucratic conflicts among their rank and file, mainly over pay scales and status, the dominant functional ethos in the legal system was professionally legal. Legal norms governed the work of judges, who in criminal trials exercised controls over police and prosecutors with little sense of appropriate evidence.[13] The protections provided in the HIR, though not elaborate, were generally respected by police and prosecution, who were sensitive to judicial oversight. Soeprapto held off grumbling politicians, bringing one or two of them to trial, while Soekanto tried to keep reasonably tight reins on the police. Professional advocates, the most accomplished lawyers in the country, were few in number but active and respected by public lawyers in and out of the courts.

How well the legal system worked depended most fundamentally, however, on the toleration of political leaders, who if they usually ignored the difficulties of the courts, prosecution, and police, also did not intervene much in other respects. It was a condition, in effect, of liberal parliamentary ideology, largely predicated on the rechtsstaat (negara hukum, or "law-state") assumptions which parliamentary parties had implanted in the provisional constitution of 1950. Accepting these assumptions constrained leaders to recognize the necessary (relative) autonomy of the legal system, which was essential to their own political legitimacy. (That many of them easily gave up these principles in the late 1950s, or in any case barely defended them, is another matter.) For their part, the police, prosecution, and courts, both ideologically and institutionally, also had much to gain from exercising their independence responsibly.

---

[12] The leadership of the Supreme Court was something of an exception. Its first chair, Kusumaatmadja, fiercely defended the prerogatives of the Court, but he died in 1951 and his successor, Wirjono Prodjodikoro, was much weaker and less inclined to ward off political pressures. At the onset of Guided Democracy, Soeprapto and Soekanto were dismissed, but Wirjono remained in office until driven out by junior judges and students in early 1966.

[13] A comparison of judicial decisions in the 1950s, published consistently in the the Madjalah Hukum (later Madjalah Hukum dan Masjarakat, Journal of Law and Society), with those that appeared desultorily after 1961, is instructive on this point.

GUIDED DEMOCRACY

None of these conditions survived Guided Democracy, which overturned the parliamentary principles, undercut the ideological supports of legal process, and enthusiastically took advantage of the ready-made repressive potential of the procedural regime left behind by the colonial administration. The relatively weak parliamentary state, surrounded by active political parties and labor, peasant, and other organizations, gave way to concentrated state power, with Soekarno at its symbolic pinnacle and an army fully engaged politically since the proclamation of martial law in early 1957. The Guided Democracy regime set aside institutional controls in favor of a surface unity, gutted parliamentary authority, rendered the parties marginal except to the extent they could mobilize supporters on the streets, and subordinated legal process, on the one hand to the unfinished revolution and on the other to the exigencies of raw political conflict. My concern here is not with the politics of Guided Democracy, any more than it is with that of the parliamentary system, nor with the merits or rationales of either, but only with the consequences of each for the workings of the legal system and the conception and treatment of crime.

Under Guided Democracy's ideological impulses towards revolutionary action, national unity, the rediscovery of local tradition, and global justice, definitions of criminality began to mutate, the results occasionally but not always rendered in statutory form.[14] Both the civilian and military sides of Guided Democracy's government became increasingly sensitive to crimes against the state, sedition, and economic subversion, which produced a presidential regulation of 1963 that eased evidentiary rules and provided for the death penalty. (Execution rarely if ever happened during the parliamentary years, and did not become common under Guided Democracy, in fact.) But ideological and political conflict generated quite different understandings of criminal behavior. The Communist Party focused on economic crimes, particularly violations of the land reform act of 1960, while army leaders concentrated on unlicensed demonstrations and unapproved meetings, especially on the left, and Islamic leaders occasionally protested against apostasy, failure to marry properly according to *shariah* rules, and so on. Who should be regarded as a criminal, by what criteria, and how seriously, depended largely on one's political commitments, anxieties, fears, and prospects, but not necessarily the law, except among professional private lawyers, to whom few saw reason to listen. Murder, rape, theft, arson, and assault still counted, but in their routineness seldom excited much interest, as a glance at newspaper headlines from about 1960 onwards will show.

Nor were they all that interesting to the formal legal system, which, challenged ideologically by Soekarno and pressed explicitly into political service, was quickly

---

[14] Characteristically, as law and legal process were increasingly marginalized under Guided Democracy the volume of legislation grew and diversified, partly because much of it came directly from President Soekarno or his various ministers in the form of decrees, decisions, and regulations, and partly too because the army, legally empowered by martial law, become an additional source of regulations. The old codes remained extant, but were intruded upon more and more by ad hoc legislation that whittled away, amended, superseded, and suspended bits and pieces of the legal corpus. How little most of it counted, however, is indicated by how long it took actually to publish new law, and how seldom anybody, not least judges, caught up with it.

shaken out of its robed distinction.[15] In 1959 Chief Public Prosecutor Soeprapto was dismissed. All his successors were politically linked. The first was Gatot Tarunamihardja, from whom Soekarno hoped for legal harassment of army officers; the latter, many believed, discretely ran him over with a truck. Gatot's successor, Goenawan, favored by army leaders, proved to be so abusive that they forced his removal. The national police were absorbed into the armed forces as its fourth arm, and the office of commandant became politically sensitive: only one commandant after Soekanto, Hoegeng Imam Santoso, appointed after the coup of 1965, was known for his commitment to the institutional independence of the police, which eventually lost him his job.

The judiciary was more problematic, for judges were more sensitive than other public lawyers to the issue of autonomy. But in 1960 Supreme Court (*Mahkamah Agung*) chair Wirjono accepted Soekarno's invitation to join the cabinet, sweeping aside the principle of separation of powers so important to judges (and professional advocates) but dismissed contemptuously by Soekarno as a Western import. Judges were demoralized, but it was only the beginning.

In short time, the entire criminal procedure regime was critically restructured, with telling consequences for judges, prosecutors, police, defense attorneys, and the criminally accused. As a reward for its political services, in 1960 the public prosecution was extracted from the Ministry of Justice and given its own ministry. The police force, equally important and long in competition with the prosecution for control over preliminary investigation, also was allowed its own cabinet rank ministry.[16] Judges, however, remained subject to Ministry of Justice administrative supervision, which easily evolved into political control. The implicit rearrangement of institutional status according to political rather than professional legal norms was quickly reflected in the growing public prominence of prosecutors, the widespread depression of judges, and a shift in the career ambitions of law students from judicial to prosecutorial position.[17] Even the pretense of judicial independence disappeared in 1964 with a law (No. 19/1964) granting the president explicit power to intervene in judicial process for the sake of national interest. In the same year local conferences were initiated of military, police, prosecutorial, judicial, and district (*kabupaten*) officials, who met monthly or so to deal with security and related issues. So far as the lower courts (*pengadilan negeri*) were concerned, this arrangement meant that judicial decisions were now subject to pre-judicial political hearings and a variety of pressures. It worked especially to the advantage of prosecutors.[18]

---

[15] This was true literally, as prosecutors gave up their black robes in favor of military style uniforms, and not longer afterwards (in 1963) judges followed suit. Only advocates hung on to their togas, now usually in tatters, throughout. In early 1966, following the coup, judges enthusiastically donned robes again, and so eventually did *jaksas*, but neither recovered the symbolic significance of them. Advocates, however, began to afford better robes.

[16] On prosecutor-police and prosecutor-judge tensions from the 1950s onward, see Daniel S. Lev, "The Politics of Judicial Development in Indonesia," *Comparative Studies in Society and History* 7,2 (1966).

[17] As in most civil law (by contrast with common law) countries, law students are recruited after graduation directly into government service either in the judicial or prosecutorial corps. During the early 1960s law students were well aware that one route to wealth and influence was through the prosecution. Judgeships had little wealth, influence or even respectability to offer to any student eager to get ahead.

[18] In fact, in April 1964 Wirjono Prodjodikoro issued a *Mahkamah Agung* circular (8/1964) regretting that the frequent discrepancy between the punishments demanded by prosecutors

Judicial process was transformed not by any significant amendment to the HIR (or the colonial law on judicial organization) but as a result of the priorities emphasized by prosecutors, police, and, reluctantly at first, judges. The first priority was to convict those whom the government wanted convicted. From 1961 on it was exceedingly rare for any political prosecution, or for that matter any other case in which the government or an influential official wanted a conviction, to result in acquittal.[19] Such cases relied heavily on the procedural advantages of the anti-subversion act and, particularly against critics, the "hate spreading" (*haatzaai*) articles of the old criminal code (*Kitab Undang-Undang Hukum Pidana*, hereafter KUHP), which was put to more use in independent Indonesia than in the colony. But in essence these procedural and substantive rules were window dressing, for the subjugation of judges provided the principal engine of judicial transformation.

A close second priority, by all accounts, was to take advantage of the opportunities for self-enrichment fostered by the first priority.[20] Once the political loyalty of the judicial complex was assured, legal officials were allowed unimpeded discretion to manage their responsibilities as they saw fit. The corruption of the legal system set off by Guided Democracy was impressively predatory, though it pales by New Order standards. Essentially disregarding whatever Soekarno insisted were the revolutionary purposes of Guided Democracy, the now unfettered bureaucracy transformed itself into a gigantic corporate enterprise specializing in public services. Low salaries and inflation explain part of the problem, and greed much of the rest, but it is important to recognize the extent to which the government was unwilling to impose controls, not only because it could little afford to do so financially but also because it could not afford the political costs of alienating its own bureaucratic base.

No agency geared up better for business than the prosecution, whose leverage lay in opportunities for extortion. Prosecutors rendered incompetent by integrity either left or were shunted aside to routine criminal cases stipulated in the criminal code. Many others, from top to bottom, devoted themselves to redefining anyone with noticeable wealth as serviceably criminal. Particularly vulnerable were ethnic Chinese businessmen, but anyone lacking useful connections would do. The charge did not matter much—economic crimes such as hoarding and smuggling, or slander, or any misdemeanor that could arbitrarily be transformed into a threat of something more—for in reality the legal procedures for trial and punishment involved kidnapping (arrest), holding (detention), the negotiation of ransom (preliminary investigation), and release (dropping the charge).

---

and the decisions rendered by judges had caused unfortunate questions and rumors to spread at large. Perhaps, but it is more likely that prosecutors had complained. Judge Wirjono instructed lower judges, especially in important cases, to confer with prosecutors before the latter submitted their indictments and recommendations of punishment (*requisitoir*). If the differences between them remained substantial, judges were required to discuss the cases with the appellate chair in their jurisdictions. *Varia Peradilan* [Judicial miscellany. The monthly journal of the judicial corps] III,7-8-9 (February-April 1964): 163. Some judges complained obliquely, but without success.

[19] From 1961 through 1997 in hundreds of political cases, the one or two acquittals that come to mind applied to distinctly minor or mistakenly arrested figures.

[20] The prosecutor's entrepreneurial advantage lay in control of preliminary investigation, which explains, in part, why police were so eager to take it away. A few years into the New Order, the prosecution was finally punished for past sins by having to turn preliminary investigation authority over to the police.

If, as sometimes happened, a detainee or his family refused to pay up, the case went to court. This possibility, along with a concern on the part of prosecutors for the efficient management of judicial work, led to an intimate arrangement between prosecutors and willing judges that laid the foundation of what later became known as the judicial mafia. Prosecutors offered judges a share of the proceeds in exchange for an assured conviction. Underpaid, reduced in status, demoralized now in the ranks of mid-level bureaucrats, and subject to attacks of cynicism, many judges took the bait and were addicted.

Despite a long-lasting rivalry between judges and prosecutors that never fully abated, they now became allies of a sort, not altogether friendly, for judges remained resentful of the high-flying prosecutors, but working more or less comfortably in cahoots. One result was that criminal litigation became noticeably more efficient than civil litigation. Civil cases were slow and frustrating, often because one or other litigant in a commercial case might see advantage in delay—to allow inflation to reduce the real costs of a settlement, for example. One means of resolving commercial disputes was to transform them into criminal prosecutions, which expanded the boundaries of legally recognized crime in interesting ways. All that was required was a willing prosecutor or police official, who, for a cut, would charge a debtor with theft or embezzlement. Detained, the debtor could either pay up, often with an additional tip for the prosecutor or police official, or go to court on the criminal charge, with much the same result.

Institutional controls disappeared. Again, the bureaucratic foundation of Guided Democracy made it unlikely that regime leaders—many of whom were themselves on the take—would challenge any significant bureaucratic bloc. The press was contained, cautious, or taken up with the grand issues of political conflict. Only the private legal profession complained loudly about judicial corruption, but its voice was too weak to have much effect. The influence of the advocacy declined dramatically under Guided Democracy, precisely because it was private at a time when the public bureaucracy had become dominant. The relatively few professional advocates in practice then, about 250 nationwide, were increasingly marginalized by judges, prosecutors, and police, who shared in common a bureaucratic collegiality reinforced by frequent collusion. Still, on occasion particularly capable and courageous advocates could lay bare the corruption of prosecutors who put to personal use cars and homes seized as "evidence" or otherwise violated a procedural code that had become, de facto, all but meaningless.

THE NEW ORDER

Following the coup of October 1965, the wholesale corruption of the legal system became a principal premise of both the condemnation of Guided Democracy and the demand for reform, formulated as the restoration of the *negara hukum*, the rule of law. The New Order regime promised as much, but with the army now in control of the state, the new political leadership had little interest and no compelling need to carry through on the promise. As the strong state of Guided Democracy was largely the creation of the army, the political dimensions of it appealed to New Order military leaders as they had to their predecessors. Now under military command, the bureaucratic base of the regime was reorganized here and there, streamlined where necessary for the sake of economic growth and more effective political control, but for the most part was subject to the same conditions and enjoyed the same privileges adumbrated by Guided Democracy. If anything, the New Order made explicit the rules that were only implied earlier: it required of its bureaucracy unity and unconditional political loyalty, in exchange for which civil servants, most importantly high-ranking bureaucratic officials, were tacitly assured insulation from reform pressures and leeway to see to personal interests.

Consequently, while General (later President) Suharto paid lip service to legal reform, little of it was forthcoming, for whatever else such reform meant, it necessarily implied the imposition of institutional constraints.[21] Until 1990 the Suharto government consistently avoided any such concessions. Once this position became clear, corruption in the judicial system, as elsewhere in the bureaucracy, expanded exponentially, for the growing New Order economy provided wonderfully rich rewards compared with the modest pickings of Guided Democracy. (Civil cases now became a lucrative source of income, encouraging remarkable judicial innovations—e.g., one [at least] first instance court chairman auctioned off potentially rewarding cases to interested judges, who then auctioned favorable decisions among litigants. Selling decisions became quite common.) Occasional dismissal of blatantly corrupt prosecutors and judges had little if any effect.

The Yap Thiam Hien trial of 1968 nicely illustrated the conditions and the issues. In a notorious case Yap, a well-known, courageous professional advocate, had accused a high police official, Mardjaman, and a prosecutor, Simandjuntak, of extortion against Yap's client, the owner of a company called PT (Ltd) Quick. In early 1968 the police official and prosecutor retaliated by having Yap arrested and detained for six days before the Jakarta press and a few officials forced his release. In itself this event, much celebrated in the press, seemed a promising departure from Guided Democracy practice. But Mardjaman and Simandjuntak thereupon brought a charge of criminal slander against Yap, which the public prosecution pursued in the first instance court of Jakarta. The trial revealed much about fundamental issues in the early New Order. Few doubted that Yap's accusation was true, but the prominent prosecutor chosen for the case, Dali Mutiara, was at pains to spotlight the real stakes. The following excerpt is extracted from a biography of Yap that I am writing:

> Dali's summation focused less on legal than more serious issues. On the one hand he defended Simandjuntak and Mardjaman, and on the other hand, he launched an extended *ad hominem* assault on Yap, whom he accused, as a BAPERKI [an ethnic Chinese political organization banned in 1966] figure, of wanting to make a political come-back and trying to make hay of such ideas as the rule of law and human rights. But the brunt of his argument, in reply to the question of public interest raised by Yap, was that defaming state officials could hardly be said to be in the public interest, but instead was done in the interest of a client and Yap's own interest in his fee. He hedged his bets a bit, insisting that if it happened that the allegations against Mardjaman and Simandjuntak were proved, they were the acts only of individuals, not the police and prosecution. "But by blowing up the matter even though unproven, the accused purposefully 'assailed' State

[21] See Daniel S. Lev, "Judicial Authority and the Struggle for an Indonesian Rechtsstaat," *Law and Society Review* 13,1 (Fall 1978).

institutions and the official corps of the government in their entirety in order to obtain political advantages for himself; that is, he tried to picture the acts of the witness . . . Simandjuntak as identical to the acts of the entire corps of prosecutors, and similarly the acts of. . . Mardjaman as identical with all the Police Generals or Military [ABRI] generals." Alerting the army officer corps to its interests was a considered stroke.

Dali concluded with an adage about the famous prime minister of the fourteenth-century empire of Majapahit, who said to his admiral, Lembu Nala, about to lead an armada to Bali: "Only one thing need I say to you, if there is a flame, put out that flame while it is still small, before it burns down your house."

But whose house? Yap and his counsel, in separate summations, addressed the ambiguous moral of Dali's story as they took up the issue of public interest. The defense team called attention to Yap's trial as a test case not only for the right of advocates to defend their clients, but for the political quality of the New Order, indicated by the widespread public attention to the case in and even out of the country. The Indonesian people, they said, were now eager for truth and justice, sick of corruption and the lip service of those who called themselves leaders. Quoting *Jaksa Agung* [Chief Public Prosecutor] Sugih Arto himself on the need to clean up the prosecution and eliminate tolerance for official corruption, they pointed out that Dali Mutiara's *requisitoir* [indictment] nevertheless read like a defense of Mardjaman and Simandjuntak and Lies Gunarsih [their associate in the PT Quick matter] who were not the accused in this case.

Judge Soetarno Soedja, noticeably hostile to Yap throughout the well-reported trial, decided in favor of the officials. A few years later Yap was acquitted by the Supreme Court, then chaired by an older, model liberal judge, Soebekti. But Yap's trial had made the point that judges, prosecutors, and police would not easily relinquish their prerogatives. The government consistently backed them up.

As legal officials were assured of their insulation, abuse and corruption in the judicial system skyrocketed, at huge costs to both civil and criminal litigants. For the criminally accused, the problem does not lie primarily in the law, but rather in legal process all along the line from arrest through trial. The law, whether the KUHP, the HIR, or the new code of criminal procedure of 1981 (KUHAP), does not lack provisions barring abuse. But few officials within the judicial order are much concerned to heed them, non-officials have little power to compel them to do so, and political leaders have little interest in holding them to rules that potentially could be applied to themselves. The New Order elite and its many dependents, a privileged political and social stratum, require their own insulation.

The consequences of these structural conditions for the definition and management of crime are far reaching. For one thing, they almost automatically inject considerations of class into the practical classifications of criminality. Political or social prominence, for example, is on the face of it exculpatory. Murder is not an indictable offense, or at least not subject to conviction, if committed by members of well-connected, well-known, or well-heeled families. (There have been several such non-cases since the mid-1970s.) The same is true of rape.[22] Corruption is a crime only if committed sufficiently far down in the bureaucracy to be safely indictable.[23] Juvenile delinquency, a growing problem among the children of the new rich in major cities, provokes official reactions mainly in the form of cover-ups.

Among the less privileged recipients of justice, in criminal cases as in civil cases, money is often the sine qua non for success: it can buy an acquittal, a lesser charge, or better treatment in prison. Collegiality among criminal justice officials, on the one hand, and their disdain for private lawyers, on the other, renders professional advocates and their clients vulnerable to manipulation and exploitation.[24] Under-the-table money—so common that it is often above the table—has become a standard procedural stratagem, as it were, in both civil and criminal cases. The effect on counsel, who have little choice but to adapt or quit, is captured perfectly in John Pemberton's contribution to this volume. Judicial cynicism engenders cynicism among just about everyone else connected in any way with the courts or merely aware of their reputation.

Where bribes are not in the offing, judges, prosecutors, and police have an interest in disposing of cases efficiently and maintaining good working relationships. They also have a compelling interest in keeping abuse quiet. In both conventional and political cases, prominence, even among critics, provides a measure of protection against severity and often an assurance of soft treatment in detention. But the less well known (or well off) the criminally accused, the more likely is he or she to be beaten or tortured (sometimes to death) by the police, usually in pursuit of a confession, prosecuted routinely, sentenced quickly by a judge, and treated miserably in prison.[25]

---

[22] The non-prosecution that set the standard for rape occurred in 1970, when Sum Kuning, a young village girl who sold eggs in Yogyakarta was raped. It was commonly supposed that a local aristocrat and his friends, among them the son of an army officer, were responsible. They were investigated, but Sum Kuning herself was tried, on the charge in effect of having spread false rumors. She was acquitted. The affair set off an uproar in the local and national press, but was never resolved. See Kamadjaja, Slamet Djabarudi, Soetijono Darsosentono, Soewindo, and J. C. Sudjami, eds., *Sum Kuning* (Yogyakarta: U.P. Indonesia, 1971).

[23] Law no. 3 of 1971 on the suppression of corruption is to all intents and purposes a dead letter. The frequent pronouncements by government ministers about the need to control corruption have long since lost the public's attention.

[24] Some defense counsel have gained admission to the inner circle, however, by way of the judicial mafia, the collusive collaboration of prosecutors, judges, and advocates to arrange the profitable disposition of cases.

[25] Official abuse of power in criminal jurisdictions has been documented (and protested) since the beginning of the New Order, often building on criticism of Guided Democracy practices. For a brief selection of significant items see: S. M. Amin, *Polemik dengan Berita Yudha* [Polemic with the daily Berita Yudha] (Jakarta: "Hudaya," 1970); Eddy Damian, ed., *The Rule of Law dan Praktek Penahanan di Indonesia* [The Rule of Law and Detention Practices in Indonesia] (Bandung:"Alumni," 1968); R. Sario, *Masalah Penahanan dan Djaminan Hak-Hak Azasi Manusia* [The Detention Problem and the Guarantee of Human Rights] (Jakarta: Yahya, 196?); Abdul Hakim G. Nusantara, Luhut Pangaribuan, and Achmad Santosa, *Studi Kasus Hukum Acara Pidana* [Case Studies in Criminal Procedure] (Jakarta: Djambatan, 1986); ELSAM, *Ke Arah Ratifikasi Konvensi Anti Penyiksaan* [Towards Ratification of the Anti-torture Convention] (Jakarta: ELSAM, 1995); Hans Toolen, ed., *Indonesia and the Rule of Law: Twenty Years of 'New Order' Government* (London: Frances Pinter, 1987). A great deal of relevant material has been published by the Indonesian Legal Aid Foundation (YLBHI).

While the law is honored only in the breach or ignored with impunity by judicial institutions, it is cited incessantly by reform organizations, particularly the Indonesian Legal Aid Foundation (YLBHI), the Institute for Social Study and Advocacy (ELSAM), professional advocates, and, more timidly, by the press. The issues are by and large officially stonewalled. Just about every death or serious injury that occurs after arrest is represented as the result of an accident. The new code of criminal procedure of 1981 (KUHAP) provides for a pre-judicial hearing in which police abuses during arrest or detention may be challenged and are subject to damages. Occasionally these hearings have led to judicial findings of an error or abuse and (quite limited) damages have been awarded, but judges are usually reluctant to fault fellow officials.

Conventional criminal cases are one thing, political cases another, though they share a few conditions in common when they involve less prominent figures. From the beginning of the New Order era, political crime has been taken more seriously and treated with more elaborate machinery than any other. In some ways its procedures are more efficient and less corrupt than civil legal process. These procedures are also basically not legal and seldom pretend to be. They are essentially discretionary, with the merest pretense of symbolic legality backed up by a widely understood privilege of power. The New Order was, after all, initiated in late 1965 with an extraordinary slaughter of citizens, mainly members of the Communist Party, justified by political decision and capability. In 1966, a thin legal process (military tribunals and civil courts) applying questionable rules ex post facto, combined with actions even less ostensibly legal (the arrest and detention for about fifteen years of scores of thousands, without evidence or trial) devastated what remained of Guided Democracy's left wing and served as a lasting reminder of the government's power.

Since then political crime has been managed by two distinct but hierarchically related institutions: one the civil judiciary, the other the more influential military-based Command for the Restoration of Security and Order (KOPKAMTIB).[26] The latter was allowed broad discretionary authority, unobstructed by public procedural rules, to deal with all issues of security, which in the circumstances of New Order public policy meant both political security narrowly conceived and the security of economic policy—i.e., control of the labor force—broadly understood. Its conception of relevant crime consisted of any opposition, serious criticism (by private persons, organizations, or the press), demonstrations, efforts at labor organization or the expression of labor discontent that regime leaders believed to be threatening or potentially so. From the apex in Jakarta down to the regional security offices, the modes of operation have ranged from threats through arrest, detention, interrogation, with or without torture, and sometimes worse. At once an internal intelligence organization, an administrative agency, and a court, the security regime has often acted literally as a law unto itself.

It might also send its detainees on to formal trial, however, in which case the civil courts have been consistently obedient to the security apparatus. No significant political trial has ever resulted in an acquittal. It is unlikely, moreover, that most

---

[26] The KOPKAMTIB has been replaced by the BAKORSTANAS, with more narrowly prescribed responsibility and authority, but there is no need here to distinguish sharply between the two, for both have involved larger institutional networks with similar consequences for their targets.

judges, from first instance through to the Supreme Court (*Mahkamah Agung*), have needed to be told what to do. Reluctant judges (or prosecutors) are simply not assigned to political cases. Judges willing to handle particularly difficult cases have sometimes been rewarded with promotions.

The foregone conclusion of conviction renders both the substantive and procedural law of crime only peripherally relevant. It matters only to defense counsel, in part because it is their only weapon other than money, but also because they can use it to demonstrate the extent to which prosecutors and judges ignore or misuse the law. In political cases defense reminders of the meanings of the *negara hukum* are standard fare.

Relatively few KUHP provisions make up the bulk of indictments. They are drawn mainly from Book Two, parts I (crimes against public security), II (lese majesté, in effect, against the president, formerly the King and Governor-General), and V (crimes against public order). Parts II and V include the much used "spreading hate" (*haatzaai*) articles that punish slanderous attacks on, or insults to, the President and high officials of the state, or prejudicial statements about racial minorities.[27]

The most effective procedural law at the disposal of prosecutors in political cases is the anti-subversion act, promulgated first as a presidential regulation in 1963 but upgraded into a law in 1968.[28] Basically, it makes it easier to proceed against the accused, relaxes rules of evidence, and allows for more drastic sentences, including death. It also signals to judges that a case has political implications. It is a prosecutor's dream, reducing the work required. During the 1970s and 1980s prosecutors with weak cases were often tempted to transform conventional criminal violations into subversion issues, though some (not all) judges, not to mention professional advocates and legal aid organizations, objected loudly. Occasionally this tactic is still used.

For the rest, the new procedural code (KUHAP), like the HIR before it, is a study in the marginalization of law. Even so, the KUHAP is a minor milestone in modern Indonesian political-legal history: significantly, the first major code revision in the independent state had to do with criminal procedure, which everywhere defines limits on the uses of state power against individual citizens. It made several concessions to the demands of legal reformers, who in the circumstances tend to be self-conscious political reformers as well. Among the provisions, for example, was the right of an accused person to be represented by professional counsel starting from the time of arrest. The concessions, however, required implementing legislation that was not forthcoming, a common tactic rendering even minor reforms otiose.

Even apart from this problem, otherwise useful procedural protections are often enough simply swept aside, despite the protests of advocates, as judges either follow the lead of prosecutors or rule conveniently to complicate the defense or facilitate the

---

[27] These *haatzaai artiklen* have been condemned by political critics and journalists since 1950, but every government of independent Indonesia has found them just as useful as the colonial administration did—perhaps more so. The advantage of them for political leaders, as for prosecutors, is that they are exceedingly flexible and can be made to apply to just about any statement or act found objectionable, so long as judges go along. As in the law of slander, truth is no defense.

[28] It was a conscious choice, not a mere oversight, to adopt the anti-subversion act as a law in 1968, for much the same reason that succeeding governments since 1950 could have, but did not, rescind the *haatzaai artiklen*.

prosecution.[29] The problem has at times been embarrassingly evident in the *Mahkamah Agung*, when politically or financially problematic decisions of Supreme Court judges have been hastily and arbitrarily overturned at the explicit request of high political authority made directly to the Chair.[30]

One consequence of this subjugation of the judiciary—or, from a different perspective, its abdication—is that it leaves the definition of crime primarily up to political leadership, unmediated by any specialized institution capable of exercising restraint according to relatively disinterested principles. As a result, in dictating crime policy, as in much else, the daily interests, concerns, and objectives of political leadership—especially, as many critics insist, the presidential family—determine the flexible dimensions of criminality. It can be argued that the New Order regime has not been oblivious to growing social anxieties about crime.[31] One of its more democratic policies appears to have been the (extra-legal and extra-judicial) killing of a few thousand "delinquents" in the *Petrus* (mysterious killings) sweeps of the early 1980s, which generated widespread applause and for which President Suharto openly took credit.[32] Even here, however, there is considerable doubt whether the primary purpose of the action was public safety or the elimination of once useful tools who had turned problematic.

Moreover, at various levels of the regime, from the political top to the administrative base, there are alliances with organized street gangs that generate financial returns—from protection rackets in the markets to cuts for local officials—and provide available strong arms for political action. Official connections with or investment in the underground is hardly peculiar to Indonesia, but the extent of it raises questions about who exactly is a criminal and what is criminal activity. So of course does widespread corruption and the failure of every promise to deal with it, the inability of the police to deal with crime in elite circles, the successful "escape" from prison of a flush businessman, for just a few examples.

The answer to these questions— who is a criminal and what is a crime?—cannot be found reliably in the Indonesian criminal code or collected statutes. Some think the law a good place to start, but others find it much too limiting. The distribution of status, wealth, and power accounts, in Indonesia as elsewhere, for varying

---

[29] For instance, defense demurrers on basic legal issues are almost inevitably denied, or the claim by an accused person that his or her confession was gained under torture is dismissed, without further investigation, on grounds of lack of proof or denials made by prosecutors or police. For further examples, see Abdul Hakim G. Nusantara et al., *Studi Kasus*.

[30] On the evolution of the Supreme Court and its problematic management of such cases, see the rich and detailed Leiden dissertation by Sebastiaan Pompe, "The Indonesian Supreme Court: Fifty Years of Judicial Development, " PhD dissertation, Leiden University, 1996.

[31] An expanding urban middle class has evinced increasing anxiety over its security. Uncertain statistics indicate that they do have something to worry about, but so do others who are less well off. For one study, see Mulyana W. Kusumah, *Kejahatan dan Penyimpangan: Suatu Perspektip Kriminologi* [Crime and Deviation: a Criminological Perspective] (Jakarta: YLBHI, 1988).

[32] On the issues set off by the *Petrus* affair, see David Bourchier, "Crime, Law and State Control in Indonesia," unpublished paper, 1988. Bourchier argues that after an initial period of popular approval a reaction set in as people began to understand the implications of the "mysterious shootings." Maybe, but this was not my impression from conversations with various informants during the mid to late 1980s. For Suharto's comment, see his *Otobiografi*, as related to G. Dwipayana and Ramadhan K. H. (Jakarta: Citra Lamtoro Gung Persada, 1988), pp. 364-367, in the first withdrawn edition.

perspectives on the problem. For many behind the moat in a political elite that has profited hugely over the last three decades, whole segments of society are now, or potentially, criminal: labor, a peasantry grown increasingly landless, various NGOs, critics, reformers, political and social activists, and anyone who doubts the motives and credentials of the New Order regime and questions its legitimacy.

A salient target of this doubt, expressed in widespread public anger and contempt (and now and again shoes, rocks, curses, and knives), is the judicial system, which in some ways has become a surrogate for the regime or its replica in miniature. The entire judicial structure—courts, prosecution, police, and prison administration—operating within a fortress of bureaucratic privilege, has become known in part for its exploitation of a public which it seems to hold arrogantly in contempt.

REFORM?

Lacking adequate organized power, that exploited public cannot do much about changing the regime or reforming it substantially without help from within the regime itself. Public opinion, however, has begun to have at least slight effect. Growing protests during the 1980s against New Order leadership, policies, corruption, and lack of institutional controls, and increasing demands for attention to human rights and fair legal process eventuated in two concessions by the government in the early 1990s. One was judicial and the other quasi-judicial, and neither was expected by anyone to mean much more than previous promises had, including those in the code of criminal procedure.

The first was the creation of administrative courts (PTUN) in five major cities. Intended to hear suits against government agencies, these tribunals had been provided for in basic legislation on the judiciary since the Guided Democracy period, but the government was unwilling to establish them. The conception of them went against the grain, implying the possibility of governmental imperfection. Perhaps more important, granting citizens a dedicated means of suing government offices threatened bureaucratic invulnerability. In 1985, however, at a time of rising domestic and international criticism, a new law provided for the administrative courts, which were finally established five years later. Given the reputation of the civil courts, however, and the recruitment of PTUN judges from them, along with growing public cynicism, expectations did not run high.

The second concession also met with serious skepticism. Following a military massacre in East Timor at the end of 1991 that provoked severe international criticism—and finally broke through the blockade of information about East Timor within Indonesia—the government took the initiative by establishing in 1993 a new National Commission on Human Rights (KOMNAS HAM), whose membership included some trusted regime insiders but also others regarded as independent. In general, it was viewed initially as little more than a ploy.

Institutional reforms, however, often have unintended trajectories of their own. The impact of the PTUN and the KOMNAS HAM should not be blown out of proportion, though it should not be dismissed either. They did not result in anything like fundamental change, nor did they develop much purchase within the regime. What they did was to highlight the decrepitude of other institutions, to attract the interest of the public, and perhaps to encourage some reform circles for a time.

Two possible influences on these institutional innovations deserve mention. One is that neither had a history or institutional memory. They could, if tempted, set their own precedents. The second is that they appeared at a time of, indeed as the result of, growing political protest, widespread disgust at corruption and abuse of authority (even among many who profited from the New Order), and the noise of daily complaints about the bureaucracy, courts, and political leadership.

At first the administrative courts seemed unremarkable. They were not entirely free of corruption, evidently, and they had little more success than the civil courts in enforcing their decisions. But they provided a setting for any administrative judge willing to rule against a powerful political figure on the merits. In 1996 a PTUN judge in Jakarta, Benyamin Mangkoedilaga, did just that by ruling in favor of the editor of the weekly *Tempo*, Goenawan Mohamad, who had sued the Minister of Information for closing down his journal. Moreover, the appellate PTUN upheld him. Startling as these decisions were, it is telling that all the PTUN judges did was to apply the unequivocal provisions of the press law. The Minister, Harmoko, promptly appealed to the pliable Supreme Court, which predictably overturned the PTUN decisions, but too late to overcome the slight edge of optimism honed by Judge Benyamin. (Judge Benyamin was promptly moved to the appellate PTUN in Medan; perhaps a routine promotion, it was commonly interpreted as administrative punishment.)

Similarly, members of the KOMNAS HAM opted to take their charge seriously, examining human rights issues around the country, evaluating them openly, and rendering judgments that were unenforceable but that nonetheless put the government on the defensive. The daily press took increasing notice, while two or three KOMNAS HAM members became outspoken advocates on human rights problems and the need for government attention.

Against the overwhelming power of the New Order regime, none of this amounts immediately to a great deal, nor again should its significance be exaggerated. The PTUN and KOMNAS HAM encouraged reformers and many others, who began to flood the PTUN with cases and the KOMNAS HAM with protests against national and local government agencies, military actions, and more. KOMNAS HAM, with less authority but more visibility than the PTUN, began to seem like a loose cannon to a few military officers, who suggested that it was time for the institution to quiet down and remember who created it.

Their work also inevitably called attention to the decrepitude, corruption, and political subservience of the civil judiciary, which may have encouraged a few unhappy judges to make their own statements. Whatever the reason, in 1996 one Supreme Court judge, Adi Andoyo, did so by inviting the public prosecution to investigate a case of collusion between Supreme Court judges and a party to a case before them. Almost immediately he became a public hero. When the new Supreme Court chair, Soerjono, encouraged President Suharto to dismiss Adi Andoyo, professional advocates, law students, and others protested, demonstrated, and even mounted a hunger strike or two. Judge Adi Andoyo soon retired anyway, but the flap had its own influence on reform interests.

No one seriously supposes that New Order leadership will soon give in to pressures for fundamental reform. The stakes are too high. But neither is it likely that the pressure will ebb soon, for the stakes have become equally high outside the regime. Politically fragmented as it is, the reform movement nevertheless enjoys an ideological consensus of sorts that insists on imposing limits on government authority and making public institutions less dangerous and more serviceable to society. This consensus, molded by experience, will sustain a long argument over many issues. Most recently, in August 1997, a debate began over a draft law on the national police submitted to Parliament. The Indonesian Legal Aid Foundation and three private lawyer associations protested the draft, insisting among a range of demands that the police should be withdrawn from the armed forces, that its discretionary authority should be limited, and that it should be subject to controls.[33] It is only one of many issues on which practicing lawyers, legal scholars, NGOs, activist groups of various sorts, the press, and many others have begun to weigh in.

Nearing its end, as New Order leaders lose authority and rely increasingly on raw power to control a population growing less patient, a wider debate has been joined over the quality of the political system, state-society relations, the economy, justice, and much else in modern Indonesia. Crime enters into this debate at many points. One dimension of it, however, may be particularly significant in Indonesia's political evolution. Against the regime's view that its critics, imaginary Communists, and labor leaders, among others, are the first order of criminality requiring attention, legal aid and human rights NGOs, professional advocates, and assorted reformers have long argued that political leaders themselves, and much of the official apparatus, are criminally culpable. Not everyone believes this, and many who do see nothing wrong with it, but there is enough support for the insight, and a deep enough sense of outrage about it, that no successor political elite can afford to ignore it.[34]

---

[33] *Republika*, August 19, 1997.

[34] This paper was completed in September 1997, as the economic crisis was gathering steam that, along with a tidal wave of political protest, finally forced President Soeharto to leave office in early May of 1998. The issues raised during late 1997 and early 1998, and that remain a principal focus of the reform movement, have to do significantly with the failures of the legal system. Every institution of the criminal law--courts, prosecution, police, prisons, the military security appartus--has been faulted, to put it mildly. After nearly forty years of abuse of authority, there is little reason to be optimistic about how easy it will be to improve criminal procedure. This same history, however, has made many citizens particularly sensitive to official abuse and will keep the issues alive and the pressure for reform heavy.

OPEN SECRETS:
EXCERPTS FROM CONVERSATIONS WITH A JAVANESE LAWYER, AND A COMMENT

John Pemberton

The following excerpts are drawn from a series of extended conversations with a Central Javanese lawyer (*advokat*), a specialist in criminal defense. The conversations took place in August 1996, just weeks after the violent takeover of the Indonesian Democratic Party headquarters in Jakarta on July 27 and the mass demonstrations that followed. Given such conditions, the lawyer preferred to remain anonymous. At many points in these conversations explicit reference was made to details specific to the locale of the lawyer's practice, noting particular persons, businesses, organizations, and events close to home. In light of the wish for anonymity, I have deleted such details, in some cases simply deleting the narrative episode entirely, in other cases changing the place name of his town to "here" or "around here." At many other points, however, the lawyer's comments extended naturally to a variety of locales—Karanganyar, Solo, Kartosuro, Yogya, Jakarta—and in doing so made clear the fact that his descriptions of conditions informing legal practice are by no means peculiar to his hometown. As he often indicated, there is nothing particularly unique about these conditions in his region or, for that matter, his own experiences as a lawyer. Despite personal stories that may appear, at times, extraordinary, such stories are widespread among Indonesian lawyers and reflect pervasive social and political conditions. This was a point repeatedly brought home by the lawyer interviewed here.

A second point to be made by way of introduction to the present excerpts concerns tone. The pervasiveness of conditions giving rise to the narrative stuff of experiences recalled here makes the stories simultaneously shocking and routine— that is, shocking in their very routineness. Hence, just as I would stress the widespread nature of such stories, I would note as well a certain tonality registered here which is common, a personal tone not unusually cynical, yet deeply edged, born from astonishment and frustration (not professional resignation) and all the while bouyed by a pronounced humor, generated by the author's awareness of his own inevitable complicity, and a sense of passionate detachment. While recording the interviews—the four excerpts translated here follow sequentially the order in which they emerged in long, informal conversations held late during August nights when temperatures were relatively cool and the normal business of everyday life temporarily distant—the lawyer often warned me that I would surely become bored. He was painfully aware of the repetitive nature of such stories, of their numbing potential. It is precisely this force of repetition that threatens to be lost in excerpted interviews where narratively dramatic moments appear, as it were, highlighted. I hope the reader will find that this is not the case with these excerpts. To the extent that some (if any) highlights appear, such moments could just as easily have been located elsewhere in the untranslated portions of the conversations. Which is to say I trust that the narrative passages translated here remain as unsettlingly boring, as unacceptably repetitious, as the lawyer knew them to be. Again, what is surprising, perhaps shocking, about such stories is just how unsurprising they have become. This too was brought home in conversation, repeatedly.

EXCERPT ONE

Q: How would you compare those who are called criminals [*kriminal*] nowadays with those in the past?

A: Of course I don't have firsthand knowledge about the old days but one often hears that there used to be robbers, thieves, burglars, that sort of thing, pickpockets in the market, and so on. And for the most part they were just making a living, satisfying basic needs. Sure, some sought luxury but basically it was about necessities. That's what I've heard. But criminals nowadays, it's certainly not just about livelihood. Instead, it's to throw around lots of money, to show off, getting drunk, gambling. It's clear that this kind of thing's increased. What's even more serious is that this criminal activity is very often tied, either directly or indirectly, to the *aparat* (officialdom), whether it's the military or the police. Now, when I say directly or indirectly, there are those cases where members of police are directly, I mean physically, involved. In a robbery, for example. But more common is the indirect. For example, they loan or rent out guns. There are several very recent cases of this here. Also, there are cases where the police—and this is common—have acted as fences, you know, purveyors of stolen goods. They buy things really cheap. You can find these characters at bus terminals or at night on the edges of town. Army men are behind this. Maybe they use other people but it's clear that behind this are members of the army. So this perhaps is a different kind of criminal. There are a lot of things going on here, John. You asked about criminals in the old days. Those are what I would call "pure" [*murni*] criminals, like *maling* [Javanese: thief, burglar]. But these other ones—here, the boundaries blur. Perhaps you could call it more refined. Like debt collectors, for example. This is clearly often the work of men in the army or police. *Jago* types,[1] like bodyguards, using illegal methods, you know, threats, coercion, and so on.

---

[1] *Jago* here refers to macho endowed figures recalling notoriously powerful bandits and local strongmen from the Javanese past. See the essay by Henk Schulte Nordholt and Margreet van Till in this volume.

Q: Some people say that what we now call criminals, in the old days, were perceived as heroes in their own villages and neighborhoods . . .

A: Sure, I've heard that, often. And there's a saying used by thieves in the old days, "Don't shit in your own room" [Javanese: *aja ngising ing kamaré dhéwé*]. But now, there's a real tendency to operate close to home, in their own territories. And they're not at all embarrassed about doing this.

Q: And the neighbors?

A: They're really concerned about this. There have been several cases here where these kinds of people were arrested and released and then beaten—even beaten to death—by their own neighbors.

Q: And the police response to this?

A: Often they try to process it officially but when the whole neighborhood acts this way, en masse, it's really impossible for them to prosecute. But probably most often, the neighbors don't do anything about it at all. They just try to look out for themselves and keep out of it.

. . .

Q: I've heard that criminals are in some way tied to the elections.

A: In elections, especially in '77 and '82, there were a lot of youths associated with the campaigns that I knew were criminals. Now, when I say criminals here, I don't mean "pure" criminals—they're not professional thieves or anything like that. They're just into collecting protection money, acting as the squeeze, "debt collectors" in quotation marks, and so on, *jago* types—you know, those people where it's not clear where their money's coming from but their life is really very good. These were recruited within one organization, AMPI [Indonesian Renewal Younger Generation]. Now, contestants from all three parties used these recruits who, personally, couldn't have cared less which party won.

Q: The PPP[2] party too?

A: Some, but far less than the other two. I'm not saying that because I'm sympathetic to PPP but I'm certain that those are the facts. So in '77 and '82 a lot of these were recruited to spearhead the campaigns. And many of them knew the campaign contestants for the DPR [The People's Legislative Assembly]. And in fact they were very intimate with the *aparat*. Obviously if they were this intimate with the government, this gave them various means—for example, if they were arrested, it was easy for them to get off. And this intimacy gave them a new kind of confidence. There were many new cases in the late '70s and early '80s. For example, in a neighborhood near here a thief was caught and beaten by the youth in that

---

[2] PPP: The United Development Party, at the time the major Islamic political party in Indonesia.

neighborhood. But then this thief turned around and threatened the neighborhood kids with retaliation, from the authorities, he said. This is fantastic—he's caught and he has no sense of wrong whatsoever. Simply revenge. They let him go and then that neighborhood prepared itself for retaliation every night after that. I don't know if there was ever any retaliation but what is clear is that they [*mereka*, i.e., these new criminal types] had become really brazen. So this kind of thing reached a pinnacle and then there was Petrus.[3] And right after that this kind of activity decreased drastically, for a time. But now, there's actually more criminal activity than in the early '80s, just before Petrus.

Q: More?

A: And they're even bolder now. In the '80s you didn't hear that often of robberies that were accompanied by mugging or killing. But nowadays a house is robbed, the daughter or wife is raped, and then the owner is killed. This is quite different. This kind of thing has increased.

Q: Why?

A: I don't know. But take, for example, someone who owes money—not only does he not pay the debt but then he turns around and murders the person who's owed money. This is increasing. Why? I don't know. . . . The murder rate was much lower in the early '80s. And I certainly wouldn't be confident in saying that criminal activity has now decreased, although newspapers several times have reported that the rate of criminal incidents in Central Java has decreased although the total number has increased. I'm positive the rate has not decreased. That's a lie. There are many, many cases that go unreported. And what's interesting is the question of why people don't report the cases.

Q: Why?

A: Many people have experienced that if you report these things, it becomes a real hassle. I've experienced this. I had something that was stolen, I reported it, it wasn't certain at all that I was ever going to get my things back, but I had to put out a lot of money to help "find out." And imagine, this happens to me, a lawyer, experienced in the world of law. You can imagine for someone else, even more a hassle. You're

---

[3] "Petrus" derives from *penembakan misterius* ("mysterious shootings") and/or *penembak misterius* ("mysterious marksman") and refers to a prolonged, nation-wide series of killings during 1983-1984 carried out by the Soeharto regime as part of its early 1980s "Elimination of Crime Operation." Although the killings were initially performed as a clandestine operation— hence the name—it soon was common knowledge that the government was responsible for these nightly raids when "criminals" were kidnapped and shot at point-blank range, their corpses left as threatening reminders of the "need" for law and order. Eventually, Soeharto himself claimed credit for the killings. In December 1983, Adnan Buyung Nasution estimated the death toll at four thousand; outside estimates would soon double this figure. For a summary of Petrus events and reports, see Justus M. van der Kroef, "'Petrus': Patterns of Prophylactic Murder in Indonesia," *Asian Survey* 25 (1985): 745–759. See also, *Tapol* 58 (1983): 1–5; 61 (1984): 8–10; 62 (1984): 9; 64 (1984): 10–11; and 65 (1984): 18. For a discussion of the implications of Petrus, see Jim Siegel's essay, "A New Criminal Type in Jakarta: The Nationalization of 'Death,'" in this book.

summoned, you're called in, but you don't know when they'll see you. You wait, you wait. You have to go home, you come back again, you have to give them some money, you wait, and so on. Now this next thing is not going to be easy to say but I've got to tell you. Sometimes I really feel sorry for these underlings at the police station. They ask me for money "for paper." Paper! He says, "Please help me out, for paper, we need paper." And the thing is, I'm sure he's not lying.

Q: A moment ago you said that AMPI worked as the spearhead for campaigns. How?

A: In the '77 and '82 elections there were a lot of groups like that around but the one that was most visible was AMPI. They were pleased, very pleased, to have obvious ties to the *aparat*. They were invited to official receptions, to ceremonies, all these official things at government offices. They were present. But we knew who these people were, we knew.

Q: And the emergence of Pemuda Pancasila [Pancasila Youth]?[4]

A: I'm not sure exactly when they were officially born. I didn't pay much attention to this early on, but by the end of the '80s, Yapto emerged on the scene.[5] It appears that the AMPI organization was displaced by Pemuda Pancasila. Now, Pemuda Pancasila is even more obvious in its recruiting from the community of hoods [*kaum preman*]. Their leaders are explicit about this with an idealistic rationale of giving the recruits "direction." All this is nonsense. In fact, this was simply a way of giving them legitimacy and organizing them at the same time. For example, they often ask for donations—"obligatory," in quotation marks, donations. Many are "debt" collectors, bodyguards, and so on.

Q: And what do people think of PP [Pemuda Pancasila]?

A: When faced with this organization, many are cynical. But what is certain is that this organization appears close, very close, to the government *aparat*. For example, the head of this thing now in Solo, Fredy. Everybody in Solo knows who he is.

Q: So who is he?

---

[4] Pemuda Pancasila designates a nationally recognized "youth" organization commonly perceived as: 1) made up of marginal, mainly urban youth, many of whom are well on their way to becoming thugs (particularly practiced in extortion) if they are not already so; 2) claiming "patriotic" devotion to Pancasila (the five basic principles of the Republic of Indonesia), as well as to certain government/army officials, by parading in quasi-paramilitary fashion; and 3) having suddenly appeared on the scene during the early 1980s in conjunction with the Petrus killings and, from that time on, headed by one Yapto, a Solonese said to have had ties with Bu Tien Soeharto. While the institutional history of Pemuda Pancasila can, in fact, be traced back to circa 1960 and the Sukarno era, in 1980 Yapto Soerjosoemarno substantially reorganized the remnants of this original institution. For an insightful history of Pemuda Pancasila and speculations on the organization's position in post-Soeharto times, see Loren Ryter, "Pemuda Pancasila: The Last Loyalist Free Men of Soeharto's Order?," *Indonesia* 66 (October 1998).

[5] See footnote 4 above.

A: He used to be a bodyguard at the Solo Movie Theater in the late '70s. Before that, people knew him as a *jago* type around Solo. Now he's director.

Q: And Fredy's relationship with the authorities?

A: Close, of course, close. His position is strengthened precisely because it is acknowledged by the authorities. He is recognized by them. I guarantee that their [i.e., Pemuda Pancasila] lobby—his and his network's lobby—with the *aparat* is stronger than that of organizations that have been time tested, like HMI [Islamic Student Association] for example. PP's lobby is much stronger. They have an organization, it's official. . . . But everybody knows who Fredy is.

EXCERPT TWO

Q: Those you refer to as criminals with ties to the *aparat*—are these ties more often to the military or to the police?

A: Generally, the police, generally.

Q: Is there competition between the military and the police for such ties?

A: Obviously. I know the military version of this. For example, there have been incidents in the last few years which have not really been exposed. A couple of years ago, for example, I forget exactly how many, the police station in Kartasura was bombarded by army men. This was at two in the morning. I don't know whether or not someone died. It was quickly hushed up. Or, again, at the soccer stadium there in Solo, there was music concert by someone, I forget his name, some famous guitarist from Sweden or some place. Members of the police on duty at the event were beaten up by members of KOSTRAD [Army Strategic Reserve Command]. And there are many individual cases, many. A lot of people in the military obviously can't stand the police and say so. And, you know, I can certainly understand this. I've often been pissed off by them. They arrest someone who really shouldn't be arrested, then they don't arrest someone that they really ought to, don't do a thing. Even some police have complained to me about this, about being so lazy in pursuing serious cases. Here's a concrete example. I received, over time, many reports associating criminal activity with a certain car dealership. You know, in other words, time after time criminal cases came up that had a tie to this dealership. I don't need to name which one it is to you, John, but everyone around here knows. I gave all this data to the police but that failed. I had a lot of data, I'd worked hard on this. Wasn't too popular with the dealership bosses. So that's a small example. The police receive a report, with plenty of proof, and finally I'm told to stop—by the police—don't want to "offend" anyone.

Q: So are people more cynical about the police or the military?

A: Without a doubt, the police. For sure.

Q: For sure?

A: Absolutely. As I said before, even though news reports say that criminal rates have gone down, this is not the case. People often don't report crimes, mostly because it feels like such a hassle. . . . And detention itself has become a commodity [*komoditi*].

Q: Commodity?

A: Take, for example, cases where there's really not enough evidence to detain someone. But the police are brazen enough just to go out there and arrest them anyway. For this arrest and detention, the police receive money from the person who reported the crime. Then, of course, the family of this prisoner very often pays off the police so he'll go free. This is what they sell—this is what I mean by a commodity. Even though, under Indonesian law, detention before trial is not a "must" but rather something that "may" be implemented. It's not required but the police tend to detain. Pardon me, not just the police, John, but judges too very often tend toward detention. This has no legal basis. You report so-and-so and I say I'll arrest him depending on how much you're willing to pay. And then his faction comes along and pays for his release. This is the commodity system. In many, many cases, detention is not necessary. I'll give you an example. I'm a lawyer. My position and identity is clear to everyone. Okay, suppose one day I'm in an accident. My car is run into by a motorcycle. And I guarantee it's not my fault—the motorcycle just runs into me. Now, the motorcyclist dies. Again, it is not my fault. So, here's the question: should I flee? That'd be crazy. If I did that, of course I'd look guilty. But the police often use this as an excuse—possible fleeing. And I'm detained so that my family will have to shell out a lot of money. This kind of thing is an open secret [*rahasia umum*]. This sort of commodity transaction has now spread through the ranks of lawyers. As a lawyer, I will be asked by my client to give the money to the police so my client's enemy will be detained. This is widespread now.

Q: And so if this is normal, an open secret, and everybody knows it, then the term "criminal" properly refers to whom?

A: They're all criminals [*semuanya kriminal*]. [laughs] They're all criminals, John. It's just up to whoever has power to say who's a criminal and who's not.

Q: You know this as a professional, a lawyer . . .

A: People may not be familiar with all the details but what everybody knows is this: if arrested, you give money. To get out of jail, you give money. You go to court, you give money. No matter what happens, you give money. Everybody knows this. Everybody knows.

. . .

Q: So when you said they're all criminals . . .

A: Of course, those who are called *kriminal*, you know, literally, are people like thieves and so on. These people tied to the *aparat* are not called *kriminal* but, in material terms, they're really criminals too. So, we are talking about the law, right?

Q: Right.

A: Well, one conclusion might be that the court of law, it's name ought to be changed. It shouldn't be called a house of justice [*kantor pengadilan*] but instead an auction house [*kantor lelang*]. An auction house for cases. Why do I say such a thing? From my own experience. This is not just a fantasy, John. I hear from older lawyers that of course in the past sometimes they tried to do this kind of thing but the judges refused. But now the judge himself calls me or the prosecutor calls me or a policeman calls me—they're the ones who ask me, "Do you want your client to be helped or not? Does your client have enough for a donation or not?" So they're actively pursuing this. They're the producers and they're offering their wares. As I was saying, in the old days lawyers tried to get the ear of the judge. But now it's not like that. The judges are selling. "Do you have money or not? If you don't, I'll make an offer to your adversary." Now when I get a telephone call like this, I'm no longer surprised. I treat it as a proper thing. [smiles] At first, I was shocked. Now, no. Now I feel that it is natural. Perhaps I'm wrong but it has finally come to feel completely normal.

Q: If that's the case and all this is an open secret, why do you think people are interested in the law at all? For example, after the recent July incident, I was impressed by how closely people followed the details of proceedings. And of course, people follow news reports on trials of criminals, as well. What's all this attention about?

A: I wouldn't say that people are necessarily following these events or reading newspapers about these cases or even a case like this recent one in July because they have any hopes in the justice system. They often just want to see how the case develops.

Q: Develops?

A: You know, how events will turn out.

Q: Like a story?

A: Exactly. News reports can appear very dramatic but, actually, the facts often aren't all that extraordinary. . . . So John, let me tell you a story, just another story. There was this judge who lived out of town but his job was here. I'd never dealt with him. First time I met him was one morning, very early in the morning. He came to my house at 7:00 a.m. This was years ago and I had really just begun practicing, still green. Perhaps he knew that. So he comes to my house really early in the morning and says that he'd been in an accident with his car and he needed to repair his car so that he could pick up his kid later that afternoon. He said he'd like to borrow two million rupiah. Remember, I had been a practicing lawyer for barely a year and in front of me was the judge. I said, "Sure, later I'll bring it over to your office." So I did this later on that morning and with much feeling of respect. He said he'd return it in two or three days, with the idea that instead of just coming back to town and giving it to me that evening he'd give it to me when he saw me two or three days later. Without any ill-feeling whatsoever I said, "That's fine." I must confess that I did this with a certain amount of self-interest, thinking "Ah, now I've got a powerful lobby with the judge." I thought, "Great, if I present a case, perhaps now it'll go smoothly." OK, I didn't ask for that money back. Time passed, I still didn't ask for it and one day he calls me up and says [in *ngoko*, that is, in low Javanese] "Come on over to my office at 1:00. I want to return that money." So I waited for him until the office closed and I thought maybe he'd forgotten. Then, the second time, I was even dumber. I was in court and when I left the courthouse, I ran into him. He said [in *ngoko*], "Listen, I've got this check for five million. I'm going to cash it at the bank. Wait here and I'll be back around 2:00." So I waited. Then it rained. 3 o'clock and he hadn't come. 3:30, no, 4, no. By 5 o'clock, he still hadn't come. Then I thought, "What a jerk." So I called him up at his house in the country. He said, in a tone that was still pleasant, "I went home because it rained." And I said, "That's fine." John, I really wasn't trying to get my money back. This went on for quite a long time. Finally, little by little, he paid most of the money back. Then he came again to my office. This time he said he wanted to borrow three million. "Yes, sure." I was really stupid, truly stupid. "Sure," I said, "but sometime if I should need money. . . ." "Oh, absolutely," he said. This was fasting month and he added, "I'll pay you back very soon." At that time I was doing well. I could've lost three million, and it really wouldn't have changed things that much. This was about two weeks before Lebaran.[6] In short, he borrowed the money and two weeks later he says to me, "Tomorrow is Lebaran." Then he shows me a check for ten million—he really liked showing off checks—and says, "I've got to go to the bank and cash this check." This is a judge, John. He says, "I'm going to the bank. How long are you going to be in your office? I want to return your loan. Hey, I'll tell you what, I'll go to the bank and then I'll stop by and give it directly to your wife." I said fine. I was already thinking about the holiday. And I'm already thinking, tomorrow I've got to go with my wife and family to visit relatives and I'm thinking I won't have to go to the bank because I'll have this three million. 6 o'clock I go home and of course the first question I ask my wife is, "Did he come with the money?" The answer was no. Now you can imagine, in my pocket was a ten-thousand rupiah bill. And tomorrow was Lebaran. For gas alone that's not enough. There was no way I could pay for everything I needed to buy for Lebaran, for the rice and all the rest. Perhaps you can understand. So I called him up. His response was, "So if it's not there, what are you going to do about it?" For me, that was the Lebaran from hell. That evening I had to go around like a beggar, asking for money from here and there so I could make the trip. OK, so after Lebaran, I met him at the courthouse and there were a lot of people around. And because he had no sense of remorse, none at all, I couldn't help but say [in *ngoko*] in front of all those people as he smiled when he passed by, "This judge is just like a prostitute." But I was not yet satisfied. So I followed him right into his chambers. Several prosecutors were there, too. Actually, if he had apologized, I probably would have backed off. But he appeared defensive and my anger grew. It was like I'd lost my head and I said "You just told

---

[6] Lebaran is an annual national holiday when millions of Indonesians return to their village homes at the end of the Muslim fasting month to beg forgiveness from family elders and, with much festivity, to celebrate the ending of the fast.

me I needed to behave responsibly. That's fine. I'd just like to add to that. From my perspective, a pimp is more respectable than you." I said, "Go ahead, take me to court. The worst thing that could happen is that I could lose my lawyer's license." I'd really lost my senses, John. "Even if I lost my license, it's no problem," I said. "I'll still be driving my car." Then that judge began to cry. He actually cried. And I said, "The money's not the issue but just don't toy with me." After that, I went to the chair of the court, still not satisfied. Finally, I took this thing to court. And through a court decision, this guy paid me back. I still have the decision papers. I paid dearly for that one. Such nonsense. Bored with these stories aren't you?

Q: Not really . . .

A: But given the present conditions it would be impossible to contest a judge like that.

EXCERPT THREE

Q: Do you find satisfaction in your work?

A: No.

Q: Why not?

A: I no longer feel it's important to read law books, no longer important to prepare an argument based on precedents. That kind of thing is no longer important. It's more important that I know whether or not my client has enough money to pay the judge. There's no satisfaction in this at all. It's meaningless. I'd planned to stop in a few years. My plan was that in 1998 I would stop completely and perhaps I'd act as a consultant. Nothing more than that. Never go to court again. But, as you know, something happened and I could no longer afford to lose the income.

Q: And if the situation in the courts is really . . .

A: For a long time I've known that the judicial system is not—what should I say?—clean. I'd heard that for a long time before I became a lawyer and I of course had a certain impression of how things might work. But when I began to practice, what was happening was way, way beyond even my imagination. Way beyond the capacity of my imagination. I'd never thought that the judge—you can just picture this—the *judge* called me into his office to discuss a case that I was presenting. He called me to ask me how much I'd be willing to pay to win this case and of course at that time other judges were present. I was too embarrassed to respond. Too embarrassed. But he wasn't at all. He said, "It's OK. Just go ahead and say what you need to say." But I couldn't understand this. Now, at first I was embarrassed. At first. There were others present and what was strange was that they just said, "You don't need to feel awkward about doing this. Go ahead." This was what was difficult for me to imagine. [laughs] But finally, of course, I had to adjust. If I didn't adjust I was dead. It would be impossible to win a case. All the clients would avoid me. And in fact that happened at first.

Q: So when you first started out, you still had faith in the judicial system, you still had some sort of hope?

A: Of course.

Q: And now?

A: Under these conditions, forget it—impossible. For example, there's the argument that raising various salaries would stop this. Bullshit. In fact, it'll just up the stakes.

Q: So, given the state of the judicial system, if there's to be some sort of social change, by what means would this come about?

A: The government is in power. They don't need to pretend that they don't know about this. They know. It's a lie that they don't know. All of us know. Everyone knows. Take the most common case in the neighborhoods and listen to the language. People no longer say that they're going to get a divorce. They say they're going to *buy* divorce papers. Buy. Everybody knows this.

Q: Everyone . . .

A: There're these types called "judicial candidates" [apprentices] who perform as clerks, working in the courts and so on. Most of these have already become go-betweens for this sort of thing. They're already brokers. They're still in training, so you know what will happen after they become judges. And once they become judges, in order to be moved to a place with good prospects, like a city, they pay for that. There was a judge in town here, John. I was close to him. He was just an ordinary judge. He got himself upgraded to a more lucrative district. And after just two years there he was able to build a deluxe house back in town here—truly deluxe, just two years. Now he's moved to Jakarta. And he jokes with me—he says, "Hey kid, move to Jakarta. There are no envelopes [*amplop*] there, just shopping bags, the big plastic ones." So everybody sells whatever they can sell. Army people sell their power, police do the same, and so on. Everyone in the *aparat* makes an effort to sell. Everyone. . . . So a courthouse is just a place for bargaining, a market. I used to be embarrassed but now I can say this: that's all there is, no alternative. The judge says, "C'mon. How much can you go for?" Or he'll say, "C'mon, man, why don't you go out and look for x-number of millions?" So I can genuinely say, I'm no longer embarrassed. Genuinely, John.

Q: No alternatives?

A: You wonder about this? I've been cussed out by clients. In my early years a judge asked me to ask my client for money. I didn't convey the request. I didn't say anything at all to my client about this. At that point, I felt that I had an airtight case. I was quiet. Understand my point?

Q: Yes. . .

A: We lost the case. Then, without my knowing, my client went to visit the judge at home. I'm not sure exactly what the judge said but the main thing was, he told the client that he had asked me to ask for money but that there was no response from me. And the judge was correct. Correct. I'm not saying that he was wrong. He really did ask me to do this and I really didn't do it. And I can't tell you how pissed my client was. He was truly angry. And my client's anger was justified. He asked me, "Why didn't you convey the judge's request to me? It's my right to decide, not yours." That's correct. Correct. And I thought, "He's not wrong." If he wanted to pay or not, that was not for me to decide. When you think of it, any message coming from the judge, I should have conveyed to my client. So, you see, I tried to hold out for awhile. That proved impossible, things dissolved. People can talk a lot about idealism but, on the ground, this is the way it is. I didn't convey the request and these were the results. I was at fault. I was going to say, John, that it's very complex but really it's not so complex.

Q: And the longer this goes on?

A: The more out of control it is.

Q: So where would controls come from?

A: Without extreme measures, don't even hope.

Q: Extreme?

A: Change 'em all. You assume that after awhile my senior colleagues would achieve a certain awareness. Bullshit. Not possible. Three generations later, just the same.

Q: Change 'em all?

A: Everyone who signs up to become a government employee—a judge, a prosecutor—they already know what their wages are going to be, they already know. So why do they take these positions? The answer is clear.

Q: Earlier you said, they're all criminals.

A: Right, criminals all [*kriminal semua*], John.

Q: Often in the newspapers, I read about sensational cases pertaining to people you'd call "pure" criminals. Perhaps they're just scapegoats, no?

A: The characters you see in the newspapers are real criminals, classics. I don't think they're scapegoats. But what I'm describing here is more evil, more dangerous. Like I said, when detention becomes a commodity, or when the police take over debt collection, manipulating the law—this is far more dangerous. So protection for the people is going to come from where? If the people are pressed by a debt collector who's a criminal, a real criminal, fine. We can send for police protection. But when the police themselves have already become the debt collectors, with the law in their hands, where are you going to turn now?

EXCERPT FOUR

Q: When an incident happens, newspapers often look for what they call the puppeteer behind it all, like the recent incident in Yogya, where a journalist was killed . . .

A: The Yogya case, right. You know, news reporters are not exempt from this kind of thing. Each profession wants to give the appearance that it's clean. But, in fact, reporters often try to get money out of people. Now with this Yogya case, it's quite possible that the reporter's drive to crack this case was based on less than idealistic motives. It's possible. That's all I can say to you about this right now. No one's exempt. I've often noted to friends, "If there's a judge or a policeman or a prosecutor who's been murdered by someone, I of course don't approve of such a thing, but in many cases I can certainly understand."

Q: Do you think there's a profession that tends to be relatively cleaner than that of lawyers?

A: John, reporters wouldn't necessarily be one of them. There's a reason for them to sell. Of course there are exceptions.

Q: Returning to the idea of a puppeteer behind it all. Does this idea represent more the perspective of the *aparat* or of the people?

A: The *aparat*. For sure. But they're not necessarily wrong. Not necessarily, John. For example, in cases where a number of people feel that their rights have been bypassed. They justly feel this way. It's pure [*murni*]. Then there emerges someone who begins a movement defending these rights. This is proper, in my opinion. But there are times when these so-called defenders of people's rights are primarily concerned with their own interests and just turning events to their own advantage. I don't accept this. In Indonesia I see a lot of cases like this, which are not really concerned with the needs of the people being mobilized, who just become a kind of tool for personal ends and after the moment of demonstration has passed the people demonstrating don't get a thing out of it. This is common.

Q: But don't you think factory workers ever move on their own?

A: As far as I know, this hasn't happened around here. They've always been mobilized by certain individuals, individuals that I happen to know. I've never seen a demonstration here where the workers weren't following one person or another.

Q: How about the case of the demonstration against [the textile factory] Batik Keris in Solo?

A: Turn off the tape recorder and I'll tell you who was the puppeteer behind it . . . .

. . .

Q: OK, suppose it does occasionally happen that a factory has been infiltrated by external groups. Why would the workers want to follow such people?

A: They're given beautiful dreams. Like the recent case in a factory in the town of Karanganyar.

Q: There are those who say that factory heads actually want to raise wages but can't afford to do this because there is so much pay-off, protection money, to the military or police.

A: Right, I've heard this and agree generally with the idea that if factory wages were higher, in fact workers would feel more settled and jobs would seem more permanent. The question is, who can cut off this protection money? Who can stop the flow? The workers don't protest this, per se. They just get angry at the businessmen. The factory administrators get caught in between since this can only be stopped at the top.

Q: Couldn't you bring a case of protection payoff to court?

A: How could you prove such a thing in court?

Q: Certainly a lot of people know that such money is given.

A: To whom? Where's the proof? This is hard for the law to track. Politics is the only solution. I'm sure the government knows all about this but how can it be proven?

Q: Do you mean it can't be proven?

A: How?

Q: A witness, say, to the money being passed.

A: Legal proof is not really possible. To whom, on what date, with signatures, exact amounts, and so on.

Q: You gave the examples of judges discussing such things in complete openness.

A: They all know they're implicated. There's no secret at all. The only way to change this is by means of a revolution, in quotation marks.

Q: Quotation marks?

A: I'm not talking about a revolution by force, of course. But there has to be action at the very top. Real action. Get rid of them all. That's why I said if you just raise the salaries of the judges that won't do it. They're already accustomed to receiving supplementary income and they wouldn't want to let go of this other income. I'll be concrete, John. I just had a judge change a legal decision, you know, a ruling that was already conceptualized, already written, ready to go for the typist and signature.

And I did that for just five hundred thousand rupiah. That's all it took. Perhaps I wouldn't have been surprised if it had been five million. This is about prestige, you know. Five million would have been a request that I could still respect. But half a million! I find this difficult to comprehend.

COMMENT

Despite my opening question in these excerpts, there was an implicit reluctance on the part of this lawyer, throughout our conversations, to extend the term *kriminal* to the past. That remains a time zone haunted by terms like *maling* (Javanese: thief, burglar), registered in Javanese, that summon up various quasi-professional skills and magical talents used to dupe victims and, increasingly, to elude colonial-era captors armed with modern institutional designations like *crimineel*.[7] When juxtaposed to intrusions into social life brought by figures like *det kolektor, bodigard, aparat*, and even *kriminal*, that zone now appears to have been motivated by relatively pure intentions. One might even call such characters of the past "pure criminals."

Yet no sooner has this been said than it is suggested that there are others who really "ought" to be called *kriminal*—many policemen, some army men, judges, lawyers, and still others—but who are not and hence represent perhaps a "different kind" of criminal, a new type of criminal. Blurring boundaries of identification and posturing in official trappings, this "different kind" of criminal appears as the antithesis of pure. It may very well indicate real criminality, with truly criminal license to mask one's identity, to extract obligatory "donations." It may signal a newly pervasive criminality where police perform as debt collectors or, more precisely, debt collectors perform as police.

With such a criminality comes unprecedented confidence among the extortionists and altered territorial relations. "Don't shit in your own room,"[8] a classic Javanese axiom from the shadow zone of *maling*, is now flagrantly violated by these characters who ought to be called *kriminal*. What is criminal here is the violation itself, the violence of the trespass at home. Even neighbors newly mobilized to attack one of their own suddenly find themselves threatened with fierce retaliation which is perhaps backed by the police. Or, again, money is extracted, locally, by all-too-familiar muscled young patriots taking "donations." The well-worn term *jago*, with faded traces of local heroism, becomes typified—*jagoan*—and detached from an increasingly distant world of Javanese specifics. *Jago* thus comes to mean *bodigard* or, better yet, bodyguards now perform *jagoan*. The patently Indonesianized figure for this? Pemuda Pancasila. But everybody knows who Fredy is.

Like the term *kriminal*, *komoditi* inserts itself into the Indonesian landscape at unannounced points. It first emerges in these interviews, significantly enough, with reference to detention practices in police stations. Within this system of justice, the

---

[7] For a marvelous introduction to *maling* logics, see George Quinn, "The Javanese Science of Burglary," *Review of Indonesian and Malaysian Affairs* 9 (1975): 33-54.

[8] "Don't shit in your own room" (*aja ngising ing kamaré dhéwé*) was/is more than a mere metaphor, among *maling*, for territorial propriety and local loyalties. As late as 1996 an older Central Javanese woman complained to me of waking up one recent morning only to find human feces in the middle of her livingroom floor and her jewelry missing. She contacted an expert in magical practice (*dukun*) to reestablish spiritual force fields around her house and ward off further violations by this cunning *maling*.

kriminal, or more exactly, criminal suspicion, is itself commodified and suspects are ushered in and out of jails. ("First the punishment, then the crime," Pramoedya would say.) With bodies shuttled back and forth across the threshold of detention, in routine accordance with how much money has passed whose hands, there appears here almost perfect congruence between *kriminal* and *komoditi*.

But just as criminality, this "different kind" of criminality, would conceal its own powers of violation by camouflaging itself as Pancasila Youth or uniformed policemen, so too the commodity here masks the implications of money's transgressive powers and poses as police department detention policy or, in the end, a judicial decision. "Like I said, when detention becomes a commodity, or when the police take over debt collection, manipulating the law—this is far more dangerous . . . . If the people are pressed by a debt collector who's a criminal, a real criminal, fine. We can send for police protection. But when the police themselves have already become the debt collectors. . . . " This double masquerade, of the *kriminal* and the *komoditi*, which conflates the roles of police protector and debt collector, of judicial decision and the decisive force of money—first the fine, then the decision—is what makes this other type of *kriminal* "more evil, more dangerous" than the classical *maling*. One might even say that this other type is the figuration of true criminality.

Perhaps to counter such a criminal force, the courthouse ought to be renamed and revealed for what it already is: an auction house. This would be a public gesture, acknowledging a scene of open bidding. Perhaps then, standards of measure would return: to reverse a decision that had already been formalized, with only the signature pending, would command a respectable five million rupiah. The fantastic realism informing such a thought derives, of course, from the very routineness of a system already in practice, a system in which lawyers who do not pass on to clients a judge's request for money deny clients their most basic right. "So I can genuinely say, I'm no longer embarrassed."

This routineness of transaction, *amplop* after *amplop*, shopping bag after shopping bag, yields stories, one after another, told not with embarrassment, nor simply out of anger (although anger is frequently tangible), but in tones that are variously edged, sometimes detached, more often intimate, occasionally bemused, almost always engaged—tones that convey the sense of *rahasia umum*, an "open secret." This ubiquitous phrase emerged in the excerpts here early on and did so, significantly, (along with *komoditi*) in connection with detention. But it is implicit everywhere, every time it is said, "everyone knows"—which car dealership is implicated, that divorce papers must be bought, that "if arrested you give money. To get out of jail, you give money. You go to court, you give money. No matter what happens, you give money. Everybody knows this."

And along with this everybody knows who Fredy is. It is an open secret that those in the *aparat*—that ominously technical term which calls to mind most immediately the police and the army but then reaches up into government implicating *oficials* and their underlings before reaching out to judges and beyond— can be *kriminal* as well. So, too, for lawyers who broker deals, maintaining relations. "They're all *kriminal*," said the lawyer, smiling, knowing that I knew this meant him as well. Everyone knows because everything must be bought—even divorce papers—thus implicating even the most pedestrian of transactive souls, government employees for example. "*Kriminal* all." Given the alleged purity of their status, only *maling*—classic Javanese thieves—remain potentially unimplicated.

All of this, and more, is an open secret. Under such conditions, the secret itself, while generating much talk and many stories, is no longer scandalous. For this is the point where the scandal is not the secret but the apparent fact that everyone knows. ("They all know they're implicated. There's no secret at all.") What becomes scandalous is the very openness of the open secret. This, then, is the point where the structure of privileged knowledge, upon which a secret rests, appears to collapse; but it is not a necessarily optimistic point of total exposure. While there was once a certain sense of community through complicity in the sharing of a secret that was widespread enough to be called "open," yet still endowed with a hint of privileged access, now, with the openness of the secret stretched to the point where it can no longer be enframed as such, where the fact that everyone knows that everyone knows is constantly disclosed, reference points are lost and uncertainties emerge, even within the routines of everyday life. Perhaps one should say they emerge precisely within these routines.

As noted at the outset, the conversations excerpted here took place just weeks after the events of July 1996, weeks that suggested the possibility of more widespread mass movements sometime in the future. Yet this possibility is approached with caution by the Javanese lawyer, who acknowledges the purity of people's feelings of outrage when rights have been bypassed, but acknowledges as well competing motives guiding mass mobilization. "The only way to change this is by means of a revolution in quotation marks." Perhaps this is what has now happened, in the 1998 wake of the terror posed by *komoditi* writ large in the form of the IMF. "Get rid of them all," said the lawyer. Much has changed. But Fredy has still not gone away. Everyone now knows this, too.

A New Criminal Type in Jakarta: The Nationalization of "Death"[1]

James T. Siegel

" . . . One should seek to prevent the regeneration of the body that we bury. Murder only takes the first life of the individual whom we strike down; we should also seek to take his second life, if we are to be even more useful to nature. For nature wants annihilation; it is beyond our capacity to achieve the scale of destruction it desires."

de Sade, *Juliette*, vol. 4

"Each sees the other do the same as it does; each does itself what it demands of the other, and therefore also does what it does only insofar as the other does the same. Action by one side only would be useless because what is to happen can only be brought about by both."

Hegel, *Philosophy of Spirit*
(A. V. Miller translation)

A. KILLING THOSE IN ONE'S OWN IMAGE: COMMUNISTS AND CRIMINALS

Most peoples of the world kill those they want to consider other than themselves: Hutus and Tutsis murder each other as do Serbs and Croatians, to take only recent examples. There is another type of massacre, however, in which one kills those in one's own image. The Indonesian nation holds three clear examples. The

---

[1] A portion of this essay has been excerpted from *A New Criminal Type in Jakarta: Counter-revolution Today* (Chapel Hill, NC: Duke University Press, 1998) with the kind permission of Duke University Press.

I should like to thank several people who commented on the paper either when it was given in 1997 at the University of Tokyo (Komaba) or in typescript. They are Professors Kitagawa Sakiko, Sekimoto Teruo, Yamashita Shinji, and Uchibori Motomitsu, as well as others present at the colloquium in Amsterdam in 1997 where the contributors to this volume gathered.

Indonesian revolution began in 1945 and culminated in 1949 with the transfer of sovereignty from the Dutch to the independent Indonesian state. In 1948 during the revolution nationalists fought communists, who were also nationalists, resulting in a number of dead that has never been estimated but which, it is agreed, was large. There was no doubt that both sides were comprised of "Indonesians." Then in 1965 there occurred the massacre of Indonesian communists and those accused of being communists. This is clearly the largest in scale of these three examples, with many hundreds of thousands, perhaps more, murdered. In 1983-84 the event I will focus on in this essay occurred. At that time, "criminals," many of whom had until that point been employed by the government party, were killed by the thousands by the government.

There are other incidents of major violence in Indonesia, such as the revolution against the Dutch, from 1946 to 1949, and the aggression against East Timor. In the first case one has to count not only Dutch deaths, but also the killings of Indonesians considered traitors either because they formed part of the Dutch armed forces or their civilian bureaucracy or because they were ordinary civilians thought to have betrayed the nation. No reliable figures on the number killed are available. In the case of East Timor, a foreign territory was invaded and annexed and, as a direct or indirect result, it is estimated that a third of the population, over two hundred thousand people to date, have died. But from our point of view, this case, like the revolution, is ambiguous; nonetheless it is clear that, as during the revolution when many were killed because they were Indonesian traitors, the Indonesian government considers East Timorese Indonesians and kills them on that assumption. One can add to these incidents and examples the aggression against Muslims in West Java and elsewhere.

One further example that should be added to this list is the violence against the "Chinese" at various times in Indonesia's history. I put "Chinese" in quotes because aggression against them is inextricably bound up with the definition of their citizenship, their loyalty to the nation, and their participation in the revolution. The insistence that they are not Indonesian, determined with regards to citizenship or sentiment, is, of course, always set against the possibility that they are members of the nation, just like "us" from an Indonesian point of view. Except for "Chinese," the question of who is Indonesian in these cases seems not to have been debated.

Even in the memorialization of the revolution against the Dutch, it seems difficult for Indonesians to think that national violence was directed against those clearly not Indonesian. Here it is instructive to visit the army museum in Jakarta. The dioramas of the revolutionary struggle in this museum show the attacking Indonesian forces but very little of the Dutch enemy. By contrast, in a separate part of the museum, there are bloody shirts from slain Indonesian Muslims and other vivid reminders of the violence practiced against those who it is said betrayed the nation. It is hardly the case that Indonesia lacks xenophobia, but even when there are other identifications than "Indonesian," the word is still important in defining the target of aggression. And when "Indonesian" cannot be used to define the object of aggression, as with the Dutch whom one would expect to appear in the dioramas but do not, the enemy is simply not represented. One has the impression that Indonesians can only picture a victim of their lethal force if the victim is a reflection of the aggressor.

Each act of large-scale violence raises various specters from the history of the nation. The explanation of why Indonesians murder those like themselves has to take account of these differences. Here I will treat only one example, the massacres of criminals in 1983-84. At that time presumed criminals, most of them tattooed, were murdered by soldiers in mufti. Typically, Jeeps loaded with masked, armed men drove to the homes of supposed criminals in the middle of the night, abducted them, repeatedly stabbed or shot their victims, and left the bodies on the streets or in rivers where they became spectacles.[2] This incident, though certainly the smallest in terms of the number of individuals murdered, is especially important because in my opinion it shows how an idea of death existed which the state wanted to control. This notion was associated with the criminal, and the criminal, in turn, has a particular relation to the development of Indonesian nationalism.

Indonesian nationalism arose in an historical context which witnessed the development of the lingua franca of the Indies, Melayu, not only for commercial purposes, but for new forms of communication as well, especially in newspapers and books. In these latter forms, the same stories reached the major groups of the Indies. Many of these stories were translations from the literatures of the world. Some were stories whose native languages had previously limited their audience to only specific ethnic groups. And some concerned criminals, especially thieves and murderers. These criminal stories were written by meztisos who, at the turn of the century, were in danger of losing their privileged relations with their Dutch fathers. These stories, in my opinion, were a way for meztisos to align themselves with the colonial power against criminals whom they pictured as "natives." The latter, they in effect said, were a menace to the Dutch who remained unaware of the danger. In the evolution of anti-Dutch activities, "criminals" often played important roles, and this was notably true during the revolutionary period.[3] One might therefore expect that nationalists would reevaluate these criminals, turning them into nationalists or perhaps proto-nationalists. This, however, has not happened. Criminals have rarely been included amongst the esteemed figures of history in Indonesian discourse.

The "criminal," always on the edge of Indonesian society but never outside it, never the foreigner, is a figure who exists within the context of Indonesian nationalism. Most recently he has been fit into the context of the notion of "the people," or *rakyat*. The word *rakyat* in many Indonesian societies referred to the followers of a leader. They were in the first place retainers supported by those who had local political authority. The word evolved in the context of nationalism to mean

---

[2] For reports on these killings see John Pemberton, *On the Subject of "Java"* (Ithaca: Cornell University Press, 1994), pp. 311-318, and Justus van der Kroef, "'Petrus': Patterns of Prophylactic Murder in Indonesia," *Asian Survey* 25,7 (July 1985): 745-759. Van der Kroef quotes the director of the Indonesian Legal Aid Society as estimating the numbers killed at 8,500. This report was issued some months before the killings came to an end.

[3] For an interpretation of the role of translation and stories of criminals in Indonesian nationalism, see Pramoedya Ananta Toer, *Tempo Doeloe* (Jakarta: Hasta Mitra, 1982) as well as James T. Siegel, *Fetish, Recognition, Revolution* (Princeton: Princeton University Press, 1997). Pramoedya Ananta Toer has conducted an important discussion of the role of the lingua franca in the development of Indonesian nationalism. It is contained in various articles published in the newspaper for which he wrote before it was closed down by the government. A list of these articles can be found in footnote 3 to the Introduction of Siegel, *Fetish, Recognition, Revolution*. For the history of criminals in one region of Indonesia during the revolution see Robert Cribb, *Gangsters and Revolutionaries: The Jakarta People's Militia and the Indonesian Revolution of 1945-49* (Sydney: Allen and Unwin, 1991).

"the people." It referred, in different times and different contexts, to the audiences at political rallies and to those who associated themselves with the nationalist movement before the revolution. During the revolution, the relation of leaders to followers became problematic. The educated Indonesians who claimed to lead the revolution often had to be pushed into action by the youth who did the fighting. The cleavage between leaders and followers was marked by the struggle of some of the latter for a social revolution beyond the anticolonial struggle.[4]

With the achievement of independence, President Sukarno claimed to speak for the people in continuing the revolution. But from another perspective, when Sukarno spoke for the people, he integrated them into the state and thereby limited their social revolutionary impulses. It cannot be doubted, however, that a great many thought that their president spoke for them. When Sukarno was displaced and the New Order of President Suharto began, populist politics was put aside. "The people" was transformed from a term of address, as it had earlier been understood under Sukarno when he spoke to "the people" in their own name, into merely a term of reference under Suharto. Since 1965, "the people" have lacked a voice to speak for them.

It was just at this point, when "the people" had been suppressed, that a notion of criminality developed in Indonesia. Shortly after the change of regime, a newspaper called *Pos Kota* began publishing. It was started by supporters of the New Order, one of whose founders later became Minister of Information, and it was, and still is, devoted nearly exclusively to criminality. The news magazine *Tempo*, modeled on *Time* and also a New Order creation, had a rubric, *Kriminalitas*, which was given over to crime and distinguished from other topics such as "Law" and "The Nation." The criminals of *kriminalitas*, emerging from anonymity to cause discomforting surprise, are the continuation of the idea of "the people" adapted to the conditions of the New Order. They arose at a time when the division between classes had become heavily marked by disparities in material conditions, while explicit definitions of, and distinctions between, the wealthy and the poor were suppressed as they still are. It

---

[4] The history of the Indonesian revolution reveals two strategies. One leads to independence from Dutch rule via negotiation. The other, led by groups of youth without national organization and without much ideological coherence, was more radical in its demands and more violent in its actions. Benedict R. O'G. Anderson examines the second of these strategies in *Java in a Time of Revolution* (Ithaca: Cornell University Press, 1972). It is the story of how youths forced their national leaders into more extreme stances, including the proclamation of independence. Youthful revolutionaries also threatened to displace the Indonesian political class left in place after the Japanese occupation, itself the heir of colonial policies. Anderson's study of the role of youth in the revolution, showing as it does their independence from recognized national leaders and their revolutionary tendencies, is part of the foundation of the present work. The early study of George Kahin, *Nationalism and Revolution in Indonesia* (Ithaca: Cornell University Press, 1952) gives a picture of the rise of nationalism and a history of the revolutionary period focusing on its leaders. The immense question of popular participation in nationalism and revolution has been treated from different points of view. Recent regional studies include most notably Audrey Kahin, ed., *Regional Dynamics of the Indonesian Revolution: Unity from Diversity* (Ithaca: Cornell University Press: 1985). A synopsis of accepted views of the course of the revolution published after Kahin's seminal work can be found in Anthony J. S. Reid, *The Indonesian National Revolution* (Hawthorn, Victoria Australia: Longman Australia, 1974). Quite important because it points the way to understanding the formation of nationalist ideas as they mediated regional origins is the study of Rudolf Mrázek, *Sjahrir, Politics and Exile in Indonesia* (Ithaca: Cornell Southeast Asia Program, 1994). Mrázek's pioneering work opens the way to a wholly new sort of study of the formation of the nation.

was a time when communication between various parts of the nation was felt to have been severed; this remains an implicit fear due to official ideology in which the nation is conceived of as a family even as criticism is censored. "Criminals" are "the people" who, lacking a voice, burst onto the public scene nonetheless.

Examined from the point of view of class, fear of communists has the same source as that of fear of "criminals." Both spring from the distinction drawn between the educated upper classes and those "below" them. Such a statement is, of course, too general, failing as it does to take into account differences, for instance, between Muslims and leftists, as well as local social fissures which sometimes mark divisions independent of class differences. Nonetheless, the criminals of 1983-84 were not equated with communists as one might well have expected. Criminality has its own history, separate from that of communism in Indonesia, although both are effects of the formation of the Indonesian nation rather than concepts originating in local formations. Not every element that emerges from the underside of the Indonesian national body is equated with every other element whose position it shares. Their common class definition, however, would make the expectation of such an equation unsurprising, particularly since, in my opinion, fear of revolution colors both the words "communist" and "criminal."

One might compare Indonesian violence to an intermittent civil war in which, by definition, members of the same nation kill each other. The 1948 battle and massacre —not war—between communists and nationalists approaches this concept. Yet the notion of vengeance complicates the comparison. The belief, widespread amongst Indonesians but certainly false, that in 1965 had communists not been murdered those who did the killing would have been the victims of the communists instead capitalizes on the events of 1948 for its justification. This belief in turn justifies a fear of communist vengeance in the years since 1965. However, there is no evidence at all that communists tried to take revenge in 1965 for the events of 1948. Indeed, communists were widely expected to take power by constitutional means. Before they had the opportunity to do so, however, leading generals, some of their aides, and some of their family were murdered in a presumed coup attempt. Communists were blamed for these murders and accused of wanting to overthrow the regime. This justified killing them by the hundreds of thousands. But the motivation for the coup has remained unclear while scholars have doubted the role of the communists and even suggested that Suharto himself staged the presumed coup. In short, reliable evidence for vengeance on the part of communists does not exist.[5] On the other hand, no one can doubt that since 1965 many Indonesians have feared communist revenge. Vengeance is not claimed by the murderers themselves; it is the one whom one kills, who, it is claimed, wants revenge.

The difficulty in thinking in terms of civil war or social revolution is that it presupposes a social division, such as that between brothers or between members of different classes, to which words such as "communist" and "criminal" refer. The odd place of vengeance complicates this reference. Instead of indicating a clear sociological and political position, "communist" and, in a different way, "criminal,"

---

[5] There were, for example, reports of blank sheets of paper found in communist headquarters which, it was claimed, were lists of those targeted for death by the communists, presumably readable if one had the right chemical formula to develop the writing. See Benedict Anderson and Ruth McVey, *A Preliminary Analysis of the 1965 Coup in Indonesia* (Ithaca: Cornell Modern Indonesia Project, 1971), p. 116, note 2 to part two. Stories of such lists were widespread at the time. There is no reliable evidence of their existence.

indicates, I will claim, something confused and even ghostly on the part of those dominant in the nation. Of course nothing precludes the victims from eventually generating a more political and sociological idea of vengeance for themselves and consequently making these terms take on a clearer sociological meaning. But here we speak of the consciousness of the dominant classes. Certain fears haunt them, requiring various figures to justify those fears, and yet these fears are not fully explicated even after one understands Indonesia's class divisions.

Since the 1980s at least, Indonesian political leaders have spoken of "organizations without bodies" to describe a presumed communist resurgence. The Indonesian state has gone to great lengths to keep track of not only those communists released after years in prison, but their descendants as well. This seems to indicate fear of something they cannot locate, even when they know precisely who is a communist and who is the son or daughter of a communist. Put differently, the ruling elite cannot find a face or a name for their fears. The people they feel to be menacing them always appear as ordinary and like themselves, and require, therefore, more and more surveillance in order to prevent them from disappearing.

One might think that those Indonesians today who fear vengeance are merely expressing guilt for their crimes. I believe there is an element of truth in this. But one would expect that guilt for an historical crime would be answered by the survivors of that crime. One might expect there to be a culture of vengeance. But the survivors of the massacres of 1965-66 have done very little indeed to claim their own history. They have, for the most part, been content to reclaim their rights as Indonesian citizens who are no different than their neighbors. There has been little, for instance, in the way of clandestine publishing.[6]

Perhaps for this reason, fear of retaliation has focused on imaginary enemies. What marks the fear of communism is a fear of specters; a fear that the descendants of communists will take revenge for the murders of their parents and grandparents. As a result, there is a great impulse to find "evidence" for such motivations of revenge in whatever expressions of political discontent manage to appear in public. Thus the regime bans historical novels on the grounds that they are "code books" used for indoctrination and that there exist organizations which have no form.[7]

---

[6] One always has to exempt Pramoedya Ananta Toer from this statement. He continued to publish abroad when his books were banned in Indonesia. For remarks on the attitude of former prisoners see my obituary of "Joebar Ayoeb," *Indonesia* 62 (October 1996): 123-124.

[7] The term "organization without form" (*organisasi tanpa bentuk*) has some interesting usages. In 1988 the Attorney General, Ali Said, banned a book by Pramoedya Ananta Toer, Indonesia's most accomplished writer and a political prisoner for fourteen years who, like eighty thousand others suspected of being communists, was never brought to trial. The Attorney General stated that the book was an example of the "infiltration of society which went unfelt by it." He went on to say that the communists had now decided that "organizations without form [*organasasi tampa bentuk*] are best."(*Kompas*, Ali Said, June 10, 1988). The head of an Indonesian intelligence agency, General Sudomo, said Pramoedya's book was "a form of instruction and reference book for PKI (Indonesian Communist Party) members and their sympathizers." For him, Pramoedya's book was a code book. Break the code and one sees, behind and within the lines of the text, its true sense. "The conclusion that this book contains Marxism and Marxism-Leninism was reached after careful and deep consideration," he added. He said also that if these teachings "are not wiped out, it is obvious that public order will be at an end." (*Jayakarta*, June 10, 1988).

In 1995, thirty years after the killings of accused communists, Lt. General Soeyono, speaking for the Coordinating Body for National Stability known by its acronym Bakorstanas, said, " . . . problems raised by the PKI now are being brought to the surface again by certain

Indonesians today feel it necessary to respond to something which they feel inhabits Indonesian society and which they cannot identify. Sometimes this fear is expressed through suspicions of or actions against "criminals," such as those massacred in 1983-84. Sometimes it is expressed through fear of communists or other social groups presumed dangerous.

The specters that inform Indonesian massacres vary along with the incidents. Even when one seems to reach a fundamental division between "the people" or "the masses" and "the elite" or the "middle class," one finds that one cannot substitute one figure of the underclass for another. Not only does each have its particular historical development, but identifications of each are precarious. In the case of lower class criminals, for instance, no stereotyped visage has developed. Criminals appear in *Pos Kota* in small photographs usually with a black bar across their eyes. One can find these same faces in other papers and magazines without the bar. One sees behind this photographically imposed mask or veil only the face of ordinary Indonesians. The face of the criminal does not reveal menace and evil. It mediates rather, as we shall see, a realm of "death," leading toward a force which the state felt it lacked and which, in mastering the criminal, it hoped to obtain for itself. The face of the criminal is familiar, not strange; or, rather, strange in its familiarity.

It was, as I shall explain, this mediating role that made the criminal a target of the violence of the state. The Indonesian criminal is, then, not an "other," different from oneself. His face, rather, is an object one sees through, as one sees through spectacles or telescopes. At the same time, given his historical determination, he is an Indonesian, a member of the same nation to which those who killed him belong or who, often enough, applauded his murder. He is a version of oneself whom one either feared or envied because of his association with death. Precisely because he is not different from oneself, what he possesses is potentially one's own. One can imagine standing in his place, a perspective which I shall argue the forces of the Indonesian state actually took up.

---

groups who agitate as they did. We have to anticipate." What he anticipated, of course, was what he claimed had occurred already and which he said could easily occur again. He "anticipated," without giving evidence, that the people involved would be, or are, the grandchildren of the dead communists. A reporter from the magazine *Tiras* asked him if there were "indications" (*indikasi*) of PKI agitation. He responded, "The clearest indicator [*indikator*] is that the struggle is the same and there is a red line from the family too. Maybe from grandchildren who hope to revenge their ancestors. This is what we detect now." From an interview entitled "Skenario dan Agitasi yang Sama" [The Same Scenario and Agitation], *Tiras* 37,1 (October 12, 1995): 63. I am indebted to Takashi Shiraishi for calling my attention to this article.

Asked for the symptoms the general added that this form of detection (*terdeteksi*) was "general." 1995 was also the year in which General Soeyono, repeating the claim of the Attorney General in 1988, again accused Pramoedya Ananta Toer and others of inspiring "organizations without form" which carried out activities resembling those of communists. François Raillon, "Indonésie 1995: La République quinquagénaire," *Archipel* 51 (1996): 179-196. As the reporters of the news magazine *Tiras* put it, paraphrasing the words of another general, General R. Hartono, "There's no getting around it, we have to really set up our radar and be on the alert." "The New Left: Is it the Vehicle for a Comeback?" *Tiras* 37,1 (October 12, 1995): 64. To be on the alert for what has already happened is, of course, another version of the fear of vengeance, as the generals stated. But revenge that comes through spectral organizations and code books such as those of Pramoedya is a strange sort of vengeance.

On the one hand, Indonesians kill those they see to be in their own image. On the other hand, the targets of their murderous impulses have their own spectral histories, as communists differ from criminals, for instance. But behind the faces of communists and criminals there is a common sense of menace whose origins cannot be securely located in historical events.[8] That there is more than one figure of the menace inherent in Indonesia could indicate different sources for different menaces. Or it could indicate that whatever the source of national menace, no figure adequately represents it. Whichever the case, the threat is located in the faces of ordinary persons, faces not substantially different, in fact, from those Indonesians who govern them.

It is the commonality of visage that made a notion of power accessible to the officials of the state, producing the new criminal type I am about to describe. The menace of *kriminalitas* was an attraction to the state. It was a lethal power which the state wanted for its own. It is my thesis that the state itself took on the form of a criminal in order to obtain this power. The result was, therefore, contrary to those cases I mentioned at the beginning of this essay. The massacres of Hutus and Tutsis or Serbs and Croats are between peoples deeply implicated in each other. In these massacres peoples similar to each other strove to make each an "other" to themselves. One could say, following a process which has frequently been described in many places, that these groups tried to make a part of themselves foreign in order that they could then expel it and therefore leave themselves ethnically "pure." In the case of Indonesian criminals, by contrast, the Indonesian state imitated the criminal, striving to become like him. In the process a new understanding of "death" arose, one with a national rather than a local or familial frame of reference. It is this phenomenon that I call the "nationalization" of death.

B. THE UPPER-CLASS CRIMINAL

Kriminalitas is, in my opinion, the successor to important political terms.[9] But I do not want to give the impression that *kriminalitas* occupies a central place similar to

---

[8] There is no space for me to describe further the origin of the menace that haunts Indonesia. I have spoken of it in detail in Chapter One of *A New Criminal Type in Jakarta* from which a portion of this essay is excerpted.

[9] Here it is of some value to consult the dictionaries. No major dictionary of Indonesian has an entry "kriminalitas" before 1983, perhaps because early dictionaries of Indonesian often did not include words derived from European languages. I thank Daniel Lev for telling me that the word occured in the Sukarno period, though its use clearly was much restricted by comparison with the Suharto period. In 1983, which is to say, during the New Order, the *Kamus Bahasa Indonesia* [Dictionary of Indonesian] (Jakarta: Pusat Pembinaan dan Pembangunan Bahasa Deptemen Pendidikan dan Kebudayaan, 1983) gave this definition: "*kriminalitas* n, events with a criminal character; acts which violate the criminal law; bad deeds; in this archipelago, robbery, armed smuggling and sales of various drugs are reflected in statistics." The same dictionary has the entry "*kriminal*" with the definition "bad deeds (violation of the law) which can be judged according to statutes." By contrast, the major Indonesian dictionary of the Sukarno period, which, as I have said, has no entry for "*kriminalitas*," gives this definition for "*kriminil*": "bad deeds (violations of the law which can be judged according to statutes)." W. J. S. Poerwadarminta, *Kamus Umum Bahasa Indonesia*, 4th edition (Jakarta: Balai Pustaka, 1966).

It is worth noting that the term I have translated as "bad deeds" (*kejahatan*) is a word in everyday use which reflects standards of behavior derived from common sense, the heir of

what "the people" once held in Indonesia or as crime currently does in the United States. Most of the time, *kriminalitas* is mere diversion, comparable to *faits divers*, for which there is no exact English equivalent.[10] Dictionaries translate *faits divers* as "miscellaneous news items." But *faits divers* differs from *kriminalitas* since the latter are usually crime stories. The equivalent in America in the tabloids includes the incredible: the world's longest zucchini, so big it stretches the imagination, or "Satan Appears in Houston," for instance. Indonesian *kriminalitas* combines both senses: it is the criminal as the fantastic, even the unbelievable. Such criminals are sensational but not memorable, exciting without being important. It is this forgettable character that I should like to emphasize. The stories of *kriminalitas*, unlike the stories of criminals of prenational times, rarely become part of cultural memory, although there are partial exceptions. For the most part, they claim only to be what people—other people—are talking about. And, indeed, this is their other important characteristic for us.

For the greater part of the time, *kriminalitas* seems to exist at the edge of memory. It eases its way into awareness and stimulates interest, while somehow lacking significance and yet stretching credulity. But at the moment when criminals are massacred they enter explicit political awareness. Drawing them into such awareness is, indeed, the attempt to make something memorable that otherwise exists only hazily, but with implications of force, and to claim this power for the government. This is the moment when the new criminal type of Jakarta, the Indonesian state and its president, comes into view.

Kriminalitas and the attempt of the state to control it depends on journalism. It was through journalism that stories of the massacres of criminals reached most people and the idea of *kriminalitas* itself was developed. There could be no nationalization of death without the power of communication that journalists offered and the standardization of thinking they provided. The press invents new types of criminals. One, central to our story, is not the criminal as residue of the people, but the upper-class murderer. He is important to our explanation of how the Indonesian state tried to nationalize death. It is out of this figure that the state came to picture itself as criminal.

---

both traditional and religious ideas. One translation includes "sinful," for instance. If one looks at the substance of *kriminalitas* judged by its appearance in newspapers, it consists mainly of robbery, rape, incest, fraud, and murder. If the substance of the idea is known and if it already has a name—*kejahatan*—one has to ask what it means that it is given another name. Furthermore, one has to ask why this new name is not Indonesian in origin. A new signifier, known to be foreign, comes to denote an indigenous idea. The implication is that there is a further reference, one beyond whatever one might delimit by making an inventory of particular acts that fall under "*kedjahatan*."

Previous to the New Order, "bad deeds" were not criminal acts unless the law was invoked. The blurring of the boundáry between "bad deeds" and "criminal acts" reflects the resurgence not of earlier concepts but of sentiments attributable to prenational times which are, one can say, "nationalized." The question is what "nationalization" means in this context.

[10] For an excellent discussion of *faits divers*, see Roland Barthes, "Qu'est-ce qu'un scandale?" in Roland Barthes, vol. 1, *Oeuvres complètes*, ed. Éric Marty (Paris: éditions du Seuil, 1995), pp. 784-786 (originally published in *Lettres Nouvelles*, March 4, 1959). See also "Structure du fait divers," ibid., pp. 1309-1316 (originally published in *Médiations*, 1962).

The upper-class criminal has figured in newspapers since at least the early 1980s. For the sake of convenience, we will describe an example from the 1990s. This criminal takes his form, amongst other places, in *Pos Kota*. On August 28, 1993, the newspaper had a headline that read "Policeman Killed and Then Burned on a Rubber Estate in Cianjur," Cianjur being a city located between Jakarta and Bandung. Above this headline in smaller bold letters was: "Kidnapped from a Police Post by Plotters with Motor Vehicles." Villagers discovered a burning body and, after putting out the fire, found it to be that of a police agent. The story as it eventually unfolded is that two cars drove up to a police post in East Jakarta and the passengers requested help, asking Sergeant Bambang Sumarno to follow them. Once at the house of IA, the initials of one of the criminals, IA had a servant bring them coffee and then tried to get Sergeant Bambang's pistol. There was a struggle in which IA stabbed the sergeant seven times, killing him. He then put his body in the car trunk, had the servant clean up the blood, and went in a new red sedan to the village where they burned the body.

By the first of September, the criminals had been caught. There were three of them and they were of a type that *Pos Kota* takes pleasure in writing about, namely university students, "*oknum mahasiswa*," which can be translated as "certain students" or perhaps "student types." *Pos Kota* enjoys showing the corruption of the privileged classes, and particularly their children. Since this is the sort of scandal preferred as well by the middle-class press, it does not indicate much about the political stance of *Pos Kota*. When the story unfolds, *Pos Kota* reports that the motive for the killing was unclear. What is certain is that IA, the ringleader of the three, wanted a pistol. *Pos Kota* at some points makes this seem merely a perverse desire, in this way distinguishing it from a more mundane, functional need for a weapon. "The penis and some of the fingers of the corpse were destroyed by the fire" they report on the second day of their accounts.[11] Later, they confirm that the policeman had, in fact, been castrated before the body was burned, placing these criminals amongst the *sadis*, a word coined during the New Order and derived from the English term "sadistic."

The criminals[12] when they are identified turn out to be the sons of prominent people. IA, the ringleader, is first noted as the son of a real estate developer. This claim is dropped without further mention when they learn that he is the adopted son of someone on the Supreme Court. His mother is never mentioned. A good deal of the later accounts focuses on the fact that the father, who is wanted by the police for questioning, never shows up at the police station. We have then not only the presumed guilt of a middle-class son, but the implication that his father had something to do with the crime as well.

One asks: "who is the victim?" *Pos Kota* tells us only about Serka Bambang's police career, nothing about his personal life. They say more about his wife,

---

[11] One should note that castration has been a favorite topic of the press and of movies in Indonesia for several years now.

[12] I call them criminals because in *Pos Kota* there are stories almost exclusively of arrests. One seldom gets to the trials. It is assumed that the police arrest the correct person. An editor of *Pos Kota* told me that the trial takes place such a long time after the arrest that people have lost interest. In any case, this editorial policy effectively makes the police and not the courts the instrument of justice.

emphasizing her origins in a village. So we have a crime against the police committed by someone who, given his social position, seems unlikely to have felt any animus against the victim or his wife. As *Pos Kota* obliquely presents it, the crime was directed at the power of the police; thus the castration. And it was committed for the purpose of using that power outside the law; hence the policeman's pistol used against him. However, the criminal, an adopted son of a supreme court justice, is, genealogically speaking, a representative of the law.

The attitude toward the police is ambiguous. There are accusations of police corruption, such as the selling of bullets to IA by a police agent. But the police are thought to be essential. The attack against them is particularly frightening. *Pos Kota* quotes villagers from the place where the body was found, for instance. "A resident told how fear had come over nearly everyone in Pasar Angin. 'They are daring enough to torture and even kill the police. They wouldn't hesitate with ignorant people like us . . .'"[13] We could rephrase the statement this way: "The police are the ultimate or near ultimate barrier against aggression and they themselves have been attacked. Therefore 'we' are not safe." The more the sons of the upper class are wild, violent, and destructive, and the more the upper class as a whole, including its agent, the police, is corrupt, the more the police and the state as a whole are necessary. This not an absolutely original logic, and it clearly is not impeccable. But it is altogether common in Jakarta. I never heard anyone complain that it was contradictory or incoherent.

In examining this logic, one has to notice how the identity of the victims of the criminals has shifted and expanded. It is not merely the police who have been the object of aggression. It is also innocent villagers. One such innocent villager appeared in the quotation I just gave. For this conservative logic to be persuasive, one has to appreciate the particular vulnerability of this class of victims. They are not merely innocent and they are not merely unintended victims; in this case they were also without the defenses that traditionally would have been available to them. Regarding the first point, the killing actually had nothing to do with the spot where the body was found; the spot was chosen precisely because it was located some distance from the scene of the murder and the policeman's workplace. The murderers wanted nothing to do with the villagers. Their aim was either the capture of a pistol, the practice of sadism against the police, or both. Even if there were a further motive, it did not concern the villagers. Villagers need the police because they cannot themselves guard against a danger they not only cannot anticipate but also cannot fathom, as we will see. They nonetheless stand guard for the five days between the discovery of the murder and the arrest of the criminals, fearing that, for some reason, these criminals will return.

After the capture of the criminals, villagers talk of their fear. One says that now they are "relieved" (*lega*) and "grateful" (*berterima kasih*) to the police. Their anxiousness (*kecemasan*) is gone. One tells a reporter this:

> According to Apip, they were not afraid of ghosts [*hal-hal gaib*] though he had to admit that there were some who felt that way too. "We were very worried, afraid that we would be the target of these people who were wandering around out there for five days."[14]

---

[13] *Pos Kota*, August 31, 1993.

[14] Ibid., September 2, 1993.

They are not afraid of ghosts, which is quite surprising. That is, it is not the spirit of the murdered policeman or spirits connected with the murderers who might bother them. This absence of ghosts is not a relief but a difficulty. The traditional locus of danger does not apply here. Were it to do so, they could rely on traditional remedies, such as amulets and magical or religious experts. But not fearing ghosts they do not know what to fear, and thus their anxiousness is increased.

Their fear is reflected in the illnesses afflicting those who had most to do with the corpse. One example is Utom, the man who discovered the body and put out the fire. "According to Utom, from the moment he was putting out the fire with water, his stomach was upset and he felt nervous. He continued to put out the fire even though he kept vomiting. But he kept going until the fire was out."[15] The report goes on to say that the body had been soaked in ten cans of gasoline and that it needed a lot of water to extinguish it. No one else would help Utom. Now he is ill, and he can't afford to go to the local clinic or to a doctor. He has a name for his sickness: "He said he was traumatized by this very disturbing event."[16] It is not the effects of fire that made him ill, it is the "very disturbing event." His illness is not fully described by its physical symptoms. It is "trauma," the English word, that he uses. Here the word seems to mean that the symptoms cannot be accounted for by physical causes and that the effects are more than physiological. "Trauma" in that sense is similar to ghostly possession. But it is made explicit that the illness is not caused by ghosts. It is caused by something having to do with this new sort of criminal or something to do with the burning of a policeman's body. Another villager, Enoh, "who had the opportunity to witness it also fell ill."[17] Simply seeing the corpse, "witnessing" it, causes illness. We must ask what "it" refers to here. What is there so particularly disturbing about the event; why is it different from the disturbances caused by ghosts, who are also associated with death; why is the effect described by the English word "trauma," while ghosts are explicitly excluded as the source of fear?

A partial answer can be found in the villagers' fear that the criminals will return. That the villagers fear a return itself suggests the behavior of ghosts who reappear at the site of death. Apip, the villager quoted above, says that they are not afraid of ghosts, they are afraid of the criminals. But the criminals are like ghosts not only in the way they are thought to "haunt" the scene of burning but also because they inhabit special sites inaccessible to those who are visited by them. Ghosts, one knows, lurk at the site of death; these criminals "roam around out there" (*berkeliaran di luar*).[18] The difference between their locus and the usual haunts of the criminals is, in fact, the difficulty requiring an explanation. Villagers can, and do, guard themselves against the sort of local criminals, thieves in particular, who come from places they know about. They can guard themselves against ghosts whose locales they can divine. But the origins of this new sort of criminal are hazy to them.

Pos Kota carried the following strange report about the choice of a place to dispose of the body:

---

[15] Ibid., September 3, 1993.

[16] Ibid., September 3, 1993. "Dia mengaku karena trauma oleh peristiwa yang sangat meggemparkan itu."

[17] Ibid.

[18] Ibid., September 2, 1993.

> The location chosen shows a new "modus" because up till now in every murder in Jakarta where the body has been disposed of in Cianjur the corpse was thrown out on the edge of the Jakarta-Bandung road. This time it was eighteen kilometers from the Jakarta-Bandung road.[19]

The paper uses the word "modus." This identifies the murderers as a special class of individuals belonging to the category "criminals," those who break the law according to certain methods with which the police are familiar. These particular criminals, however, are innovators. The policeman was stabbed to death in the house of the murderer. The body was transported quite some distance from there in order to be able to burn it and, no doubt especially, to dissociate it from the murderers. The village, as we have said, was chosen because it had nothing to do with these criminals or with this particular policeman, and perhaps, in addition, because it was outside the usual pattern of locations where corpses are discarded after killings in Jakarta. The villagers could not anticipate the danger. They were victims of the murderers, victims of "trauma," for a reason that one has to label, "no particular reason." The suggestion of *Pos Kota* in trying to define the murderers as "criminals," as that category is known to the police, is that they are even then different from the usual, known type. In relation to them, the villagers, in turn, are not exactly "villagers," people who live in a certain way in a certain place and have a delimited set of relationships, in short, a certain identity. They were just "anyone" at all, anyone who did not know the murderers and who was outside the circle of people who matter, or who even knows people who know someone who matters. To the murderers these villagers were anonymous and conveniently ignorant, perfect nobodies who had no part in any circuit of knowledgeable people who might trace the murderers.

The "shock," which is the other word besides "trauma" used by the villagers to describe their state, is first caused by the strangeness of the crime. But its effects continue after the crime is solved. No understanding of the crime could account for its effects on the villagers because the story has nothing to do with them. Nothing in their identities could help to account for why they had to suffer. By the same token, the murderers are without a known place from the perspective of these victims. The murderers come from "Jakarta," but "Jakarta," or rather the criminals' "Jakarta," is a place to which the villagers have no access. Unlike ghosts, who usually have some sort of story to account for their appearances in a particular place, no story, not even one that accurately described the murderers' motivation, could account for why they progressed, as *Pos Kota* reported, from a discotheque to the police station, to a wealthy Jakarta neighborhood, finally arriving at the place where they burned the body. Murder alone is not enough to create a new effect, "trauma." Murder has been known for a long time without "trauma." "Trauma" and "shock" are words from the vocabulary of the middle class. They are brought into the village not only with a violent event, but with violence that originates where "trauma," the word, originates on the Indonesian scene. "Trauma" and "shock" come with the intrusion of the ruling class as it makes itself felt to the underclass not merely in the event itself, but through the reporting of *Pos Kota*. The place that one knows one does not know about and cannot fathom used to be the abode of ghosts. Now, in this report of *Pos*

---

[19] Ibid., August 29, 1993.

Kota, it is the discotheque, the university, the places where youth smoke ganja, and the walled houses of the wealthy.

It is crime that brings the lower-class readers of *Pos Kota* into the upper-class world. It is the beginning of communication between these worlds. The newspaper which reports and even produces their story is thus a mediator between cultural realms. It produces a story which links classes, a story which makes the very choice of the villagers as secondary victims of members of the upper class reasonable, and this reasonableness is understood in terms of both class and "modern" communications. The "traumatized" villagers, we will see, are transformed by the end of the story from being onlookers entirely outside the focus of the story into becoming characters sought out as the center of interest.

The transformation of the narrative into one that shows the paternalistic nature of class relations is a result of the police's role. The police not only are given credit for catching the criminals, they also assuage the fear of the villagers. A large group of policemen go to the village to pray for their dead colleague and at the same time to thank the villagers who helped by recovering the body while it was still recognizable. Thus the narrative describes an effort by the police to put the soul of their comrade at rest and at the same time to still the effects of the murder on villagers. It is an act of mourning, putting the murder behind the villagers and reestablishing the police not merely as catchers of criminals and protectors of the peace, but as religious figures who reassure. Utom, aged forty-eight, is said to be *"tengah mengalami shock,"* "continuing to suffer shock," and was earlier said to be unable to afford to go to a clinic or see a doctor. The police doctor arrives with the visiting group of police officers, however, and tells him, "Stop worrying. We'll take care of everything. Its all in the hands of the police now."[20] I am unable to reproduce in English the paternalistic, reassuring, yet still dismissive tonality of this comment. The peasant tells the reporter that he never expected that his efforts to put out the fire would take such a toll on him. The police give him a trophy. They also congratulate another villager who helped extinguish the fire, and they contribute 100,000 rupiahs toward the costs of the ceremony they attend. If relations between the classes are initiated, it is because *Pos Kota* turns actualities into typical events. If relations between the classes are also made harmonious, it is because *Pos Kota* shows the police functioning not as catchers of criminals; they are, rather, assuagers of "trauma," if such is possible, and recognizers of civic actions.

The fear of the authors of these stories is that certain people do exist and function outside the channels of communication that run between classes. This is a reasonable fear given the dissipation of the populism of the Sukarno epoch. The remedy for this state of affairs is mass forms of communication and stories such as the one recounted above where communication is initiated by the elite. But we are a little ahead of ourselves.

The lack of traditional supernatural beliefs surrounding this incident intensifies the interest in death. One indication of this is the attention paid to witnesses. These are not witnesses to the crime but witnesses to the last moments of the victim. There is, for instance, the testimony of the sergeant's colleague who was present at the post when the kidnappers arrived. They summoned the sergeant to follow them, alleging some troubles at home.

---

[20] Ibid., September 4, 1993.

"His motorcycle wouldn't start, but finally the engine caught and Bambang followed the two cars," Rumini stated.

That was the final exit of the member of the police with the strong body and thick mustache. Because the next day Master Sergeant Bambang Sumarno was come across with his body burned in the rubber grove in Pedaja Village, Cikalong Kulon, Cianjur.[21]

In this mingling of the metaphorical and the factual, disappearance from view is equated with dying. But Serka Bambang disappears only to reappear again, this time as a corpse. *Pos Kota* again insists on a purely visual connection to the deceased when it interviews the widow after the criminals have been caught. In their issue of September 5, they show the widow in the same way they have in each of the three previous pictures of her. She stares into space, focusing on nothing around her, or she looks at the ground, perhaps even having her eyes closed. These are signs of her grief, of course; her mind is numbed and her thoughts are doubtless with her late husband. When she speaks, she says that she wants to see. The headline of the article reads "Even Though Bitter, No Vengeance: Mrs. Herlin Wants to See the Face of Her Husband's Killer." It reads in part:

> Mrs. Herlin Widrastuti expressed her desire to see directly the faces of the three student-types who are accused of killing her husband, Master Sergeant Bambang Sumarno. "Let me be at peace. Even though bitter, I will not seek vengeance," she said with a peaceful expression on her face.
>
> I want to know the one called IA, the stepson of the high official of the Supreme Court, said Mrs. Herlin Widrastuti.[22]

In an earlier report she had called for the severest punishment of the criminals. Here she says nothing of the sort. Later, she will repeat that she does not want vengeance and trusts the police to act appropriately. She only wants to see the murderers. She does not want to know IA as a person, which would mean, for instance, wanting revenge. She disregards him as a person, leaving him to the authorities. But for her peace of mind, she wants to see him. She wants, in other words, to see him without knowing him; to see him without trying to see behind his face into his thoughts, his motives, or his feelings.

Mrs. Widrastuti puts a face on the criminal, as it were. One could imagine that to put a face on the criminal would be to identify him, to make him an image of criminality, or to create a picture of an undesirable other. This, however, does not seem to be the logic behind this widow's actions. To see him without knowing him is to disregard his criminality in favor of his connection with her deceased husband. He is the best example of a witness to her husband's disappearance and therefore to her memory of him. Through IA, Mrs. Widrastuti has a connection to her husband. It is, of course, not the memory of him as he was alive. Mediated as it is through the face of the murderer it has something to do with his death.

The criminal here has a special connection with death. IA saw what Mrs. Widrastuti cannot: her husband at the moment he died. IA for Mrs. Widrastuti is like a camera which can preserve something for someone not present when the picture

---

[21] Ibid., August 28, 1993.

[22] Ibid., September 5, 1993.

was taken. Roland Barthes, speaking about a photograph of a prisoner who tried to assassinate the American Secretary of State in 1865 and who was to be executed after his picture was taken, states that the prisoner dies two deaths; a first time in history soon after the photograph was made, and a second time as he is recreated again in the photograph with Barthes present. IA, the murderer, is in this case also the preserver not merely of the dead husband's last moment alive, but also of him past that moment, as though he could live again in the way the soon-to-be executed prisoner did for Barthes; which is to say in a register where he is at once both dead and alive. Mrs. Widrastuti no longer concerns herself with the murderous deed of IA. Instead of breaking her link with her husband, IA preserves it and, it seems, preserves this connection beyond death. This criminal makes the dead reappear and in that sense he produces within himself a state equivalent to the simultaneous presence and absence registered by the traditional village ghost.

But the class identity of IA is significant. Mrs. Widrastuti is characterized as a villager who remains in her affinities a villager. From her statements, she appears to be a person much like the villagers who found her husband's burning body. In the end, IA, the adopted son of a supreme court justice, shows how the upper class controls death. It may well be, and it is even likely, that low-class murderers too could have the same ability to stand between the living and the dead. But if so, they not only do not link social classes together, they threaten whatever stability exists between them. They also challenge the myth being forged out of violence in the pages of *Pos Kota*. As it stands, IA is the living embodiment of the man he killed. He has, from this report, absorbed Serka Bambang and so, like the police who cure "trauma," he has both assuaged grief and shown the bond between supreme court justices, their high-living university student sons, and helpless villagers. The murderer himself, then, is the best witness not to the crime but to his victim, putting him to death yet still keeping him present. It is this new form of ghost that villagers fear will reappear before them.

This upper-class criminal, embodying his victim, intruding on other low-class victims, links upper and lower classes, reestablishing the bond between them which eroded in the course of the New Order. That the bond passes through death and "trauma," redefining the first and introducing the second, is an effect of nationalization, "death" being no longer what it was in Sundanese or other regional worlds. Death is instead defined in terms of "Indonesia," a construct created through a network of national ties made technologically possible in Suharto's regime which augment previously existing local social relations.

C. MORE "TRAUMA," ANOTHER NEW CRIMINAL

The upper-class criminal may foster solidarity between classes. But his urge to violence has to be thought of separately from his social function. I do not want to reconcile these facts; they merely exist side by side, or at least have done so in the New Order up until this moment.

The intrusion of the ruling classes on the lives of the underclass took a flagrant turn in 1983 and early 1984 when headlines like this one appeared: "Flat On His Face in the Gutter Covered With Stones A Man Tattooed With a Picture of a Naked

Woman Found Stabbed One Hundred Times."[23] By 1984 bodies of dead tattooed men were found in many places in Indonesia and had been reported in the press nearly every day for a year. These killings were labeled *"Petrus,"* a neologism made up of two words, *"penembak"* or *"shooting"* and *"misterius"* or *"mysterious."*

Long before the *Petrus* killings, *Pos Kota* featured reports of dead bodies discovered in public places. But the *Petrus* corpses were different, in the first place because they were generally tattooed. The killings were not a mystery for long. The government, though it first denied its involvement, soon identified itself as the perpetrator. The victims were known as *"gali,"* itself an acronym for "the savage class." *Gali* were for the most part petty criminals, members of gangs. Many of them had worked for the government party, GOLKAR, during the elections the previous year, and were then subsequently discharged to go back to their old ways.[24] Typically, the *Petrus* killings involved masked men arriving at night in jeeps and abducting their victims, who were found dead on the street the next day.

Pos Kota's stories featured little besides the descriptions of corpses, the finding of them, and the way in which the news was reported to the police. *Tempo,* which had special features on the subject, reported more details. It presented the statement of the army commander in Jogjakarta, Central Java, who was responsible for many such murders. He claimed that the criminals were organized, brutal, and taking in huge sums of money. He was particularly concerned that they upset tourists and that, consequently, Indonesia would have a poor reputation abroad.[25]

President Suharto saw these *gali* as incarnations of inhuman cruelty who created a generalized and destabilizing fear. Here is a passage included in his *Autobiography,* but subsequently excised from later editions:

> The real problem is that these events [*Petrus*] were preceded by fear and nervousness amongst the people [*rakyat*]. Threats from the criminals [*jahat*], robberies, murder and so on all happened. Stability was shaken. It was as though the country no longer had any stability. There was only fear. Criminals [*jahat*] went beyond human limits. They not only broke the law, but they stepped beyond the limits of humanity. For instance, old people were first robbed of whatever they had and then killed. Isn't that inhumane? If you are going to take something, sure, take it, but then don't murder. Then there were women whose wealth was stolen and other peoples' wives even

---

[23] Ibid., January 3, 1984.

[24] For descriptions of the events labeled *"petrus"* see John Pemberton, *On the Subject of "Java"* and Justus M. van der Kroef, *"'Petrus': Patterns of Prophylactic Murder in Indonesia."* The political explanation for these killings—that the government wanted to disengage itself from criminals who, having lost their governmental ties, went back to crime and caused disruption—is only partially satisfactory. It does not explain, for instance, why the government proceeded illegally, disguising the soldiers who murdered these men, nor why they were killed rather than arrested and tried as had been the case from time to time in the past.

[25] "Ada dor, ada ya, ada yang tidak" ["Shootings: Some Agree, Some Don't"], *Tempo,* August 6, 1983, pp. 12-16.

raped by these criminals and in front of their husbands yet. Isn't that going too far? [26]

One might speak like Suharto and say, "if you are going to kill, sure, kill, but once is enough." It is a serious comment. Can one kill more than once? What is the point of twenty stab wounds or in some cases even a hundred, or a dozen, bullet holes in a single victim? It is no different in its excessiveness from the manifestations of the *sadis*. Perhaps it is for display; the display of force and the willingness to use it.

President Suharto continued:

> Doesn't that demand action? Automatically we had to give it the *treatment* [in English], strong measures. And what sort of measures? Sure, with real firmness. But that firmness did not mean shooting, bang! bang! just like that. But those who resisted, sure, like it or not, had to be shot. Because they resisted, they were shot.[27]

In response to the *sadis*, when the criminals resisted, soldiers shot them. In Suharto's account the actions sound like the legitimate operation of the law. But of course the soldiers who shot were disguised, often with their faces covered. Furthermore, stories from families of victims do not report resistance. The "firmness" of the government is a display of strength. But this strength is derived not from its authority as the law but from another source no different, judging from the state of the corpses, from that of the criminals. Attributing *sadis* to the criminals, the government was provoked to act as they did.

It would have been possible to proceed legally, or at least with the appearance of legality, in putting down "criminals." Confessions of criminals, registered in law courts, for instance, would have produced a different effect. Their admissions, false or true, of the atrocities they committed would have simply put them outside the pale of normal society and distinguished them from the government which, as such, acts with steady, legal procedures. In this way, the government would be perceived as acting from motives wholly different from those of the criminals. But by excessively wounding these *gali* and accusing *gali* of acting in just that way, the government, and President Suharto himself, implicitly identified themselves with their victims even as they asserted their difference from them. It is the imitation of the criminal that is predominant, while the assertion of difference at this point was mere camouflage. This is what makes this Indonesian case different from the African or European examples cited earlier. In these latter cases, the attempt is to create an "other"; in the Indonesian case there is the assertion of identity with the victims. It is an example of murdering those professed to be like oneself.

Difference was asserted by the Indonesian government through a claim of superior power; a claim that rested, of course, on maintaining an identification with the *gali*. The government, as we have repeatedly said, turned *gali* into corpses

---

[26] *Soeharto: Otobiografi: Pikiran, Ucapkan, dan Tindakan Saya [Autobiography: My Thoughts, Speech and Acts]*, ed. G. Dwipayana and Ramadhan K. H. (Jakarta: PT Citra Lamtoro Gung Persada, 1988), p. 364.

[27] Ibid. The last two sentences in Indonesian are: "Tetapi yang melawan, ya, mau tidak mau harus ditembak. Karena melawan, maka mereka ditembak." The word I translate as "resist" is *"melawan"* which could also be rendered, "act as an enemy." The sense is that the soldiers came up against an opposing force.

intended to indicate not merely the danger of anyone daring to act as they were presumed to act, but also the unlimited power, inherent not merely in the sadistic quality of these criminals but in something beyond even that that made it necessary to kill each of them several times. The power of the government, when it is unrestricted, is claimed to be equal to the power of its adversaries. The force of the government was made equivalent to the power attributed to these corpses precisely because the victims were murdered multiple times.

The government's claim to superior power rests on showing that such a power exists, and it is for this goal that multiple wounds serve a purpose. This strategy was prepared for by the existence of *kriminalitas* as reported in the press before (and after) the *Petrus* incident with its inherent violence and its always incipient expressiveness. But until the *Petrus* incidents, this was kept within the boundaries of the *faits divers*. Something more was necessary for there to be a question of national importance.

The government acted against a strength which was "inhuman." By acting in the same manner as the criminals whom they opposed acted, illegally and violently, the government claimed to capture this strength for itself. It tore it out of the grasp of the criminals, one might say, as though this power was transferable.

President Suharto said this about the fact that the corpses were left in the streets and the rivers: "So the corpses were left where they were, just like that. This was for *shock therapy*"[in English].[28] "Shock therapy" means to shock in order to cure. This therapy is directed not at "criminals" but at the general populace. The corpses were left where they were, he says, "So that the crowds [*orang banyak*] would understand that faced with criminals there were still some who would act and who would control them."[29] Practicing this therapy, President Suharto is in the same position as IA and his friends who "traumatized" villagers. And, of course, he is utilizing the same means, the display of murder victims. Presumably the initial anonymity of the actions, the appearance of masked men at night, and the abductions of men from their families, were part of "shock therapy," little different than terrorizing.

But if there were terror one might expect that people would flee from the sight of the *Petrus* corpses. The opposite was the case. They became, as we have seen, attractions, not only to newspaper readers but also to people on the streets where the bodies were distributed. The attractive power of corpses—confined, however, to those known as *Petrus* corpses—indicates something about them that people, including the president, found fascinating even if it was terrorizing.

The corpses were made into warnings, a form of sign. One can ask how such signs can be constructed. It is not merely that to be warnings these corpses needed the explanations given in the press. They were more than merely illustrations of what others said. These "criminals," of course, were never brought before the courts; they were merely criminals by accusation. Their tattoos were enough to indicate their *kriminalitas.* They bore a mark which, the state declared, identified them as "criminals." Simply by virtue of having incisions on their skin, rather than because of specific crimes they were judged to have committed, they were condemned to death.

The tattoo, in the eyes of the government, did not represent what the wearer of the tattoo intended. It spoke beyond any such intention, signaling that its bearer was targeted and distinguishing the corpses of *gali* from other dead bodies. It was the sign of a menace that was not measurable by the history of the person, even if the

---

[28] Ibid., p. 364.
[29] Ibid.

person concerned was in fact a *gali*. Had it been otherwise, the newspapers would have given the criminal history of the people killed. Instead, the tattoo, after death, proclaimed a menace. It indicated that each such bearer had attracted a lethal power. And it indicated, furthermore, that this mark had a power of attraction quite apart from any deeds actually committed or any intention of the person. As the statement of President Suharto shows, the attraction of this mark was its indication of a power attributed to *kriminalitas* greater than the force manifested by the acts of any particular criminal.

Through this disarticulation of the person from the marks on his body, the tattoo announced an ahistorical force. It was, of course, just this force that the government claimed for itself. In this context, the tattoo also marks the bearer as unrecognizable, as no longer the person, for instance, who boasted of his sexual prowess through his tattoos, but rather as one who was a conduit of communication capable of summoning the government to him despite his intentions.

The corpses left in the streets keep vivid the moment of disappearance from life, retaining that moment in the present. It is in that way that *gali* were turned into communiqués. "He was murdered" or perhaps "We murdered him" is the substance of the warning. The dead person was a notice posted to others. He was the essential element of Suharto's "shock therapy." His dead body displayed in public turned him into a messenger for his killers. The corpse was endowed with "death," which means the capacity to transmit "trauma" and to create "shock," quite unlike the corpses of those who died within the world, for instance, governed by Javanese culture. The *Petrus* corpses, made into warnings, spoke; but they spoke, of course, for the government.

They spoke principally through their tattoos. These marks came to mean that the persons bearing them had within themselves a supernatural power evidenced by their attraction of death. Their corpses brought the force of "death" as close to the living as it could come. It is this that made them fascinating. This, I posit, is why Mrs. Widrastuti wanted to see the murderer of her husband, the person who had seen her husband last, and who kept him present to her not as a person but as he existed in both his last moments alive and just after his death. Seeing the murderer she was close to the force inherent in this new form, "death."

The indication of the power of "death" was the murder committed by the government, as though had the government not committed the murder there would be no "death" in this new sense. The historical context supplies the possibility of this new referent for death. Before these events there was already an amorphous force, *kriminalitas*, thought to inhere in, but beyond the control of, Indonesian society. There are also effects produced by the revolution and by the formation of the Indonesian nation in relation to the family which I do not have the time to go into here.

The case of Serka Bambang, however, shows that the historical reading of the reference of "death" is insufficient. The bewildering effect of his corpse on the villagers who discovered it had nothing to do with tattoos. It had, however, everything to do with the sudden intrusion of unknown, unaccounted for murder victims into spaces where they could not have been anticipated. The power of the corpse, its capacity to open up references which could not be controlled, is essential. To know why, one would have to ask how it was that the defenses against death usually in place did not work. It is not as "death" in either the national or the local sense that this intrusion took place. It was, rather, from the first the intrusion of death that had no available context. It was death that occurred in a place where the nation was split between classes that were feared to be alienated from one another and thus lacking common references. It is only on this foundation, if one can use that word, that national "death" was formulated.

There remains a difference between the *Petrus* corpses which attracted attention and the corpse of the police agent that "traumatized" the villagers. The attraction of any tattooed *Petrus* corpse was possible because the corpse was attributed a power and that power was considered already restrained, if not completely dominated, once each corpse was made into a sign. The very presence of the corpse on the street came to mean what the government wanted it to mean. But only on condition that before the corpse spoke for the government it spoke for itself, as it were, creating fear of the sort found in the rubber tappers' village. The attraction was the power of the corpse; but that power had to be thought to be under control before the corpses could be approached.

The attractive force of the corpse rested on an unresolved contradiction. On the one hand, the corpse contained a power; on the other hand, that power had passed into the hands of the murderers. The same contradiction applied to the corpse of Serka Bambang. But the corpse was still active through its effects not only so long as the murderers were at large, but even after their arrest. So long as no one claimed to have taken that power for himself, "trauma" ensued. The police who returned to the village, claiming everything was in their hands, shifted the balance of assumptions toward control. As the widow wanted to see the murderer, the villagers had to see the police who had achieved control of him. The murderer blends into the figure of the police and, because of his manner of controlling "criminality," into the face of President Suharto, the instigator of "shock therapy."

But I do not want to leave the impression that the Indonesian government ended in full control of this force. There is a paradox in their notion of the power of the corpse such that its power always exceeds the power of murderers. Each corpse came to indicate not the person of the criminal killed but a power associated with death in general and therefore beyond itself. The dead bodies of *gali* may have demonstrated that the government can control this power but only on the contradictory assumption that leaves this power in a form that is always elsewhere and therefore beyond the government's control. Had the government full control of this power, the power would evaporate, or be routinized into the merely human power of government as we know it. The reference of the power of *kriminalitas* and of the government is never exhausted. However many *gali* the government killed, they could not be sure that they had subdued this supernatural force and taken it for their own. They killed more. The massacre founded itself on a logic in which each murder demanded another. Only in that way could the source of power beyond the state at once be said to exist and to be controlled by it. The nationalization of death is a result of this terrible transaction between the state and its citizens.

FLYING A KITE:
THE CRIMES OF
PRAMOEDYA ANANTA TOER[1]

Hendrik M. J. Maier

This is the letter which the President of the Republic Indonesia, General Soeharto, wrote to political prisoner no. 641, Pramoedya Ananta Toer:

> To:
> brother Pramudya Ananta Tur
> in Tefaat, Buru

I received a report of the Commander for the Restoration of Peace, Security and Order, General Sumitro, about the situation of you and your brothers.

An error for a human being is natural; however, that naturalness should also have a natural sequel. That is to say:

"Honesty, courage, and ability to recover the road that is true and made true."

May the Very Great and Very Merciful Lord give protection and guidance while you recover that road. Amen.

Try and ask Him for help.
Jakarta, November 10, 1973

> President of the Republic of Indonesia
> (signature)
> Soeharto,
> General of the Indonesian National Army TNI

And this was the reply:

To the respected
Father President of the Republic of Indonesia,
General Suharto

---

[1] This essay was written before the so-called Reformasi began and General Soeharto resigned as the Father-President. The ban on Pramoedya Ananta Toer's books has not yet been lifted.

With respect:

Shocked and moved I was in receiving a letter from you, Father President, because so far it was inconceivable that a political prisoner be given such a great honor. A thousand thanks and the highest possible appreciation for the very valuable time and attention which Father President has bestowed upon me.

It is very true what you wrote in your letter, dd. November 10, 1973: "an error for a human being is natural" and "should also have a natural sequel."
Most respected Father President,

My parents, and maybe this is the case of parents in general, taught me to always love truth, justice, and beauty, knowledge, archipelago and nation. With those supplies I entered the world, and on my journey I left traces which everyone can judge. That is why your letter that makes an appeal to "honesty, courage and ability to recover the road that is true and made true" is like an appeal of my own parents, making the value of their supplies shine. A great mind forgives errors and a strong hand reaches out to the weak.

A thousand thanks for the prayers which Father President has sent up to the One and Only because there is no true protection and guidance without Him.

Always try and ask.

> Respectful greetings
> from Political Prisoner No. 641,
> Pramoedya Ananta Toer.

***

The innuendoes are puzzling, the allusions cryptic, and it is tempting to explore the Malay double-talk that passes between these two Javanese men in words such as *wajar* (natural), *benar* (true), *mohon* (ask), *saudara* (brother), and *bapak* (father). Yet most important in this connection is, of course, the word *kekhilafan* that is used by the President. "Error," "mistake," "slip" all translate this word, the dictionaries tell us. *Kekhilafan* is not as bad as a "crime," the experts explain, and not worth a punishment . . . a correction should do.

Political Prisoner No. 641 has made "a natural error," is the President's verdict; what exactly that error consists of and what exactly is "natural" about that error remains unclarified, but the consequence is clear: Political Prisoner No. 641 should recover the true road. "The true road" is another concept that remains unclarified, but then, Father President does not owe a clarification to anyone. The President of the Republic Indonesia, General Soeharto—maybe we should write "Suharto," as Pramoedya does, and maybe we should write "Pramudya," as Soeharto does—wants to block his addressee's path and stop him from starting a discussion about freedom of speech, about the right to have a trial. He wants to make it clear that he, the General, the President, was in the right and in the true from the very first moment he put his pen to paper or asked one of his secretaries to type out his voice, creating a document which he then signed. Make sure you find the Lord's protection and guidance, brother, and pray to Him. That should do. But why does the President address Pramoedya as "brother"? Perhaps to suggest a familiar intimacy or a spiritual complicity which is not appreciated in Buru?

Political Prisoner No. 641, shocked and moved, tells "the honored Father President of the Republic Indonesia, General Suharto" that his suggestion that "honesty, courage and the ability to recover the true road that is made true" reminds him of the teachings of his parents. Do the words of Father President really sound like the words of Pramoedya's own parents, or is this irony? And is General Suharto himself the great mind, the strong hand who forgives errors? Political Prisoner No. 641 adds that he is grateful about Father President's willingness to pray for him because, indeed, only the Lord could give him true protection. But then, does the Lord truly protect him? And how to interpret Pramoedya's last sentence against the background of the President's last sentence: is it an imperative as well, or is it, rather, a confirmation?

Here the correspondence stops.

***

The two letters can be found on pages 31 and 32 of the book the Indonesian author Pramoedya Ananta Toer launched in Jakarta, February 6, 1995, under the title of *Nyanyi Sunyi Seorang Bisu—Catatan-catatan dari P. Buru* (Silent Songs of a Mute Man, Notes from the Island of Buru).[2]

"Silent Songs" opens with a short explanation of its content and form, "Memories at the 70th birthday." It tells us that the book is a compilation of "valuable notes that were irregularly written down, from time to time, whenever the situation allowed it, during the ten years the writer was held prisoner on Buru," and that the Indonesian edition was preceded by the publication of a Dutch translation.

The explanation is followed by one page of Biodata.

"Name: Pramoedya Ananta Toer, nationality: Indonesian, Political prisoner: number 641. Born: in Blora, February 6 1925. Occupation: author. Period of imprisonment: 14 years (1965-1979). Accusation: not clear. Trial: never. Salemba prison October 13 1965—July 1969, Nusakambangan: July 1969—August 16 1969, Buru: August 1969—November 12 1979, Magelang/Banyumanik: November-December 1979, "free": December 12 1979. Duty to report to Kodim Jakarta Timur: once a week (about 2 years), then once a month."

Over these data: a photo of the author taken, as the subtitle tells us, one day after his release from Cipinang prison, Jakarta 1961. A grim man on a dark picture, frantically typing away.

Then, in two pages, the introduction Pramoedya had written in Jakarta, 1988, for the Dutch edition that had appeared in 1989. One of the officials on the Island of Buru, we are told, could not bear seeing the prisoners' plight and gave them a well-meaning piece of advice: "Deal with all this as if you are playing with a kite: if the wind blows, let the kite go, if there is no wind, take it in—and if you do not do that you will be exterminated," and Pramoedya comments: "If I had not followed that advice, these writings would never have been printed, and the writer would have

---

[2] Pramoedya Ananta Toer, *Nyanyi Sunyi Seorang Bisu—Catatan-catatan dari P. Buru* (Jakarta: Lentera, 1995).

been a salted fish in a piece of bleached cotton." Know how the wind blows, in short, and act accordingly: this reads like a summary of the efforts Pramoedya, author, has undertaken to have himself accepted by his society.

At the time the Dutch translation was published, there must have been a lot of wind so that Pramoedya could let his kite freely play in the sky: "It has been suggested that some parties will be furious, those who want certain experiences—nodes in the wider network of experiences which eventually tie the experiences of everyone and everybody in the same period together—to be eliminated merely because of the axiom that crime sets a taboo on witnesses. Too bad: experiences are the right of the one who has them in order to do with them what he wants to, and there is no force that can seize them from him. At the most, other people can bring them into discredit, and to carry out that intent a warehouse of motives can be collected, the more so when funds and power and authority are available to do so." To paraphrase the writer, experiences are the possession of the individual who can operate in the safe knowledge that they are part of a larger whole because he is part of a larger whole. The author of "Silent Songs" is still a member of a community despite his designation as a criminal, and on the back cover this idea is formulated in the widest possible sense under a picture of the writer embracing his wife: "This is a social document about the experiences of the author which are, at once, a part of the experiences of the nation. These are the notes of Pramoedya Ananta Toer during his imprisonment on the Island of Buru 1969-1979."

The text itself—almost three hundred pages of fragments and bits and pieces, polyvocal and heterogeneous—is followed by a number of appendices. I—An explanatory list of those who died in Buru. II—A letter of warning from the commander of the camps at the time (1972): "On the basis of the [Indonesian state ideology] Panca Sila, the Government of the Republic of Indonesia has brought you to Buru with the intention you will return to the natural [*wajar*] road and become Indonesian human beings with the Panca Sila so that you will become good citizens." III—Some information about the area that was occupied by the camps. IV—Maps of the area. V—A report by the author himself about his damaged hearing. VI—A copy of the official letter of the author's release from his "temporary detention," and a number of photographs of life in Buru.

Nyanyi Sunyi Seorang Bisu is closed off by the epilogue that the book's editor, Joesoef Isak, wrote for the Dutch translation. It evokes the difficulties that ex-political prisoners are facing in Indonesian society after their so-called release: ". . . in Indonesia there are two groups of citizens: those who enjoy civil rights and those who do not."

***

Nyanyi Sunyi was launched at a party in Pramoedya's house in Jakarta. Authors, journalists, activists, and foreigners were invited to rub shoulders and celebrate the author's seventieth birthday as well as his forty years of marriage with Maemunah Thamrin. News of the party even made it into some of the metropolitan newspapers. A social event indeed.

The ban on "Silent Songs of a Mute Man" was made public on May 12, 1995, in a a muted series of announcements. Apparently the *Jakarta Post*, the leading English-language daily in Jakarta, was given the scoop and so first announced the news; only a few days later some of the national Indonesian newspapers followed suit and published a statement of identical import, communicating the message that Pramoedya's activities were a sensitive subject, and maybe irrelevant at that. The fact that the Attorney General's decree was dated April 19—that is, some three weeks before the ban was made public through the press, the channel which Indonesian authorities often use to give their decisions and rulings a wider publicity—makes it even more difficult to make sense of the deliberations that had led to this intervention in public life. The book "contains misleading writings which could create a wrong opinion about the government of Indonesia," was Attorney General Singgih's opinion. "Allowing the circulation of the book will cause commotion or restlessness which can disturb public order." All copies of *Nyanyi Sunyi* should be withdrawn from circulation, the officials declared, and people who had a copy in their possession were requested to hand it in at the nearest Prosecutor's office. Those who had the authority to maintain public order—prosecutors, police, and other law-enforcement officers—were asked to confiscate the copies they could lay their hand on.[3]

The ban on *Nyanyi Sunyi* had, shortly before, been preceded by a renewed ban on yet another book of Pramoedya's, one that had been made available in Central Java only. *Tjerita dari Blora* ("Tales from Blora," first published in 1952) had been reprinted some years before, and although it had already been officially banned, copies were resurfacing again in Yogyakarta in the second half of 1994 so that the Prosecutor's office of Central Java felt obliged to issue a warning again. Bookstores were ordered to remove all copies of the book from their shelves, and citizens who possessed a copy were requested to hand it in because it contained "political messages which could undermine the state ideology of Panca Sila and the 1945 Constitution"; this directive was formulated in a phrase that, by then, had become a familiar one.

Bans had been recurrent phenomena in Indonesia throughout the New Order, yet both influential citizens and the media had, for the most part, avoided publicly speaking out against these administrative interventions in the name of freedom of expression (or in the name of "honesty, courage and ability," to use the words of Father President). These two concrete cases of repression, however, led to angry reactions in Jakarta which were widely publicized. Intellectuals felt compelled to regroup themselves in networks of loyalty and hostility and saw to it that their opinions were quoted and discussed in the leading national newspapers; after all, not only the authorities can use newspapers to express their statements and opinions. Goenawan Mohamad, for instance—editor-in-chief of the weekly *Tempo*, he was himself involved at the time in a bitter fight with the Minister of Information, who had banned the periodical—called it nonsense to maintain a general embargo on Pramoedya Ananta Toer's work in this day and age. Others followed suit. The well-respected essayist and poet Subagio Sastrowardoyo, for instance, was quoted as saying that in Indonesia the habit of reading was restricted to a small group and that fact in itself should be a reason to avoid banning too many books. In his view, the ban on Pramoedya's work was even more inappropriate since the book had been shaped by eternal and universal values that are characteristic of all real "literature." The critic H. B. Jassin, whose 1952 essay on *Tjerita dari Blora* served as an introduction to the new edition of the book, also supported the idea that the ban of Pramoedya's

---

[3] See *The Jakarta Post*, May 13, 1995.

work should be lifted. Asked for his opinion by the *Jakarta Post*, he stated that communism should no longer be made an issue in Indonesian literature. "Those days have passed."

Then the Attorney General's office relaxed its instructions slightly. The head of its Office for Societal Relations (*Humas*) suggested that Pramoedya's books could still be used for research, but insisted that not everybody should be given the chance freely to read them because many people would not be able to make sense of them in the correct way. The roads of Law and Order are unfathomable, and the Attorney General's decrees are usually hard to interpret, as they are designed to confirm stability and create rumors simultaneously. The statement of *Humas* sounded at least like a faint echo of the call for openness which President Suharto had made some months before, but it also sounded like a defensive reaction to the remonstrations of leading intellectuals in Jakarta. Perhaps it could also be read as a response to the confusion which the Coordinating Minister of National Development, Ginandjar Kartasasmita, had created with his speech for the National Congress of Books in which he had argued in favor of making banned books available to institutions of higher education. Interestingly enough, Ginandjar only mentioned books that were written by Europeans—he claimed that an economist should be able to read Marx's *Das Kapital*, just as a political scientist should be able to read Hitler's *Mein Kampf*—and he left it to others to be more courageous and give examples of Indonesian books significant to scholars. The Administration should try to decentralize its activities, the Coordinating Minister suggested, and the authority to ban books should no longer be monopolized by the Attorney General. Committees of experts should be formed who could decide if certain books contained "lies and crimes" and decide whether a ban was needed or not.

Given these sorts of public reactions, it seemed as if the times were indeed changing in 1995, although the subsequent remarks of the Minister of Education and Culture must have been like a cold shower for those who tried to take Father President's call for openness seriously: "Why use books that are banned?" he challenged. "Just use the books that are available, there are still so many books that are not banned!" This is the statement of a cynic who does not visit bookstores. One just wonders to what extent this attitude influences the Indonesian government's approach toward the problems of censorship, artistic creativity, and freedom of speech, and to what extent the Administration, despite its frequent statements calling for the construction of a proper national identity, worries about the commodification that is taking hold of Indonesian culture. It's a miserable statement, off target. More than anyone else, the Minister of Education and Culture should have been the one to express his anxiety about ominous cracks that presage the collapse of Indonesian literature as a pillar of National Indonesian Culture.

The hesitation of the Attorney General and his subordinates in making a decision about the Pramoedya ban reflects the confusion within the judiciary. Lawyers, judges, and prosecutors are operating in a system the basic purpose of which is not the observation of laws and rules, but the enforcement of the government's will; deeply infiltrated as they are by politicians and military officials, agencies assigned to oversee and enforce the Law are prone to comply with pressures from those in power.[4] The calls for openness (*keterbukaan*) by president Suharto—and, echoing him,

---

[4] See, for instance, Adam Schwartz, *A Nation in Waiting—Indonesia in the 1990s* (St. Leonards: Allen & Unwin, 1995), p. 245.

by his subordinates—were still resounding at this time, even if rather vaguely and distantly, and obviously both the judiciary and the public prosecutor, equally shaky and dependent officials, had no idea how to integrate the Republic's rules and regulations with the President's promises, the General's moods, and the citizens' opinions so as to arrive at a coherent plan of action. Did Father President really mean to say that the time had come to open up the possibility for discussing national history in a more balanced way? Were the general and his friends, men typically eager to maintain stability and suspicious of every kind of dynamics, really loosening their iron grip? Had Father President really opened a space for dialogues and conversations?

In the first weeks after it was launched, *Nyanyi Sunyi* was available in some book shops, and those who took an interest in Pramoedya, in Buru, in the more ominous face of the New Order, and in renegade voices were given the time, so it seems, to purchase a copy of the book. It was not a bestseller. Discussions about recent history are anathema to those who have made it their business to praise the glorious achievements of the New Order. "Literature" is an activity practiced by only a few.

***

Between the date when *Nyanyi Sunyi* was published and the date when it was banned, a book appeared that pretended to offer a balanced and objective picture of the debates and polemics that marked the years between 1960 and 1965 in Jakarta and beyond, of "what had really happened" in those turbulent years of discussions and dialogues about the future of Indonesia. While the timing of this book's publication may have been fortuitous or arranged, the effect remains the same. *Prahara Budaya* (Cultural Hurricane), a compilation of essays and articles, had been edited by D. S. Moeljanto and Taufiq Ismail, two of the intellectuals who had signed the so-called "Cultural Manifesto" (*Manifes Kebudayaan*), a Manifesto which in 1963 had called for creative freedom.[5] The Manifesto had been banned in 1964, and at that time its signatories had been the target of abuse and criticism by those who regarded them as renegades of the Revolution. But then the military coup of 1965 had brought them back into the limelight, whereas those who had challenged their authority found themselves in jail, silenced, ignored, and ridiculed.

Not surprisingly, Taufiq and Moeljanto present the Manifesto itself as the ultimate hero of *Prahara Budaya*, and the explanatory remarks appended to the documents make it clear that there should be no mistaking the good guys and the bad guys of this tale. Given this slant to the book, it is not surprising that it was strongly recommended as reading for the cadre-members of Golkar, the party that the regime had made its main tool in the political arena, and which it used to nip every form of dialogue in the bud, turning every form of discussion about principles and ideas into an effrontery.

Prahara Budaya showed once again that the mist of the events surrounding the dissemination of the Cultural Manifesto of 1963 is still hanging over intellectual life in the nineties. Or rather, it showed how successful the signatories of the Manifesto and their friends have been in creating the myth that describes their own repression,

---

[5] See D. S. Moeljanto and Taufiq Ismail, *Prahara Budaya—Kilas-balik Offensif Lekra? PKI dkk (Kumpulan Dokumen Pergolakan Sejarah)* (Bandung: Misan & HU Republika, 1995).

terror, and intimidation at the hands of those who confronted them in writings and debates in the years preceding the military coup of 1965. Even thirty years and one generation later, they still reveal a deep hostility—pretended or not, contrived or not—toward the people who had allegedly terrorized cultural life in the early sixties, and of these people Pramoedya has been designated the greatest evildoer, the epitome for everything bad, intolerant, and criminal. The book, Moeljanto and Taufiq Ismail claimed without a grain of irony, should serve as a warning of what happens when intimidation and repression take control over culture and when "politics is the general."

The immediate pretext for the publication of *Prahara Budaya* had apparently been a meeting held in Jakarta in August 1993 during which the poet Sitor Situmorang had spoken. An outspoken opponent of the Cultural Manifesto who after the military coup d'état had spent some ten years in jail on charges that were never clarified, Sitor had tried to explain the politics of the situation, explicitly addressing representatives of the younger generation, who were confused once again about a dispute that dealt with issues they could not relate to in the present situation of repression and intimidation. The meeting had been rather widely reported in newspapers and journals; just like *Prahara Budaya* some months later, it had created unease and annoyance among intellectuals in Jakarta and beyond. Why bring those painful events back into public memory? Why did Sitor, of all people, try to dispel the myth that signers of the Manifesto had been victims of intimidation and terror, intimating that the prelude to the massacres had been a time of heated discussions when there was so much wind that many kites could fly?

"Cultural Hurricane" is a strange book, and it is difficult to agree with the editors' claim that the book offers a balanced picture of the atmosphere in the early sixties by way of presenting essays, poems, short stories, and cartoons of people from all the parties involved in the discussions. The introductions to the various sections lack the coolness required of any persuasive, objective argument. Nor is the book comprehensive in its report of the era; the selection of historical information offered by the editors shows a kind of strange amnesia. Pramoedya Ananta Toer's year-long detention as the result of his publication of a book on the Chinese in Indonesia in 1960, for instance, is passed over in silence; so is the involvement of the army in the events that took place after the publication of the Manifesto, and the polemics stirred up by Hamka's alleged plagiarism, to mention just three issues that certainly contributed to the tensions among intellectuals in the last years of the Old Order. The omission of Hamka's problems contributes to, and is characteristic of, the book's general neglect of the role Islamic writers and intellectuals played in the discussions about the task and responsibility of artists and intellectuals. Given Taufiq's sympathies for the influential Organization of Indonesian Islam Intellectuals (ICMI), founded some years before by Suharto's close protégé, Habibie, in an attempt to rally and reorganize Muslim support for the New Order, this neglect is suspicious, to say the least. Had Islam-inspired authors not tried to join the discussions? Had they perhaps not been able to formulate a clear stance? And speaking of intimidation, suppression, and the complicity between government and intellectuals, it is amazing that the compilers did not realize that they were looking into a convex mirror of their own situation and were unable to see correspondences with the situation around them. Bookkeepers can be very dangerous, the more so when they are angry about the past, ignorant about the present, and not interested in the future.

Prahara Budaya was given mixed reviews. For those who are interested in the period—and as Taufiq Ismail and Moeljanto wrote in the introduction, the book is particularly meant for those who do not know about the time and were not involved—the book offers many articles that are still worth reading; it is a useful publication in that it offers documents that had been unavailable ever since Taufiq and his friends regained an undisputed authority in Indonesian literary circles in 1966. However, "Cultural Hurricane" did not become the bestseller it clearly aspired to be, and it did not really lead to the heated discussions the editors seem to have expected. As a matter of fact, it raised a number of large questions that the editors had not intended or foreseen. Were Indonesian intellectuals in general, apart from those who had been made criminals after 1965, actually interested in recent history at all? It would seem that those who had come out on top were overcome by a certain embarrassment about their willingness to accept the intimidation of the New Order. What had happened to the Indonesian nation, the *bangsa Indonesia*? Did it still exist? Was there any reason to be proud and satisfied with the state of the nation? Those who were too young to know what happened from their own experience showed diffidence if not indifference toward the nation's recent history and its implications. Were there not issues at stake that were more important than the recent past? What of freedom of speech, for instance, as well as censorship, propaganda, intimidation, and silence? The occasional outbursts of virulent anti-communism by writers such as Mochtar Lubis were heard with amazement, but raised no energetic response. The calls for more openness by the old guard, duly published in national newspapers, did not evoke much more than a frown here and there. The rumors of "who was close to whom" and "who did not like whom" in the discussions that were triggered by the ban on Pramoedya's books were a topic of discussion for newspapers and journals, but not for the younger intellectuals. They were more interested in the present situation than in the past and wondered how to break the laws and rules that in theory may be meant to hold the nation together but in practice institutionalize the nation's heterogeneity and sooner or later generate acts that negate that very solidarity.

***

Why was "Silent Songs" banned? The official justification has already been quoted above. The book was supposed to "contain misleading writings which could create the wrong opinion about the Government of Indonesia."[6] What's more, "allowing the circulation of the book will cause commotion or restlessness which can disturb public order." Those sentences would seem to demand a close reading, had they not been used on so many previous occasions that they have almost completely emptied themselves of concrete meaning. Given the pompous rhetoric of the New Order, the word "misleading" has certainly lost its aura of precision, and so has the phrase "to disturb public order." But then, even the most conventional phrases, though downtrodden and dead, should still refer to something. No doubt, seen from the perspective of the authorities, as presented by the Attorney General, Pramoedya's *Nyanyi Sunyi* did indeed create a wrong opinion about the Government: "Buru" was not a prison-camp where people were indoctrinated,

---

[6] See, for instance, *The Jakarta Post*, May 13, 1995.

maltreated, and if necessary killed in the aftermath of a massive massacre, but a place of rehabilitation and re-education where some individuals who had been led astray by an evil ideology were shown the path to becoming good and God-fearing citizens again, worthy members of the Indonesian nation. And of course "Silent Songs" could have created some commotion in a society pervaded by fear, silence, and ignorance; the book's descriptions about the methods of detention were not very edifying or flattering, to put it mildly. Moreover, Pramoedya's representation of facts and events pertaining to the years before 1966 contradicted official interpretations; his words could have easily led to undesired discussions among those who did not fully support the New Order and were looking for a springboard to help launch their criticisms.

Secondly, the book is about Buru, and the negative connotations of the name "Buru"—the book's cover alone is telling, as it shows a Javanese farmer working the land behind barbed wires—should be eradicated from collective memory according to the government. Insofar as the word "Buru" was to remain part of Malay discourse at all, it should refer to a mysterious and awe-inspiring black hole. "Silent Songs," however, describes Buru realistically, in all its horrors: the bogeymen are mentioned by name, their stupidities and cruelties are explicitly described, their system ridiculed. Those were sufficient grounds to ban "Silent Songs." The New Order's mythology was undermined by the book, and the New Order's ideological vision should be implemented without disruptions and questions.

Another reason for the ban may have stemmed from the quality of the book itself. The Malay of *Nyanyi Sunyi* is powerful and painful in its anger and frustration. The form in which the tales of horror, the ideas about history and culture, the recollections of senseless punishments of defenseless people, called "criminals," are presented·is compelling and persuasive—and therefore, according to the official censors, erroneous. Besides, although Pramoedya may have been known as a writer of literary prose, this book is certainly not a novel, or a collection of short stories, or an autobiography. It does not fit in the box of "literature," which the New Order had designated as a basically harmless genre. "Silent Songs" is a mixture of political comments, historiography, personal reflections, and reminiscences, pictures of life in Buru, descriptions of those who died, and some photographs which merely strengthen the sober, realistic impression of the book as a whole. It could make its readers think; they could easily be confused and therefore they should be protected from that confusion. In their efforts to keep control over the representation of the world, the New Order's authorities had to try to silence Pramoedya's representation of the facts.

Moreover, those who were more or less directly involved in deciding that Pramoedya's book should be repressed must have had personal reasons for banning it as well, apart from considerations of security, order, literature, and representation. It is telling that on its back cover "Silent Songs" is characterized not only as a description of personal experiences but also as a description of the experiences of a nation, a sentence that must have touched a nerve or two. For many Indonesians, the memories of the sixties are painful and disturbing. Most families lost some members in the turmoil. Why be reminded of the recent past? Why evoke those experiences which could so easily unsettle one's peace of mind? Repression is a natural way of dealing with trauma, horror, and confusion, and in order to maintain a kind of integration not only every individual but also every nation needs some form of repression. In an authoritarian regime such as the New Order those who question publicly whether repression is a proper government tool are, by definition, outsiders who willfully block the officials' efforts to construct a comprehensive, reassuring personal and national history—and outsiders are criminals. With his book Pramoedya acted as a gadfly, reminding authorities of traumatic events in their personal lives and, therefore, in the life of their nation.

Last but certainly not least, those who chose to ban the book were probably provoked by the identity and reputation of the author himself. The book was not written by an anonymous or unknown person, but by Pramoedya Ananta Toer. As the book of Taufiq and Moeljanto illustrates time and again, in the mythology created to describe the nation's intellectual life in the Old Order, Pramoedya has been portrayed as the epitome of all terrorizing, intimidating aggressors, the greatest threat to the happiness and peace of mind authorities were striving for. Yes, *Tjerita dari Blora* and *Keluarga Gerilja* (Guerrilla Family), a compilation of tales and a novel, respectively, had been widely acclaimed as the provisional climax of "modern Indonesian literature," and they had made him the great author of the Revolution. But something had gone wrong with him. He had made a serious if not a "natural" error. He had become a "communist," a "Stalinist," and he had terrorized and intimidated intellectuals in the sixties, silencing them, muffling them, threatening them. This man was a criminal, in short, who should be denied the right to make a contribution to the "National Construction" which was undertaken in the New Order. This individual simply did not have the right to challenge the authorities with his statements and publications. And if he claimed to speak in the name of the nation, he should be silenced.

***

Those in power may have felt awe for Pramoedya, the individual. They may have feared Pramoedya, the author, and his words. Their consciences may have been troubled. They were eager to preserve Law and Order through a complex set of rituals whose rules they established. In retrospect, the ban on "Silent Songs" in May 1995 was just one logical step in the series of bans that had frustrated Pramoedya's efforts to make his voice heard and accepted in Indonesia ever since his release from Buru in 1979.

This recurrent pattern of challenge and censorship began in September 1980 when *Bumi Manusia* (later translated as "This Earth of Mankind") was launched. Just as in the case of *Nyanyi Sunyi Seorang Bisu*, the launching was embedded in a public performance of an overtly political character: Pramoedya himself presented a copy of the book to the then vice-president, Adam Malik. Pictures of the Vice-president with Pramoedya, Joesoef Isak, and Hasyim Rachman, the three men who had established the publishing house of Hasta Mitra in Jakarta ("the publishing house for books with quality") appeared in some of the leading newspapers in Jakarta and beyond.

The first edition of *Bumi Manusia* did not keep its own origins secret: *Karya Pulau Buru*, the front cover tells us in very inelegant letters, "Work of the Island of Buru," and in case the readers did not yet believe their eyes, the message is repeated on the back cover, which also tells us that *Bumi Manusia* is the first volume of a multi-volume project. Three volumes were to follow, together covering the period between 1898 and 1918, the period of the National Awakening "which Indonesian literature has hardly ever touched upon, the beginning period of the influence of rational thinking, the beginning of the growth of modern organizations which also means the beginning of the birth of democracy, on the model of the French Revolution." These three additional volumes would be titled *Anak Semua Bangsa* ("Child of all Nations," "it tells the introduction of the hero to his own context and the world, insofar as his thinking can reach it"), *Jejak Langkah* ("Footprints," "it tells about the birth of the first modern Native organizations"), and *Rumah Kaca* ("House of Glass," "it tells about the efforts of the colonial Dutch Indies Government to make the Indies a glass house in which it can see every movement of its inhabitants and in which it can do whatever it wants against the players in the house by using the exorbitant laws"). All four of them "had been written while (the author was) in exile on Buru," the back cover states, and they "had first been narrated in an oral form to the comrades of Unit III Wanayasa," a statement that is confirmed by the final words of *Bumi Manusia*: Buru, Oral 1973. Written 1975 (*Buru. Lisan, 1973. Tulisan 1975*).

Those sentences could easily lead to further reflection. It would be tempting, for instance, to wonder to what extent they refer to the present state of things in Indonesia, in particular the phrases that tell us how *Rumah Kaca* should be read. It would be tempting, too, to take up the word "exile," make a link with older Malay literature in which scribes presented themselves as being in exile, and thus identify Pramoedya as a modern Malay writer. We might wonder what the author and publisher meant by the word "rationalism," or by the statements that "Indonesian literature has hardly ever touched upon the period of National Awakening" and that "democracy had been the result of this Awakening." With which period of Indonesian history are these four books actually dealing? Did they perhaps suggest parallels between the colonial order and the New Order?

In Indonesia, *Bumi Manusia* became a bestseller. It went through five editions and sold altogether tens of thousands of copies. By the time it was banned on May 29, 1981, forty thousand copies had been sold, the publishers claimed, and that is very unusual for a work of its kind; in Indonesia, books that are advertised and treated as *sastra* (literature) usually sell no more than four or five thousand copies over a long period of time. If anything, Pramoedya's success indicated that there still was a market for the old-fashioned "realist literature" that had dominated metropolitan literary life in the fifties but had been marginalized in the alienating atmosphere of the seventies. While the leading authors such as Iwan Simatupang, Putu Wijaya, and Danarto had indulged in forms of "surrealism" or "a-realism," Pramoedya had simply continued his work as a "realist," in the spirit of Mochtar Lubis, Armijn Pane, Hamka, and Mas Marco who, each in his own way, had been masters in representing real life.

When *Bumi Manusia* was first published, Pramoedya was interviewed several times, and in those interviews he expressed his opinions in the clear, uncompromising manner he had always used. The Indonesian nation was running aground, he said. The ideals of the Revolution were being squandered. Those in power were corrupt and immoral. To those members of his audience who had grown up in the fifties and before, these verdicts must have sounded familiar. Here was an author who still believed in the moral authority of "literature," in the obligation of authors to educate the people, in their responsibility to speak out about national affairs in the name of the people, and in their right to be actively involved in political life. "This Earth of Mankind" was meant to make Indonesians more familiar with the emergence of nationalism, Pramoedya told his interviewers again and again; it was meant to increase the awareness among Indonesians of being part of a nation. Yes, of course he addressed young people, by far the largest group of readers in Indonesia, in particular. They did not know where "Indonesia" came from. They had lost their roots. They had lost the nationalist fervor necessary to create a just and prosperous society.

In order to reach as many readers as possible, Pramoedya emphasized, he had made a conscious attempt to imitate the smooth forms of language that had made the so-called "popular novels" so easily readable. This remark suggests that Pramoedya, just back from a long period of exile, knew very well that not only nationalism had run aground in the New Order, but that two of its most prominent manifestations, its literature and its language, also appeared to be stranded. However, read against the background of the smoothly composed tales of Ashadi Siregar or Yudhistira and the cute prose of Marga T and Mira W, *Bumi Manusia* belies Pramoedya's claim that it was designed for easy accessibility. In terms of its topics and themes, his novel about the rise of nationalism stands out as radically different from, say, Ashadi's *Cintaku di Kampus Biru*, Marga T's *Karmila*, or any of the books emulating them that deal with contemporary urban life. In terms of its words, phrases, and sentences, it operates on a radically different level: the Malay is more complex, not to say more forbidding, than of any of the tales that are categorized as *sastra pop*, "popular literature." It was rhetorically different from the others, yet it shared the aim of the work of these popular authors: to instill Malay with new energy in order to protect its function as the "national language" and subvert the crippling double-talk of officials and bureaucrats.

Bumi Manusia had almost unanimously been welcomed in the media as an important book. Even *Kompas*, the authoritative Jakarta newspaper that was to become a close accomplice of the regime, had the courage to publish a positive review, full of praise and admiration. The novel, it was suggested, tried to open a discussion about the past which had been neutralized by professional historians. Some critics even had the courage to intimate that "This Earth of Mankind" could teach us something about the present state of things. The positive reception of the book posed problems for the authorities, and so did the author himself, who publicly spoke out and garnered support not only from certain Indonesian intellectuals and critics, but also from supporters abroad. Here was a former political prisoner who claimed to have the right to be a member of the Indonesian nation and wanted to make use of his freedom of speech. *Karya Pulau Buru* (Work of Buru) was meant to be a first step towards rehabilitation or, in official terms, towards the resocialization of one who had been made a criminal. It took the authorities quite some time, however, to define a stance in response to these challenges.

As in the case of "Silent Songs of a Mute Man" fifteen years later, some feelers had been sent out before the Attorney General decided to issue an official statement, dated May 29, 1981, in which the circulation of *Bumi Manusia* and its sequel, *Anak Semua Bangsa* (published some months later) was prohibited within the jurisdiction of the Republic of Indonesia.[7] The Ministry of Education and Culture had not waited for this decision; by September 27, 1980 it had already issued a decree that banned *Bumi Manusia* from all the institutions under its jurisdiction; moreover, it forbade civil servants to buy or possess a copy of *Bumi Manusia* because a careful study had shown that the book "dealt with class conflict and therefore could cause unrest."

---

[7] *Surat Keputusan Jaksa Agung Republik Indonesia nomor KEP-052/JA/5/1981 tentang Larangan Peredaran Barang Cetakan Berjudul 'Bumi Manusia' dan 'Anak Semua Bangsa'*

Clearly the Ministry exceeded its authority with this action. The fact that the judiciary did not act to revoke the arbitrary ban serves as another indication of its incompetence to command respect for the legal system and its inability to maintain the rule of law.

Around October 10, 1980, newspapers and journals in Jakarta received warnings via telephone (a common method in modern Indonesia since the message remains anonymous and unrecorded, the source cannot be traced, and the message is clear in its covertness) instructing them not to publish reviews of the book or polemics responding to it. The editors of Hasta Mitra were summoned to the office of the Attorney General repeatedly; they were urgently requested to operate with care and caution, first because the book was still under review by the security services and a ban was under consideration, later because Pramoedya was a former political prisoner and was not allowed to write or publish. In a public statement following these meetings, the editors expressed their amazement about the fact that the security forces had been asked to evaluate the book: was the office of the Attorney General itself not able to do so, or rather, should the office not do so? Besides, what about the writings of other former political prisoners that were appearing in journals and magazines? Didn't the appearance of these articles show a praiseworthy tolerance on the part of the authorities? Why was Pramoedya Ananta Toer singled out? And so far as the Attorney General's requests were concerned, they were hard to understand. Was the book banned or was it not? To add to this confusion, on October 23, 1980, the Attorney General explicitly informed the press that he had not banned the book. The uncertainty remained however. As officials contradicted one another in public, the literary public gradually lost its interest in the affair.

In the beginning of 1981 Hasta Mitra published the sequel to *Bumi Manusia*, called *Anak semua bangsa* (Child of All Nations). Critics welcomed the book as yet another landmark in the development of "modern Indonesian literature," but this time some distinct hesitations could be detected. Perhaps the novel was too thick, too heavy for the average readers in Indonesia. Perhaps readers preferred short stories or popular novels to yet another dense and multivocal text. Perhaps the parallels with the present were all too clear. And perhaps Pramoedya was a communist after all. The novel's glorification of the resistance of poor Javanese farmers and workers was very suspect.

Again the publishers were given several warnings, and again Hasta Mitra issued statements in which it reported to the public its discussions with the state's authorities. They explained why it was not correct to read *Bumi Manusia* and *Anak Semua Bangsa* as novels that propagated Marxism-Leninism—"these are just tales about the sufferings of the natives in the colonial system."[8] It questioned the validity of the anger that was expressed in "certain circles" about the re-emergence of Pramoedya Ananta Toer and about his candidacy for the Nobel Prize for Literature. "Their evaluation is very subjective and contrived; it is anachronistic, prochronistic, and parachronistic in the way it mixes up the colonial period with the present-day."

With the appointment of a new Attorney General, the mist of confusion was blown away, the wind died down, and Pramoedya and his friends had to take their

---

[8] See, for instance, Hasta Mitra's summaries of the affair in *Risalah ringkas kronologis mengenai penerbitan buku 'Bumi Manusia'* (Jakarta, November 20, 1980) and *Surat Terbuka Penerbit Hasta Mitra Tentang Larangan Kejaksaan Agung terhadap Buku Bumi Manusia dan Anak Semua Bangsa* (Jakarta, June 5, 1981).

kite in: an official ban was issued. In the ten months that had passed since its first publication, *Bumi Manusia* had reached a fifth edition. In four months *Anak Semua Bangsa* had reached a second edition.

"Those who keep, own or trade the aforementioned printed matters are obliged to hand them over to the Attorney General or his local representatives, so that they can be sent forward to the Attorney General of the Republic of Indonesia," the official formulation ran.[9] The ban was based on several considerations. *"Bumi Manusia* and *Anak Semua Bangsa* had given cause to reactions in various sectors of society and had developed and influenced the situation of public security and order"—this word-for-word translation of the original should show how uneasy, not to say how incorrect and incomplete, the formulation was. The two books had been "carefully studied," and experts had concluded that they showed that "the skill and agility of the author's pen could smuggle the teachings of Marxism-Leninism in by way of historical data in a refined and well-disguised manner." The content of the books was clearly "in conflict with the resolution of the Provisional People's National Assembly, dated July 5, 1966, regarding the dissolution of the Indonesian Communist Party as well as its declaration that it is a banned organization within the territory of the Republic of Indonesia and that every activity to spread or develop the ideas or teachings of Communism/Marxism-Leninism is banned." In an attempt to strengthen the legitimacy of the ban, some more resolutions and decisions by various institutions were added, one of them dated 1963. As if the law does not merely follow the illusions of the day. As if the law had not become a tool in the hands of those in power.

That was not the end of the tale. By now many people owned a copy of the two novels; they were supposed to hand them in, but how to trace those who did not? How to parry the criticism of intellectuals and politicians abroad who made public protests in defense of Pramoedya? What to do with references to the books in subsequent essays and articles that appeared in the Indonesian press? How to react to the publication of Pramoedya's work in Malaysia where it was welcomed as a great and impressive contribution to Malay literature?

The ban discouraged neither the publishers nor the author. True heirs of Tirto Adisoerjo, the hero of the novels, and Mas Marco, who was to play a prominent role in the two volumes still to come, they did not let themselves be intimidated; in interviews and flyers Hasta Mitra continued to demand the right to join the national conversation about Justice, Humanity, and Prosperity. Was the government's policy not meant to integrate former political prisoners into society? If Pramoedya had committed a criminal act, why was he never given a trial? Did the government not subscribe to freedom of speech?

In the second half of 1985, *Jejak Langkah* (Footsteps) appeared, soon followed by a historical study about the main protagonist of the tetralogy, Minke alias Tirto Adisoerjo, entitled *Sang Pemula* (The Beginner). On October 16, 1985, the publishers were ordered by the authorities to see to it that further distribution of these two publications was halted, pending a study by the Attorney General's office. Of course, Hasta Mitra refused to obey; such an order was not an accepted procedure in Indonesian law, and the publishing house did not hesitate to issue a public statement on the matter, showing the civil courage that was needed to continue the public debate which these tales had initiated.

---

[9] See *Surat Keputusan KEP-052/JA/5/1981.*

It was to take seven months before an official ban on the two books was issued on May 1, 1986. "The historical novels entitled *Jejak Langkah* and *Sang Pemula* are historical novels that start out from the concepts of social contradiction and class struggle, based on Socialist Realism, which is the type of literature which is adhered to by Communists," the statement read, and "these writings contain influences which could disturb public order." Not a very careful formulation, if only because *Sang Pemula* was not a novel at all.

In 1988 the drama of complicity was repeated once more. *Rumah Kaca* (Glass House), the fourth volume about Minke, was published, and only some months later banned (June 8, 1988) on the basis of exactly the same considerations that had caused *Jejak langkah* to be removed from circulation two years before. A drama of challenge and repression ensued. Operating from the margins, Hasta Mitra persisted in its efforts to test the government's flexibility in an atmosphere which, for a while, seemed to be growing more tolerant of intellectual and even ideological discussions.

For the sake of completeness, it should be mentioned that not only books by Pramoedya that were published during the New Order were subject to a ban. His book *Hoa Kiau di Indonesia* (The Chinese in Indonesia), an exploration of the presence of the Chinese in Indonesia, published in 1960, had been banned during Sukarno's Old Order. The author's balanced attitude toward the nation's small but powerful Chinese minority was sufficient reason for the Army, General Nasution in particular, to detain him for almost a year without a trial: another punishment without an accusation, without a crime. Pramoedya came out of prison as an embittered and wiser man. Hardly anyone had taken the trouble to speak out for him, and his grudge against Nasution as well as his distrust of his fellow colleagues-authors found an outlet in the cultural column which the radical nationalist newspaper *Bintang Timur* made available to him. In *Lentera* he could not only voice his anger but also develop radically new ideas about Indonesian culture which ran against the grain and caused a growing anxiety among intellectuals in Jakarta and beyond.

Hoa Kiau, the tetralogy about Minke alias Tirto Adisoerjo, *Sang Pemula*, *Nyanyi Sunyi*—all were banned after some muddled hesitations. Each of these cases shows that the authorities in Jakarta were fearful of this particular man, and that laws and regulations are not only the reflection of people's experiences and feelings but also interventions upon them. An author could be made a criminal. Speaking out could be made a crime.

***

How is a book banned in Indonesia in the New Order? The principle is simple. Every book can be published, but within forty-eight hours after publication at least two copies have to be submitted at the office of the Attorney General or one of his regional representatives, and the appropriate official is then supposed to study the text. The actual agents and instigators of a possible ban remain invisible, their deliberations unclear, but they can decide that further circulation of the book should be stopped and all its copies be withdrawn, either in the whole country or in certain regions only. A decree to that effect is issued and is then given greater publicity.

This form of repressive censorship is just one of the options open to authorities in Indonesia to keep the flow of information and communication under surveillance. An author can also be indicted on charges of sowing unrest or immorality, and then be brought to trial, sentenced, and sent to prison. A short-cut is also possible: the author can be sent to prison right away before a trial takes place, thus denying the author the opportunity to defend himself against charges in public and perhaps make himself a hero. Conversely, the author himself could lodge a complaint that he had been rendered unable to do his work; if the authorities are willing to consider his case and do not succeed in intimidating the author, a trial is held during which his complaint is rejected. A more effective way of banning books, however, is to make sure that publishers will not consider publication at all of materials that are considered sensitive and harmful to societal stability. Such a method could be called a subtle form of preventive censorship—and until recently, authorities in Indonesia have shown themselves as effective in preventive as in repressive censorship. An occasional anonymous telephone call, some well-designed rumors, a well-publicized speech by a Minister, a nocturnal threat here and there—these are very adequate tools for deflating any spirit of anger and resistance.

Every state is held together by a set of laws, and the publication of printed matters is usually covered by a set of laws as well. In Indonesia, the law governing the publication of printed matter echoes the colonial days; the considerations that the Attorney General or any of his regional representatives have used to justify their surveillance are still inspired by the so-called *Haatzaai artikelen*, a number of paragraphs in the law code that Dutch administrators formulated, not without many difficulties and deliberations, during the second decade of this century in order to keep intellectual life in the Indies under control and to stop activists and politicians from "sowing hate" among the local population.

The *Haatzaai artikelen* constituted an intriguing form of censorship in that they tried to find and maintain a delicate balance between the need to grant a certain degree of free speech, on the one hand, and maintain civic order and morality, on the other hand. Everything could be printed and published, but Authorities reserved the right to judge that a certain publication threatened to upset public order so that they could step in and have the publication destroyed and the author and publisher sued, imprisoned, exiled, or killed. Needless to say, the guardians of morality and order in the Indies had Power on their side which allowed them to intervene at will. Following a calculated strategy of restraint and tolerance, these interventions often resulted in an eerie complicity between authorities and those individuals who were taking the liberty to question Law and Order. In their confrontations by way of newspapers or books both parties could not but gain—the authorities made it clear that there were limits to individual freedom, while individuals acquired fame and respect by calling for freedom—and both parties were fully aware of this complicity.[10]

As is the case everywhere else, censorship in the Indies was intended to sow fear and insecurity. As is true of everywhere else, it is hard to say how well censorship in the Indies effectively worked to preserve Law and Order and stop people from sowing dissension. Writers and journalists such as Mas Marco, Sneevliet, and Semaoen felt challenged rather than discouraged by the *Haatzaai artikelen*. They did not allow themselves to be intimated, but instead explored the boundaries of openness and dialogue, and, like true knights, they made it a point of honor to be arrested, tried in the name of Justice, Truth, and Honesty, and then be made

---

[10] See J. M. Coetzee, *Giving Offense: Essays on Censorship* (Chicago and London: University of Chicago Press, 1996).

criminals. In the same tradition of repression and diffidence, in the same play of complicity, some fifteen years later young nationalist leaders such as Hatta and Sukarno would be willing to pay for their desire to resist this and every other form of repression with exile and detention. Their public resistance and defiance made them heroes and examples in "the movement."

The principle of repressive censorship was retained once Indonesia became an independent nation. The *Haatzaai artikelen* themselves were reformulated, preserving the delicate balance between the individual's freedom and the state's stability. In Suharto's New Order, restrictions on public discussions and publications established to maintain Law and Order are inspired by what officials in the eighties have called considerations of SARA: offensive references to *suku* (ethnicity), *agama* (religion), *ras* (race), and *antar-golongan* (social groups) are considered offences that justify an authority's decision to intervene at any time in the name of tranquillity and peace, of Law and Order. Two other topics were made taboo as well: the relevance of the activities of the President and the authority of the State-ideology of Panca Sila and the Constitution of 1945 could not be debated.

"Allowing the circulation of the book will cause commotion or restlessness which can disturb public order": this phrase could have been written by a Dutch colonial official eighty years earlier. Claiming they had the right to speak out in the name of the Indonesian people, Pramoedya Ananta Toer and his friends did what Mas Marco and Sukarno had done in the colonial days—they flew their kites, knowing that they ran the risk that the wind would die down and they would be caught.

Now it has always been hard to know when the Attorney General, a major representative of the authorities, will step in and use his powers to control the level of public dissent. Banning a book takes place in a certain context, in a certain *sikon* as Indonesian has it: in certain situations, under certain conditions. A ban is inspired by concrete political considerations rather than by legal ones, and authorities rule and intervene by referring, often arbitrarily, to societal developments, safe in the knowledge that the very arbitrariness of repressive censorship tends to create more fear and uncertainty than systematically imposed preventive censorship could ever create.

A ban has to be implemented. A decision is made, the ruling is published or made public, and the press then plays an important role in making this ruling known to "the people." Cases of censorship in Indonesia—not only "communist" but also Islamic writings have been hit in the past decades—not only show that the administrative apparatus lacks the power and acumen to see to it that the ban is effectuated but also that the judiciary is unwilling to question the legality of these rulings. Another question is, of course, whether "the people" are willing to follow the ruling and submit the banned books to the authorities involved once they have been publicly told to do so. Once a book is officially banned, copies may not appear in the open anymore, but it does not seem to be a very common practice to hand them in, if only because people are afraid of showing the authorities that they have acquired something forbidden and thereby make themselves suspect of committing subversive activities. In these days of repression, for some Indonesian citizens having a forbidden book may be like having a forbidden fruit; it is good to keep it, stealthily look at it now and then, wonder why it should be forbidden at all—and then take a bite. In modern Indonesia, in other words, reading a "literary" book can still be an act of resistance, selling "literature" can still land someone in prison. An author can still be an object of suspicion, anger, and envy on the part of the government that, in its monological obsession with societal control, feels compelled to monitor not only transmissions by e-mail, the Internet, and fax, but also the circulation of "literature."

***

On several occasions, Pramoedya Ananta Toer has reflected on his role as an author in Indonesia and, in a more general sense, on the role of "literature" (*sastra*) in Indonesia. The best exposé may be the speech he wrote for the ceremony at which he was to receive the Magsaysay award in Manila in 1995.[11] It reads like a summary of wisdom from an experienced but embittered man who is looking back on what has happened to him since his release in 1979 and taking stock of his achievements.

Pramoedya distinguished three kinds of *sastra*. First, there is the form of literature that glorifies the caste of warriors which, securely in power, denies every small movement toward progress and gives the people the idea that the past is better than the present. This kind of *sastra* is born in the lap of Power. Second, there is the "literature" that merely entertains. It is an indirect tool of those in power, used to make sure that the members of a society remain unaware of the way Authority is being wielded. It suggests to readers that the present time and the status quo are best. The third kind of *sastra* is the kind Pramoedya has tried to practice. It offers courage, new values, a novel world-vision, and human dignity to its readers and it makes individuals aware of the role they can play in society. It shows the readers a pathway to a better future, and it provides them with the vitality and enthusiasm to "move."

Every literary work, Pramoedya adds, is the autobiography of an author in a certain phase and situation in his life. It is the autobiography of someone who is, simultaneously, an individual and a member of the community of human beings, offering to add his experiences to the aggregate of mankind's collective experiences. "An author evaluates the situation of life he and his society are in; he cannot feel but dissatisfied, cornered, repressed by the current state of things. He shouts, struggles, rebels. And then he is called an opponent, a rebel, the source of a revolution, all by himself, in all his muteness." Literature is written with the name of the author clearly in evidence. One knows where it comes from, and the source of any literary work is an individual who does not have a police or military force to support him, let alone a gang of contract killers. How could an author be a danger to a state? "He just tells a story about the possibilities of a better life within a pattern of renewal of the moldy and old state of things, without elasticity left."

Indonesia has changed several times and, Pramoedya claims, never has literature played a role in these changes. That very fact makes the ban on literary work so strange and the designation of an author as a criminal so hard to grasp. Developments in literary life have followed a different pattern from social life; at the most a literary work is able to disturb "the elite of power" in its sleep and make it afraid it will lose its grip on the people. "Censorship had to be established to give the people with authority the opportunity to sleep without having to educate

---

11 Pramoedya himself did not go to Manila; his wife accepted the prize in his name. See *Polemik Hadiah Magsaysay* (Jakarta: Institut Studi Arus Informasi, 1997), in particular pp. 228-234.

themselves." What he, Pramoedya, has tried to do in his work is to tell his public about certain phases in the journey of the Indonesian people and to formulate an answer to the question: what has happened to this nation?[12]

***

The adventures surrounding the publication of "Silent Songs" were a repetition of the adventures surrounding Pramoedya's previous publications in Suharto's New Order. By having his writings published, the author had reached out for a public, making it clear that he wanted to engage with society, the authorities, and the Law. He accepted the state if only by repeatedly asking for a trial that could give a decisive answer to the question of why he had been violating the Law, why he had made an error, and why he had been made a criminal. He was eager to join public discourse and become a member of civil society, and time and again he made himself heard asking the same set of questions: what have I done wrong? What has been my crime? Why am I punished this way?

The logic governing crime, judgment, and punishment seems a simple one: a person acts, he is accused of having committed a crime, his crime is proven, he is declared a criminal, and then he is punished. In the case of Pramoedya—and this seems to apply to individuals who have been the victims of every form of censorship in Indonesia—the accusation is left out, or rather the accusation is preceded by the punishment. The final sentence of "Silent Songs" gives an apt summary of this reversal: "What political prisoners are accused of is actually what they are expected to have done—it is the method in political crime which I have only recently come to understand." He might have gone on to say: those in power expect us to have done the things of which they accuse us, but what exactly should we not have done? In Suharto's letter, another summary of this mechanism is offered; Suharto explains that

---

[12] In *Nyanyi Sunyi Seorang Bisu* Pramoedya had already given an explanation of his authorship which had found its climax in the four volumes he published in the eighties. He wanted to write a great novel: "I intended to write a novel about the period of National Awakening. I had started in Unit III but now I started to doubt because sooner or later it would be read by others, not only by me. To rely on my memory would mean looseness and awkwardness. If I wrote it and it was inaccurate, people would accuse me of falsifying history, and of course history is not my field. And every falsification of history could easily lead to social calamities. I wanted to write a great novel once in my life; every author has this ideal of producing an eternal work which will be read for ages to come, and better still: which will be read by mankind in the whole world, for ever and ever. I am an author, and there is nothing extraordinary about me, neither in national nor in international terms. I had started my preparations long before 1965; I had collected authentic materials and interviews. I had read and I had published the materials I had found little by little in the media in order to get corrections or additions (from readers), and it all had cost me quite a lot of money. Having the necessary books typed out in the National Museum alone cost me ten thousand rupiah for every hundred pages in 1962, and that did not include the payments to the people that helped me to type out articles from the many old newspapers I myself had collected. It did not include the help I received from students of (the University of) Res Publica either. I was determined to write a novel again at the time I was forty years old. That was exactly my age when I entered jail in 1965 and everything I had collected with so many hardships and expenses was destroyed by the hands of people who did not understand . . . someone can have 'pride' because of his documentation, but the documentation itself has not been a source of 'pride.' Rather, it is the backbone, the power, the compass for reality, and with it a creative work is constructed. . . . I postponed writing my novel while I trained myself to remember things and grope into the dark." Pramoedya Ananta Toer, *Nyanyi Sunyi*, pp. 89-90.

a person has made an error and that error demands a sequel rather than a cause. In Indonesia's New Order, so it seems, events and activities are not supposed to have causes but only effects and sequels, or in other words, an author is punished without yet having committed a crime. First comes the punishment and then the crime, so to speak. Is there not irony in the correspondence between Pramoedya's definition of an author, the Attorney General's verdict, and Suharto's definition of error, in that they all point at the effect of a deed rather than a cause?

In one of the first chapters of his "Silent Songs," Pramoedya asks his interrogator Fuad Hassan—the leader of an inter-university psychological team that had come to Buru not to interrogate the prisoners but "to know the real contents of the heart and thoughts of the brothers"—to justify his, Pramoedya's own, stay in Buru. It is a strange interrogation during which Pramoedya pretends not to understand his situation. "I feel I am not treated according to the law. Never have I been sentenced by a court. I am an author, I write with a clear name. If there is a mistake [*kesalahan*] or a fault [*kekeliruan*] in my writings, everybody can accuse me, everybody has the right to accuse me of mistakes, most of all the Government which has *nota bene* a Ministry of Information. Why am I here? If I made a mistake, I am willing to accept a punishment."[13] He accepts the existence of the Law, making it clear that he has always desperately tried to keep inside of it, to be accepted by the State in which he wants to be a law-abiding citizen. But he is speaking of a particular sort of Law, here, not the Law of Power, but the Law that ideally reflects the experiences of the people, of the nation he is talking about. In the course of the interview, Pramoedya pretends to be naïve and unsure of this distinction. He proposes that a public discussion should be held with those who keep accusing him of being the great instigator of the polemics in the early sixties, but also acknowledges that the "others" had not reacted, that the discussion would never take place, and that no court was willing to treat his case.

Pramoedya, the self-appointed guardian of historical reality, of facts and events, simply refuses to accept the hazy, marginal situation which the New Order created around him and his comrades. He wants his situation to be defined, expressed in clear terms; his existence, his authorship has to be legitimized, so to speak, to be accepted by the Law, by the State's authorities. In his efforts to force recognition of his identity by the Law, he has built up a complicity with the regime just like Sukarno and Marco did in the colonial days. They, too, did not turn away from authorities and their prospective censors. Instead, they, too, invited the authorities to participate with them in a discussion about the foundations of power, to participate like equals. If there is a difference between Pramoedya and his predecessors, it lies in the fact that Pramoedya was never given a trial during which he could vent his anger and grasp the opportunity to label the authorities' treatment of him, correctly, as an injustice.

The crime is made to be a rough one, retroactively, because the punishment for that crime has already been rough. In the course of his punishment, Pramoedya was first sent into exile in the physical sense; the descriptions of his experiences in Buru tell us how violent and humiliating this punishment was. Then he was also sent into a spiritual exile, while the authorities continued to caress him. Yet the author is almost grateful for this treatment, since it gives him the feeling of being alive, of

---

13 Pramoedya Ananta Toer, *Nyanyi Sunyi*, p. 9.

being taken seriously. When it succeeds in eliciting fear and respect from him, its victim, this treatment ironically gives him the feeling he is powerful and important.[14]

This is how Pramoedya pictures Minke alias Tirto Adisoerjo alias himself as seen from the perspective of a secret agent:

> He was not a criminal, he was not a rebel. He was a native intellectual who just very much loved his people and his fatherland, tried to bring his people ahead, tried to establish justice in his lifetime, for his people in the Archipelago, for all the people on this world of human beings. And he was fully in the true . . . he belonged to the group of people who were basically good, not bad. He was clearly not a criminal.[15]

***

By way of interviews, essays, and articles, the criminal Pramoedya Ananta Toer has managed to maintain a degree of visibility in Indonesia. The numerous translations of his work that have appeared abroad have given him an almost unassailable authority among his peers in Indonesia and also made him fairly invulnerable to attacks by authorities. By showing youth, by example, how to resist authority, he became a source of embarrassment for the older intellectuals in Jakarta and beyond because he reminded them of the past which they had tried to repress. The interpretation of events between 1960 and 1965, including the events in literary life, had been fixed once and for all. According to that fixed interpretation, members of the Institute of People's Culture, *Lekra*, affiliated with the Communist Party, had terrorized those who refused to agree with its ideas about culture and literature, had intimidated them, had seen to it that they were removed from any official positions and their books banned. Period, discussion closed. And yet this fixed interpretation has been challenged, sometimes inadvertently by those who were aiming to discredit *Lekra*. When writers such as Abdul Hadi, Taufiq Ismail, Ikranegara, and Lukman Ali chose to open up old wounds and describe the crimes Pramoedya and his comrades had supposedly committed, they had no problem finding an eager and well-paying publisher, but even this good fortune could have an adverse effect, since by feeding Pramoedya's notoriety their efforts granted Pramoedya further opportunities to question the authority of the New Order and challenge the Laws of Power.

Of course, the authorities do have some justifications easily available for explaining the decreed punishments against Pramoedyato to those who would speak out on his behalf. One of them is summarized in Suharto's own words: the author has made an error and needs to be re-educated so he can find the true road again and thus become a loyal representative of the Indonesian people. This is an inconclusive statement which cuts off every kind of discussion if only because it comes from the apex of state Power in which accusation and crime concur and the legal system has become ritualized.

A more precise statement is formulated in the decrees by which Pramoedya's books were successively banned. They declared that national security and social

---

[14] Coetzee, *Giving Offense*, p. 38.

[15] Pramoedya Ananta Toer, *Rumah Kaca (Buku Ke-IV, Sebuah Roman Sejarah)* (Jakarta: Hasta Mitra, 1988), p. 6.

stability were endangered by this author's works. Pramoedya himself must have been flattered by the idea that "literature" was still thought powerful enough to derail society as a whole. It must have made him feel like a master and a martyr both, as it confirmed the importance of authors no matter how little respect they are usually shown in Indonesia. It vindicated, so to speak, his claim that he was writing in the name of the Indonesian nation, that he had an historical mission to fulfill in the name of the Indonesian people.

Did these decrees not show the powerlessness of the Suharto regime and constitute an admission that it needed the authors' compliance to help prop up its existence? The Attorney General's decrees must have confirmed Pramoedya's idea that he was not an enemy but a rival of the state's authorities, a potentially powerful leader who had to be silenced to prevent him from gaining followers among those groups in Indonesian society that were able to evoke the very dynamism which the New Order tried to repress. It must have reminded him of the discussions in the early fifties when people still believed that "literature" was of central importance in the construction of a widely supported national culture, a time when authors felt they had the right to be heard and respected. The echoes of Takdir Alisjahbana are audible. The megalomania of *Poedjangga Baroe* and of those who created the notion of "Generation of '45" is implicit in these decrees.

Pramoedya's novels are manifestations of the "great novel" for which the older Indonesian critics had been waiting for thirty years, the great work that would prove "Indonesian literature" had grown up at last and could compete with other literatures. However, *Bumi Manusia* and its sequels may have arrived too late on the scene to make "Indonesian literature" mature in the way that generation dreamed it might, too late to generate a literature of great and densely constructed novels that would deal with love, life, and death in a deeply philosophical way, full of intricate plays between voices that evoke a comprehensive picture of the world. Malay writing in Indonesia had taken another path in the sixties and seventies in which *sastra pop*, short stories, and poetry readings set the tone, in close correspondence with the wishes of the ideologists of the New Order. *Bumi Manusia,* no matter how much it was admired by almost everyone who read it and did not read it, was to remain an anomaly just like its successors. Maybe Pramoedya Ananta Toer is to be the last great representative of the notion of the *sastra Indonesia* which was created by the metropolitan intelligentsia in late-colonial times and now is in decline.

The image that was recently used by a journalist of the *New Yorker* who paid a visit to Pramoedya is a marvelous one in that it symbolizes Pramoedya's conclusion of his own attempts to place his literary work within the Law and to be accepted as a mouthpiece and representative of the Indonesian nation: "Indonesian author vents his fury in a garbage dump."

***

Of course Pramoedya is more than the creator of novels that may have arrived too late on the literary scene to make much impact. He is also a man who has systematically refused to abide by the monologues of the New Order, and through these actions he has become a symbol of resistance in a society dominated by the New Order and its imposition of a shared morality that treats every critical remark on its authority as a serious threat to that society as a whole. In the same *New Yorker* article, Pramoedya's situation relative to the New Order is formulated as follows:

"Pramoedya remains a thorn in the side of the authorities, stubbornly critical of the government and a magnet for idealistic young people. These read underground copies of his works and visit his home . . . to talk politics."

Surveillance is needed to preserve the monolith; troublemakers should be won over, silenced, or expelled. In New Order Indonesia, one hears resounding echoes of the late-colonial state, which created agitators on the Eastern Islands and then imposed a system of arbitrary censorship and silence to retain order, thus setting precedents for its successors. Once again, the hum of social engineering can be detected in the air, driven by the idea that society is malleable and that the Indonesian people need a strict and authoritarian regime to control them for their own benefit. No wonder New Order policy makers frequently rely on the plans and publications of the late-colonial state. The Project that has been implemented throughout the past thirty years has not tolerated voices of dissent; in the opinion of the powerful in Jakarta, a single grain of sand could disrupt the machine and sooner or later lead to explosions of social unrest. Therefore a network of security forces has been set up and continuously expanded so as to keep everything and everybody "in a distinctive and institutionalized pattern of control: militarization, comprehensive domestic political surveillance, and intermittent but persistent state terror."[16] As a result, fear has taken hold of daily life, more often than not sublimated under blind obedience or mute apathy. It requires a certain kind of moral confidence and intellectual courage to speak out. Silence is safe, gossip and slander are free, howling in sync with the authorities is profitable, and corruption, moral as well as financial, has been spreading like wildfire.

An undigested history and an uncontested present are the result. An observer can only wonder how so many millions of people have managed to sensibly survive—if they ever did—with the traumas that the early sixties inflicted on their hearts, and how they have come to terms with the government's monologue on national construction—if they ever have. Only on rare occasions has the official interpretation of the events that led to the massacres of 1965-1966 been openly challenged. Every critique of the regime has had a hard time making itself heard, even when it comes from abroad where political refugees and their sympathizers have often showed an astonishing lack of direction and unity.

Since the late eighties, this strict regime of tranquillity and stability has been interrupted by short periods of relative openness. *Keterbukaan* (openness) has become a magical word, suggesting a certain tolerance which could be turned into a clampdown at any time, unpredictable and sudden. With its policy of combining intimidation and caprice, supplemented by the spread of rumor and slander, the authoritarian Suharto regime may have established more effective control than it ever could have managed by imposing a policy of more consistent totalitarianism. The people outside the direct circle around Father President can only guess to what extent these alternating movements—intimidation and caprice, tolerance and openness—reflect tensions, personal or ideological, within the ruling elite itself and to what extent these vacillations are all part of a well-designed strategy for sowing the uncertainty that allows the authorities to act against "subversive" elements at any time. Efforts to engage the common man more actively and whole-heartedly in the

---

[16] See Richard Tanter, "The Totalitarian Ambition: Intelligence Organizations in the Indonesian State," in *State and Civil Society in Indonesia*, ed. Arief Budiman (Melbourne: Monash Papers on Southeast Asia 22, 1990), p. 214.

National Construction have been lacking. Democracy à la Indonesia, hailed by the power-brokers in Jakarta as a genuine expression of Indonesian norms and values, manifests itself in forms of political consensus that on all levels are manipulated from above. The parliament in Jakarta is a shining pinnacle of powerlessness and pompousness, with members appointed in carefully orchestrated elections. The judiciary has lost the independence necessary to defend the Law. Most Indonesians are very badly informed about the mishaps, conflicts, and crises in their own country, and about the tensions and conflicts within the circles of the ruling elite in particular. News and information about the occupation of East Timor, the unrest in Irian Jaya, the tensions in Aceh, the labor conflicts, and the strains between Muslims and Christians are filtered and blocked. Knowledge about incompetence and corruption mainly resides within the realm of gossip and tales; the financial scandals, the commercial deals are all part of public knowledge, but these crimes are hardly ever effectively proven, let alone punished, by authorities.

Until the economy collapses, there will be a consensus among Indonesians that the New Order has accomplished a great deal. Agricultural methods have been improved, with impressive results. The economy has been diversified. Public health services are better than they ever were before. The infrastructure has been upgraded. There are more and more cars and motorcycles in the streets, more and more TV sets in the houses. Everything is done in the name of *Pembangunan* (Construction), a term that has been brought home to the people by way of a monolithic and all-pervasive propaganda machine which has succeeded in silencing almost every form of radical nationalism or religionism that could aim at actively engaging the people in the construction of the nation. Orders progress from the top down and are called advice. Government blueprints are accepted without changes and called deliberations and democracy. Discussion closed. Only a few people have been heard warning that the economic boom is built on quicksand. Only some people have been heard protesting that the regime has barred the largest part of the nation from active involvement. And here a person like Pramoedya steps in, fearless, indifferent to intimidation, with his "Silent Songs of a Mute Man." The discussion is not closed, he says. We should have a conversation and see how the people are best served. Once again the secret agent in "Glass House" summarizes it all in his description of the man he has to follow:

> He does not break the law. There is no law that can forbid him to act, not a colonial law, not a Dutch law that has been brought to the Indies. But every movement that steers to a concentration of power is a potential danger for the Government. Such a movement could reduce the Government's prestige, it could impose its wishes upon the Government and eventually it could oppose the Government. Unrest is the fruit of every concentration of power—but only when the Government begins to feel its prestige is hurt, it can act against such a movement.[17]

***

The case of Pramoedya Ananta Toer tells us how an author can be made a criminal when he refuses to accept the monolithic state that curbs his freedom to

---

[17] Pramoedya Ananta Toer, *Rumah Kaca*, p. 8

express himself and, more importantly, tries to teach him intolerance. He is a criminal not only because he represents annoyance and nuisance; he is a criminal because he acts as a mirror, showing "the others" what has happened to them as a result of accepting the lessons and constructions of the New Order.

The reactions to *Bumi Manusia* were positive but the daily worries of how to make a living, the attempts to survive, soon muted most of the voices that had been raised in support of Pramoedya and his work. These understandable, human reactions ultimately stifled the initial enthusiasm for the book, and one could discern efforts among people, particularly intellectuals, to justify the growing indifference. Why bother about an author who should be distrusted and who allegedly had committed crimes? Some kind of guilty resentment could be felt in literary circles when the literary master resurfaced. Perhaps other writers felt some guilt about their own silence in the face of repression and intimidation, and felt resentment about the past. Driven by fear, opportunism, and the urge for self-preservation, people have followed the rules and regulations that the Indonesian state has laid down. In a way, they must have felt like collaborators, and that cannot be a pleasant feeling.

Only gradually, it seems, have critics and authors come to realize what has happened to themselves and to the nation, and one can ask to what extent Pramoedya has helped make the people aware that the ideas of the New Order have sunk into their bone and marrow. Only at the time "Silent Songs" was banned did intellectuals get their act together and protest in public for a week or two. Had the repression not yet been long enough? And after that, the silence, the indifference, the rumors set in again.

Pramoedya not only chided the literary world in the eighties, he also rebuked Indonesian historiography by his presentation of the National Awakening and the "Movement" in his four novels that offer a wide panorama based upon colonial life around the turn of the century. Who in Indonesia knew of Tirto Adisoerjo, the first native journalist? Who was willing gratefully to acknowledge the influence of Western science and culture? As if his four volumes were not enough to turn literary life upside down, forcing readers and critics to rethink their preference for surrealism and their tendency to ridicule *sastra pop*, Pramoedya also edited some Malay tales that had originally been published around 1900, in the days of the rise of Tirto Adisoerjo alias Minke, that is. His anthology, entitled *Tempo Doeloe*, opens with an introduction in which he returns to the idea he had already explored in the tumultuous days before his exile on Buru. According to Pramoedya, modern Malay literature had not started with Marah Roesli's *Sitti Noerbaja* of 1922, as Indonesian critics and textbook-writers, their vision obscured by the shadows of Western scholarship, had for so long assumed. No, Indonesian literature began with the tales of authors such as Francis, Kommer, and Lie Kim Hok that had been published around the turn of the century, in the days of budding nationalism. Inspired by the same desire to challenge accepted views, Pramoedya edited and republished *Hikayat Siti Mariyah*, a very unusual Malay tale by the mysterious Hadji Moekti. "The Tale of Siti Mariyah" had originally been published in 1917 and could easily compete with *Sitti Noerbaja,* or with *Bumi Manusia,* for that matter, in breadth of vision, volume and vitality. It evoked the days of the Movement, the start of the Indonesian nation, the beginnings of a new vitality—and it was banned.

Looking back from the late nineties, one is amazed by the sterility of literary life in the New Order, as though there were an implicit social contract between authors and authorities not to disturb one another. "Literature" (and writing as a whole) is caught in a web of hollow and elusive phrases which the writers themselves would probably call "permitted dissent." The sense of adventure, at the level of both language and ideas, is absent, the courage squarely to confront Authority is vanishing, and this dull status quo gets perpetuated in a press that avoids engaging any issues and conflicts that could break their financial necks. Newspapers and weeklies have played it safe in a "mannered knowingness," as Anderson recently characterized this drab atmosphere which is only subverted by an occasional poetry reading, loaded with complaints and criticism.[18]

Writers and authors have taken refuge in Aesopian tales, full of innuendoes and allusions which are permitted by the authorities because they act as a kind of a safety valve. Censorship can inspire the imagination and so can self-censorship, but eventually this muffled state becomes so complete and pervasive that even the authors themselves are no longer aware of it, leaving the writing of explicitly offensive and confrontational poetry and prose to madmen and clowns who should not be surprised when sooner or later they are arrested, punished, and shoveled away under the epitaph: "Communist." Like Wiji Thukul. Like Pramoedya Ananta Toer.

Iwan Simatupang, and after him Danarto, Putu Wijaya, and Budi Darma, the heroes of the literary life that the metropolitan scene created in the seventies, questioned the force of realism, the notions of cause and effect, and the generally accepted ideas of verisimilitude. Seeking alternatives to the literature shaped by such notions, they explored their fragmentary personal experiences in complicated, not to say hermetic, forms of Malay. Their products were tales with unclear, faceless, and often nameless protagonists, plots that defied common-sense logic, descriptions that leaned on older (oral) forms of telling, and themes that were hard to connect to everyday reality in the way established authors in the fifties tried and often managed. The interaction between language and life was no longer as clear is it used to be, and in tales such as *Ziarah, Godlob, Telegram,* and *Kritikus Adinan*—to mention a characteristic publication from each of these authors—*sastra* moved farther and farther away from everyday life, alienating the limited number of readers it still could claim, escaping from conventional meanings, flying away into a never-never

---

[18] In a now well-known talk he gave in Leiden some years ago, Goenawan Mohamad has tried to give a description of this sterility without, however, giving a clear suggestion how to escape it:

"'The official and national language spends most of its time not in the wry or witty words of writers but in closed classrooms, between office walls, in seminars and conferences or in innocuous and interpersonal chatter of distant acquaintances. There is no element of sensuousness. In the monotonous environment in which it lives, the concrete world seems not to exist; it is not relevant. The word has already changed into an amorphous mass that is present in the mind as nothing more than generic signs. Our language has been ripped from the world, stripped of shape, smell, color and form, cleansed of the grit and grafitti, the rumpus and commotion, that make up real life. And it is this language which for reasons of 'limited time and space' the press and other form of mass media feed back to the public in a bland but easily digested stew. Lack of spice in language has become the norm and the powers that be, the political powers, have adopted it with relish. It has been made the lowest common denominator, the common languge for the public as well as for the bureaucrats who force its use on everyone, insisting on its ready acceptance by all." Goenawan Mohamad, "*Pasemon:* On Allusion and Illusions," in *Menagerie* 2 (1993): 125-126.

land which was very hard to link up with anyone's actual experiences. No wonder authors can no longer speak in the name of the nation.

Suharto and his administrative apparatus have castrated a generation of writers, robbing them of their generative power, the power of being historical witnesses who could tell others about what is happening before their very eyes. Rejecting realism and strict moralism, the tales of the seventies and eighties were preoccupied with an experimental freedom and playfulness that confused the critics, alienated those who thought that "literature" still had a role to play in the New Order, and discouraged new and young readers, who subsequently turned away from *sastra* as a crucial manifestation of national culture. The latter effect could only please the authorities who were eager to silence discussion on the literary front. It looked as if a source of possible dissent and unrest—clearly authors played a significant political role in the early sixties—was neutralizing itself by making itself inaccessible. Literary life, in other words, no longer needs to be reined in by very much repressive censorship and intimidation in order to force it to walk in line with the national ideology of Panca Sila. Censorship, invisibly and facelessly operating along various patterns of power, has done an excellent job; literary life has eliminated itself as a force of vociferous dissent, leaving only some authors and writers wandering on the savannas, to use Pramoedya's image, where they run the risk of being made criminals. Their calls to question the state's authority, to challenge its monologues, to resist its interpretation of history are hardly heard. It must feel like living in a glass house . . . and Pramoedya knows how it feels to be made a criminal without a cause.

***

A censor acts or claims he acts in the interests of a community. In actuality, he relies on and wields the outrage of that community, or he imagines its outrage and then manipulates this handy fiction, his own invention. Sometimes he even imagines both the community and its outrage, but goes about his business just the same, in the safe knowledge that he is protected by the silent support of those in Power.

Who is this punisher, or what is the punisher? Who is entitled to tell an author that he deserves a punishment so that he can be said to have committed a crime? A censor is invisible, he never parades himself, he remains in hiding, and if he is a good censor, we will hardly notice his work.

That is why the fourth volume of Pramoedya's novels on the rise of Indonesian nationalism should shock us all, and not only because it tells us in detail how a censor works: the tale is told by the secret agent Pangemanann who, French-educated, full of dreams about freedom, equality, and fraternity, realizes too late that he has fallen into Power's trap and become one of its creatures. The reader is suddenly made aware of the fact that the tales that Minke, the hero of volumes one, two, and three, has told us in the first-person singular have been touched by this very censor who admits that he has brushed them up before giving them to us to read. The censors are among and in us, so to speak, and if anything, we should try to keep our kites flying high in the air.

NOTES ON CONTRIBUTORS

Joshua Barker recently received his PhD in anthropology from Cornell University.

Caroline S. Hau holds a PhD in English from Cornell University and is currently teaching at the University of the Philippines. She is a member of the organization Kaisa Para sa Kaunlaran.

Daniel S. Lev is professor of political science at the University of Washington in Seattle.

Hendrik M. J. Maier is professor of Malay literature at Leiden University.

Rudolf Mrázek is professor of history at the University of Michigan in Ann Arbor.

Henk Schulte Nordholt is professor of history at the University of Amsterdam.

John Pemberton is associate professor of anthropology at Columbia University.

Vicente L. Rafael is associate professor at the Department of Communication, University of California at San Diego.

John Sidel teaches political science at the School of Oriental and African Studies in London.

James T. Siegel is professor of anthropology and Asian Studies at Cornell University.

Margreet van Till is a PhD candidate in history at the University of Amsterdam.

Peter Zinoman is assistant professor of history at the University of California, Berkeley.

SOUTHEAST ASIA PROGRAM PUBLICATIONS
Cornell University

Studies on Southeast Asia

Number 37   *Sumatran Sultanate and Colonial State: Jambi and the Rise of Dutch Imperialism, 1830-1907*, Elsbeth Locher-Scholten, trans. Beverley Jackson. 2003. 332 pp. ISBN 0-87727-736-2.

Number 36   *Southeast Asia over Three Generations: Essays Presented to Benedict R. O'G. Anderson*, ed. James T. Siegel and Audrey R. Kahin. 2003. 398 pp. ISBN 0-87727-735-4.

Number 35   *Nationalism and Revolution in Indonesia*, George McTurnan Kahin, intro. Benedict R. O'G. Anderson (reprinted from 1952 edition, Cornell University Press, with permission). 2003. 530 pp. ISBN 0-87727-734-6.

Number 34   *Golddiggers, Farmers, and Traders in the "Chinese Districts" of West Kalimantan, Indonesia*, Mary Somers Heidhues. 2003. 316 pp. ISBN 0-87727-733-8.

Number 33   *Opusculum de Sectis apud Sinenses et Tunkinenses (A Small Treatise on the Sects among the Chinese and Tonkinese): A Study of Religion in China and North Vietnam in the Eighteenth Century*, Father Adriano de St. Thecla, trans. Olga Dror, with Mariya Berezovska. 2002. 363 pp. ISBN 0-87727-732-X.

Number 32   *Fear and Sanctuary: Burmese Refugees in Thailand*, Hazel J. Lang. 2002. 204 pp. ISBN 0-87727-731-1.

Number 31   *Modern Dreams: An Inquiry into Power, Cultural Production, and the Cityscape in Contemporary Urban Penang, Malaysia*, Beng-Lan Goh. 2002. 225 pp. ISBN 0-87727-730-3.

Number 30   *Violence and the State in Suharto's Indonesia*, ed. Benedict R. O'G. Anderson. 2001. Second printing, 2002. 247 pp. ISBN 0-87727-729-X.

Number 29   *Studies in Southeast Asian Art: Essays in Honor of Stanley J. O'Connor*, ed. Nora A. Taylor. 2000. 243 pp. Illustrations. ISBN 0-87727-728-1.

Number 28   *The Hadrami Awakening: Community and Identity in the Netherlands East Indies, 1900-1942*, Natalie Mobini-Kesheh. 1999. 174 pp. ISBN 0-87727-727-3.

Number 27   *Tales from Djakarta: Caricatures of Circumstances and their Human Beings*, Pramoedya Ananta Toer. 1999. 145 pp. ISBN 0-87727-726-5.

Number 26   *History, Culture, and Region in Southeast Asian Perspectives*, rev. ed., O. W. Wolters. 1999. 275 pp. ISBN 0-87727-725-7.

Number 25   *Figures of Criminality in Indonesia, the Philippines, and Colonial Vietnam*, ed. Vicente L. Rafael. 1999. 259 pp. ISBN 0-87727-724-9.

Number 24   *Paths to Conflagration: Fifty Years of Diplomacy and Warfare in Laos, Thailand, and Vietnam, 1778-1828*, Mayoury Ngaosyvathn and Pheuiphanh Ngaosyvathn. 1998. 268 pp. ISBN 0-87727-723-0.

Number 23   *Nguyễn Cochinchina: Southern Vietnam in the Seventeenth and Eighteenth Centuries*, Li Tana. 1998. Second printing, 2002. 194 pp. ISBN 0-87727-722-2.

Number 22   *Young Heroes: The Indonesian Family in Politics*, Saya S. Shiraishi. 1997. 183 pp. ISBN 0-87727-721-4.

Number 21   *Interpreting Development: Capitalism, Democracy, and the Middle Class in Thailand*, John Girling. 1996. 95 pp. ISBN 0-87727-720-6.

Number 20   *Making Indonesia*, ed. Daniel S. Lev, Ruth McVey. 1996. 201 pp. ISBN 0-87727-719-2.

Number 19   *Essays into Vietnamese Pasts*, ed. K. W. Taylor, John K. Whitmore. 1995. 288 pp. ISBN 0-87727-718-4.

Number 18   *In the Land of Lady White Blood: Southern Thailand and the Meaning of History*, Lorraine M. Gesick. 1995. 106 pp. ISBN 0-87727-717-6.

Number 17   *The Vernacular Press and the Emergence of Modern Indonesian Consciousness*, Ahmat Adam. 1995. 220 pp. ISBN 0-87727-716-8.

Number 16   *The Nan Chronicle*, trans., ed. David K. Wyatt. 1994. 158 pp. ISBN 0-87727-715-X.

Number 15   *Selective Judicial Competence: The Cirebon-Priangan Legal Administration, 1680–1792*, Mason C. Hoadley. 1994. 185 pp. ISBN 0-87727-714-1.

Number 14   *Sjahrir: Politics and Exile in Indonesia*, Rudolf Mrázek. 1994. 536 pp. ISBN 0-87727-713-3.

Number 13   *Fair Land Sarawak: Some Recollections of an Expatriate Officer*, Alastair Morrison. 1993. 196 pp. ISBN 0-87727-712-5.

Number 12   *Fields from the Sea: Chinese Junk Trade with Siam during the Late Eighteenth and Early Nineteenth Centuries*, Jennifer Cushman. 1993. 206 pp. ISBN 0-87727-711-7.

Number 11   *Money, Markets, and Trade in Early Southeast Asia: The Development of Indigenous Monetary Systems to AD 1400*, Robert S. Wicks. 1992. 2nd printing 1996. 354 pp., 78 tables, illus., maps. ISBN 0-87727-710-9.

Number 10   *Tai Ahoms and the Stars: Three Ritual Texts to Ward Off Danger*, trans., ed. B. J. Terwiel, Ranoo Wichasin. 1992. 170 pp. ISBN 0-87727-709-5.

Number 9   *Southeast Asian Capitalists*, ed. Ruth McVey. 1992. 2nd printing 1993. 220 pp. ISBN 0-87727-708-7.

Number 8   *The Politics of Colonial Exploitation: Java, the Dutch, and the Cultivation System*, Cornelis Fasseur, ed. R. E. Elson, trans. R. E. Elson, Ary Kraal. 1992. 2nd printing 1994. 266 pp. ISBN 0-87727-707-9.

Number 7   *A Malay Frontier: Unity and Duality in a Sumatran Kingdom*, Jane Drakard. 1990. 215 pp. ISBN 0-87727-706-0.

Number 6   *Trends in Khmer Art*, Jean Boisselier, ed. Natasha Eilenberg, trans. Natasha Eilenberg, Melvin Elliott. 1989. 124 pp., 24 plates. ISBN 0-87727-705-2.

Number 5   *Southeast Asian Ephemeris: Solar and Planetary Positions, A.D. 638–2000*, J. C. Eade. 1989. 175 pp. ISBN 0-87727-704-4.

Number 3   *Thai Radical Discourse: The Real Face of Thai Feudalism Today*, Craig J. Reynolds. 1987. 2nd printing 1994. 186 pp. ISBN 0-87727-702-8.

Number 1   *The Symbolism of the Stupa*, Adrian Snodgrass. 1985. Revised with index, 1988. 3rd printing 1998. 469 pp. ISBN 0-87727-700-1.

SEAP Series

Number 19   *Gender, Household, State: Đổi Mới in Việt Nam,* ed. Jayne Werner and
             Danièle Bélanger. 2002. 151 pp. ISBN 0-87727-137-2.

Number 18   *Culture and Power in Traditional Siamese Government,* Neil A. Englehart.
             2001. 130 pp. ISBN 0-87727-135-6.

Number 17   *Gangsters, Democracy, and the State,* ed. Carl A. Trocki. 1998. Second
             printing, 2002. 94 pp. ISBN 0-87727-134-8.

Number 16   *Cutting across the Lands: An Annotated Bibliography on Natural Resource
             Management and Community Development in Indonesia, the Philippines,
             and Malaysia,* ed. Eveline Ferretti. 1997. 329 pp. ISBN 0-87727-133-X.

Number 15   *The Revolution Falters: The Left in Philippine Politics after 1986,* ed.
             Patricio N. Abinales. 1996. Second printing, 2002. 182 pp. ISBN 0-
             87727-132-1.

Number 14   *Being Kammu: My Village, My Life,* Damrong Tayanin. 1994. 138 pp., 22
             tables, illus., maps. ISBN 0-87727-130-5.

Number 13   *The American War in Vietnam,* ed. Jayne Werner, David Hunt. 1993.
             132 pp. ISBN 0-87727-131-3.

Number 12   *The Political Legacy of Aung San,* ed. Josef Silverstein. Revised edition
             1993. 169 pp. ISBN 0-87727-128-3.

Number 10   *Studies on Vietnamese Language and Literature: A Preliminary Bibliography,*
             Nguyen Dinh Tham. 1992. 227 pp. ISBN 0-87727-127-5.

Number 9   *A Secret Past,* Dokmaisot, trans. Ted Strehlow. 1992. 2nd printing 1997.
             72 pp. ISBN 0-87727-126-7.

Number 8   *From PKI to the Comintern, 1924–1941: The Apprenticeship of the Malayan
             Communist Party,* Cheah Boon Kheng. 1992. 147 pp. ISBN 0-87727-125-9.

Number 7   *Intellectual Property and US Relations with Indonesia, Malaysia, Singapore,
             and Thailand,* Elisabeth Uphoff. 1991. 67 pp. ISBN 0-87727-124-0.

Number 6   *The Rise and Fall of the Communist Party of Burma (CPB),* Bertil Lintner.
             1990. 124 pp. 26 illus., 14 maps. ISBN 0-87727-123-2.

Number 5   *Japanese Relations with Vietnam: 1951–1987,* Masaya Shiraishi. 1990.
             174 pp. ISBN 0-87727-122-4.

Number 3   *Postwar Vietnam: Dilemmas in Socialist Development,* ed. Christine White,
             David Marr. 1988. 2nd printing 1993. 260 pp. ISBN 0-87727-120-8.

Number 2   *The Dobama Movement in Burma (1930–1938),* Khin Yi. 1988. 160 pp.
             ISBN 0-87727-118-6.

Cornell Modern Indonesia Project Publications

Number 75   *A Tour of Duty: Changing Patterns of Military Politics in Indonesia in the
             1990s.* Douglas Kammen and Siddharth Chandra. 1999. 99 pp.
             ISBN 0-87763-049-6.

Number 74   *The Roots of Acehnese Rebellion 1989–1992,* Tim Kell. 1995. 103 pp.
             ISBN 0-87763-040-2.

Number 73   *"White Book" on the 1992 General Election in Indonesia,* trans. Dwight
             King. 1994. 72 pp. ISBN 0-87763-039-9.

Number 72   *Popular Indonesian Literature of the Qur'an*, Howard M. Federspiel. 1994.
170 pp. ISBN 0-87763-038-0.

Number 71   *A Javanese Memoir of Sumatra, 1945–1946: Love and Hatred in the
Liberation War*, Takao Fusayama. 1993. 150 pp. ISBN 0-87763-037-2.

Number 70   *East Kalimantan: The Decline of a Commercial Aristocracy*, Burhan
Magenda. 1991. 120 pp. ISBN 0-87763-036-4.

Number 69   *The Road to Madiun: The Indonesian Communist Uprising of 1948*,
Elizabeth Ann Swift. 1989. 120 pp. ISBN 0-87763-035-6.

Number 68   *Intellectuals and Nationalism in Indonesia: A Study of the Following
Recruited by Sutan Sjahrir in Occupation Jakarta*, J. D. Legge. 1988.
159 pp. ISBN 0-87763-034-8.

Number 67   *Indonesia Free: A Biography of Mohammad Hatta*, Mavis Rose. 1987.
252 pp. ISBN 0-87763-033-X.

Number 66   *Prisoners at Kota Cane*, Leon Salim, trans. Audrey Kahin. 1986. 112 pp.
ISBN 0-87763-032-1.

Number 65   *The Kenpeitai in Java and Sumatra*, trans. Barbara G. Shimer, Guy Hobbs,
intro. Theodore Friend. 1986. 80 pp. ISBN 0-87763-031-3.

Number 64   *Suharto and His Generals: Indonesia's Military Politics, 1975–1983*, David
Jenkins. 1984. 4th printing 1997. 300 pp. ISBN 0-87763-030-5.

Number 62   *Interpreting Indonesian Politics: Thirteen Contributions to the Debate,
1964–1981*, ed. Benedict Anderson, Audrey Kahin, intro. Daniel S. Lev.
1982. 3rd printing 1991. 172 pp. ISBN 0-87763-028-3.

Number 60   *The Minangkabau Response to Dutch Colonial Rule in the Nineteenth
Century*, Elizabeth E. Graves. 1981. 157 pp. ISBN 0-87763-000-3.

Number 59   *Breaking the Chains of Oppression of the Indonesian People: Defense
Statement at His Trial on Charges of Insulting the Head of State, Bandung,
June 7–10, 1979*, Heri Akhmadi. 1981. 201 pp. ISBN 0-87763-001-1.

Number 57   *Permesta: Half a Rebellion*, Barbara S. Harvey. 1977. 174 pp.
ISBN 0-87763-003-8.

Number 55   *Report from Banaran: The Story of the Experiences of a Soldier during the
War of Independence*, Maj. Gen. T. B. Simatupang. 1972. 186 pp.
ISBN 0-87763-005-4.

Number 52   *A Preliminary Analysis of the October 1 1965, Coup in Indonesia (Prepared
in January 1966)*, Benedict R. Anderson, Ruth T. McVey, assist.
Frederick P. Bunnell. 1971. 3rd printing 1990. 174 pp.
ISBN 0-87763-008-9.

Number 51   *The Putera Reports: Problems in Indonesian-Japanese War-Time Cooperation*,
Mohammad Hatta, trans., intro. William H. Frederick. 1971. 114 pp.
ISBN 0-87763-009-7.

Number 50   *Schools and Politics: The Kaum Muda Movement in West Sumatra
(1927–1933)*, Taufik Abdullah. 1971. 257 pp. ISBN 0-87763-010-0.

Number 49   *The Foundation of the Partai Muslimin Indonesia*, K. E. Ward. 1970. 75 pp.
ISBN 0-87763-011-9.

Number 48   *Nationalism, Islam and Marxism*, Soekarno, intro. Ruth T. McVey. 1970.
2nd printing 1984. 62 pp. ISBN 0-87763-012-7.

Translation Series

Language Texts

A. U. A. Language Center Thai Course, Reading and Writing Text (mostly reading), 1979. Reissued 1997. 164 pp. ISBN 0-87727-511-4.

A. U. A. Language Center Thai Course, Reading and Writing Workbook (mostly writing), 1979. Reissued 1997. 99 pp. ISBN 0-87727-512-2.

KHMER

Cambodian System of Writing and Beginning Reader, Franklin E. Huffman. Originally published by Yale University Press, 1970. Reissued by Cornell Southeast Asia Program, 4th printing 2002. 365 pp. ISBN 0-300-01314-0.

Modern Spoken Cambodian, Franklin E. Huffman, assist. Charan Promchan, Chhom-Rak Thong Lambert. Originally published by Yale University Press, 1970. Reissued by Cornell Southeast Asia Program, 3rd printing 1991. 451 pp. ISBN 0-300-01316-7.

Intermediate Cambodian Reader, ed. Franklin E. Huffman, assist. Im Proum. Originally published by Yale University Press, 1972. Reissued by Cornell Southeast Asia Program, 1988. 499 pp. ISBN 0-300-01552-6.

Cambodian Literary Reader and Glossary, Franklin E. Huffman, Im Proum. Originally published by Yale University Press, 1977. Reissued by Cornell Southeast Asia Program, 1988. 494 pp. ISBN 0-300-02069-4.

HMONG

White Hmong-English Dictionary, Ernest E. Heimbach. 1969. 8th printing, 2002. 523 pp. ISBN 0-87727-075-9.

VIETNAMESE

Intermediate Spoken Vietnamese, Franklin E. Huffman, Tran Trong Hai. 1980. 3rd printing 1994. ISBN 0-87727-500-9.

* * *

Southeast Asian Studies: Reorientations. Craig J. Reynolds and Ruth McVey. Frank H. Golay Lectures 2 & 3. 70 pp. ISBN 0-87727-301-4.

Javanese Literature in Surakarta Manuscripts, Nancy K. Florida. Vol. 1, *Introduction and Manuscripts of the Karaton Surakarta*. 1993. 410 pp. Frontispiece, illustrations. Hard cover, ISBN 0-87727-602-1, Paperback, ISBN 0-87727-603-X. Vol. 2, *Manuscripts of the Mangkunagaran Palace*. 2000. 576 pp. Frontispiece, illustrations. Paperback, ISBN 0-87727-604-8.

Sbek Thom: Khmer Shadow Theater. Pech Tum Kravel, trans. Sos Kem, ed. Thavro Phim, Sos Kem, Martin Hatch. 1996. 363 pp., 153 photographs. ISBN 0-87727-620-X.

In the Mirror: Literature and Politics in Siam in the American Era, ed. Benedict R. O'G. Anderson, trans. Benedict R. O'G. Anderson, Ruchira Mendiones. 1985. 2nd printing 1991. 303 pp. Paperback. ISBN 974-210-380-1.

To order, please contact:

Cornell University
SEAP Distribution Center
369 Pine Tree Rd.
Ithaca, NY 14850-2819 USA

Online: http://www.einaudi.cornell.edu/southeastasia/publications/
Tel: 1-877-865-2432 (Toll free – U.S.)
Fax: (607) 255-7534

E-mail: SEAP-Pubs@cornell.edu
Orders must be prepaid by check or credit card (VISA, MasterCard, Discover).

Milton Keynes UK
Ingram Content Group UK Ltd.
UKHW032217141223
434411UK00012B/306